Dearest Sylvia

Dearest Sylvia

**An Airman's
Love Letters from
World War II**

ANTHONY S. MAZZA

Edited by G.J. Mazza

gatekeeper press

Columbus, Ohio

Dearest Sylvia: An Airman's Love Letters from World War II

Published by Gatekeeper Press
2167 Stringtown Rd, Suite 109
Columbus, OH 43123-2989
www.GatekeeperPress.com

The views and opinions expressed in this book are solely those of the author and do not reflect the views or opinions of Gatekeeper Press. Gatekeeper Press is not to be held responsible for and expressly disclaims responsibility of the content herein.

ISBN (hardcover): 9781662903748

Table of Contents

Introduction

My father never spoke about the war. Whenever the subject came up, he steered the conversation in another direction. He never mentioned his time in the U.S. Army Air Forces during World War II. He had no interest in attending reunions of those who served alongside him, and he did not understand those who wanted to reconnect with their former comrades in arms to reminisce about their wartime experiences.

My father's younger brother, my uncle Greg, also served in the Army Air Forces at the same time as my father. My uncle and father were even stationed in Italy together toward the end of the war in Europe, flying on at least one mission in separate airplanes in the same formation. Uncle Greg offered me some insight into my father's aversion to talking about the war. He told me that when he visited my father's camp in Italy, beside my father's cot was a picture of my mother, a smiling young woman in a white nurse's uniform. Uncle Greg said that "Tony," the name my father's friends and family called him, carried the picture of my mother with him wherever he was stationed during the war. Her picture was the first thing my father set up when moving into new lodging. My mother was the axis orienting his life during a time when military orders could require him to move at any time.

Uncle Greg recalled that when he was in my father's quarters in Italy, my father gestured to the picture of my mother and said, "Greg, when the war is over, I am going to go home and marry that woman. I will put the war behind me, and I will never think about it again."

After the war, my father did as he said. He went home; he married his sweetheart; and he put the war firmly behind him.

This volume of letters, what anyone would certainly recognize as love letters, are from my father, Anthony S. Mazza, to my mother, Sylvia M. Jacobs, during World War II. The letters span the time period from August of 1943 to March of 1945. For the most part, the letters detail my father's experience in the Army Air Forces, first as a cadet, then as a navigator-trainee, and finally as a flight officer aboard a B-24 Liberator Bomber. The letters, as one would expect, are filled with a young man's longings—for the war to be over and to go home to the woman he loved.

The letters are about an everyday man who served in the military during World War II, and they are addressed to an everyday woman on the home front. The young woman was in nursing school at the time, anticipating that she, too, might volunteer to contribute to the war effort. The letters are surely not unlike those that thousands of other servicemen wrote during the same time period, and I suspect there is little in the letters that distinguishes them based on historical or literary merit. The primary audience for the collected letters is a narrow one, the descendants of Anthony Mazza and Sylvia Jacobs, so they may come to appreciate their family's heritage. Nonetheless, the letters may also be of some interest to scholars of the period or writers of historical belles-lettres, as the correspondence chronicles the details of ordinary life in the mid-1940s, from what is being served for dinner to what is being played on the radio.

The letters clearly reflect their time. In some circles, my father was an outsider because he was a second-generation Italian American. Based on his own experience, he identified with and avidly supported the civil-rights struggles of others in American society who were discounted based on race or ethnicity.

Nonetheless, the Army Air Forces in World War II were racially segregated. Integration did not come to the U.S. military until 1948. My father also recognized women as equals, celebrating my mother's nursing career and criticizing Victorian notions that women should be subservient to men in the home. Yet, to contemporary sensibilities, some of the passing references in the letters to women and people of differing races and ethnicities may be jarring.

In the interim, we have come to understand, especially from traditionally oppressed groups, that many of the things we have learned and said about them are deeply offensive. Listening thoughtfully to the experiences of marginalized voices is an ongoing process, one that continues to challenge us today to examine the misinformation we have learned about people who are different than we are.

I have not altered the language in the transcribed letters, even though it has made me uncomfortable at times, because it reflects the world in which the writer lived. I have for the most part followed a similar approach to the text itself, keeping syntax flaws and misspellings and inserting clearly marked additional punctuation or capitalization changes only to aid the reader. This volume includes facsimiles of the original letters so that readers may choose to focus on them exclusively or compare copies of the original, handwritten texts to the annotated transcriptions.

In publishing my father's love letters to my mother, I have had to confront the question of whether doing so may be a breach of intimacy, that I should respect the privacy of a correspondence that was never meant to be public.[1] In weighing this matter, I have

---

[1] C. Thi Nguyen and Matthew Strohl, "Cultural Appropriation and the Intimacy of Groups," *Philosophical Studies* 176, no. 4 (2019): 982-83.

given considerable thought to how my mother treated the letters. Toward the end of her life, my mother carefully went through her personal papers, deciding what to throw away and what to keep. She knew that what she retained would be left for her children. In her possession at the time were some of her own letters that she had written to my father during the war, which my father had kept. She chose to discard all her letters. She did not make the same decision about my father's letters. It is impossible to know her thoughts. Perhaps she could not bring herself to destroy letters that sustained her at the beginning of her relationship with my father, when they were parted for long periods of time. I believe that she kept the nearly eighty letters that comprise this collection because she wanted her children to read them, hoping they would see the young man with whom she fell in love. She also implicitly understood that her children were likely to share the letters with others.

The letters themselves contain significant lacunae. For example, there are eight letters in November of 1944, whereas there are no letters from early January to June of 1944. It is unlikely that there were no letters during this months–long lapse. Whether these letters were lost or subject to my mother's deliberate omission, I do not know.

One of the most frustrating aspects of the collected letters is that my father's letters end on March 27, 1945, just as he arrives at the warfront and begins undertaking bombing missions. Did he not write after April of 1945? Were the letters during this period lost?

Although the letters do not document my father's wartime sorties, I found in his files, to my astonishment, a small handwritten notepad that filled in the gap. According to his own notes, which other military records corroborate, my father flew six missions between March 27 and April 25, 1945, before the war in Europe ended on VE Day, May 8, 1945. I have included his

4

mission notes in Appendix A. Although my father only flew six missions, he had a distinguished flying record, earning the Air Medal for meritorious service and the Purple Heart on his last mission for suffering wounds in combat.

The omission of any letters from my father from April 1945 onward may be consistent with one of the reasons that my father never spoke about the war: remorse. My older sister, Mary Ann Mazza Crawford, told me that in his later years, our father was keenly aware that the bombing missions he flew during World War II most likely resulted in the deaths of not only hostile Axis forces but also civilians on the ground. As a religious man, my father understood his duty as an American soldier, but he profoundly regretted that he had any part in the taking of human life.

My mother, like my father, had a sober view of the war. As a child, I remember watching with my family a documentary on television about World War II. I was just beginning to come to a dim awareness that there was a great war before I was born, and I was trying to understand it in the terms of winning or losing in children's games. That evening, as my mother was tucking me into bed, I asked her, "Mom, so is it right? Did we win the war?" I remember her response because it left me so confused: "Oh, honey," she said, "No one ever wins a war."

In the end, the significance of the letters collected here is that they are part of a long love story. My parents survived the war and wed on June 26, 1948. They built a life together, being married for more than 46 years, raising children, and enjoying grandchildren.[2] Based on these letters, one might be tempted to think of their story in cinematic terms: after suffering through the war, the earnest young airman returns to the arms of his patient sweetheart as

---

[2] For a short history of the Mazza and Jacobs families, see Appendix B.

bells ring, the victory parade engulfs them, and they live happily ever after. In some respects, this narrative is true, but life is, as we all know, more complicated. My parents had many joys in life, but they also had serious struggles. Some of them were no doubt a consequence of the war. Yet, the relationship that they built during the war years, to which the collected letters attest, was one that sustained them throughout their lives despite adversity.

One of the recurring themes in the letters is the reliance on "mental telepathy" to span the distance between my father and mother. My father writes that when he cannot reach my mother because the mail is too slow or the telephone is unavailable, he can still contact her via "mental telepathy," inviting her into his life and spending time with her. One wonders whether their mutual cultivation of this capacity may explain the endurance of their bond.

One of my favorite passages in the letters that provides an insight into my parents' relationship is my father's reflection on the short military leave he spent with my mother in October of 1944:

> Still can't help but think of the wonder-ful time I had with you last week. [It] went so fast that even now I can hardly be sure that it was real and not one of those wishful thoughts stored in that cranium of mine. Next time[,] I'll have to rope that gremlin who keeps pushing the clock around so fast when we are together and I am not looking[;] it will be up to you to keep one eye on him, the other on me. I'll keep both eyes on you!![3]

I found this letter helpful when I spoke at my father's funeral. Although my parents, like all parents, had many shortcomings,

---

[3] Letter from Anthony S. Mazza to Sylvia M. Jacobs (November 3, 1944).

perhaps the greatest gift they gave to their children was that we knew that they loved each other.

In bringing these letters to print, I am grateful to my brothers and sisters, who entrusted me with the task of maintaining our father's letters and presenting them in a way that we may share them. Our collective memories have often worked together to recall half-forgotten people and family stories. My sister Mary Ann Mazza Crawford was often the source I would consult in verifying family lore. My brother Louis Mazza, the family archivist, would immediately send me scanned family photographs, military records, and other relevant documents I requested. My brother Mark Mazza provided help with proofreading and thinking through publishing questions, and my sister Michelle Mazza Robertson not only helped me retrieve a missing letter, but she also provided invaluable moral support. I am also most grateful to my wife, Cherie Brown, who patiently endured the late nights I spent putting together this collection of letters as we sheltered in place during the pandemic summer of 2020. She would often provide feedback and useful suggestions in bringing this project to completion. Although I made an effort to transcribe the text accurately and to track down references, I am aware that gaps remain and that I may have inadvertently made some errors. I ask in advance for the readers' pardon and welcome corrections.

If he had lived, my father would have celebrated his hundredth birthday on February 6, 2021. I hope these letters bring to life again the young man I did not know, a man who had every hope for the life ahead of him.

G.J. Mazza
May 2021
Silver Spring, Maryland

Anthony S. Mazza
(ca. December 1944)

Sylvia M. Jacobs
(ca. October 1944)

9

1943

ARMY AIR FORCES
B. T. C. # 10
GREENSBORO, NORTH CAROLINA

August 3, 1943

Dear Sylvie,

Here at last is that much discussed letter that we talked of in my pre-army days. There is so much to tell that I hardly know where to begin. I think that in order to get more things in, I shall take them in chronological order. On Sunday August 1st, I reported at the post office at 10:00 P.M. We received our orders but were not "shipped" until 2:00 P.M. The Penn. Railroad provided two of the oldest coaches they could find for our group which consisted of 68 men. These coaches looked old enough to me to have been erected in Lincoln's time. Worst of all they were placed directly behind the engine; the result was a shower of dirt and cinders. On arrival at Greensboro, we resembled a bunch of Penn. coalminers. Our train headed east to Harrisburgh; from there to Baltimore md, Washington D.C., through Virginia to Greensboro. The mountain sides in Penn, covered with forrests, were beautiful to behold. Nothing can beat them for scenery. Through Virginia, I saw acres of tobacco plantations; the home of "Lucky Strikes". The houses are mostly delapodated

12

August 3, 1943

From: Pvt. Anthony S. Mazza
            Army Air Forces
            B.T.C. –10 T.G.-1183
            Flt. F Barracks T-167
            Greensboro, North Carolina

To: Miss Sylvia Jacobs
            2334 Atmore St.
            N.S. (12) Phg., Pa.

Letterhead: Army Air Forces
            B.T.C. #10
            Greensboro, North Carolina

[1*]   August, 3, 1943

Dear Sylvie,

Here at last is that much discussed letter that we talked of in my pre-[A]rmy days.[4] There is so much to tell that I hardly know where to begin. I think that in order to get more things in, I shall take them in chronological order. On Sunday[,] August 1st, I reported at the post office at 10:00 PM.[5] We received our orders but were not "shipped" until 2:00 P.M. The Penn. Railroad provided two of the oldest coaches they could find for our group[,] which consisted of 68 men. These coaches looked old enough to

---

[4] "67 Leave Here for Air Cadet Training: Will Take Pre-Flight Preparatory Work in North Carolina," *Pittsburgh Post-Gazette*, August 2, 1943.
[5] The time reference is more likely to be 10:00 AM.

shacks; one of our homes would look like a mansion in comparison. Our Camp is located on a site that was once a swamp; it was drained and roads paved with tar & slag. The entire area is covered with cypress, cedar and pine and barracks are located beneath them. There are about 35,000 men at this center all of whom are taking Basic Training. I shall have the rank of private while here and the period that I shall remain will be about 28 days; then I shall be sent to a college for 5 months before sent to classification center where Greg is now.

We arrived yesterday morning at 8:00 A.M. after riding for 18 consecutive hours without a bit of sleep. Processing began immediately with a physical examination followed by a lecture of rules & regulations of the camp. We were introduced to our Commanding officer who, of all things, is English. Our meals are very good and I have nothing to complain about in that respect. We were then issued barracks and of all things I land an upper berth bed. It is quite a struggle getting in and out, hard to make the bed, and hotter than ever in warm weather for hot air always rises (Old science axioms). They have been giving us (ZnO) zinc oxide tablets. I haven't the slightest idea what they are for (that is in your field) but they taste & look like chalk. All of the afternoon yesterday was spent in getting outfitted. Just take a peek in George's Duffle bag and you will know what I have. We also have gas masks; I don't remember if George has one or not.

me to have been erected in Lincoln's time. Worst of all[,] they were placed directly behind the engine; the result was a shower of dirt and cinders. On arrival at Greensboro, we resembled a bunch of Penn. [c]oalminers [*sic*]. Our train headed east to Harrisburg, from there to Baltimore, Md.[,] Washington[,] D.C., through Virginia to Greensboro. The mountainsides in Penn[.], covered with forests, were beautiful to behold. Nothing can beat them for scenery. Through Virginia, I saw acres of tobacco plantations[,] the home of "Lucky Strikes."[6] The houses are mostly delapadated [*sic*] [1R*] shacks; one of our homes would look like a mansion in comparison. Our camp is located on a site that was once a swamp; it was drained and roads paved with tar + slag. The entire area is covered with cypress, cedar[,] and pine[,] and [the] barracks are located beneath them. There are about 35,000 men at this center[,] all of whom are taking [b]asic [t]raining. I shall have the rank of private while here[,] and the period that I shall remain will be about 28 days; then I shall be sent to a college for 5 months before [being] sent to [the] classification center where Greg is now.[7]

We arrived yesterday morning at 8:00 A[.]M. after riding for 18 consecutive hours without a bit of sleep. Processing began immediately with a physical examination followed by a lecture of rules + regu-lations of the camp. We were introduced to our commanding officer[,] who, of all things, is English. Our meals are very good[,] and I have nothing to complain about in that respect. We were then issued barracks[,] and of all things[,] I land

---

6 Lucky Strike was a popular American cigarette brand in the 1930s and 1940s. Allan Brandt, *The Cigarette Century: The Rise, Fall, and Deadly Persistence of the Product That Defined America* (New York: Basic Books, 2007), 75.

7 Gregory (Greg) E. Mazza (b. March 10, 1922; d. June 18, 2007) was Anthony Mazza's younger brother. He was also serving at the time in the Army Air Forces.

ARMY AIR FORCES
B. T. C. # 10
GREENSBORO, NORTH CAROLINA

2.

Our day is to end at 5:30 P.M; that is we are to have free time. Last night we didn't for we had to have our bedding supplies ---- We won't be paid overtime either. We should be in our barracks at 9:30 P.M. for the lights go off then but we are not held to that. We can stay out late but have to crawl to our bunks in the dark. We, as aviation cadets, are confined for a period of 7 days; I can't visit the fair city of Greensboro. Our location is about 1½ mile from there. After our 7 day confinement we will be permitted leave every night into the city 'till 11:00 P.M. Last night I went to bed after 40 hrs. of excitement wondering what would happen next. I slept very little for the fellow beneath me spent most of the night coughing & snoring. Too bad I am a light sleeper; I'll have to figure some way to stop him ------ Maybe you could help with some bright idea.

This morning we dashed in formation at 5:30 A.M. before our barracks. We had to be in uniform there in less than 15 minutes. Guess who was there first? You're right. ---- me. I had everything laid out nice & neat the night before and was all set. 5:30 is my time anyway

16

an upper[-]berth bed. It is quite a struggle getting in and out, hard to make the bed, and hotter than ever in warm weather[,] for hot air always rises (old science axiom). They have been giving us (ZnO) zinc oxide tablets.[8] I haven't the slightest idea what they are for (that is your field)[,][9] but they taste + look like chalk. All of the afternoon yesterday was spent in getting outfitted. Just take a peek in George's[10] [d]uffle bag and you will know what I have. We also have gas masks; I don't remember if George has one or not.

[2*] Our day is to end at 5:30 PM; that is[,] we are to have free time. Last night we didn't[,] for we had to have our bedding supplies - - - - We won't be paid overtime either. We should be in

---

8 James P. McClung and Angus G. Scrimgeour, "Zinc: An Essential Trace Element with Potential Benefits to Soldiers," *Military Medicine* 170, no. 12 (2005): 1048-52.

9 Sylvia Jacobs (b. June 2, 1923; d. December 14, 1994) was studying to become a registered nurse at St. John's General Hospital School of Nursing in Pittsburgh, Pennsylvania. Founded in 1896, St. John's General Hospital, located in the Brighton Heights section of the North Side of Pittsburgh, closed in 1995. Christine Davis, "St. John's General Hospital," *PHLF News*, June 2003, https://phlf.org/wp-content/uploads/2015/05/164_PHLF_NEWS_2003_06.pdf.

10 George Jacobs (b. January 18, 1921; d. March 12, 2009), who later became a physician with a general practice on the North Side of Pittsburgh, was Sylvia Jacobs' older brother. He and Anthony Mazza were in the same high school class at David B. Oliver High School, 2323 Brighton Road, Pittsburgh, Pennsylvania 15212. They graduated in June of 1939. *The Omicron* (Pittsburgh, PA: The Class of June, 1939, David B. Oliver High School, 1939), 31, 40, 62, 69. The high school closed in 2012. Eleanor Chule, "Students Team to Ease School Closing," *Pittsburgh Post-Gazette*, March 11, 2012. Sylvia Jacobs, Class of 1941, and Gregory Mazza, Class of 1940, also attended Oliver High School. *The Omicron* (Pittsburgh, PA: The Class of June, 1941, David B. Oliver High School, 1941), 42; *The Omicron* (Pittsburgh, PA: The Class of June, 1940, David B. Oliver High School, 1940), 10, 42.

to get up.

We rushed to chow and from there back to barracks to clean up room & make beds. The rest of the morning was spent in lectures about Chemical Warfare & gas mask. We had to learn all about that for tomorrow will be gas mask day. We will have to wear it all day. An officer in a little jeep rides all about the place with tear gas bombs throwing them near all personal. I hope I won't do any crying; I am all set with my mask though and have practiced several times tonight so I am sure I can hold my breath & get it on in time. We also got lectures on the mess hall and its care. no longer will the boys in aviation cadets be put on K.P. they shall serve as "mess attendants." (Who are they trying to kid.)

We saw a movie on "Swim & Live" but when I feel that bump on my forehead from swimming at Riverview, I began to wonder. This afternoon we had all our equipment checked and have been charged with all of it. One thing missing and we must pay. We were told of the Physical Ed. program that we must endure very shortly. Two 1 hr programs per day including a 2½ mile cross country run. Also obstacle courses. I see where I shall be a pretty tired boy soon!

I guess that as I am writing this letter you are all set for that vacation.

18

our barracks at 9:30 P.M.[,][11] for the lights go off then[,] but we are not held to that. We can stay out late but have to crawl to our bunks in the dark. We, as aviation cadets, are confined for a period of 7 days; I can't visit the fair City of Greensboro. Our location is about 1½ mile[s] from there. After our 7[-]day confinement[,] we will be permitted leave every night into the city 'till [sic] 11:00 P[.]M. Last night[,] I went to bed after 40 hrs. of excitement[,] wondering what would happen next. I slept very little[,] for the fellow beneath me spent most of the night coughing + snoring. Too bad I am a light sleeper; I'll have to figure some way to stop him - - - - - Maybe you could help with some bright idea.

This morning[,] we dashed in formation at 5:30 A.M. before our barracks. We had to be in uniform there in less than 15 minutes. Guess who was there first? You[']re right. - - - - Me. I had everything laid out nice + neat the night before and was all set. [Five-thirty] is my time anyway [2R*] to get up.

We rushed to chow and from there back to barracks to clean up [the] room + make beds. The rest of the morning was spent in lectures about chemical warfare + gas mask[s]. We had to learn all about that[,] for tomorrow will be gas[-]mask day. An officer in a little jeep rides all about the place with tear[-]gas bombs throwing them near all personal [sic]. I hope I won't do any crying; I am all set with my mask[,] though[,] and have practiced several times tonight so I am sure I can hold my breath + get it on in time. We also got lectures on the [m]ess hall and its care; no longer will the boys in [the] aviation cadets be put on K.P.[12] [T]hey shall serve as "Mess attendants [sic]." (Who are they trying to kid[?])

---

[11] The time reference is not clear, as the number has been written over. One may read either 8:30 PM or 9:30 PM.

[12] Kitchen Patrol or Police (i.e., working in the kitchen to prepare meals).

ARMY AIR FORCES
B. T. C. # 10
GREENSBORO, NORTH CAROLINA

3.

Did you say something about "Everything for the best." I disagree heartily and look back at all the fun I would miss and all the good times we could have providing I was there. Lets see --- Wed. we'd go to a show. . Thurs. dancing to the tune of ♪ Babe Rhodes ♪. Friday we'd take it easy and play tennis followed by a good swim. Saturday for supper followed by dancing at the Roosevelt Hotel.... I can dream can't I. .... That is if you would accept.

I cannot thank you enough for that medal and I assure you that at all times it will be around my neck. I could kick myself for the boner I pulled Saturday at 4:35 P.M when you gave me the gift. Remember when Phil said he wanted a drink of water? Well he did that so that I could talk to you alone. What did I do? I just tagged along saying that I was thirsty too. Wow I'll never live that down. You did look marvelous in that uniform-. blue eyed -- blue skirt -- perfect match. Another little bit and I would

20

We saw a movie on "Swim + Live," but when I feel that bump on my forehead from swimming at Riverview,[13] I begin to wonder. This afternoon we had all our equipment checked and have been charged with all of it. One thing missing and we must pay. We were told of the Physical Ed. Program that we must endure very shortly. Two 1[-]hr[.] programs per day including obstacle courses. I see where I shall be a pretty tired boy soon.

I guess that as I am writing this letter[,] you are all set for that vacation. [3*] Did you say something about "Everything for the best"[?] I disagree heartily and look back at all the fun I would miss and all the good times we could have[,] providing I was there. Let[']s see - - - Wed.[,] we'd go to a show.[14] Thurs.[,] dancing to the tune of Babe Rhodes.[15] Friday[,] we'd take it easy and play tennis followed by a good swim. Saturday[,] out for supper followed by dancing at the Roosevelt Hotel.[16] - - - I can dream can't I[?] - - - - That is[,] if you would accept.

---

[13] Anthony Mazza's residence in Pittsburgh at the time was 817 Woods Run Avenue, adjacent to Riverview Park, which had a public swimming pool. "3 City Draft Boards List More Selectees," *Pittsburgh Sun-Telegraph*, July 21, 1943.

[14] Following this sentence, there is a simple miniature line drawing of two people sitting next to each other, presumably seeing a film or play together.

[15] Hand-drawn musical notes appear before and after the reference to Babe Rhodes. The Babe Rhodes Orchestra was popular during the Big Band Era in Pittsburgh, often featured on local radio programs. "Today's Radio Programs," *Pittsburgh Post-Gazette*, February 1, 1944.

[16] Constructed in 1927, the Roosevelt Hotel, 607 Penn Avenue, Pittsburgh, Pennsylvania, is currently an apartment building known as the Roosevelt Building. "The Roosevelt Building," accessed June 20, 2020, https://therooseveltbuilding.com.

have played sick providing you would attend
me. You must send me a picture of you
one in uniform and one without ---- I mean in civilian
dress. --- One in a Catalina.

I sure did enjoy Wed + Friday night last
week and hope you did too. I really have
something to look forward to. I think
I've said enough for tonight and close
with plenty of love.

XX (I'm used to being)
rationed)

Love
Anthony

I cannot thank you enough for that medal[,][17] and I assure you that at all times it will be around my neck. I could kick myself for the boner I pulled Saturday at 4:35 P.M[.] when you gave me the gift. Remember when Phil[18] said he wanted a drink of water? Well[,] he did that so that I could talk to you alone. What did I do? I just tagged along saying that I was thirsty[,] too. Wow[,] I'll never live that down. You did look marvelous in that uniform[19] - - - blue[-]eyed - - blue skirt - - perfect match. Another little bit and I would [3R*] have played sick[,] providing you would attend me. You must send me a picture of you[,] one in uniform and one without - - - - I mean in civilian dress. - - - One in a Catalina.[20]

I sure did enjoy Wed[.] + Friday night last week and hope you did[,] too. I really have something to look forward to. I think I've said enough for tonight and close with plenty of love.

only XX[21] (I'm used to being rationed)   Love[,]
                                                            Anthony

---

[17] Sylvia Jacobs and Anthony Mazza were Roman Catholics. The medal that Sylvia sent was a religious medal, presumably sent with prayers to keep Anthony safe during the war.

[18] The reference is most likely to Philip Ventura (b. July 14, 1922; d. June 26, 1971), Anthony Mazza's fraternal first cousin, the son of Angeline Rose (Angelarosa) Mazza Ventura Branca, the sister of Anthony Mazza's father. See Appendix B.

[19] The reference is presumably to Sylvia Jacobs' uniform as a nursing student.

[20] The reference is to a one-piece bathing suit made by Catalina, a swimwear brand.

[21] In written correspondence, an X is a conventional way of indicating a kiss.

Free

GREENSBORO
AUG 4
11:30 AM
1943
N. C.

PVT. ANTHONY S. MAZZA
B.I.C.-10 T.G.-1183
Flt. F Barracks T-167
Greensboro, N. Carolina

Miss Sylvia Jacobs
2334 Atmore St.
N.S. (12) Pgh., Pa.

24

ARMY AIR FORCES
B. T. C. # 10
GREENSBORO, NORTH CAROLINA

Aug. 12, 1943

My dear Sylvia,

It seems that mail takes much longer to get from Greensboro to Pgh than I anticipated. I wrote my last letter to you on Wednesday and it arrived on Saturday; I couldn't write those first few days because we were continuously on the move being outfitted and receiving a very critical Physical examination. I could have written a card but I think you deserve more than that from me. I knew that you would leave for Camp Rosary and am certainly glad that you received my letter before starting. I would be only punishing myself if I delayed writing to you, for all the letters that may come, yours and those from home I deem the most important and I'm no masochist.

So you may be a Jr. Lifeguard before you leave. That's fine because then I'll give you the chance to "save" me. Camping is wonderful when there is water nearby. This camp here in N.C. would be more attentive to me if it had a huge lake or pool on or near its premises, but there isn't a pool within a twelve mile radius. In fact, it hasn't rained a drop since I've been here—

26

August 12, 1943

From: P.A.C. A.S. Mazza
                B.T.C.–10 T.G. 1183
                Sq.-F T-167
                Greensboro, N. Carolina

To: Miss Sylvia Jacobs
                2334 Atmore St.
                N.S. (12) Pgh., Pa

Postmark: 10:30 AM [?]
                Aug. 13, 1943
                Greensboro, N.C.

Letterhead: Army Air Forces
                B.T.C. # 10
                Greensboro, North Carolina

[1*]   Aug. 12, 1943

My dear Sylvia,

    It seems that mail takes much longer to get from Greensboro to Pgh[22] than I anticipated. I wrote my last letter to you on Wednesday[,] and it arrived on Saturday; I couldn't write those first few days because we were continuously on the move[,] being outfitted and receiving a very critical [p]hysical examination. I could have written a card[,] but I think you deserve more than

---

[22] Pittsburgh, Pennsylvania.

The water too is terrible for it is highly chemically treated. I find myself drinking more pop and Coca Cola than I ever did before in order to quench my thirst. When you receive this letter, your stay at camp will have been over, and I hope you have had a real enjoyable time and rest. You deserve a good rest after working most every day at that hospital, especially working on those various shifts. I hope too that there weren't many "casualties" while you were on duty.

Did I give you the impression that I was mad? If I did, I think you were over generous in giving me A+. I'll be content with a straight A grade, however. When you say that when the war is over nothing will be rationed that is awful --- --- but I like it. For that, you get A++ in your letter and I've increased the kisses to 3. (I'm not stingy). Your letter was far from dry and I reread it much more than 3 times.

I thought that there would be little drilling if I happened to get into the Air corps but I was quite wrong. The Air Cadets must be in more perfect condition than any other group and therefore we are getting quite a workout. Most of this drill, I've had with the R.O.T.C. when at Tech, so all I do is go through the motions without learning very much new.

that from me. I knew that you would leave for Camp Rosary[23] and am certainly glad that you received my letter before starting. I would be only punishing myself if I delayed writing to you, for of all the letters that may come, yours and those from home I deem the most important[,] and I'm no masochist.

So you may be a Jr. Lifeguard before you leave. That[']s fine because then I'll give you the chance to "save" me. Camping is wonderful when there is water nearby. This camp here in N.C. would be more attractive to me if it had a huge lake or pool on or near its premises, but there isn't a pool within a twelve[-]mile radius. In fact, it hasn't rained a drop since I've been here.

[1R*] The water[,] too[,] is terrible[,] for it is highly chemically treated. I find myself drinking more pop and Coca[-]Cola than I ever did before in order to quench my thirst. When you receive this letter, your stay at camp will have been over, and I hope you have had a real[ly] enjoyable time and rest. You deserve a good rest after working most every day at that hospital, especially working on those various shifts. I hope[,] too[,] that there weren't many "casualties" while you were on duty.

Did I give you the impression that I was mad? If I did, I think you were over generous in giving me [an] A+. I'll be content with a straight A grade, however. When you say that when the war is

---

[23] Camp Rosary, founded in 1941, continues today as Camp "R" under the auspices of the Pittsburgh Catholic Youth Association. The camp was located within the Laurel Hill State Park near Somerset, Pennsylvania. "Camp Rosary Opens at Laurel Hill," *Somerset Daily American*, July 5, 1941; "Catholic Nurses Set to Run Camp Rosary," *Pittsburgh Press*, August 8, 1941; "Laurel Hill Park Covers over 4,000 Acres of Land," *Cumberland Sunday Times*, 1952; "Camp 'R' Session Filling up Quickly," *Somerset Daily American*, June 25, 2007; "Camp 'R,'" Catholic Youth Association, accessed June 20, 2020, https://www.activityhero.com/biz/4046-camp-r-rockwood-pa.

ARMY AIR FORCES
B. T. C. # 10
GREENSBORO, NORTH CAROLINA

2.

We are starting to get the evenings off after 5:30 P.M. and thus I am able to catch-up on my mail.

Mother received a letter from one of the big officials at Randolph Field commending Gregory on the wonderful work that he had done and is doing thus far. I really have something to work forward to; a goal to shoot at.

I've been walking about with my chest poking out the last couple of days. We had an examination last week for mental aptitude. I scored an I.Q. of 135. 100 is average. With 110 score, one can be recommended for officers' candidate school. With 115 score, one can attend the army A.S.T.P. program which is something like what Joe is doing now with the Navy. It will eventually lead to an Officer's Commission. Look at the possibilities I may have should I not make cadets. 150 is "Genius." Who wants to be a genius anyway? I am content as I am.

I attended mass at the Army Camp last Sunday. Over 3,500 attended at the one mass

30

over[,] nothing will be rationed, that is awful - - - - - - but I like it. For that, you get [an] A++ on your letter[,] and I've increased the kisses to 3. (I'm not stingy). Your letter was far from dry[,] and I reread it much more than 3 times.

I thought that there would be little drilling if I happened to get into the Air Corps[,] but I was quite wrong. The Air Cadets must be in more perfect condition than any other group[,] and therefore[,] we are getting quite a workout. Most of this drill, I've had with the R.O.T.C.[24] when at Tech,[25] so all I do is go through the motions without learning very much new.

[2*] We are starting to get the evenings off after 5:30 P.M.[,] and thus I am able to catch-up [sic] on my mail.

Mother received a letter from one of the big officials at Randolph Field[26] commending Gregory on the wonderful work that he has done and is doing thus far. I really have something to look forward to[,] a goal to shoot at.

I've been walking about with my chest poking out the last couple of days. We had an examination last week for mental

---

[24] The Reserve Officer Training Corps.

[25] The reference is to the Carnegie Institute of Technology in Pittsburgh, Pennsylvania, which merged in 1967 with the Mellon Institute to become Carnegie Mellon University, located at 500 Forbes Avenue, Pittsburgh, Pennsylvania. Herbert G. Stein, "New Carnegie University to Emerge Here," *Pittsburgh Post-Gazette*, September 15, 1966; "Carnegie Mellon University," accessed June 20, 2020, https://www.cmu.edu/. After the war, Anthony Mazza completed a B.S. in chemical engineering from Carnegie Tech and worked as a metallurgist for steel companies in Pennsylvania and Indiana.

[26] Randolph Field, near San Antonio, Texas, was a flight-training facility for the U.S. Army Air Forces during World War II. "Randolph Field Historic District," National Park Service, accessed June 20, 2020, https://www.nps/articles/randolph-field-historic-district.htm.

the chapel couldn't hold them all so we had mass said in a theater. Soldiers are permitted to eat meat on Fridays by order of the bishop. The Chaplains here are on the order of those we saw in that picture --- Remember? I have yet to meet anything like them in civilian life; they really understand young men's problems.

One of the fellows across from me had his radio sent from home. Harry James is now serenading as I am writing this letter. One piece that I'll never forget and shall always like --- "You'll never know." If any of the tubes break, we will pitch in to keep the radio in condition at all times.

Last night I went to the post Library and looked at my position on the map. It really isn't so far as it seems. There are 59,000 people in the fair city of Greensboro. I am also reading, with an eye towards the future, "Air Craft Instruments."

There are 4 movies on the Post and during the past week I saw: "What's Buzzing Cousin." also "Stormy Weather" at the price of 15¢.

Our physical training program is quite rugged. We exercise for ½ hour; then run for the other half. This goes on twice each day. The boys call it "pysical tortura". There is many a "kink" in my limbs at present, but they will loosen shortly. Tennis helped plenty

32

aptitude. I scored an I.Q. of 135. [A hundred] is average. With 110 score, one can be recommended for officers' candidate school. With 115 score, one can attend the [A]rmy A.S.T.P.[27] program[,] which is something like [what] our Joe[28] is doing now with the Navy; it will eventually lead to an [o]fficer's [c]ommission. Look at the possibilities I may have[,] should I not make cadets. [One hundred fifty] is "Genius." Who wants to be a genius anyway? I am content as I am.

I attended [M]ass at the Army Camp last Sunday. Over 2,500 attended the one [M]ass—[2R*] the chapel couldn't hold them all[,] so we had [M]ass said in a theater. Soldiers are permitted to eat meat on Fridays by order of the bishop.[29] The chaplains here are on the order of those we saw in that picture - - - Remember? I have yet to meet anything like them in civilian life; they really understand young men's problems.

One of the fellows across from me had his radio sent from home. Harry James[30] is now serenading as I am writing this letter. One piece I'll never forget and shall always like - - - - "You'll

---

27 The Army Specialized Training Program during World War II trained selected recruits to become junior officers and acquire much-needed technical skills. Louis E. Keefer, "The Army Specialized Training Program in World War II," ASTP ASTU 3890, accessed June 20, 2020, http://www.pierce-evans.org/ASTPinWWII.htm.

28 Joseph (Joe) L. Mazza (b. November 7, 1924; d. December 22, 2015) was Anthony Mazza's younger brother. He became a physician, and his practice was in North Hills, the northern suburbs of Pittsburgh, Pennsylvania.

29 At the time, the religious discipline for Roman Catholics in the United States was to abstain from meat on Fridays.

30 Harry James (b. March 15, 1916; d. July 5, 1983) was a bandleader and popular trumpeter during the Big Band Era. "The Life of Harry James," Regal Artists Corporation, accessed June 20, 2020, http://www.harryjamesband.com/aboutharry.asp.

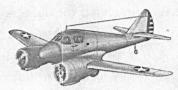

ARMY AIR FORCES
B. T. C. # 10
GREENSBORO, NORTH CAROLINA

Another popular piece that you and I know quite well is coming from the radio. It is a harmonica arrangement of "Tango Dela Rose." Another fellow just come in with some ice cream I've ordered. - - - - - All the comforts of home, Oh! yeah.

I think I better stop writing now for I am looking forward to your next letter tomorrow and thus I must have something to tell you when I answer that. I don't think I'll have to tell you to be good - - - - - You are. (I mean that in more ways than one)

Here they are:

XXX -

Love

Anthony

P.S. Say hello to the rest of your family for me.

Never Know."[31] If any of the tubes break, we will pitch in to keep the radio in condition at all times.

Last night[,] I went to the post [l]ibrary and looked at my position on the map. It really isn't so far as it seems. There are 59,000 people in the fair [C]ity of Greensboro. I am also reading, with an eye towards the future, "Air Craft Instruments."

There are 4 movies on the [p]ost[,] and during the past week I saw: "What's Bugging [*sic*] Cousin[,]"[32] also "Stormy Weather[,]"[33] at the price of 15¢.[34]

Our physical training program is quite rugged. We exercise for ½ hour; then run for the other half. This goes on twice each day. The boys call it "physical torture." There is many a "kink" in my limbs at present, but they will loosen shortly. Tennis helped plenty.

---

[31] Although she did not release a recording of the song until much later in her career, Alice Faye first sang "You'll Never Know," written by Harry Warren and Mack Gordon, in the film *Hello, Frisco* in 1943. In 1943, there were a number of hit recordings of the song, including one by Dick Haymes in June for Decca Records and one by Frank Sinatra in July for Columbia Records. *Hello, Frisco*, directed by H. Bruce Humberstone, featuring Alice Faye, John Payne, and Lynn Bari (20th Century Fox, 1943); "You'll Never Know by Alice Faye," Second Hand Songs, accessed June 20, 2020, https://secondhandsongs.com/performance/63854.

[32] *What's Buzzin', Cousin?*, directed by Charles Barton, featuring Ann Miller, Eddie "Rochester" Anderson, and John Hubbard (Columbia Pictures, 1943).

[33] *Stormy Weather*, directed by Andrew L. Stone, featuring Lena Horne, Cab Calloway, and Bill Robinson (20th Century Fox, 1943).

[34] Taking into account the inflation rate, $1.00 in 1943 would be equivalent to $15.31 in 2021. Fifteen cents would be equivalent to $2.30 in 2021 dollars. US Inflation Calculator, accessed May 1, 2021, https://www.usinflationcalculator.com/.

Free

A.S. MAZZA
15.T.C.-1° T.G. 1183
Sg - F T- 167
Greensboro, N. Carolina

GREEN[S]
AUG 13
10ᵀᴴ AM
1943
N. C.

Miss Sylvia Jacobs
2334 Atmore St.
N.5. ('1) Pgh, Pa

[3*] Another popular piece that you and I know quite well is coming from the radio. It is a harmonica arrangement of "Tango Dela Rose [*sic*]."[35] Another fellow just came in with some ice cream I ordered. - - - - - All the comforts of home. Oh! Yeah.

I think I better stop writing now[,] for I am looking forward to your next letter tomorrow[,] and thus I must have something to tell you when I answer that. I don't think I'll have to tell you to be good - - - - - You are. (I mean that in more ways than one[.])

Here they are: Love[,]
XXX   Anthony

P.S. Say hello to the rest of your family for me.

---

[35] Filippo Schreier wrote the music for "Tango Delle Rose" in 1928; Gigliola Cinquetti wrote Italian lyrics, and Aldo Bottero wrote English lyrics. "Filippo Schreier and Tango Delle Rose," walkerhomeschoolblog, accessed June 20, 2020, https://walkerhomeschoolblog.wordpress.com/2017/12/29/filippo-schreier-and-tango-delle-rose/. The melody is also known as Tango de la Rosa, Tango des Roses, or Song of the Rose. "Tango Delle Rose" was featured in the popular 1942 film *Casablanca*, sung uncredited by Corinna Mura in the role of a cabaret singer. "Corinna Mura," IMDb, accessed June 20, 2020, https://www.imdb.com/name/nm0613389/mediaviewer/rm3457689088; *Casablanca*, directed by Michael Curtiz, featuring Humphrey Bogart, Ingrid Bergman, Paul Henreid, and Claude Rains (Warner Bros., 1942).

Sun. Aug. 15, 1943

Dear Sylvia,

I had my own plans as to how I would take advantage of the liberty I was to get today but general headquarters had some plans of their own. We were notified last night that our services were desired and that we would be needed vitally as "mess attendants." We told them that we have as yet to get Sunday off and that it is the only day of the week that we can have to ourselves but they just smiled and said "report tomorrow morning at 4:00 A.M." We all tied a towel at the head of our beds and were awakened at 3:30 A.M. K.P.'s eat before the others so our meal began at 4:30 A.M. We had Wheaties with milk plus bacon, flap jacks, toast and honey dew melons. During the morning, it was my job to split and quarter the melons. Since we serve food in cafeteria style, another task was to feed the toaster and pass toast out to the boys who promptly came for breakfast at 5:30 A.M. Then when breakfast was over, with a bucket of hot water & brush, I scrubbed down the tables; then mopped the floor of the mess hall, also in the kitchen about the stoves.

We were to have steak for dinner so I had to cube the steaks and finally pass out soup at the dinner meal. Again I scrubbed & mopped the mess hall tables; then the floors. From 3:00 P.M. to 5:00 P.M., I did exactly nothing but sprawl out on a bench and try to sleep. We had a juke box where we played tunes over & over. They included "you'll never know", "Mess

38

August 15, 1943

From: P.A.C. A.S. Mazza
       B.T.C. – 10 T.G. 1183
       Sq F BKS – 167
       Greensboro, N. Carolina

To: Miss Sylvia Jacobs
       2334 Atmore St.
       N.S. Pgh., Pa

Postmark: 11:00 AM
           August 16, 1943
           Greensboro, N.C.

Letterhead: Army Air Forces
             Greensboro
             North Carolina

[1*]   Sun.[,] Aug. 15, 1943

Dear Sylvia,

I had my own plans as to how I would take advantage of the
liberty I was to get today[,] but general headquarters had some
plans of their own. We were notified last night that our services
were desired and that we would be needed vitally as "mess
attendants." We told them that we have as yet to get Sunday
off and that it is the only day of the week that we can have to

you". "Don't get around much anymore" + "Wait for me Mary".

This kind of work really can get you down if you let it, but we had plenty of fun ragging one another and discussing who had the easiest or hardest job. When serving food, we would include a sales talk to the boys. this kept spirits very high. I have just finished the detail at 8:00 PM before writing this letter.

So far we have learned to become excellent housewifes. We can make our bunks, keep our articles neat and clean; yes, even wash our own clothes. Most every night one cleans his undies in bed. On Mondays, boys are all lined up rubbing their clothes as hard as they can to remove dirt and seriously discussing the best methods of removing "tattle tale grey". ---- maybe I shouldn't tell you all the things I can do. They may be held against me.

I have been waiting for that second letter you promised but I imagine you were quite engrossed at your work at camp since your stay was so short. I received your card and agree that the mountains and landscape in that area can't be beat for natural beauty. I was at Laurel Ridge Camp -- Y.M.C.A. last year and would like some day to go back there to spend a couple of weeks by the lake and camp grounds.

Yesterday, we had dress parade and had to pass in review. The sun was so hot that boys collapsed while standing at attention for 45 minutes. Over 200 were victims; there weren't ambulances for them all. As one man fell, he was carried to the back of the lines and the next man would move up one. I felt pretty good when I found that I was still standing when the parade and ceremonies were over a

ourselves[,] but they just smiled and said[,] "[R]eport tomorrow morning at 4:00 AM." We all tied a towel at the head of our beds and were awakened at 3:30 AM. K.P.'s [*sic*] eat before the others[,] so our meal began at 4:30 A.M. We had Wheaties with milk plus bacon, flap jacks [*sic*], toast[,] and honey dew [*sic*] melons. During the morning, it was my job to split and quarter the melons. Since we serve food in cafeteria style, another task was to feed the toaster and pass toast out to the boys who promptly came for breakfast at 5:30 AM. Then when break-fast was over, with a bucket of hot water + brush, I scrubbed down the tables[,] then mopped the floor of the mess hall, also in the kitchen about the stoves.

We were to have steak for dinner so I had to cube the steaks and finally pass out soup at the dinner meal. Again[,] I scrubbed + mopped the mess hall tables[,] then the floors. From 2:00 PM to 5:00 PM, I did exactly nothing but sprawl out on a bench and try to sleep. We had a juke box [*sic*] where we played tunes over + over. They included "You'll [N]ever [K]now,"[36] "Miss [1R*] [Y]ou[,]"[37]

---

[36] See *supra* note 31.

[37] "Miss You," by Charles Tobias, Harry Tobias, and Henry Tobias, written in 1929, was a popular song in 1942-43, with a number of hit versions aired on the radio, including one by Dinah Shore on Bluebird Records in 1942 and one by Bing Crosby on Decca Records in the same year. B. Lee Cooper, "Charting Cultural Change, 1953-57: Song Assimilation through Cover Recording," in *Play It Again: Cover Songs in Popular Music*, ed. George Plasketes, 43-76 (Burlington, VT: Ashgate, 2013), 55.

ARMY AIR FORCES
GREENSBORO,
NORTH CAROLINA

It seemed that the largest and huskiest looking ones would topple first. It wasn't a slow faint but reacted very sudden and the victim hit the ground without stumbling.

Gosh Sylvia --- it seems that I am here quite a long time for I have adapted myself to these surroundings. You have the same set up at the Hospital, while you are in training; to a certain degree, it resembles army life.

Another trait I am acquiring is the art of singing. We are compelled to sing in ranks as this is to boost morale and also improve lung capacity so that we can sing at high altitudes later on. To sing the songs once or twice isn't so bad but after marching 3 or 4 miles and singing the same song 10 times or more is simply disgusting.

As I am writing this letter, one of the boys is getting up a collection of pennies in order to get a dog for a mascot. We won't get it now but when we land at college. Card games still flourish but I won't have any part of that. There are 4 fellows from our neighborhood with me in the Aviation Cadet program. Their names are Ralph Kalnas, Leonard Slevence, Julius Shoffer and Andrew Jerome. You may know them.

Last night we gave one of the fellows the works; someone put crackerjumbs in his bed while another put a water can before the door

42

"Don't [G]et [A]round [M]uch [A]nymore[,]"[38] + "Wait for [M]e[,] Mary[.]"[39]

This kind of work really can get you down if you let it[,] but we had plenty of fun razzing one another and discussing who had the easiest or hardest job. When serving food, we would include a sales talk to the boys; this kept spirits very high. I had just finished the detail at 8:00 PM before writing this letter.

So far[,] we have learned to become excellent housewifes [*sic*]. We can make our bunks, keep our articles neat and clean[,] yes, even wash our own clothes. Most every night one cleans his undies in [L]ux.[40] On Mondays, boys are all lined up rubbing their clothes as hard as they can to remove dirt and seriously discussing the best methods of removing "tattle tale [*sic*] grey."[41] - - - -

---

[38] In 1940, Victor Records released Duke Ellington's instrumental composition "Never No Lament." Duke Ellington and His Famous Orchestra, "Never No Lament," written by Duke Ellington, recorded May 4, 1940, Victor, No. 26610-A. After Bob Russell wrote lyrics to the melody in 1942, popular versions appeared under the new title "Don't Get Around Much Anymore." Glen Gray and the Casa Loma Orchestra with Kenny Sergeant and the Le Brun Sisters, vocalists, "Don't Get Around Much Anymore," by Duke Ellington and Bob Russell, released July 27, 1942, Decca, No. 18479B; The Ink Spots, vocalists, "Don't Get Around Much Anymore," by Duke Ellington and Bob Russell, recorded July 28, 1942, Decca, No. 18503B; "Don't Get Around Much Anymore," Second Hand Songs, accessed June 20, 2020, https://secondhandsongs.com/work/10904.

[39] Dick Haymes, vocalist, "Wait for Me, Mary," by Charlie Tobias, Nat Simon, and Harry Tobias, recorded May 27, 1943, Decca, No. 18556B; "Dick Haymes, (vocalist)," DAHR, accessed June 20, 2020, https://adp. library.ucsb.edu/index.php/talent/detail/149417/Hames_Dick_vocalist.

[40] In 1943, Lux was not only a popular brand of bath soap, but it was also a popular laundry soap. "Soap Prices Set Up for City Area Shops," *Harrisburg Telegraph*, May 14, 1943.

[41] A popular radio advertisement at the time advised consumers to banish "tattletale gray" from their laundry. "Silhouettes from the Nashville Army Air Center (AAFC)," *Nashville Banner*, April 22, 1943.

you can imagine the results. He didn't take the incident too well and made plenty of fuss; that means that he is on the spot as far as the rest of us are concerned and you can bet that he will have many more pranks played on him in the near future.

We were to hear Grace Moore in a concert this week but she didn't arrive due to illness.

It seems that I can go on writing hours telling about myself until I shall ~~itter~~ surely become egoistic. Will wait for reports from you so some evening you can spend some time with me by writing. I think I had better close now as the bugle will blow very soon and I want to take a shower, shampoo & shave. I sent my love to you and this time!

X X X X Surprised?

Love
Anthony

P.S. Excuse this letter for I'm not feeling too sharp after being up since 3:30 A.M. I'll surely do better next time.

44

Maybe I shouldn't tell you all the things I can do. They may be held against me.

I have been waiting for that second letter you promised[,] but I imagine you were quite engrossed at your work at camp since your stay was so short. I received your card and agree that the mountains and landscape in that area can't be beat for natural beauty. I was at Laurel Ridge Camp - - Y.M.C.A. last year and would like some day to go back there to spend a couple of weeks by the lake and camp grounds [sic].

Yesterday, we had dress parade and had to pass in review. The sun was so hot that boys collapsed while standing at attention for 45 minutes. Over 200 were victims; there weren't ambulances for them all. As one man fell, he was carried to the back of the lines[,] and the next man would move up one. I felt pretty good when I found that I was still standing when the parade and ceremonies were over.

[2*] It seemed that the largest and huskiest[-]looking ones would topple first. It wasn't a slow faint but reacted very sudden[,] and the victim hit the ground without stumbling.

Gosh[,] Sylvia - - - it seems that I am here quite a long time[,] for I have adapted myself to these surroundings. You have the same set up [sic] at the [h]ospital, while you are in training; to a certain degree, it resembles [A]rmy life.

Another trait I am acquiring is the art of singing. We are compelled to sing in ranks as this is to boost morale and also improve lung capacity so that we can fly at high altitudes later on. To sing the songs once or twice isn't so bad[,] but after marching 3 or 4 miles and singing the same song 10 times or more is simply disgusting.

As I am writing this letter, one of the boys is getting up a collection of pennies in order to get a dog for a mascot. We won't get it now but when we land at college. Card games still flourish[,] but I won't have any part of that. There are 4 fellows from our

P.A.C. A.S. MAZZA
10.T.C.-10 T.G. 1183
Sq F BKS-167
Greensboro N.Carolina

Free

Miss Sylvia Jacobs
2334 Wharton St.
N.S. Pgh, Pa

46

neighborhood with me in the Pre-Aviation Cadet program. Their names are Ralph Kalnas, Leonard Derence, Joseph Shaffer, and Andrew Jerome.[42] You may know them.

Last night we gave one of the fellows the works; someone put crackercrumbs [*sic*] in his bed while another put a water can before the doors—[2R] you can imagine the results. He didn't take the incident too well and made plenty of fuss; that means that he is on the spot as far as the rest of us are concerned[,] and you can bet that he will have many more pranks played on him in the near future.

We were to hear Grace Moore in a concert this week[,] but she didn't arrive due to illness.[43]

It seems that I can go on writing hours[,] telling about myself until I shall surely become egotistic. Will want for reports from you[,] so some evening you can spend some time with me by writing. I think I had better close now as the bugle will blow very soon[,] and I want to take a shower, shampoo + shave. I sen[d] my love to you and this time:

XXXX Surprised?

Love[,]
Anthony

P.S. Excuse this letter for I'm not feeling too sharp after being up since 3:30 AM. I'll surely do better next time.

---

42 The men from Pittsburgh mentioned here were Leonard A. Derence of 3153 Shadeland Avenue, Andrew A. Jerome of 3123 Brighton Road, Ralph G. Kalnas of 3134 McClure Avenue, and Joseph J. Shaffer of 1239 Superior Avenue. "67 Leave Here for Air Cadet Training," *Pittsburgh Post-Gazette*, August 2, 1943.

43 Grace Moore (b. December 5, 1898; d. January 26, 1947) was an American operatic soprano known as the "Tennessee Nightingale." Bruce Eder, "Grace Moore: Artist Biography," AllMusic, accessed June 20, 2020, https://www.allmusic.com/artist/grace-moore-mn0000198358.

ARMY AIR FORCES
GREENSBORO.
NORTH CAROLINA

Aug 19, 1943

My darling Sylvia,

Have received your long sought for letter and must tell you that it was a treat to read for it contained all the little things I like to hear! I don't like the idea of you answering them but want you to have a reply for each individual letter I send. This letter couldn't be written sooner for I was detailed to Guard Duty during the past 24 hours. I would have written even though I didn't get an answer from you as yet. I am glad to hear you enjoyed camping but I knew that before you wrote. I am glad to hear that you were made an honored guest and you bet I'm glad I know you. You've been on my honor list for quite some time though. (Don't I move to the head of the class for that remark) I'm sorry to say I don't know what a "Honeymoon Salad" is like, but I'm glad to give you the opportunity of explaining it to me. I'll take a guess as to the weigh you gained --- 3 lbs --- How good am I at guessing? Now its your turn. Guess how many lbs I gained? (Its all solid though).

I'm thrilled that you think so much of those wings and more so at the fact that you wear them on the left side. I'll give you every chance to earn them once I get home.

48

August 19, 1943

Postmark: [The envelope is missing.]

Letterhead: Army Air Forces
              Greensboro
              North Carolina

[1*]   Aug[.] 19, 1943

My darling Sylvia,

Have received your long[-]sought[-]for letter and must tell you that it was a treat to read[,] for it contained all the little things I like to hear. I don't like the idea of you[r] answering them but want you to have a reply for each individual letter I send. This letter couldn't be written sooner[,] for I was detailed to [g]uard [d]uty during the past 24 hours. I would have written[,] even though I didn't get an answer from you as yet. I am glad to hear you enjoyed camping[,] but I knew that before you wrote. I am glad to hear that you were made an honored guest[,] and you bet I'm glad I know you. You've been on my honor list for quite some time[,] though. (Don't I move to the head of the class for that remark[?]) I'm sorry to say I don't know what a "Honeymoon Salad" is like, but I'm glad to give you the opportunity of explaining it to me.[44] I'll take a guess as to the weigh[t] you gained - - - 2 lbs[.] - - - How

---

[44] This is an old joke. What is a Honeymoon Salad? Lettuce alone (i.e., let us alone). In subsequent years, the answer to the joke became embellished: lettuce alone with no dressing. Barry Popik, "Honeymoon Salad," The Big Apple (blog), August, 30, 2009, https://www.barrypopik.com/index.php/ new_york_city/entry/honeymoon_salad_lettuce_alone_and_no_dressing.

How did you like riding the Turnpike? I thought it a well built highway but after a while I got tired of looking at everything the same. I prefer a road that twists and bends, goes up and down, and gives a picturesque panorama of the terrain. I would very much like to dance the "Virginia Reel" with you. I can picture you as the girl that danced that part in "Rodeo" at the Ballet. I'll dance the male role however. Be sure you have "softey shoes." Here goes stomp! Stomp! Stomp! and so on into the night.

You mentioned the moon and wishing that I might be there. I beat you to that for on Wednesday night I was assigned to guard duty and was on guard for twenty four hours at 2 hours on duty and 4 hours off. My watch was from 4:00 PM to 6:00 PM, 10 PM to 12:00 PM. etc. I was armed with a very potent weapon --- a mace. It was my detail to guard the camp reservoir from would be sabateurs. If anyone passed and didn't give the proper pass word and countersign, I had instructions to bash his brains in. My first watch wasn't so bad as I watched the sun begin to set. I knew it would be quite lonely on the next watch so I asked who would I like to tag along for company from 10:00 PM to 12:00. Guess who got the nod? Yup. Your right as usual. You. I called you by mental telepathy first at Ce 4546 but you weren't there. .. next at 11 9924 and asked for Miss Sylvia Jacobs please. Of all things you were taking a shower. Twenty minutes later you answered. I asked if you would like to take a stroll with me. You hemmed and hawwed --- but I finally talked you into it. Zoom and

50

good am I at guessing? Now it[']s your turn. Guess how many lbs[.] I gained? (It[']s all solid though).

I'm thrilled that you think so much of those wings and more so at the fact that you wear them on the left side. I'll give you every chance to earn them once I get home.

[1R*] How did you like riding the Turnpike? I thought it a well[-]built highway[,] but after a while[,] I got tired of looking at everything the same. I prefer a road that twists and bends, goes up and down, and gives a picturesque panorama of the terrain. I would very much like to dance the "Virginia Reel" with you. I can picture you as the girl that danced that part in "Rodeo" at the [b]allet.[45] I'll dance the male role however; be sure you have "safety shoes." Here goes stomp! stomp! stomp! and so on into the night.

You mentioned the moon and wishing that I might be there. I beat you to that[,] for on Wednesday night[,] I was assigned to guard duty and was on guard for twenty[-]four hours at 2 hours on duty and 4 hours off. My watch was from 4:00 PM to 6:00 PM[,] 10:00 PM to 12:00 PM[,] etc. I was armed with a very potent weapon - - - a mace. It was my detail to guard the [c]amp reservoir from would[-]be saboteurs. If anyone passed and didn't give the proper pass word [*sic*] and countersign, I had instructions to bash his brains in. My first watch wasn't so bad as I watched the sun begin to set. I knew it would be quite lonely on the next watch[,] so I asked who[m] would I like to tag along for company from 10:00 PM to 12:00. Guess who got the nod? Yep. Your [*sic*] right as usual.

---

[45] *Rodeo* is a one-act ballet, written in 1942 by the American composer Aaron Copland and choreographed by Agnes de Mille. "Rodeo: Ballet in One Act," Aaron Copland, accessed June 20, 2020, https://www.aaroncopland. com/works/rodeo-ballet/.

You. I called you by mental telepathy first at Ce 4546[,] but you weren't there – – – next at Li 9924 and asked for Miss Sylvia Jacobs[,] please. Of all things[,] you were taking a shower. Twenty minutes later[,] you answered. I asked if you would like to take a stroll with me. You hemmed and hawwed [*sic*] – – – but I finally talked you into it. Zoom and

[The rest of the letter is missing.]

ARMY AIR FORCES
GREENSBORO,
NORTH CAROLINA

(A SOLDIER'S NIGHT OFF)

Aug 22, 1943

Dearest Sylvia,

At last I have seen the fair city of Greensboro. Last night being Saturday, I was able to get a pass from 6:00 PM to 7 AM. I didn't feel like going at first but when I looked at some of the laundry I had that I couldn't do myself (lack of an iron) I didn't hesitate very long. From the camp main gate, which is located near my barracks, I took a taxi and was in the heart of the city in less than 15 minutes. The price too was very reasonable at 15¢. I did find a laundry but I gave them my clothes and when I asked for a ticket to proove that I left my clothes there, they wouldn't give me one. "Just call out your name next Wednesday and you'll get them without any trouble," was their reply. So I asked for my clothes back and walked out and after going to several other places I found they all had the same system. I finally left them at one laundry but I am still wondering if I shall ever get them back for I have no proof that I left them. Next week I may have to drill in my underwear. I then started to look the town over and started to realize that I did miss city life after all and it did feel plenty good just to roam through crowded streets and stores. I had gone but two blocks when I met

54

August 22, 1943

Postmark: [The envelope is missing.]

Letterhead: Army Air Forces
              Greensboro
              North Carolina

[1*]   (A SOLDIER'S NIGHT OFF)
                                        Aug[.] 22, 1943

Dearest Sylvia,

At last I have seen the fair City of Greensboro. Last night being Saturday, I was able to get a pass from 6:00 PM to 1:[00] AM. I didn't feel like going at first[,] but when I looked at some of the laundry I had that I couldn't do myself (lack of an iron)[,] I didn't hesitate very long. From the camp main gate, which is located near my barracks, I took a taxi and was in the heart of the city in less than 15 minutes. The price[,]too[,] was very reasonable at 15¢. I did find a laundry[,] but I gave them my clothes[,] and when I asked for a ticket to proove [*sic*] I left my clothes there, they wouldn't give me one. "Just call out your name next Wednesday[,] and you'll get them without any trouble," was their reply. So I asked for my clothes back and walked out[,] and after going to several other places[,] I found they all had the same system. I finally left them at one laundry[,] but I am still wondering if I shall ever get them back[,] for I have no proof that I left them. Next week[,] I may have to drill in my underwear. I then started to look the town over and started to realize that I did miss city life after all[,] and it did feel plenty good just to roam through crowded streets and stores. I had gone two blocks when I met [1R*] one of my buddies who

55

one of my buddies who had a date with a girl in a department store. He said he was in a fix for he was to meet her at 8:00PM and he had forgotten her name and what store she worked. He had her telephone number but was too backward to call. So I (the bold one) offered to help him. I dialed the number and found no one at home. So we walked several blocks stopping at every other one to call. We made no connections. Finally we decided to go to the dance held at Hotel Henry for service men. We found the place with little difficulty but it was tremendously crowded. The orchestra was very excellant, the floor beautifully lit and polished, the band stand nicely elevated, the musicans neatly dressed, huge drapes hung in luxurious manner from windows, the place was packed to capacity but (it seems) one minor thing was missing - - - - women. (who ever heard of those creatures?) ??!! We left in a hurry and headed for the east side of the town. before long we ~~were at~~ a rink. I roller skated most of the evening going round and round and round. Too bad you weren't with me. I called by mental telepath~~y~~ but you were on duty. - - - - darn it! I think you were pretty tired too from guard duty. you mentioned something about your feet being sore. Maybe you don't care for skating very much? A little later in the evening I went to the Bowling alley beneath the Roller Skating Rink. I bowled but one line and with my trusty right arm bowled the amazing score of 75. (am I good). I am going out for national competition. (Aren't you glad you know me.) Sometime I'll let you

had a date with a girl in a department store. He said he was in a fix[,] for he was to meet her at 8:00 PM[,] and he had forgotten her name and [at] what store she worked. He had her telephone number but was too backward to call. So I (the bold one) offered to help him. I dialed the number and found no one at home. So we walked blocks[,] stopping at every other one to call. We made no connections. Finally[,] we decided to go to the dance held at Hotel Henry for service men [*sic*].[46] We found the place with little difficulty[,] but it was tremendously crowded. The orchestra was very excellent, the floor beautifully lit and polished, the band stand [*sic*] nicely elevated, the musicians neatly dressed, huge drapes hung in [a] luxurious manner from windows, the place was packed to capacity[,] but it seems one minor thing was missing - - - - - women. (Who ever heard of those creatures?)??!! We left in a hurry and headed for the east side of the town; before long we were at a rink. I roller[-]skated most of the evening[,] going round and round and round. Too bad you weren't with me. I called by mental telepathy[,] but you were on duty. - - - - darn it! I think you were pretty tired[,] too[,] from guard duty. You mentioned something about your feet being sore. Maybe you don't care for skating very much? A little later in the evening[,] I went to the bowling alley beneath the [r]oller[-][s]kating [r]ink. I bowled but one line and with my trusty right arm bowled the amazing score of <u>75</u>. (Am I good). I am going out for national competition. (Aren't you glad you know me?) Sometime I'll let you

[The rest of the letter is missing.]

---

[46] The original O. Henry Hotel, built in 1919, was located at the southwest corner of Bellemeade and North Elm Streets in Greensboro, North Carolina. The hotel was closed in the 1960s and razed in 1979. "Original O. Henry Hotel," O. Henry Hotel, accessed June 20, 2020, https://ohenryhotel.com/original/.

Aug. 25, 1943

My dear Sylvia,

I like the idea of ~~having your wrote~~ Wednesday and Fridays for I too shall commemorate those nights to letter writing and you. . . . . I'll get more mail that way too from you. (I'm a little bit selfish but I don't think you'll mind.) (I know that I won't). So its back to work for you once more and here am I still waiting for a vacation. I probably won't get one until my first furlough which seems now ages away. I keep my fingers always crossed for you until one of them now is still white while the others are tanned from the rays of the sun. I don't know if you need it that bad but my fingers are sometimes numb keeping them crossed for you. I need fingers crossed for me at all times though. My most popular song is "Wait for me Mary". What do you think of that one?

You should hear me sing (shout) Jolly, Jolly sixpence from "I've got sixpence". I think we'd make a pretty good duet if you could be heard 'neath the volumous roaring of my voluptuous voice. My lungs are rounding into very good condition - - - They were never much out of order.

Mother wrote and told me of my cousin (Margret's brother) being in the hospital. He and I associated very little together for we have nothing in common and his principles are entirely different

58

August 25, 1943

From: P.A.C. A.S. Mazza
        B.T.C. – 10 T.G. 1183
        Sq F BKS – 167
        Greensboro, N. Carolina

To: Miss Sylvia Jacobs
        3334 Fleming Ave[.]
        St. John's School for Nurses
        Pgh., (12) Pa.

Postmark: 10:30 AM
            August 26, 1943
            Greensboro, N.C.

Letterhead: Army Air Forces Basic Training Center
              Greensboro, North Carolina

[1*]   Aug. 25, 1943

My dear Sylvia,

I like the idea of having you write Wednesdays and Fridays[,] for I[,] too[,] shall commemorate [*sic*] those nights to letter writing and you. - - - - I'll get more mail that way[,] too[,] from you. (I'm a little bit selfish[,] but I don't think you'll mind.) (I know that I won't). So it[']s back to work for you once more[,] and here am I still waiting for a vacation. I probably won't get one until my first furlough[,] which seems now ages away. I keep my fingers always crossed for you until one of them is still white while the others are tanned from the rays of the sun. I don't know if you need it that

from mine. Mother also told me that she received your card and that it was very thoughtful of you. She also wishes that when you go by the post to visit her sometime. Won't you? I am glad to hear that you were honored by what mother said about you. It must have been good. I always knew mother's good judgement.

Whatever you do when playing tennis don't get too good for then you will show me up when I get my hands on a racket once more. No I didn't see "This is the Army" but will go after your recommendation.

What! you gained 5 lbs. Better watch out or next time I'll write a good lecture for you. With me, well that is a song with a different tune. I gained 5 lbs but I'm afraid to disappoint you for they are absolutely on the solid side. Your guess was far better than mine and shall concede the decision to you.

No matter what you write on or if you can't spell a word, it little matters to me as long as what you write sounds like the you I knew. As far as my spelling, I won't take any honors for that, for "scientists" don't give a hoot for English although they must put up with it. Symbols will be used as long as they explain thought. My letters are as unorthodox as I can make them.

I am hoping and praying that I shall be sent to a college within 50 miles of the city of Pgh. I shall then be able to get home almost every other week as Joe is doing now. Let's see what happens if we both concentrate our prayers on this one (selfish) item. I won't be here very long and some reports have it that we shall be gone by Sept 3rd. On Friday and four days

bad[,] but my fingers are sometimes numb keeping them crossed for you. I need fingers crossed for me at all times[,] though. My most popular song is "Wait for [M]e, [M]ary."[47] What do you think of that one?

You should hear me sing (shout)[, "]Jolly, [j]olly sixpence[,"] from "I've [G]ot [S]ixpence."[48] I think we'd make a pretty good duet if you could be heard 'neath the volumous [*sic*] roaring of my voluptuous voice. My lungs are rounding into very good condition - - - They were never[49] much out of order.

Mother wrote and told me of my cousin (Marg[a]ret's brother) being in the hospital. He and I associated very little together[,] for we have nothing in common[,] and his principles are entirely different [1R*] from mine. Mother also told me that she received your card and that it was very thoughtful of you. She also wishes that when you go by the park to visit her some-time. Won't you? I am glad to hear that you were honored by what [M]other said about you. It must have been good. I always knew and respected [M]other's good judgement [*sic*].

Whatever you do when playing tennis[,] don't get too good[,] for then you will show me up when I get my hands on a racket once more. No[,] I didn't see "This is the Army"[50] but will go after your recommendation.

---

47 See *supra* note 39.
48 "I've Got Sixpence" is a traditional folk song that became a popular World War II marching song for the U.S. military. "See Origins: I've Got Sixpence, Joly, Jolly Sixpence," The Mudcat Cafe, accessed June 20, 2020, https://mudcat.org/thread.cfm?threadid=92279,92279.
49 The script is not clear.
50 *This is the Army*, directed by Michael Curtiz, featuring George Murphy, Joan Leslie, and Ronald Reagan (Warner Bros., 1943).

2.

after that I shall be at the rifle range hitting
bull's eyes --- I hope, I hope.

All we do now from morning to night is drill
in the hot day weather. Not a drop of rain yet since
I've been here and there wasn't any 3 wks before I
came. Its a wonder that a blade of grass can be
found outside the swampy areas. I'm getting tanner
each day until maybe even you could hardly recognize me under my dark complexion.

I hope you don't mind me teasing you in
my letters but I get a kick out of it. Mental
telepathy is quite a tool to have handy and it
has made the one month that I've been here seem like
two instead of these or more. It will never approach
the real thing though.

Last Saturday evening I called once more
and had a difficult time getting you for the phone
was busy for quite some time. We talked for oh-so
short a period for there was a line extending from
the phone all the way down the hall of girls waiting
to get calls through. I was pretty mean though
and wanted to keep them waiting but you put
a stop to it. I succeeded in getting you to go
swimming with me in a pool called "High
Point" 14 miles from Greensboro. This pool
resembled "North Park Pool." I had plenty of
fun trying to duck you but got ducked plenty
myself for after all you are a Jr. lifeguard.

62

What! [Y]ou gained 5 lbs. Better watch out or next time I'll write a good lecture for you. With me, well that is a song with a different tune. I gained 5 lbs[.,] but I'm afraid to disappoint you[,] for they are absolutely on the solid side. Your guess was far better than mine and shall concede the decision to you.

No matter what you write on or if you can't spell a word, it little matters to me as long as what you write sounds like the you I know. As far as my spelling, I won't take any honors for that, for "scientists" don't give a hoot for English[,] although they must put up with it. Symbols will be used as long as they explain thought. My letters are as unorthodox as I can make them.

I am hoping and praying that I shall be sent to a college within 50 miles of the City of Pgh. I shall then be able to get home almost every other week as Joe is doing now. Let's see what happens if we both concentrate our prayers on this one (selfish) item. I won't be here very long[,] and some reports have it that we shall be gone by Sept[.] 3rd. On Friday and four days [2*] after that[,] I shall be at the rifle range hitting bull's[-]eyes - - - I hope, I hope.

All we do now from morning to night is drill in the hot[,] dry weather. Not a drop of rain yet since I've been here[,] and there wasn't any 3 wks[.] before I came. It[']s a wonder that a blade of grass can be found outside the swampy areas. I'm getting tanner each day until maybe even you could hardly recognize me under my dark complexion.

I hope you don't mind me teasing you in my letters[,] but I get a kick out of it. Mental telepathy is quite a tool to have handy[,] and it has made the one month I've been here seem like two instead of three or more. It will never approach the real thing[,] though.

Last Saturday evening[,] I called once more and had a difficult time getting you[,] for the phone was busy for quite some time. We talked for oh[-]so[-]short a period[;] there was a line extending

We played in the sand and ended by having it all over us from head to toe. After a short snack including a chicken dinner, we went canoeing on Lake "High Point." The moon was full and crystal clear and we sang perfect duets as I paddled silently across the lake while you reclined in a soft cushion at the other end of the boat, facing me. I'm afraid we got in after 12:00 A.M. that night but I couldn't help it if the transportation problem was not up to par.

I have enclosed a card which I thought best to put in an enclosed envelope, for Miss Smith might not think you gave me the correct version of her personality. also it might be embarrassing to you should someone else get it.

Imagine me sending X X X X and getting x x x X in return. Something is wrong somewhere for I like them all like the first ones.

X X X X See what I mean.

Love
Anthony

64

from the phone all the way down the hall, of girls waiting to get calls through. I was pretty mean[,] though[,] and wanted to keep them waiting[,] but you put a stop to it. I succeeded in getting you to go swimming with me [on] Sunday to a pool called "High Point" 14 miles from Greensboro. This pool resembled "North Park Pool."[51] I had plenty of fun trying to duck you[,] but got ducked plenty myself[,] for after all[,] you are a Jr. [L]ifeguard.

[2R*] We played in the sand and ended by having it all over us from head to toe. After a short snack, including a chicken dinner, we went canoeing on lake "High Point." The moon was full and crystal clear[,] and we sang perfect duets as I paddled silently across the lake while you reclined on a soft cushion at the other end of the boat, facing me. I'm afraid we got in after 12:00 AM. that night[,] but I couldn't help it if the transportation problem was not up to par.

I have inclosed [*sic*] a card which I thought best to put in an enclosed envelope, for Miss Smith might not think you gave me the correct version of her personality, also it might be embarrassing to you should someone else get it.

Imagine me sending XXXX and getting xxxX in return. Something is wrong somewhere[,] for I like them all like the first ones.

XXXX See what I mean.

Love[,]
Anthony

---

51 The reference is to North Park in Allegheny County, Pennsylvania, 10501 Pearce Mill Road, Allison Park, PA 15101. See "North Park," Allegheny County, accessed June 20, 2020, https://www.alleghenycounty.us/parks/north-park/index.aspx.

Free

P.A.C. A.S. MATZ...
B.T.C.-10 T.S.-1193
Sq F. 13th T-167
Greensboro, N. Carolina

GREENSBORO
AUG 26
10³⁰ AM
1943

Miss Sylvia Jacobs
3334 Fleming Ave
St. John's School for Nurses
Pgh; (12) Pa.

Aug 29, 1943

Dearest Sylvia,

I aimed to call you by mental
Telepathy Friday but the lines were jamed. A severe
electrical storm prevented the connection. I
finally put the call through this morning and it
worked but one way; I keep talking while you
do all of the listening. This suits me fine for
I never gave you much of a chance to say anything
anyway. I got you to spend Sunday with me here
at camp; 2 oo m and there you are. Hallo! what,
you thought you'd be at camp? Well you're wrong
for we are in a pup tent 10 miles from Greensboro
at the rifle range. I thought we'd go out somewhere
but that is impossible for there is nowhere to go and
the rain keeps pouring down. So we'll sit and talk,
if that is alright with you. Did I hear you say
yes? Well Thursday night our group was assembled
and told that tomorrow, Friday morning, we would
go to the rifle range. All were elated at the idea of
camping out and getting the opportunity to test our
skill at hitting the bull's eye. There were several
factors we didn't consider and they were the
ten mile hike with a forty lb. pack and the weather.
The march wasn't so bad for I felt that I could
go many a mile more after we had arrived. On
the way we had lots of fun singing, shouting out

August 29, 1943

From: P.A.C. A.S. Mazza
                B.T.C. – 10 T.G. 1183
                Sq F BKS – 167
                Greensboro, N. Carolina

To: Miss Sylvia Jacobs
                3334 Flemming [*sic*] Ave.
                St. John's School for Nurses
                N.S. (12) Pgh., Pa

Postmark: 7:00 PM
                August 29, 1943
                Greensboro, N.C.

Letterhead: Army Air Forces
                Greensboro
                North Carolina

[1*]   Aug[.] 29, 1943

Dearest Sylvia,

I aimed to call you by mental telepathy Friday[,] but the lines were jammed. A severe electrical storm prevented the connection. I finally put the call through this morning[,] and it worked but one way; I keep talking while you do all the listening. This suits me fine[,] for I never gave you much of a chance to say anything anyway. I got you to spend Sunday with me here at camp; zoom and there you are. Hello! What, you thought you'd be at camp? Well[,] you're wrong[,] for we are in a pup tent 10 miles from

remarks to civilians as "join the Aircorps to fly" or "Why aren't you at work, there is a war going on". Some of the boys would whistle at the beautiful southern gals but (I didn't pay much attention.) A few little tots no more than 4 years old would walk or rather stand still on the road with a piggy bank and ask to have pennies put in. I'm afraid I got rid of all my pennies that day. Some racket, they sure start young here. There is quite a contrast in homes from that of an old fashioned Southern Plantation to a darkies cabin setting back in the woods. Just as we arrived at the bivouac area, a medical officer stopped us and wanted to examine our feet for blisters. We pulled off our shoes + socks, rolled back our trousers and held our feet straight in the air as he went by. It started to rain a bit then --- the first since I have been here. There was a mad scramble for shoes, socks, and the raincoats that were in our packs. In a few minutes we were directed to the area where our tents were to be pitched. Each soldier carries a tent half and two of them make the tent and live in it after it is up. You have probably seen these small boy scout tents, well its exactly the same. The weather let up a bit and we had little trouble getting them up but instead of being permitted to dig proper trenches about the tent, our program called for swimming lessons so down to the lake we went. What a lake? It was beautifully located but muddier than the Monongahela at its worst. That is quite muddy, isn't it.

Greensboro at the rifle range. I thought we'd go out somewhere[,] but that is impossible[,] for there is nowhere to go[,] and the rain keeps pouring down. So we'll sit and talk, if that is alright [sic] with you. Did I hear you say yes? Well, Thursday night our group was assembled and told that tomorrow, Friday morning, we would go to the rifle range. All were elated at the idea of camping out and getting the opportunity to test our skill at hitting the bull's[-]eye. There were several factors we didn't consider[,] and they were the ten[-]mile hike with a forty[-]lb. pack and the weather. The march wasn't so bad[,] for I felt that I could go many a mile more after we had arrived. On the way[,] we had lots of fun singing, shouting out [1R*] remarks to civilians [such] as "Join the Aircorps [sic] to fly" or "Why aren't you at [w]ork; there is a war going on." Some of the boys would whistle at the beautiful Southern gals[,] but (I didn't pay much attention[).] A few little tots[,] no more than 4 years old[,] would walk[,] or rather stand still on the road with a piggy bank and ask to have pennies put in. I'm afraid I got rid of all my pennies that day. Some racket, they sure start young here. There is quite a contrast in homes from that of an old[-]fashioned Southern [p]lantation to a darkies [sic] cabin sitting back in the woods. Just as we arrived at the bivouac area, a medical officer stopped us and wanted to examine our feet for blisters. We pulled off our shoes + socks[,] rolled back on our haunches[,] and held our feet straight in the air as he went by. It started to rain a bit then – – – – – the first since I have been here. There was a mad scramble for shoes, socks, and the raincoats that were in our packs. In a few minutes[,] we were directed to the area where our our [sic] tents were to be pitched. Each soldier carries a tent half[,] and two of them make the tent and live in it after it is up. You have probably seen these small [B]oy [S]cout tents[;] well[,] it[']s exactly the same. The weather let up a bit[,] and we had little trouble getting them up, but instead of

71

ARMY AIR FORCES
GREENSBORO,
NORTH CAROLINA

1

We saw that picture again of "Swim and Live". The army insists that we swim using but three methods; the breast stroke, the side stroke with scissors kick and the back stroke using frog kick. In all of these the hands never go above the surface of the water. I am learning to swim all over again. We shall learn to make life preservers from our barracks bag and clothing tomorrow. As we got back from the pool, a huge thunderhead could be seen above and we hurried to our tents as fast as we could. It was quite late and near chow time so we took our mess kits and went to dinner. My what a line! It wasn't long before a new verse was added to one of our songs. The chow that they give you, they say is mighty fine.
You'll surely die of hunger just standing there in line.
Oh! I don't want no more of army life
Gee mom! I want to go home.
Then it started to rain. A regular deluge with hail included. I just got my food and dashed into the mess tent. I ate peacefully for a while thankful of the shelter, when suddenly the water

72

being permitted to dig proper trenches about the tent, our program called for swimming lessons[,] so down to the lake we went. What a lake? It was beautifully located but muddier than the Monongahela at its worst.[52] That is quite muddy, isn't it[?]

[2*] We saw that picture again of "Swim and Live." The [A]rmy insists that we swim using but three methods[:] the breast stroke [*sic*], the side stroke with sissors [*sic*] kick[,] and the back stroke [*sic*][,] using frog kick. In all of these[,] the hands never go above the surface of the water. I am learning to swim all over again. We shall learn to make life preservers from our barracks bag and clothing tomorrow. As we got back from the pool, a huge thunderhead could be seen above[,] and we hurried to our tents as fast as we could. It was quite late and near chow time[,] so we took our mess kits and went to dinner. My what a line! It wasn't long before a new verse was added to one of our songs[:]

The chow that they give you, they say is mighty fine.
You'll surely die of hunger just standing there in line.
Oh! I don't want no more of [A]rmy life[.]
Gee[,] [M]om! I want to go home.[53]

---

[52] The City of Pittsburgh, Pennsylvania, is located at the confluence of the Monongahela River and the Allegheny River, which together form the Ohio River. "Three Rivers Run through It," Popular Pittsburgh, accessed June 20, 2020, https://popularpittsburgh.com/threerivers/.

[53] "Gee, Mom, I Want to Go Home," is a traditional, satirical song about military life, which Canadian soldiers created during World War II. Members of the U.S. military quickly borrowed it. As here, the first two lines are often improvised to address current circumstances, while the last two lines, the chorus, remain constant. "Gee, Mom, I Want to Go Home," wikivisually.com, accessed June 20, 2020, https://wikivisually.com/wiki/Gee,_Mom,_I_Want_to_Go_Home.

began to accumulate at one end of the tent and burst a seam open. A group of boys were soaked to the skin from that unexpected stream. I nearly died laughing after seeing the startled expression on their faces, although it could just as easily have been me and I'm sure that I wouldn't think it very funny.

The mud began to form inches deep and after it, the rain, let up a bit, I skidded and slid back to my tent. It didn't rain very long so very little damage was done. My blankets were in my barracks bag and I was glad that I didn't have them out. At last 5 picks were salvaged to dig trenches but our group was much too large to have everyone use them. So my partner and I turned primitive and with the knife from our mess kit digged and scraped an 8" inch trench around our tent. Then it did rain hard and steady, and I crawled inside feeling quite secure. Some of the fellows didn't fare so well for water pushed inside and they were soaked. Others had their tents cave in on them and you should have heard the howls and language (maybe you shouldn't). It dried up a bit yesterday but last night it rained again most of the night and it is raining now. It looks like an all day rain. Its mud, mud and more mud. I don't see how you didn't get your feet muddy when you came but I bet that was due to the speed. You know that I wanted to write on Friday night but it was impossible. I thought about you though so that ought to put me in your good graces. Doesn't it?

Then it started to rain. A regular deluge with hail included. I just got my food and dashed into the mess tent. I ate peacefully for a while[,] thankful of the shelter, when suddenly the water [2R*] began to accumulate at one end of the tent and burst a seam open. A group of boys were soaked to the skin from that unexpected stream. I nearly died laughing after seeing the startled expression on their faces, althought [sic] it could just as easily have been me[,] and I'm sure that I wouldn't think it very funny.

The mud began to form inches deep[,] and after it, the rain let up a bit[;] I skidded and slid back to my tent. It didn't rain very long[,] so very little damage was done. My blankets were in my barracks bag[,] and I was glad that I didn't have them out. At last[,] 5 picks were salvaged to dig trenches[,] but our group was much too large to have everyone use them. So my partner and I turned primitive[,] and with the knife from our mess kit digged [sic] and scraped an 8[-]inch trench around our tent. Then it did rain hard and steady, and I crawled inside[,] feeling quite secure. Some of the fellows didn't fare so well[,] for water gushed inside[,] and they were soaked. Others had their tents cave in on them[,] and you should have heard the howls and language (maybe you shouldn't). It dried up a bit yesterday[,] but last night[,] it rained again most of the night[,] and it is raining now. It looks like an all[-]day rain. It[']s mud, mud[,] and more mud. I don't see how you didn't get your feet muddy when you came[,] but I bet that was due to the speed. You know that I wanted to write on Friday night[,] but it was impossible. I thought about you[,] though[,] so that ought to put me in your good graces. Doesn't it?

[The rest of the letter is missing.]

Free

P.A.C. A.S. MAZZA
B.T.C.-10 T.G. 1183
Sgt Brks 7-167
Greensboro, N. Carolina

Miss Sylvia Jacobs
3334 Fleming Ave.
St. John's School for Nurses
N.S. (12) Pgh., Pa

76

Sept 4, 1943

Dearest Sylvia,

It is for the best. Keep those Saturday nights wide open for I shall be on hand as soon as permissible. There must be something to a concentrated prayer for it was answered to perfection. Of all the small colleges in Western Penna, I had chosen St. Vincent as the one I would most like to attend. I can hardly believe my eyes when I returned to it from Greensboro. compared to Greensboro this is like floating on a cloud. George said that cadets at Pitt live like kings; we likeas "emperors" here. It seems I have returned to civilization once more and appreciate small conveniences that I never did before. I have a room shared by one other man. This room has wash bowl, bath, shower, shelves for putting various articles, desk, and a bed. --- with sheets! My room-mate is too most fortunate for he lives at Latrobe which is but 2 miles from the college.

September 4, 1943

From: A./S. A.S. Mazza
                    33rd College Training Detachment
                    (Air Crew)
                    St. Vincent College
                    Latrobe, Pennsylvania

To: Miss Sylvia Jacobs
                    3334 Fleming Ave.
                    St. John's School for Nursing
                    N.S. Pgh., Pa[.] (12)

Postmark: 7:00 PM
                    September 4, 1943
                    Latrobe, PA

Letterhead: 33rd College Training Detachment
                    (Air Crew)
                    Saint Vincent College, Latrobe, Pennsylvania

[1*]   Sept[.] 4, 1943

Dearest Sylvia,

It is for the best. Keep those Saturday nights wide open[,] for I shall be on hand as soon as permissible. There must be something to a concentrated prayer[,] for it was answered to perfection. Of all the small colleges in Western Penna[.], I had chosen St. Vincent as

Pennsylvania can't be beat for its natural beauty; maybe I'm prejudiced but this college sets back surrounded by mountains. At the foothills, the well cultivated land can be seen neatly divided into small patterns. The landscape about the college itself is well planned with willow and pine trees plus beautiful plots of flowers.

All of the building were built by the monks of the Benedictan Order with their own hands. Every brick was molded and formed by them!

I shall be confined to the premises for two whole weeks (campused) by Army regulations. As for week-end passes, I may get one every two wks or at least once per month. (Providing I'm not gigged). We may get passes every week from Saturday 4:00 PM to Sunday morning 2:00 AM. Sunday morning from 8:00 AM until Sunday night 9:30 PM.

I wanted to call you by phone when I arrived but since you might be at one of three places and I never did get you on the first call, I decided to let a letter suffice. I called mother and told her to give you my new address; I hope she was able to

the one I would most like to attend.[54] I can hardly believe my eyes when I returned to it from Greensboro; compared to Greensboro this is like floating on a cloud. George said that cadets at Pitt live like kings; we live as "emperors" here. It seems I have returned to civilization once more and appreciate small conveniences that I never did before. I have a room shared by one other man. This room has wash bowl, bath, shower, shelves for putting various articles, desk[,] and a bed - - - - with sheets! My room mate [*sic*] is[,] too[,] most fortunate[,] for he lives at Latrobe[,] which is but 2 miles from the college.

[1R*] Pennsylvania can't be beat for its natural beauty; maybe I'm prejudiced[,] but this college sets [*sic*] back surrounded by mountains. At the foothills, the well[-]cultivated land can be seen neatly divided into small patterns. The landscape about the college itself is well planned with willow and pine trees plus beautiful plots of flowers.

All the building[s] were built by the monks of the Benedictine Order with their own hands. Every brick was molded and formed by them!

I shall be confined to the premises for two whole weeks (campused) by Army regulations. As for week-end [*sic*] passes, I may get one every two wks[.] or at least once per month. (Providing I'm not gigged). We may get passes every week from Saturday 4:00 PM to Sunday morning 2:00 AM. Sunday morning from 8:00 AM until Sunday night 9:30 PM.

---

[54] In 1846, Benedictine monks founded St. Vincent College, a Catholic liberal arts college, located at 300 Fraser Purchase Road, Latrobe, PA 15650-2690. The college is associated with St. Vincent Archabbey. "About," Saint Vincent College, accessed June 20, 2020, https://www.stvincent.edu/about.

33RD COLLEGE TRAINING DETACHMENT

(AIR CREW)

Saint Vincent College • Latrobe, Pennsylvania

2.

Contact you with little difficulty.

Studies and classes will begin Monday. I hope to be here at least three months but wish that it could be extended the full period of five months.

I'll let you tell me all about P. H. when I get to see you. (This will be much better than (mental Telepathy.) I'm a ~~commin~~ commin to collect - - - in person soon and x's and o's will become quite authentic. Poor you. See what you get for making promises. I shall close with plenty of love.

Love

Anthony

x x o o (Wait till I get there)

I wanted to call you by phone when I arrived[,] but since you might be at one of three places and I never did get you on the first call, I decided to let a letter suffice. I called [M]other and told her to give you my new address; I hope she was able to [2*] contact you with little difficulty.

Studies and classes will begin Monday. I hope to be here at least three months but wish that it could be extended the full period of five months.

I'll let you tell me all about P.H. when I get to see you. (This will be much better than (mental telepathy.) I'm a commin['] to collect - - - - - in person soon[,] and X's and O's [*sic*][55] will become quite authentic. Poor you. See what you get for making promises. I shall close with plenty of love.

Love[,]
Anthony

xx
oo   (Wait till I get there)

---

[55] *O* indicates a hug.

Free

A/s. A.S. MAZZA
33rd College Training Detachment
(Air Crew)
St. Vincent College
LATROBE, PENNSYLVANIA

LATROBE
SEP 4
7 PM
1943
PA.

Miss Sylvia Jacobs
3334 Fleming Ave.
St John's School for Nursing
N.S. Pgh, Pa (12)

84

Free

LATROBE
NOV 10
7 PM
1943
PA.

Miss Sylvia Jacobs
3334 Fleming Ave
St. Johns School of Nursing
N.S. Pgh, Pa (12)

November 10, 1943 (Invitation)

you are invited ...

... to a party

this is the word ...

... to dress right dress informally ...

aviation students will come solo or

dual ... all dancing will be at close

interval ... cadence will be counted

by jack merlin and crew ... take off

2030* at the latrobe armory and

we'll be all squared away by 2400**

... for class 43•c•8

"Anthony"

* 8:30 p.m.
** 12 midnight.
12 november.

33rd college training detachment, latrobe, pennsylvania

December 17, 1943 (Christmas Card)

A CHRISTMAS NOTE FOR MY Sweetheart

Because I Love You So

Once again ———
          at Christmas
I want to let you know
I'm wishing all life's
          best for you
Because I love you so

We've talked and laughed together,
We've enjoyed the selfsame things
We've known the happy feeling
That true understanding brings
And when I wish you every joy
That Christmas can impart
That wish brings ———
          special love, dear
From the bottom of my heart
          "Anthony"

89

A/S. A.S. MAZZA
Sq B-1 BKS-4
N.A.A.C. A.A.F.C.C.
Nashville, Tenn.

NASHVILLE TENN. DEC 17 3 PM 1943

AIR MAIL 6 CENTS UNITED STATES OF AMERICA

Miss Sylvia Jacobs
3334 Fleming Ave
St Johns School of Nursing
Pittsburgh, Pa. (12)

Dec 24, 1943

Dearest Sylvia,

'Twas the night before Christmas
and all through the barracks not a creature
was stirring not even a "Kaydet". The
scratch of a pen touching the surface of this
paper was the only noise that broke the
stillness of the night, yet faintly humming through
the writer's ears were the words and tune of
"Silent night." Yes, it is Christmas eve once
more but to me it is quite different from
the ones I have known in the past. One
year ago, I was probably trimming the Christmas
tree laughing and happily getting the presents set
for the eventful surprises when the family
would open them the next morning. Mother
was dashing back and forth in the kitchen getting
the Turkey all set for the Christmas meal. It
was always the custom at home to put up the
Christmas tree on Christmas eve, never before.
After the tree was all trimmed we all would
go to "Midnight Mass." Today many things for
me are not the same but one thing I shall
have in common with our family wherever they
may be . . . . Midnight Mass.

One year ago faintly in my memories
were the visions of a certain girl who has
now meant so much to me. What did
she think of the card I sent her? Do you
remember its theme? I do. I haven't
received your Christmas card yet??

December 24, 1943

Postmark: [The envelope is missing.]

Letterhead: Army Air Forces Logo

[1*]   Dec[.] 24, 1943

Dearest Sylvia,

'Twas the night before Christmas and all through the barracks not a creature was stirring[,] not even a "Kaydet." The scratch of pen touching the surface of this paper was the only noise that broke the stillness of the night, yet faintly humming through the writer's ears were the words and tune of "Silent [N]ight." Yes, it is Christmas [E]ve once more[,] but to me it is quite different from the ones I have known in the past. One year ago, I was probably trimming the Christmas tree[,] laughing and happily getting the presents set for the eventful surprises when the family would open them in the next morning. Mother was dashing back and forth in the [k]itchen[,] getting the [t]urkey all set for the Christmas meal. It was always the custom at home to put up the Christmas tree on Christmas [E]ve[,] never before. After the tree was all trimmed[,] we all would go to "Midnight Mass." Today many things for me are not the same[,] but one thing I shall have in common with our family wherever they may be - - - - [m]idnight Mass.

One year ago[,] faintly in my memories were the visions of a certain girl who has now meant so much to me. What did she think of the card I sent her? Do you remember its theme? I do. I haven't received your [C]hristmas [c]ard yet??

When I mentioned all was peaceful and quiet here, I shall try to explain why. Many of the boys have been much more fortunate than I in living within 300 miles from this post while others have maybe more nerve or are more fool hardy than I. We were granted 3 day passes yesterday with the following restrictions: 1.) Not permitted outside 300 mile radius. 2.) No public conveyances could be used. I might have risked hitch hiking 700 miles to Pittsburgh, but I've too much to lose and I have worked quite hard to get this far as it is. It seems though that a great number of the boys have friends or relatives within that area and took advantage of the set-up. Personally I can't see why they couldn't have extended the pass to 4 or 5 days so that everyone could get home but the army doesn't seem to operate on that basis. To bolster our morale an amplifying system plays Christmas carols all day and every five minutes they play the ballad "I'll be home for Christmas". It is a very beautiful song with a very definite meaning.

Here is how I spent my day today. We were aroused at 5:00 A.M. as usual and had chow at 6:00 A.M. Guess what I did? Back to bed and didn't get up until it was time for dinner. Played ping pong, listened to the President, read, and studied in the afternoon. This evening I visited the boys from St. Vincent who are still in quarantine. We stopped at the P.X. and all were in a celebrating mood and wanted to toast. The result was that yours truly drank his first bottle of 3.2 beer. Also my last for quite some time for I felt as if the stuff had blown me up

94

[1R*] When I mentioned all was peaceful and quiet here, I shall try to explain why. Many of the boys have been much more fortunate than I in living within 300 miles from this post[,] while others have maybe more nerve or are more fool hardy [*sic*] than I. We were granted 3[-]day passes yesterday with the following restrictions: 1.) Not permitted outside 300[-]mile radius. 2.) No public conveyances could be used. I might have risked hitch hiking [*sic*] 700 miles to Pittsburgh, but I've too much to lose[,] and I have worked quite hard to get this far as it is. It seems[,] though[,] that a great number of the boys have friends or relatives within that area and took advantage of the set-up [*sic*]. Personally[,] I can't see why they couldn't have extended the pass to 4 or 5 days so that everyone could get home[,] but the [A]rmy doesn't seem to operate on that basis. To bolster our morale[,] an amplifying system plays Christmas carols all day[,] and every five minutes they play the ballad, "I'll [B]e [H]ome for Christmas."⁵⁶ It is a very beautiful song with a very definite meaning.

Here is how I spent my day today. We were aroused at 5:00 A.M. as usual and had chow at 6:00 AM. Guess what I did? Back to bed and didn't get up until it was time for dinner. Played ping[-]pong, listened to the president, read, and studied in the afternoon. This evening I visited the boys from St. Vincent who are still in quarantine. We stopped at the P.X.[,]⁵⁷ and all were in a celebrating mood and wanted to toast. The result was that yours

---

⁵⁶ Bing Crosby, vocalist, "I'll Be Home for Christmas," by Walter Kent and Kim Gannon, released December 11, 1943, Decca, No. 18570A; Joel Whitburn, *Joel Whitburn's Billboard Pop Hits, Singles and Albums, 1940-1954* (Menomonee Falls, WI: Record Research, 2002), 43.

⁵⁷ A Post Exchange or P.X. is a tax-free retail outlet for goods and services for military staff. "Post Exchange," Dictionary.com, accessed June 20, 2020, https://www.dictionary.com/browse/post-exchange.

2

like a balloon.)

Never a day goes by that I don't think
of you and ----- go to a movie. This
time it was our old standby Richard Arlen
and Jean Parker in "Minesweeper" — hurrah!!
Class 4D strictly. When I finish this letter
I'll be all set for Church and the end of a
perfect day. (under Circumstances.)

I must tell you what I asked Santa
Claus for Christmas. Yup, I hung my stocking
right on the window sill near the head of my
bed. What could a big boy like me want
from good old St. Nick? Should I tell you
now better not (finger in mouth) well if
you insist, I want a doll. One of those
great big mama dolls about 5 ft? It must
have blue eyes, beautiful curls and -----
figure just so. It should answer to the name
of S. M. S. I'd like to hold hands with it and
hug it every now and then and of course a
few kisses now and then would suit me
fine. Santa says things are rationed
now but maybe someday he'll take care of
my wish.

It is cold out and the weather has
the typical holiday cast. It rained slightly
and everything froze, it is just one big
sheet of ice. Maybe way up there in
the Northland, we have snow, yes? --- no?
Anyway I shall end this letter with

truly drank his first bottle of 3.2 beer[,] (also my last for quite some time for I felt as if the stuff had blown me up [2*] like a balloon[.)]

Never a day goes by that I don't think of you and - - - - go to a movie. This time it was our old standby Richard Arlen and Jean Parker in "Minesweeper" - - - hurrah!!⁵⁸ Class 4D strictly. When I finish this letter[,] I'll be all set for church and the end of a perfect day (under the circumstances).

I must tell you what I asked Santa Claus for Christmas. Yep, I hung my stocking right on the window sill near the head of my bed. What could a big boy like me want from good old St. Nick? Should I tell you now - - - better not (finger in mouth). Well if you insist, I want a doll. One of these great big mama dolls about 5 ft[.] ?[in.] It must have blue eyes, beautiful curls, and - - - - - - figure just so. It should answer to the name of S.M.J.⁵⁹ I'd like to hold hands wiff [sic] it and hug it every now and then and[,] of course[,] a few kisses now and then would suit me fine. Santa says things are rationed now[,] but maybe someday he'll take care of my wish.

It is cold out[,] and the weather has the typical holiday cast. It rained slightly and everything froze[;] it is just one big sheet of ice. Maybe way up thar in the Nortland [sic], we have snow, yes? - - - no? Anyway[,] I shall end this letter with [2R*] visions of sugar plums dancing in my head[,] for you and I are circling the floor dreamy eyed to the tune of: "I'm [D]reaming of a White Christmas."⁶⁰

Love[,]

Anthony

---

⁵⁸ *Minesweeper*, directed by William A. Berke, featuring Richard Arlen, Jean Parker, and Russell Hayden (Pamamount Pictures, 1943).

⁵⁹ Sylvia Mary Jacobs.

⁶⁰ Bing Crosby, vocalist, "White Christmas," by Irving Berlin, released October 10, 1942, Decca, No. 18429A; Whitburn, 43.

visions of sugar plums dancing in my head
for you and I are circling the floor dreamy
eyed to the tune of: "I'm dreaming of a
White Christmas"

Love

Anthony

X X X X   Christmas
0 0 0 0   quality behind
          there. No spacing
          of sugar.

P.S. Tell all your folks that I did wish them
a merry Christmas and a Happy New Year even
if I didn't send a card. Things are a bit
different and I couldn't get around to everyone.

Goodnight

The sergeant flashed a light into the eyes
of one of the boys at 4:00 PM this morning with
the following remark: "Merry Christmas,
You're on K.P."

XXXX   Christmas
OOOO   quality behind
these. No sparing of sugar.[61]

P.S. Tell all your folks that I did wish them a Merry Christmas and a Happy New Year even if I didn't send a card. Things are a bit different[,] and I couldn't get around to everyone.

Goodnight [*sic*]

The sergeant flashed a light into the eyes of one of the boys at 4:00 PM[62] this morning with the following remark: "Merry Christmas, you're on K.P."

---

[61] From April of 1942 to June of 1947, the U.S. Government rationed sugar in the U.S. because of a shortage resulting from the war's disruption in the supply chain. Sarah Sundin, "Make It Do—Sugar Rationing in World War II," Sarah's Blog (blog), January 31, 2011, http://www.sarahsundin.com/make-it-do-sugar-rationing-in-world-war-ii-2/.

[62] The reference is more likely to 4:00 AM.

1944

Jan. 8, 1944

Dearest Sylvia:

It didn't take me long to realize that something was wrong when I received your letter yesterday. The handwriting on the outside of the letter indicated that that finger of yours had not healed as it should have. It sure has been a long wait between letters but by the time that you get this letter that should all be settled for my little prayer last night did the trick. I didn't know what to think but since you have been repeatedly at fault in failing to write I thought that this was another of your offenses and was preparing to fine you heavily. Good thing I didn't take action too soon but this situation reminds me of the story of the boy who cried "Wolfe". Did you ever read it? Anyway I accept your excuse and hope that all will go well once more that your finger is healed. I thought of the possibilities of you getting worse, but when mother said that you had called at home she didn't mention anything being wrong so I assumed that you were well.

Maybe you are surprised to hear that I am still at Nashville but I'll assure you that is no fault of mine. Our shipping orders have been canceled for some reason or another and here I set waiting for the world to move. We have been alerted again and rumor has it that we may move during the middle of next week. I don't know what to believe anymore. All of the original squadron that came here with me from St. Vincent is gone for a shipment of Pilots left yesterday cleaning out our squadron. Since the Bombardiers left the middle of December, only we three Navigators

102

January 8, 1944

Postmark: [The envelope is missing.]

Letterhead: No Letterhead, Typewritten

[1*]   Jan. 8, 1944

Dearest Sylvia:

It didn't take me long to realize that something was wrong when I received your letter yesterday. The handwriting on the outside of the letter indicated that that finger of yours had not healed as it should have. It sure has been a long wait between letters, but by the time that you get this letter that should all be settled[,] for my little prayer last night did the trick. I didn't know what to think[,] but since you have been repeatedly at fault in failing to write, I thought that this was another of your offenses and was preparing to fine you heavily. Good thing I didn't take action too soon[,] but this situation reminds me of the story of the boy who cried "Wolf[."] Did you ever read it? Anyway, I accept your excuse and hope that all will go well once more that your finger is healed. I thought of the possibilities of you[r] getting worse, but when [M]other said that you had called at home[,] she didn't mention anything being wrong, so I assumed that you were well.

Maybe you are surprised to hear that I am still at Nashville[,] but I assure you that is no fault of mine. Our shipping orders have been canceled for some reason or another[,] and here I set [*sic*][,] waiting for the word to move. We have been alerted again[,] and rumor has it that we may move during the middle of next week. I don't know what to believe anymore. All of the original remain.

        Yesterday I had plenty of fun being a one-man squadron. The other two boys were put on a detail and I was the only free man left. I took P.T. all by myself, marched myself down the the drill area and walked up to the Officer in Charge, saluted and said, " Sir, B-1 all present and accounted for." "How many men have you? " "One, Sir" The Officer laughed and said, " March your squadron to the rear rank of the first platoon." At chow practically the same thing happened when I reported all of B-1 present and when asked where the rest of them were, I smartly replied that I am the rest of them.

        No doubt by now you are wondering, " Where on earth did he get the typewriter". Well, today I am known as C.Q. or Charge of Quarters. I am stationed at the Squadron headquarters to receive and pass on to the commanding officer of the section any notices of importance. I march the men to chow, call out all formations, wake the boys at 5:00, answer and take down all in-coming phone calls. There are a lot of minor details to be taked care of as the issueing of Open Post passes and knowing what to do in case of fire. Checking all the lights in all of the barracks and the fire fighting equipment. The typewriter in the office being free for the moment I am taking full advantage of it. You will have to pardon some of my misprints for after a month or so, I am out of practice again.

        I am very sorry to hear of your grandmother's death for although I have seen her but three times that was enough to convince me of how grand a person she was. I did not have to speak the same language as she to understand that. I am very thankful that I had the chance to see her that Sunday when we made the little visits to your relatives.

squadron that came here with me from St. Vincent is gone, for a shipment of [p]ilots left yesterday[,] cleaning out our squadron. Since the [b]ombardiers left [in] the middle of December, only we three [n]avigators [2*] remain.

Yesterday[,] I had plenty of fun being a one-man squadron. The other two boys were put on a detail[,] and I was the only free man left. I took P.T.[63] all by myself, marched myself down the the [sic] drill area and walked up to the Officer in Charge, saluted and said, "Sir, B-1 all present and accounted for." "How many men have you?" "One, [s]ir[!"] The [o]fficer laughed and said, "March your squadron to the rear rank of the first platoon." At chow[,] practically the same thing happened when I reported all of B-1 present[,] and when asked where the rest of them were, I smartly replied that I am the rest of them.

No doubt by now you are wondering, "Where on earth did he get the typewriter[?"] Well, today I am known as C.Q. or Charge of Quarters. I am stationed at the [s]quadron headquarters to receive and pass off to the commanding officer of the section any notices of importance. I march the men to chow, call out all formations, wake the boys at 5:00, answer and take down all in-coming [sic] phone calls. There are a lot of minor details to be taken care of[,] as the issuing of [o]pen[-p]ost passes and knowing what to do in case of fire. Checking all the lights in all of the barracks and the fire fighting [sic] equipment. The typewriter in the office being free for the moment[,] I'm taking full advantage of it. You will have to pardon some of my misprints[,] for after a month or so, I am out of practice again.

I am very sorry to hear of your grandmother's death[,] for although I have seen her but three times[,] that was enough to

---

[63] Physical Training.

I shall send my little prayer that her soul may rest in peace.

I am really sorry to hear that that finger of yours has caused you so much pain and discomfort, but do you know what that was due from? Do you know how all that trouble could have been prevented? Well, I shall tell you. It is due to lack of exercise to a certain degree, but also due to it not getting enough rest. Now, when you pick up a pencil that is one of the easist ways that I can think of resting and massaging one's finger at the same time. Since I can't be around to hold it for you, that is the next best thing I can think of.

Today, for the first time in Nashville this year it is snowing. Good old sunny southiq Just like the north but sunny only in the summer. By the way, we are stating to get new fellows in already and I have been moved to barracks 5 instead of 4. It seems that will always happen in the army making a lot of friends only to lose them almost as fast as you make them.

Well I guess I had better finish this letter for someone is waiting to use the typewriter and I won't hold him back. Sounds like the good old telephone calls that we used to have. I shall close sending plenty of love.

                                        Love as ever,
                                        Anthony
xxxxxxxxxxxxxxxxxx xxx   Anthony S. Mazza
ooooooooooooooooooooo●
Wished I could knock them
off as fast as I type them.

Did you say you had something on me. Well I had to write for almost a month this way last summer. Remember? If you cant write with your right hand, the left will due. I can read and understand it.

convince me of how grand a person she was.[64] I did not have to speak the same language as she to understand that. I am very thankful that I had the chance to see her that Sunday when we made the little visits to your relatives. [3*] I shall send my little prayer that her soul may rest in peace.

I am really sorry to hear that that finger of yours has caused you so much pain and discomfort, but do you know what that was due from? Do you know how all that trouble could have been prevented? Well, I shall tell you. It is due to lack of exercise to a certain degree, but also due to it not getting enough rest. Now, when you pick up a pencil[,] that is one of the easist [sic] ways that I can think of resting and massaging one's finger at the same time. Since I can't be around to hold it for you, that is the next best thing I can think of.

Today, for the first time in Nashville this year[,] it is snowing. Good old sunny [S]outh! Just like the [N]orth but sunny only in the summer. By the way[,] we are starting to get new fellows in already[,] and I have been moved to barracks 5 instead of 4. It seems that will always happen in the [A]rmy[,] making a lot of friends only to lose them almost as fast as you make them.

Well[,] I guess I had better finish this letter[,] for someone is waiting to use the typewriter[,] and I won't hold him back. Sounds

---

[64] Sylvia Jacobs' maternal grandmother, Anna Stulyak Kopcie, born on June 9, 1860, in present-day Slovakia, died on January 2, 1944. See Appendix B. According to a holy card among Sylvia Jacobs' memorabilia, issued by Albert A. Novak, funeral director, 3313 Brighton Road, N.S., Pittsburgh, Pennsylvania, the funeral was from Anna Kopcie's residence at 2342 Colorado Street, N.S., Pittsburgh, Pennsylvania. The requiem high Mass was celebrated at St. Gabriel's Church on Wednesday, January 5, 1944, with internment at St. Joseph Cemetery, West View, Pennsylvania.

like the good old telephone calls that we used to have. I shall close
sending plenty of love.

	Love as ever,
xxxxxxxxxxxxxxxxx xxx	/s/ Anthony
ooooooooooooooooooooo	Anthony S. Mazza
Wished I could knock them	
off as fast as I type them.	

Did you say you had something on me? Well I had to write almost
a month this way last summer. Remember? If you can't write with
your right hand, the left will due [*sic*]. I can read and understand it.[65]

---

[65] The final section consists of a scrawl, presumably written lefthandedly.

WESTERN UNION

1201

A. N. WILLIAMS
PRESIDENT

NEWCOMB CARLTON
CHAIRMAN OF THE BOARD

J. C. WILLEVER
FIRST VICE-PRESIDENT

The filing time shown in the date line on telegrams and day letters is STANDARD TIME at point of origin. Time of receipt is STANDARD TIME at point of destination

LD187 CM 9

PITTSBURGH PENN

MISS SYLVIA M JACOBS

ST FRANCIS NURSE HOME 45TH & CALVIN ST PGH PENN

SCHEDULE CHANGED, LEAVING TONIGHT. WILL EXPLAIN IN LETTER LOVE.

TONY

May 1944 (Telegram)

From: Anthony S. Mazza

To: Miss Sylvia M[.] Jacobs
             St Francis Nurse Home 45th & Calvin St.
             Pgh Penn

Postmark: 10:23 PM?[66]
             LD187 CM 9

Letterhead: Western Union

[1*]   Pittsburgh[,] Penn
Miss Sylvia M Jacobs
    St Francis Nurse Home 45th & Calvin St Pgh Penn
    Schedule Changed, Leaving Tonight. Will Explain in Letter
Love.
    Tony

---

[66] The date stamp of the telegram is difficult to read, but it appears to be in
May. As Anthony Mazza did not report for military duty until after May
1943 and he was already serving in Italy by May 1945, the date of the letter
is most likely May 1944. Moreover, Sylvia Jacobs was living on Atmore
Street in May of 1945.

United States
Army Air Forces

Dearest Sylvia:

I have just returned from the P.X. to see if I could find some token for you on your birthday, but alas! I couldn't and thus send only this card to help express my sentiments for you on that happy date. I'll round up something though the first time I get out of this prison. Was it June 12th or June 22nd? I'll send this early though and hope you get it on the 2nd. I'm busier than ever and getting along fine and hope that no other patient has imprinted their nails on your wonderful features. I've got to run along now and hope the card isn't too mushy but I mean every word that is in it.

Love

Tony

May 30, 1944 (Letter and Birthday Card)

From: A./C. Mazza, A.S.
               44-12-6 S.M.A.A.N.S.
               S.M.A.A.F.
               San Marcos, Texas

To: AIR MAIL
               Miss Sylvia M. Jacobs
               St. Francis Nurse Home
               Box 340
               45th + Calvin St.
               Pittsburgh 1, Pa[.]

Postmark: 4:30 PM[67]
               May 30, 1943 [or 1944]
               San Marcos, Texas

Letterhead: United States Army Air Forces

Card: A Hallmark Card
               50 B 752-1

[1* Letter]   [no date]

Dearest Sylvia:

I have just returned from the P.X. to see if I could find some token for you on your birthday, but alas! I couldn't and thus send

---

[67] The postmark is smudged, so 4:30 PM, as well as other details, may not be correct.

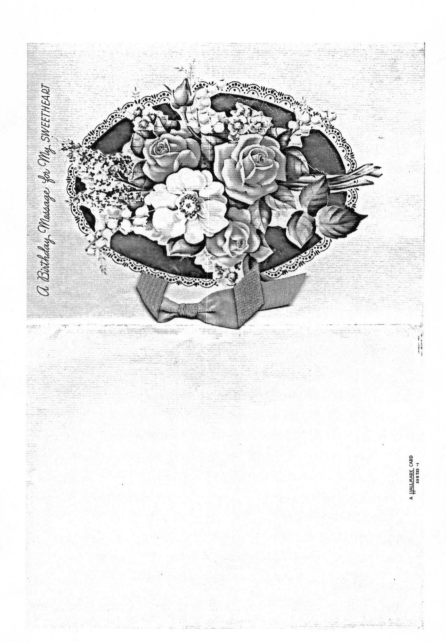

A Birthday Message for My SWEETHEART

114

only this card to help express my sentiments for you on that happy date. I'll round up something[,]though[,] the first time I get out of this prison. Was it June 12th or June 2nd?[68] I'll send this early[,] though[,] and hope you get it on the 2nd. I'm busier than ever and getting along fine and hope that no other patient has imprinted their nails on your wonderful features. I've got to run along now and hope the card isn't too mushy[,] but I mean every word that is in it.

Love[,]

Tony

X [within an] O

---

[68] Sylvia Jacobs was born on June 2, 1923, in Pittsburgh, Pennsylvania.

A/C Mezza, A.S.
44-12-6   S.M.A.A.N.S.
S.M.A.A.F.
San Marcos, Texas

AIR MAIL

Miss Sylvia M. Jacobs
St Francis Nurse Home
Box 340
45th & Calvin St.
Pittsburgh, Pa

AIR MAIL

There's a special place in my heart for you-
For you, Sweetheart, alone,

There's a special place for the memories
Of happiness we've known,

There's a special place for the dreams
we share

And the dreams we've seen come true,
And there's

worlds of love in the wish this brings
Especially for you!

HAPPY BIRTHDAY

Love
"Tony"

117

July 14, 1944 (Postcard)

From: Anthony S. Mazza

To: Miss Sylvia Jacobs
                3334 Fleming Ave.
                St. John ['s] Nurse Home
                Pittsburgh 12, Pa.

Postmark: 4:30 PM
                July 14, 1944
                Navigation School
                San Marcos, Tex.

Photo: [1*] The jumbo postcard is a black-and-white
                photograph of a dual propeller airplaine with the
                letters N43 on the side, flying over rocky terrain.
                Handwritten in blue ink on the photograph is
                an arrow with "me," which points to the second
                window on the aircraft. Jumbo Post Card Co., San
                Antonio, Texas.

Printed: [1R*] [The upper left corner of the postcard states
                the following:]
                From the Army Air Forces Navigation school at San
                Marcos, Texas, cadets fly thousands of miles over
                Texas and surrounding states. This silvery twin-
                motored AT-7 carries a trio of student navigators
                over the rugged terrain of the Rocky mountain
                foot-hills [sic]. As navigation officers later, they will
                plot the course of America's huge flying fortresses
                over enemy-held mountains and waters.

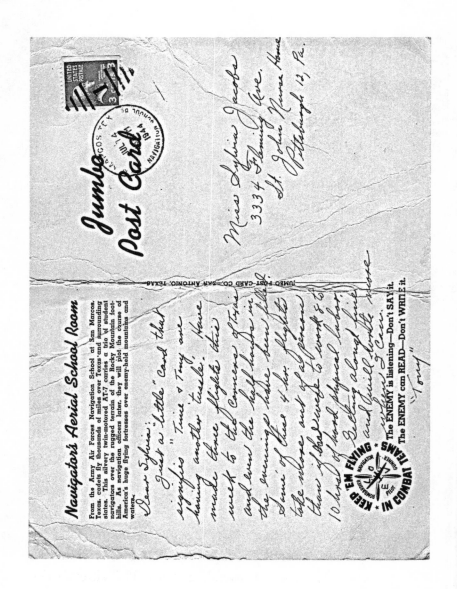

[The lower left corner of the postcard contains a logo of a small airplane in the center of a four-blade propeller. In between the propellers are the following words: "Bombadier," "Navigator," "Gunner," "Pilot." The words encircling the logo are "Keep 'Em Flying in Combat Teams." Handwritten in between the propeller blades are the letters *L, O, V, E* (i.e., Love).]

[Next to the logo at the bottom of the postcard appear the following words:]
The ENEMY is listening—Don't SAY it.
The ENEMY can READ—Don't WRITE it.

[At the top of the address section of the postcard (i.e., the right half of the reverse side of the picture) appear the words, "Jumbo Post Card."]

[1R*]   [no date]

Dear Sylvia:

Just a "little" card that signifies "Time + Tony are having another 'tussle.'["] Have made three flights this week to the corners of Texas[,] and even the half hours in the evenings have been filled. Some of these 4[-]hr. flights take more out of a person than if one were to work 8 to 10 hrs[.] of hard physical labor.

Getting along fine and will write more when I can.

"Tony"

121

United States
Army Air Forces

July 19, 1944

Dearest Sylvia:

Just returned from the base hospital, as our echelon was given the 64 Army physical for flying. This will be the last such physical before graduation, and the Army is making sure its Navigators will be able to withstand the conditions that exist in flight. The whole exam lasted but 3½ hrs and it is now only 11:00 AM, yet we have the rest of the day to ourselves . . . . that is a surprise isn't it? I don't know why that is so, but it is possibly due to the fact that we only had shots for typhus, small pox, tetanus and cholera. Two shots in each arm with a Wasserman blood test for good measure. The two men in front of me collapsed and were out like a light, a few seconds after the blood test. Every time I had the blood test it was done by suction. This time they jabbed a needle in the arm and let the blood drip into a test tube. It was coincidence that those two men fainted but yet I was surprised to find myself standing when the ordeal was complete.

I don't know the results of the

July 19, 1944

From: A./C. Mazza, A.S.
                44-12-6 S.M.A.A.F.N.S.
                San Marcos, Texas

To: Miss Sylvia Jacobs
                3334 Fleming Ave[.]
                St. John[']s Nurse Home
                Pittsburgh 12, Pa.

Postmark: 12:30 PM
                July 20, 1944
                San Marcos, Texas

Letterhead: United States
                Army Air Forces

[1*]   July 19, 1944

Dearest Sylvia:

I just returned from the base hospital, as our eschelon [*sic*] was given the 64 Army [P]hysical for flying. This will be the last such physical before graduation, and the Army is making sure its [n]avigators will be able to withstand the conditions that exist in flight. The whole exam lasted but 3½ hrs[.,] and it is now only 11:00 AM[;] yet we have the rest of the day to ourselves – – – – that is a surprise[,] isn't it? I don't know why that is so, but it is possibly due to the fact that we only had shots for typhus, small pox [*sic*], tetanus[,] and cholera. Two shots in each arm with a Wasserman blood test for good measure. The two men in front of me collapsed

of the exam but it won't be given until next tuesday but I do know that my heart beats steadily for you. I'm probably immune to everything but S. M. J. and I don't want to be immune from her.

Say, something else has been added (or shall I say subtracted) for I now weigh a mere 166 lbs. I lost over 10 lbs but didn't notice it one bit. At this rate I'll surely be "stream lined before long" but I'd better not get too "excited" about this since the scale could have been out of order.

Sorry to hear your picnic didn't turn out too well but as long as you went swimming you were "all wet" to begin with. I can see one advantage of my imaginary picnics. We never have bad weather to contend with and the Sun always shines, the temperature is moderate and a cool breeze just keeps Sylvia's hair fluttering. The grass is always at its greenest, the food at its best, the shade is just perfect and the air filled with the fresh smell of the flowers, bushes and shrubbery nearby. Close your eyes? Can you picture everything as described? Now who do you see facing you? Only 1 guess this time?

Too bad Harry James didn't have

and were out like a light, a few seconds after the blood test. Every time I had the blood test[,] it was done by suction; [t]his time they jabbed a needle in the arm and let the blood drip into a test tube. It was [a] coincidence that those two men fainted[,] but yet[,] I was surprised to find myself standing when the ordeal was complete.

I don't know the results of the [1R*] exam[,] but it won't be given until next Tuesday[,] but I do know that my heart beats steadily for you. I'm probably immune to everything but S.M.J. and don't want to be immune from her.

Say, something else has been added (or shall I say subtracted)[,] for I now weigh a mere 166 lbs. I lost over 10 lbs[.,] but didn't notice it one bit. At this rate[,] I'll surely be "stream lined [*sic*] before long[,]" but I'd better not get too "excited" about this since the scale could have been out of order.

Sorry to hear your picnic didn't turn out too well[,] but as long as you went swimming[,] you were "all wet" to begin with. I can see one advantage of my imaginary picnics. We never have bad weather to contend with[,] and the [s]un always shines[;] the temperature is moderate[;] and a cool breeze just keeps Sylvia's hair fluttering. The grass is always at it greenest[;] the food is its best[;] the shade is just perfect[;] and the air filled with the fresh smell of flowers, bushes[,] and shrubbery nearby. Close your eyes? Can you picture everything as described? Now who do you see teasing you? Only ½ guess this time?

Too bad Harry James didn't have [2*] the opportunity to play while we danced to his music. One of these days we might give him a break. Will show off with a perfect two[-]step fox trot [*sic*]. ([M]ostly trot.)

United States
Army Air Forces

2

the opportunity to play while we danced to
his music! One of these days we might
give him a break. Will show off with
a perfect two step fox trot. (mostly trot.)

The T.W.A. Hostess job doesn't seem
bad and it might be worth a try. While
you are at it, ask them if they would need
a good Navigator to go along with you on
Oceanic hops. Some navigating I would
do too with a sweet little nurse to see that
I didn't get too air sick or ---- sick??

I'll bet your home did seem empty
with almost everyone on a vacation. It
was always that way for me too when
mother would go out for a few days each
summer to my Aunts home in Glassport,
Pa. You mustn't get too jealous and
it won't be long before you will be
having your one wk (or has it been
upped to 2 wks) off.

We are still (in spite of today's collapse)
fighting for time and work piles up as
the hours go by. At this rate, it won't
be long ere another week be canceled

The T.W.A.[69] [h]ostess job doesn't seem bad, and it might be worth a try. While you are at it, ask them if they would need a good [n]avigator to go along with you on [o]ceanic hops. Some navigating I would do[,] too[,] with a sweet little nurse to see that I didn't get too air sick [*sic*] or - - - - sick??

I'll bet your home did seem empty with almost everyone on a vacation. It was always that way for me[,] too[,] when [M]other would go out for a few days each summer to my [a]unt[']s in Glassport, Pa. You musn't [*sic*] get too jeaulous [*sic*] since it won't be long before you will be having your one wk[.] (or has it been upped to 2 wks[.]) off[?]

We are still (in spite of today's relapse) fighting for time[,] and work piles up as the hours go by. At this rate, it won't be long ere another week be canceled [2R*] from our schedules.

Celestial + [r]adio missions are but one week away[,] and already we can compute our position celestially by the use of stars, moon, planets[,] and sun. There is plenty more theory to learn and flights needed for practice.

Maybe tonight I may go to a show[,] providing my arms hold up. The after[-]effects of some of these shots are terrific[,] but as yet[,] I have failed to be annoyed by them. Several of the boys are

---

[69] Trans World Airlines was a major American commercial air carrier that existed from 1930 to 2001. Elaine X. Grant, "TWA—Death of a Legend," *St. Louis Magazine*, July 28, 2008, https://www.stlmag.com/TWA-Death-Of-A-Legend/. Until World War II, all flight attendants had to be registered nurses. Neil Patrick, "The First Flight Attendants Were All Registered Nurses, This Requirement Disappeared When Many Nurses Left to Enlist During WWII," *The Vintage News*, September 11, 2016, https://www.thevintagenews.com/2016/09/11/first-flight-attendants-registered-nurses-requirement-disappeared-many-nurses-left-enlist-wwii/.

from new schedules.

Celestial + Radio missions are but one week away and already we can compute our position celestially by the use of stars, moon, planets and sun. There is plenty more theory to learn and flights for practice.

Maybe tonight I may go to a show providing my arms hold up. The after effects of some of these shots are terrific, but as yet I have failed to be annoyed by them. Several of the boys are stretched out now and don't feel very good. They'll probably be up and running around within a few hours though (maybe).

Quite an uproar is in progress now as the Physical Training Dept. "requests" our presence to P.T. at 5:30 PM. I doubt if we will be able to do much exercising, but will be there providing we can't find some means of getting out of it.

Well it is about time I bid thee adieu. Good Day

with Love &

Kisses

"Tony"

P.S.
See I told you I was an artist. That used to be an old signature of mine

128

stretched out now and don't feel very good. They'll probably be up and running around within a few hours[,] though (maybe)[.]

Quite an uproar is in progress now as the Physical Training Dept. "requests" our presence to P.T. at 5:30 PM. I doubt if we will be able to do much exer-cising[,] but we'll be there[,] providing we can't find some means of getting out of it.

Well[,] it is about time I bid thee adieu. Good [d]ay

with
X[70]   Love
X   +
X   Kisses
"Tony"

P.S. See I told you I was an artist. That used to be an old signature of mine.[71]

---

[70] Each X is within a circle.

[71] The beginning of the postscript has a short arrow pointing toward a small line drawing of a smiling face.

A/c Mazza, A.S.
43-10-6 S.M.A.A.F.N.S.
San Marcos, Texas

NAVIGATION SCHOOL

SAN MARCOS, TEXAS
JUL 20
1230PM
1944

Miss Sylvia Jacob
3334 Fleming Ave
St. Johns Nurse Home
Pittsburgh 12, Pa.

130

United States
Army Air Forces

July 23, 1944

Dearest Sylvia:

The radio is now playing a familiar tune "Good night where-ever you are". It isn't very appropriate for a beginning so we'll consider it as "Good-evening where-ever you are." A follow through is the popular song in these parts, "Amor". That too is appropriate for an ending but we'll sprinkle it through-out the letter just for a little "variety". "Long Ago & Far Away", "I'll be seeing you", "I love you" have been played in order so you can understand what type of mood I am in now and of whom each one of those melodies portrays.

Flash! ____ ! ____ (Swish) Zing! Whee ____ and bingo there you are deep in the heart of Texas. Wasn't that a fast trip? The radio stations from Pgh. to San Marcos registered state for one full second? What happened anyhow, you know you were exactly ½ sec. late. I told you that you could powder your nose and put

July 22, 1944

From: A./C. Mazza, A.S.
               44-12-6 S.M.A.A.F.N.S.
               San Marcos, Texas

To: Miss Sylvia Jacobs
               3334 Fleming Ave.
               St. John[']s Nurse Home
               Pittsburgh 12, Pa.

Postmark: 12:30 PM
               [Month and Date Unreadable] 1944
               San Marcos, Texas

Letterhead: Army Air Forces
               Greensboro
               North Carolina

[1*]   July 22, 1944

Dearest Sylvia:
    The radio is now playing a familiar tune[,] "Good [N]ight[,]
[W]here-ever [*sic*] [Y]ou [A]re."[72] It isn't very appropriate for a

---

[72] Although there were many versions of the song "Good Night, Wherever
    You Are" airing on the radio in 1944, the most popular one was by
    Russ Morgan and His Orchestra. Russ Morgan, vocalist, "Good Night,
    Wherever You Are," by Frank Waldon, Al Hoffman, and Dick Roberts,
    released May 27, 1944, Decca, No. 18598A; Whitburn, 112; "100 Greatest
    Songs from 1944," DigitalDreamDoor.com, accessed June 20, 2020,
    https://digitaldreaddoor.com/pages/bg_hits/bg_hits__44.html.

put on Raspberry lipstick after you got here. Mind if I comb your hair? I'll really do a good job – almost like the last ~~time~~. Stand up now and walk around a bit. Hmmm just as wonderful as ever. Say, that must of been some fast haul since you have on the "jumper dress". A little warm for it down here, but the evenings are cool and you won't regret wearing it. What shall we do? I'll let you guess??? I could set here and look at you all the rest of the evening but these barracks ~~isn't~~ aren't very appropriate for a young lady to visit right now. The C.O. would really rave but I've got it we'll go over to the Cadet Club and have a couple of cool drinks and talk. Too bad I couldn't have swished you down here with a ~~~~ jug of that famous iced lemon Tea but I'll see what can be done about that next time. It would have hampered your speed by offering more resistance than accounted for and thus you would have arrived ¼ second later than you did. Can't afford to have you waste time like that when I can have you here

134

beginning so we'll consider it as "Good-evening [*sic*] where-ever [*sic*] you are." A follow[-]through is the popular song in these parts, "Amor."[73] That[,] too[,] is appropriate for an ending[,] but we'll sprinkle it through-out [*sic*] the letter just for a little "variety." "Long Ago [(and] Far Way[),"][74] "I'll [B]e [S]eeing [Y]ou[,"][75] and] "I [L]ove [Y]ou"[76] have been played in order so you can understand what type of mood I am in now and of whom each one of those melodies portrays.

Flash! –! –(Swish) Zing! Wheeee and bingo[!] [H]ere you are[,] deep in the heart of Texas. Wasn't that a fast trip? The radio stations from Pgh to San Marcos registered static for one full second? What happened anyhow[?] [Y]ou know you were exactly ½ sec. late. I told you that you could powder your nose and [1R*] put on [r]aspberry lipstick after you got here. Mind if I comb your hair? I'll really do a good job—almost like the last time. Stand up now and walk around a bit. Hmmm[,] just as wonderful as ever. Say, that must of [*sic*] been some fast haul since you have on the

[73] Bing Crosby, vocalist, "Amor," by Gabriel Ruiz and Sunny Skylar, released July 8, 1944, Decca, No. 18608A; Whitburn, 43.

[74] Jerome Kern and Ira Gershwin wrote the song "Long Ago (and Far Away)" for the 1944 film *Cover Girl*. *Cover Girl*, directed by Charles Vidor, featuring Gene Kelly and Rita Hayworth (Columbia Pictures, 1944). Although a number of prominent artists released recordings of the song in 1944, including Bing Crosby (Decca), Jo Stafford (Capitol Records), and Perry Como (RCA Victor), the most popular version was by Helen Forrest and Dick Haymes. Helen Forest and Dick Haymes, vocalists, "Long Ago (and Far Away)," by Jerome Kern and Ira Gershwin, released April 29, 1944, Decca, No. 23317A; Whitburn, 71; "1944 Radio (Top 80 Song Playlist)," playback.fm, accessed June 20, 2020, https://playack.fm/year/1944.

[75] Bing Crosby, vocalist, "I'll Be Seeing You," by Sammy Fain and Irving Kahal, released April 22, 1944, Decca, No. 18595A.

[76] Bing Crosby, vocalist, "I Love You," by Cole Porter, released April 15, 1944, Decca, No. 18586A.

United States
Army Air Forces

2

to myself that much longer. (Selfish aren't
I.) Why the dance will begin in a few
minutes! May I? What? you refuse
to dance cheek to cheek? All cadets dance
that way down here and we want look
too conspicuous. Pardon me, It was
my fault. (It always is) I'll never learn
to be a professional but you are the only
person I can dance with reasonably well.
Even at that I can't do it too well, because
my mind is seldom concentrated at the actions
of my feet with you here. Darn these
blasted Texans! They would play a
Boogie Woogie Piece. Lets go outside on
the front patio. Wow! look at all
those couples cuddled up out there. Reminds
me of St Francis Alcove. Here is a
spot way back here. Shall we join
the crowd or should we study the
stars???

That is Jupiter and that is Mars
over here, we have Polaris, Regulus

"[j]umper dress." A little warm for it down here, but the evenings are cool[,] and you won't regret wearing it. What shall we do? I'll let you guess??? I could set [sic] here and look at you all the rest of the evening[,] but these barracks aren't very appropriate for a young lady to visit right now. The C.O.[77] would really rave[,] but I've got it[;] we'll go over to the cadet club and have a couple of cool drinks and talk. Too bad I couldn't have swished you down here with a jug of that famous iced lemon [t]ea[,] but I'll see what can be done about that next time. It would have hampered your speed by offering more resistance than accounted for[,] and thus[,] you would have arrived ¼ second later than you did. Can't afford to have you waste time like that when I can have you here [2*] to myself that much longer. (Selfish aren't I [?])

Why the dance will begin in a few minutes! May I? What? You refuse to dance cheek to cheek? All cadets dance that way down here[,] and we won['] t look too conspicuous. Parden [sic] me, [i]t was my fault. (It always is[.]) I'll never learn to be a professional[,] but you are the only person I can dance with reasonably well. Even at that[,] I can't do it too well, because my mind is seldom concentrated at the activity of my feet with you here. Darn these blasted Texans! They would play a [b]oogie[-w]oogie [p]iece. Let[']s go outside on the front patio. Wow! Look at all those couples cuddled up out there. Reminds me of St. Francis Alcove. Here is a spot way back here. Shall we join the crowd or should we study the stars???

That is Jupiter and that is Mars[;] over here, we have Polarus [sic], Regulus[,] [2R*] etc. (Censored.) Sorry, coach[,] but I couldn't resist.

Let[']s go back and try stepping it again. That fellow there isn't Harry James[,] but he is trying awful[ly] hard to substitute.

---

[77] Commanding Officer.

etc. (Censored.)   Sorry, Coach but I couldn't resist.

Lets go back and try stepping it again. That fellow there isn't Harry James but he is trying awful hard to substitute. We had better move away from the orchestra or the next note will break my ear drums. Crowded in here isn't it?

Time is beginning to run out on us. Let's go for a stroll through B. Street. O.K. Jay, you aren't hard to get along with one bit.

Sure I knew George Kelly. He was Sect. of Publicity on my Cabinet at O.H.S. He was 4F for a long time but they must have accepted him, if he is in uniform (wonderful deduction?) Incidently George Kelly lived on Woods Run Ave.

Give George (your brother) my regards and I'm rooting for him as hard as you are. He will make good. I seem to be getting along fairly well, but I'm not breaking any records. I could and should but the gremlins have had a wonderful time working out on me. Thankful that they haven't left the ground. Keep those prayers coming this way. Gee! time does go fast when together. Bong Bong. X O

Sure enjoyed every single second of the evening. "Buenos Noches Senorita." "Amor" (Swish!)   "Tony"

138

We had better move away from the orchestra[,] or the next note will break my ear drums [*sic*]. Crowded in here[,] isn't it?

Time is beginning to run out on us. Let's go for a stroll through B. Street. O.K. Say, you aren't hard to get along with one bit.

Sure[,] I know George Kelly. He was [sec.] of [p]ublicity on my [c]abinet at O.H.S.[78] He was 4F[79] for a long time[,] but they must have accepted him, if he is in uniform (wonderful deduction?)[.] Incidently [*sic*], George Kelly lived on Woods Run Ave.[80]

Give George (your brother) my regards[,] and I'm rooting for him as hard as you are. He will make good. I seem to be getting along fairly well, but I'm not breaking any records. I could and should[,] but the gremlins have had a wonderful time working out on me. Thankful that they haven't left the ground. Keep those prayers coming this way. Gee! Time does go fast when [we] are together. Bong Bong X O[.] Sure enjoyed every single second of the evening. Buen[a]s [n]oches[,] [s]e[ñ]orita! "Amor[,]"

(Swish!)   "Tony"

---

[78] In 1939, as a senior at David B. Oliver High School in Pittsburgh, Pennsylvania, Anthony Mazza was the president of the student body. *The Omicron* (June 1939), 62; "Merit Parade: Anthony Mazza, Oliver High," *Pittsburgh Post-Gazette*, March 21, 1939.

[79] According to the Selected Service Classifications during World War II, IV-F indicated "physically, mentally or morally unfit." "Military Classifications for Draftees," Swarthmore College, accessed June 20, 2020, https://www.swarthmore.edu/library/peace/conscientiousobjection/MilitaryClassifications.htm.

[80] Anthony Mazza's family lived at 817 Woods Run Avenue, Pittsburgh, Pennsylvania. "67 Leave Here for Air Cadet Training," *Pittsburgh Post-Gazette*, August 2, 1943.

Free

INSTRUCTION SCHOOL BR.

SAN MARCOS TEXAS 1944

v/c. Mezza, u.s.
44-12-6 S.M.A.A.F.N.S.
San Marcos, Texas.

Miss Sylvia Jacobs
3334 Fleming Ave.
St. John's Nurse Home
Pittsburgh 13, Pa

140

United States
Army Air Forces

July 25, 1944

Dearest Sylvia:

Have just returned from a flight over the Gulf. I was surprised to notice in big broad letters on the Black board as I entered the class-room. "No night class tonight." Naturally this gave me the golden opportunity to spend a few moments with thee. I'm really quite exhausted tonight so we'll spend the evening at home just chatting quietly of the things that happen in the course of a few days and munch on a bowl filled with potato chips and Iced Lemon Tea. This mission I flew this afternoon is known as a "Y" search but the pattern resembles something like this:

bay

H₂O

One must be absolutely careful to get the correct heading on each leg or he probably end up getting lost in an endless vast of water and "nothingness". A feeling of loneliness and the weight of responsibility sure feels like a burden as we student navigators sweat-out these missions for miles we keep the plane headed

142

July 25, 1944

From: A./C. Mazza, A.S.
     44-12-6 S.M.A.A.F.N.S.
     San Marcos, Texas

To: Sylvia Jacobs
     3334 Fleming Ave[.]
     St. John['s] Nurse Home
     Pittsburgh 12, Pa.

Postmark: 12:30 PM
     July 26, 1944
     San Marcos, Texas

Letterhead: United States
     Army Air Forces

[1*]   July 25, 1944

Dearest Sylvia:

Have just returned from a flight over the Gulf.[81] I was surprised to notice in big broad letters on the Black board [*sic*] as I entered the class-room [*sic*][,] "No night class tonight." Naturally[,] this gave me the golden opportunity to spend a few moments with thee. I'm really quite exhausted tonight[,] so we'll spend the evening at home just chatting quietly of the things that happen in the course of a few days and munch on a bowl filled with potato chips and [i]ced [l]emon [t]ea. This mission I flew this

---

[81] The Gulf of Mexico.

143

out into the ocean without seeing land for a good couple of hours. When my E.T.A. (estimated time of arrival) ended this evening, I gave one concentrated little prayer that we had come some where near destination. A moment later the Pilot tipped his wings and directly below us lay the destination of "Bay City." . . . ~~luck~~ Luck had still been in my favor.

Occasionaly some of the fellows get off course and today there were several who had to land at Corpus Christi & refuel. One lad takes things quite lightly as he remarked: "I don't mind these searches but it sure is some predicament to have ~~a~~ some one 'search for a searcher.'"

I probably have never explained the set up in our flying scheme, but we do have three student navigators working individually at three different seats, occasionally an instructor and of course a Pilot. One man directs the Pilot, another follows by instruments checking on the 1st Nav. while the third man works a system of navigation known as Air Plot. Last week one of the boys lost 10 minutes of time some where in his work and I had to follow him 30 miles into Mexico. From there I took over and brought the ship in.

afternoon is known as a "Y" search[,] but the pattern resembles something like this: [line drawing.][82]

One must be absolutely careful to get the correct heading on each leg[,] or he would probably end up getting lost in an endless vast of water and "nothingness." A feeling of lonliness [sic] and the weight of respons-ibility sure feels like a burden as we student navigators sweat-out [sic] these missions[,] as for miles we keep the plane headed [1R*] out into the ocean without seeing land for at least a couple of hours. When my E.T.A. (estimated time of arrival) ended this evening, I gave one concentrated little prayer that we had come some where [sic] near [the] destination. A moment later the [p]ilot tipped his wings[,] and directly below us lay the destination of "Bay City."[83]

Occasionaly [sic] some of the fellows get off course[,] and today there were several who had to land at Corpus Christi + refuel. One lad takes things quite lightly as he remarked: "I don't mind

---

[82] The ink drawing shows a squiggly line slanting upward from the left to the right at about a 45-degree angle. The word "bay" appears to the left of the squiggly line. From the right side of the squiggly line, about a quarter from the top, a straight line with an arrow moves downward at about a 90-degree angle. The straight line stops at the top of an equilateral triangle, and the arrowed straight line would have bisected the triangle if it continued. Instead, the arrowed straight line follows one of the triangle's equal sides, which is parallel to the bottom of the paper. The arrow then follows along the triangle's short side and returns to its origin at the top of the triangle by following the second equal side. However, midway along the second equal side, there is a diversion toward the triangle's interior, taking the form of three sides of a square before joining the remainder of the second equal side of the triangle and finishing where it started at the triangle's top. In the area between the squiggly line and the initial arrow and triangle is the formula "H_2O."

[83] Bay City, Texas, within Matagorda County, Texas, is about 20 miles from the coast of the Gulf of Mexico.

United States
Army Air Forces

Say, this kind of talk is getting me no where fast and sounds like a lot of bragging. 2nd Let flying go until another day and talk about the person who interests me most.

I wished I could take you up on dancing "Chus-Chics" down the hall way. One fellow just came out with a smart definition of dancing: "Hugging set to music." -- sounds more like the way I do it, doesn't it though. Well, it is different ??? ... and it depends on just who the partner happens to be.

Never did think you would see between the props of a huge Jumbo Post Card. You certainly deserve the implication of those little letters. and its too bad I'm not on hand to start the propellor twirling.

Mother informed me of the Infantile Paralysis epedemic in Pgh. We haven't heard a thing about it in this wilderness. Incidently, I passed the 64th Physical with flying Colors and again am most thankful for that. Being in perfect health surpasses the the most perfect navigator who has not

146

these searches[,] but it sure is some predicament to have some one [*sic*] search for a searcher."

I probably have never explained the set up [*sic*] in our flying scheme, but we do have three student navigators working individually at three different seats, ocasionally [*sic*] an instructor[,] and[,] of course[,] a [p]ilot. One man directs the [p]ilot[;] another follows by instruments[,] checking on the 1st Nav.[,] while the third man works a system of navigation known as Air Plot. Last week[,] one of the boys lost 10 minutes of time some where [*sic*] in his work[,] and I had to follow him 30 miles into Mexico. From there I took over and brought the ship in.

[2*] Say, this kind of talk is getting me no where [*sic*] fast and sounds like a lot of bragging. I'll let flying go until another day and talk about the person who interests me most.

Sure wished I could take you up on dancing "Chico-Chico" down the hall way [*sic*]. One fellow just came out with a smart definition of dancing: "Hugging set to music." - - - [S]ounds more like the way I do it, doesn't it[,] though[?] Well, it is different??? - - - - and it depends on just who the <u>partner</u> happens to be.

Never did think you would see between the props of a huge Jumbo Post Card.[84] You certainly deserve the implication of those fond little letters[,] and it[']s too bad I'm not on hand to start the propellor [*sic*] twirling.[85]

Mother informed me of the [i]nfantile [p]aralysis epidemic in Pgh. We haven't heard a thing about it in this wilderness. Incidentally, I passed the 64 Physical with flying colors and again

---

[84] See *supra* page 120 (Postcard from Anthony S. Mazza to Sylvia M. Jacobs (July 14, 1944)).

[85] Anthony Mazza wrote the letters *L*, *O*, *V*, and *E* in between the four propellers of the logo at the bottom of the card.

in that category. The Army, however, doesn't seem to want me to stay in that condition as tomorrow we shall be given two more additional shots of typhus & cholera.

I really don't know what to say definitely about your pursuing your education. Glad to have "the family" come through with the real decision. My puny two cents worth on the subject would be thus: Education never hurt anyone and the more out one can get the better it will be for them. Again I realize your sense of family loyalty and desire for independence (which must be considered). Beyond the many clouds, the haze of the future lifts and the Sylvia in my dreams does not need further education. (Particularly not, if I happen to be the tutor.) It really makes no difference one way or the other, as long as she keeps intact those wonderful characteristics that make Sylvia. — Sylvia (sigh) to me. Mr. Anthony has spoken — Ugh!

Shucks, we ran out of potato chips, Tea and Time. "Pucker up"!! Guess how long we held that one. I'm sure it would have broken the screen record. So long for now. Imagination sure has its advantages at night!

Love to
"Sylvia"
from Tony!

US

(XXXX)

am most thankful for that. Being in perfect health surpasses the the [*sic*] most perfect navigator who is not [2R*] in that category. The Army, however, doesn't seem to want me to stay in that condition[,] as tomorrow we shall be given two more adittional [*sic*] shots of typhus + cholera.

I really don't know what to say definitely about your pursuing your education. Glad to have "the family" come through with the real decision. My puny two cents['] worth on the subject would be this: [e]ducation never hurt anyone[,] and the more one can get[,] the better it will be for them. Again[,] I realize your sense of family loyalty and desire for independence[,] which must be considered. Beyond the many clouds, the haze of the future lifts and Sylvia in my dreams does not need further education. (Particularly not, if I happen to be the tutor.) It really makes no difference one way or the other, as long as she keeps intact those wonder-ful characteristics that make Sylvia - - - Sylvia (sigh) to me. Mr. Anthony has spoken—Ugh!

Shucks! We ran out of potato chips, [t]ea[,] and [t]ime. "Pucker up[!"] Guess how long we held that one. I'm sure it would have broken the screen record. So long for now. Imagination sure has its advantages at night!

Love to
"Sylvia"
from 'Tony'

US XXXX[86]

★

---

[86] One circle surrounds the four *X*s; lines radiate from the five-pointed star. One may infer that the "US" over the star may indicate Anthony Mazza and Sylvia Jacobs as a couple.

A/C. Mazza A.S.
44-12-6 S.M.A.A.F.N.S.
San Marcos, Texas.

Sylvia Jacobs
3334 Fleming Ave
St. John Nurse Home
Pittsburgh 12, Pa.

150

United States
Army Air Forces

August 16, 1944

Dearest Sylvia:

I can see now by your being at home that the Nurse Training program for you is practically at an end. I'll bet it seems strange to be "free" again and not to be able to get home every day. It sure has been one long grind and you must be given some credit at least for sticking it out. If I add to some of the sisters' praises, maybe your head will swell, but again I doubt that not if I'm right in character analysis. I can make mistakes however but not in this case. (Sure of myself again?). I have a half hour before a night flight so I thought I'd start this letter and end it when I can.

Couldn't help but smile at the p's & q's and immediately a scene flashed through my mind of a Court room with poor me as the defendant. A huge, harsh, stern, stone faced judge staring at me, while a long lanky scowling scoundrel of an attorney pointed his long crooked finger in front of my nose with the following quotation:

152

August 16, 1944

From: A./C. Mazza, A.S.
               44-12-6 S.M.A.A.F.N.S.
               San Marcos, Texas

To: Miss Sylvia Jacobs
               2334 Atmore St.
               N.S. Pittsburgh, Pa.

Postmark: 12:30 PM
               August 18, 1944
               San Marcos, Texas

Letterhead: United States
               Army Air Forces

[1*]   August 16, 1944

Dearest Sylvia:

I can see now by your being at home that the [n]urse [t]raining program for you is practically at an end. I'll bet it seems strange to be "free" again and to be able to get home every day. It sure has been one long grind[,] and you must be given some credit at least for sticking it out. If I add to some of the sisters' praises,[87] maybe

---

[87] The reference is most likely to the Sisters of Divine Providence, a Roman Catholic religious order, which conducted the nurses' training program at St. John's General Hospital in Pittsburgh, where Sylvia Jacobs was a student. See "Sisters of Divine Providence Marie de la Roche Province," accessed June 20, 2020, https://cdpsisters.org/. It is also possible that the reference may be to Sylvia Jacobs' own sisters, as she had six living sisters at the time.

Anything that you may say will be held against you." Imagine the perdicament???

We have been told that our graduating date will be Sept 25th should everything move according to schedule. Lets see, - - - - if I get a leave and it takes about 3 days to get to - - - - - - - - - -, about the last few days of the month will find me with - - - - - - . It would be perfect if your vacation could coincide but - - - - - OH! Well, its all a bit of wishful thinking that can come true - - - maybe. There are but 5 weeks left but they are the most important ones I have yet to face so keep those concentrated prayers coming down this way. There goes the whistle so I'm off - - - be back shortly.

                                        August 17th

It is lunch time now and I have another half hour before class time. That should give me ample time to conclude this letter - - - I hope. We flew last night to Lake Charles, Louisiana. It was but a practice hop to familiarize us with the procedure on how three star fixes are obtained while on flight. I had fair results but hope to do much better on my next mission, it will count then. We got in early this morning about 2:00 AM and believe it or not we were permitted to sleep through reveille up to 7:30 AM. It

154

your head will swell[,] but again[,] I doubt that[,] not if I'm right in character analysis. I can make mistakes, however, but not in this case! (Sure of myself again??). I have a half hour before a night flight[,] so I thought I'd start this letter and end it when I can.

Couldn't help but smile at the p's + q's[,] and immediately a scene flashed through my mind of a [c]ourt room [*sic*] with poor me as the defendant. A huge, harsh, stern[,] stone[-]faced judge staring at me, while a long[,] lanky[,] scowling scoundrel of an [a]ttorney pointed his long[,] crooked finger in front of my nose with the following quotation: [1R*] "Anything that you may say will be held against you." Imagine the perdicament [*sic*]???

We have been told that our graduating date will be Sept[.] 25th[,] should everything move according to schedule. Let[']s see, - - - - - if I get a leave and it takes about 3 days to get to - - - - - - - - - -, about the last few days of the month will find me with - - - - - -. It would be perfect if your vaction [*sic*] could coincide but - - - - - OH! Well, it[']s all a bit of wishful thinking that can come true - - - maybe. There are but five weeks left[,] but they are the most important ones I have yet to face[,] so keep those concentrated prayers coming down this way. There goes the whistle[,] so I'm off - - - - be back shortly.

August 17th

It is [l]unch time [*sic*] now[,] and I have another half hour before class time. That should give me ample time to conclude this letter - - - - I hope. We flew last night to Lake Charles, Louisiana. It was but a practice hop to familiarize us with the procedure on how three[-]star fixes are obtained while on flight. I had four results but hope to do much better on my next mission; it will count then. We got in early this morning about 2:00 AM[,] and believe it or not[,] we were permitted to sleep through reveille up

United States
Army Air Forces

2

was a treat to be able to "cuss" the bugler and roll over on the other side for a change.

I was delighted to hear that you had Doug & Eddie visit you and that too you could have dinner at our house last week. Mother wrote and told me of the fun that was had by all and one thing you must get straight right now. Mother really gets a "kick" out of putting herself out a bit. She really enjoys seeing young people together, having fun, and happy. I have never asked her to invite you home, but all that was done of her own accord and because of your own merit. You really must have applied all the charm of your personality to her and it is getting the same results it has had on me. Mother told me that you met with the sincere approval of my Uncle. He is rather "frank" with his opinions so I have every right to be proud of you.

Our relationship is a huge one, but one good thing is that there are many of us in the same age group. Now when

156

to 9:30 AM. It [2*] was a treat to be able to "cuss" the bugler and roll over on the other side for a change.

I was delighted to hear that you had Greg and Eddie[88] visit you and that[,]too[,] you could have dinner at our home last week. Mother wrote and told me of the fun that was had by all[,] and one thing you must get straight right now. Mother really gets a "kick" out of putting herself out a bit. She really enjoys seeing young people together, having fun, and happy. I have never asked her to invite you home, but all that was done of her own accord and because of your own merit. You really must have applied all the charm of your personality to her[,] and it is getting the same results that it has had on me. Mother told me that you met with the sincere approval of my [u]ncle. He is rather "frank" with his opinions[,] so I have every right to be proud of you.

Our relationship is a huge one[,] but one good thing is that there are many of us in the same age group. Now when [2R*] we could really be having so much fun together[,] the war had to spoil that. It will come[,] though[,] one of these days[,] when all that will be possible.

No, you never did meet Tom[,] and I can't possibly think how he could have met Eddie either - - - - - same situation isn't it?

---

[88] Edna Surenda (b. March 3, 1922; d. December 9, 2018) and Gregory Mazza were dating at the time, but they did not continue dating after the war. She and her siblings, however, remained longtime friends of both the Mazza and Jacobs families. Edna Surenda and Sylvia Jacobs' older sister Elizabeth Jacobs (b. December 27, 1918; d. January 28, 1988) were lifelong friends, often playing tennis and ice skating together. See *infra* page 763 (Photograph of Edna Surenda).

me could really be having so much fun together the war had to spoil that. It will come though one of these days when all that will be possible.

No, you never did meet Tom and I can't possibly think how he could have met Eddie either. . . . same situation isn't it? Don't bribe Antoinette too much or she'll create one of her own original stories to fit the occasion.

That brother of mine would beat me to the punch in congratulating you but my mental telepathy beat him by several years, I think.

You had better keep me in mind for a picture or you certainly will ruin your fair standing with me!!!!

Wow! time certainly flies here and I must sign off now.

Sending plenty of love from here to you Sylvie.

Love,
Tony

P.S. I believe you are one of the 15% but I have learned, the hard way, that it does not pay to assume.

P.S.² How are my P's & q's?

Don't bribe Antoinette[89] too much[,] or she'll create one of her own original stories to fit the occasion.

That brother of mine would beat me to the punch in congratulating you[,] but my mental telepathy beat him by several years, I think.[90]

You had better keep me in mind for a picture[,] or you certainly will ruin your fair standing with me!!!!

Wow! Time certainly flies here[,] and I must sign off now.

Sending plenty of love from here

To you[,] Sylvie:

Love[,]

Tony

P.S. I believe you are one of the 15%[,] but I have learned, the hard way, that it does not pay to assume.

P.²S.² How are my [p]'s + q's?

---

[89] Marie Antoinette Mazza Sudarich (b. June 13, 1931; d. February 14, 2001) was Anthony Mazza's younger sister.

[90] See Letter from Gregory E. Mazza to Sylvia M. Jacobs (September 22, 1944) (on file with the editor).

A/c. Jga, ES.
44-12-6 S.M.A.A.F.N.S.
San Marcos, Texas

Miss Sylvia M. Jacobs
2334 Atmore Alt.
N.S. Pittsburgh, Pa.

Aug 21, 1944

Dearest Sylvia:

Enclosed in the last letter you sent were three pages of written material that always appeals to me, but there ~~but~~ inside I found ~~one~~ page blank. Seemed rather odd and may have been done intentional or non-intentional ~~but~~ however, since I am quite a conservative this famous sheet of cellulose now contains writing matter from U.S.M. (reason for it being ~~famous~~.) ~~Hum~~ (Chuckling ~~to myself~~) It could mean I register just a blank to you. ???

Have had quite an active week-end but the better part of the evenings or nights, were spent in shooting those heavenly celestial bodies, the stars. This coming week any time you "poke" your head from a window to look up at the sky at night, you will know Tony is somewhere in an AT-7 shooting ~~stars~~ with a sextant, fumbling through an Air Almanac, 3 or 4 volumes of Astronomical tables, and ~~plotting his position somewhere in the south~~ eastern part of the U.S. Did you know that some stars can be identified by their color? If you look long enough and hard enough the big bright ones, you will be able to classify them as being either red, amber or blue. Be careful though and don't try it as you walk down the street or you will have a terrible time trying to explain the condition of your eye caused by walking

August 21, 1944

Postmark: [The envelope is missing.]

Letterhead: The first page is without a letterhead, but the second
              and third pages have the following letterhead:
              United States
              Army Air Forces

[1*]   Aug[.] 21, 1944

Dearest Sylvia:[91]

Enclosed in the last letter you sent were three pages of
written material that always appeals to me, but there [on] the
inside[,] I found one page <u>blank</u>. Seemed rather odd and may
have been done intentional[ly] or non-intentional[ly,] but,
however, since I am quite a conservative[,] this famous sheet of
cellulose now contains writing from A.S.M. (reason for it being
<u>famous</u>.) Hmm: (chuckling to myself)[.] It could mean I register
just a <u>blank</u> to you???

Have had quite an active week-end [*sic*][,] but the better part
of the evenings or nights, were spent in shooting those heavenly
celestial bodies, the stars. This coming week, any time you "poke"
your head from a window to look up at the sky at night, you will
know Tony is somewhere in an AT-7[,][92] shooting stars with a

---

[91] An *x* is above the letter *i* in Sylvia, and two small letter *o*'s, one above the
other, form the colon.

[92] The Army Air Forces used the AT-7, an airplane manufactured by
Beechcraft, to train navigators during World War II. "Beechcraft AT-7
Navigator," Pima Air and Space Museum, accessed June 20, 2020, https://
pimaairorg/museum–aircraft/beechcraft-at-7/; see *supra* page 118.

into a lamp post.

Just received two letters from my two best girls. One from mother and the other from S. - h - - A. The letter from home had the rather disappointing but inevitable news that Irey is about to be shipped across. He never mentioned a word about it while he was home. It was just like him to cause as little "fuss" over the issue as he possible could, and to make his leave enjoyed in the simplest things he wanted. All the war does strike home more than ever but there isn't much we can do but sit and pray always hoping for the best and realizing that others are in the same or even worse predicament than we. The only thing I regret most is the effect it will have on mother, she really has had about all the toughest breaks an individual can have.

Glad you liked my "musical gem" program. There is only one woman who is a "mystery" to me, but if you can help me to solve it everything will be just perfect.

Your work at the E.R. is very interesting and you must be meeting many people. The burn case you mentioned reminds me of myself about a year ago. Did I ever tell you of the beautiful

sextant, fumbling through an *Air Almanac*,[93] 3 or 4 volumes of astronomical tables, and plotting his position somewhere in the south-eastern [*sic*] part of the U.S. Did you know that some stars can be identified by their color? If you look long enough and hard enough at the big bright ones, you will be able to classify them as being red, amber, or blue. Be careful[,] though[,] and don't try it as you walk down the street[,] or you will have a terrible time trying to explain the condition of your eye caused by walking [1R*] into a lamp post [*sic*].

Just received two letters from my two best girls. One from my mother and the other from S -L- - A. The letter from home had the rather disappointing but inevitable news that Greg is about to be shipped across. He never mentioned a word about it while he was home. It was just like him to cause as little "fuss" over the issue as he possibl[y] could, and to make his leave en-joyed in the simplest things he wanted. All the war does strike home more than ever[,] but there isn't much we can do but sit and pray[,] always hoping for the best and realizing that others are in the same or even worse predicament than we. The only thing I regret most is the effect it will have on [M]other; she really has had about all the toughest breaks an individual can have.

Glad you liked my "musical gem" program. There is only one woman who is a "mystery" to me, but if you can help me to solve it[,] everything will be just perfect.

Your work at the E.R.[94] is very interesting[,] and you must be meeting many people. The burn case you mentioned reminds me of myself about a year ago. Did I ever tell you of the beautiful

---

[93] Italics added.
[94] Emergency Room.

165

2

nurse who applied the wax treatment each
day? Naturally that had something to do
with the fast cure.??? Can't realize what a mess ~~I was~~
~~of blisters~~ Yesterday, I cooled off as usual at
a swimming pool. This time to the fair city
of Austin where I brought one of my buddies
to teach me diving from the 16 ft board. I
climbed to the board and started my stuff
threw out my arms and hurtled through
the air with the greatest of ease. As I came
to the surface, my "pal" ~~had~~ crumpled up
in a fit of violent laughter and could
hardly move or speak coherently. I finally
asked him just what happened that could
cause him to react so. Imagine what
he said? He told me that ~~I looked like~~
my "swan" dive reminded him of "Bat-
man" in one of his mighty leaps through
space. I see where my diving attempts
will be shelved for a while at least.
    What! you haven't got a tan us
yet? I'm really curious to find out
how you would appear in a deep tan.

166

[2*] nurse who applied the wax treatments each day? Naturally[,] that had something to do with the fast cure??? Can't realize what a mass of blisters I was then.

Yesterday, I cooled off as usual at a swimming pool. This time to the fair City of Austin[,] where I brought one of my buddies to teach me diving from the 10[-]ft[.] board. I climbed to the board and strutted my stuff[,] threw out my arms and hurtled through the air with the greatest of ease. As I came to the surface, my "pal" had crumpled up in a fit of violent laughter and could hardly move or speak coherently. I finally asked him just what happened that could cause him to react so. Imagine what he said? He told me that my "swan" dive reminded him of "Bat-man" in one of his mighty leaps through space. I see where my diving attempts will be shelved for a-while [*sic*] at least.

What! [Y]ou haven't got a tan as yet? I'm really curious to find out how you would appear in a deep tan. [2R*] I mean "real["]

I mean real tan, now not "sun tan powder." I'll be wise to that kind of stunt so don't try to pull that trick on me.

The furlough you mentioned is still only a possibility and I really hope and pray that it will become authentic. I do plenty of powerful wishing too, but wishing just can't supplant realization. It is something to look forward to, something to build up hope, something that temporarily at least can make some dreams come true. I hope this next one can really move smoothly but not as long as there are things to settle. I'd prefer to settle 'em, It always ends up better that way. and it has always been my policy to take care of the staff assignments first. --- Rough & Ready I was known as in those days!!

Quite a bit of excitement going on as there has been a forecast of two hurricanes in the + about the Gulf. One will go through Florida and a Potential one may come up this way. We are getting set to fly a long mission probably to get the planes out of the danger area. Our destination may be Carlsbad, New Mexico and from there on to California. This should give us plenty of practice and tan now[,] not "sun tan [*sic*] powder." I'll be wise to that kind of stunt[,] so don't try to pull that trick on me.

The furlough you mentioned is still only a possibility[,] and I really hope and pray that it will become authentic. I do plenty of powerful wishing[,] too, but wishing just can't supplant [*sic*] realization. It is something to look forward to, something to build up hope for, something that temporarily at least can make some dreams come true. I hope this next one can really move smoothly[,] but not as long as there are things to settle[,] I'd prefer to settle 'em. It always ends up better that way[,] and it has always been my policy to take care of "tall" assignments first. - - - Rough + Ready I was known as in those day[s]!!

Quite a bit of excitement going on[,] as there has been a forecast of two hurricanes in + about the Gulf. One will go through Florida and a [p]otential one may come up this way. We are getting set to fly a long mission[,] probably to get the planes out of the danger [a]rea. Our destination may be Carlsbad, New Mexico[,] and from there on to California. This should give us plenty of practice[,] and [3*] experience if such is actually the case.

United States
Army Air Forces

3

experience of such is actually the case.

You certainly pulled an ~~original~~ over on me in your last letter. Really think your smart, don't you? Well you are. I do have a little come-back by the salutation of this letter as you probably have noticed by now.

(Not to be outdone!)

Saw a wonderful Movie picture at Austin yesterday too. It was "White Cliffs of Dover." As all heavy dramas, it was a tradgedy, but the story and acting were ~~very~~ superior.

Gee! I'd better get this letter off to you or you'll really be wondering what this happened. Sure did enjoy reading your letter this morning; It always gives quite a feeling to find a letter from S.M.F. waiting for me on my bunk after a tough day. You certainly have improved and should be properly complimented.

Goodnight Syl and I send my Love

"Tony"

170

You certainly pulled an original over on me in your last letter. Really think your [sic] smart, don't you? Well[,] you are. Not to be outdone, I do have a little come-back [sic] in the salutation of this letter[,] as you probably have noticed by now.

Saw a wonderful movie picture at Austin yesterday[,] too. It was "White Cliffs of Dover."[95] As all heavy dramas, it was a tradgedy [sic], but the story and acting were superior.

Gee! I'd better get this letter off to you[,] or you'll really be wondering what has happened. Sure did enjoy reading your letter this morning; it always gives quite a feeling to find a letter from S.M.J. waiting for me on my bunk after a tough day. You certainly have improved and should be properly complimented.

Good night[,] Syl[,] and I send my

Love[,]
"Tony"

---

[95] *The White Cliffs of Dover*, directed by Clarence Brown, featuring Irene Dunne, Alan Marshal, and Roddy McDowall (Metro-Goldwyn-Mayer, 1944).

United States
Army Air Forces

Dearest Sylvia: Aug 26, 1944

Since I last wrote to you, I've
had quite a bit of adventure and travel. We
have been through half of the country and
back within the last two days traveling
over 2,000 knots in the air (one knot equals
1.15 miles). I'm like the bewildered sailor
who, when asked what he had seen on
his vast travel experiences over the many
oceans, calmly replied; "I saw the sea."
My little addition to that would be, "I
saw the sky." No, it wasn't as bad as
that but it is hard to describe everything
at once. The hurricane that we expected
to come directly south of us, blew itself
out but the other one moved in from
Cuba across the Gulf gathering momentum
as it swung west-ward to Mexico. As
a precaution, a group of us were assigned
to detached service and it was our responsibility to keep the plane out of the
area and fly the training missions

172

August 26, 1944

Postmark: [The envelope is missing.]

Letterhead: United States
              Army Air Forces

[1*]   Aug[.] 26, 1944

Dearest Sylvia:

Since I last wrote you, I've had quite a-bit [*sic*] of adventure and travel. We have been through half of the country and back within the last two days[,] traveling over 2,000 [k]nots in the air (one [k]not equals 1.13 miles). I'm like the bewildered sailor who, when asked what he had seen on his vast travel experiences over the many oceans, calmly replied, "I saw the sea." My little addition to that would be, "I saw the sky." No, it wasn't as bad as that[,] but it is hard to describe everything at once. The hurricane we expected to come directly south of us, blew itself out[,] but the other one moved in from Cuba across the Gulf[,] gathering momentum as it swung west-ward [*sic*] to Mexico. As a precaution, a group of us were assigned to detached service[,] and it was our res-posibility [*sic*] to keep the plane[s] out of the area and fly the training missions [1R*] we need to fulfill our course requirements.

we need to fulfill our course requirements.

The first leg was uneventful as we headed for El Paso, Texas. Using the Sun, do it was fading in the sky for our only celestial body, we got there O.K. With but a bite to eat, we started again this time to Palm Springs, California. Over the western plains the Sierra Nevada mountain range was a thrill I'll never forget but this air travel isn't what one would desire to survey the beauties of nature in this area. But poor me, there I was shooting Polaris, Antares, Arcturus, Alpheratz and a score of other stars above, and fighting to keep awake, since it was way past my bedtime. We arrived at Palm Springs about 3:00 AM in the morning and sleepy eyed grabbed a blanket from Sect. Headquarters and soon was fast asleep in Dream Land. Palm Springs is really a beautiful spot since it is an A.T.C. base. They say there are many beautiful women, hundreds of Wacs but we never saw them at 5:00 AM that same morning just 2 hours later. Within two hours, we were back in the air heading for

The first leg was uneventful[,] as we headed for El Paso, Texas. Using the [s]un, as it was fading in the sky[,] for our only celestial body, we got there O.K. With but a bite to eat, we started again this time to Palm Springs, California. [Flying o]ver the western plains, + the Sierra Nevada mountain range was a thrill I'll never forget[,] but this air travel isn't what we would desire to survey the beauties of nature in this area. But poor me, there I was shooting Polaris, Antares, Arcturus, Alpheratz and a score of other stars above, and fighting to keep awake, since it was way past my bedtime. We arrived at Palm Springs about 3:00 AM in the morning[,] and sleepy eyed[, I] grabbed a blanket from Sect. Headquarters and was soon fast asleep in Dream Land [*sic*]. Palm Springs is really a beautiful spot since it is an A.T.C.[96] base. They say there are many beautiful women, hundreds of W[ACS,][97] but we never saw them at 5:00 AM that same morning just 2 hours later. Within two hours, we were back in the air[,] heading for [2*] Elpaso [*sic*]. The course was smooth[,] but we did

---

[96] The Air Transport Command (ATC) was a component of the United States Army Air Forces. Wesley F. Craven and James L. Cate, ed., "The Air Transport Command," in *Services Around the World*, vol. 7, *The Army Air Forces in World War II* (Arlington, VA: Office of Air Force History, 1983), 3.

[97] Created during World War II, the Women Army Corps (WAC) enabled women to serve in noncombat positions in the U.S. Army. "Creation of the Women's Army Corps," Women in the Army, accessed June 20, 2020, https://www.army.mil/women/history/wac.html.

2

El paso. The course was smooth but we did have excitement trying to avoid Guadalupe Peak 10,800 miles up as we were maintaining a flight altitude of 12,000 ft.

From El Paso to San Marcos, again it was work all the way but freak thunderstorms lit up the sky to give rather an uncomfortable feeling to the occupants of our plane. Lightning is one thing we need never fear since the plane is adequately equipped to throw off the charge. We can't be grounded since we are in the air. this being the main reason for no ill effects from a direct hit on a plane by a lightning charge.

See! there really isn't much I can say about my trip but I am trying to recuperate but I'm class all day and all night just the same. We won't begin class tonight until 8:30 PM but a ground mission will find us working

176

have excitement trying to avoid Guadalupe Peak[,] 10,800 miles [*sic*] up[,] as we were mainta[in]ing a flight altitude of 10,000 ft.

From El Paso to San Marcos, again it was work all the way[,] but freak thunderstorms lit up the sky to give rather an uncomfortable feeling to the occupants of our plane. Lightning is one thing we need never fear since the plane is adequately equipped to throw off the charge. We can't be grounded since we are in the air[,] this being the main reason for no ill effects from a direct hit on a plane by a lightning charge.

See! [T]here really isn't much I can say about my trip[,] and I am trying to recuperate[,] but it['s] class all day and all night just the same. We won't begin class tonight until 8:30 PM[,] but a ground mission will find us working [2R*] up through 12:00 PM. However, tomorrow morning we can sleep until 8:00 AM.

up through 12:00 PM. However, tomorrow morning we can sleep until 8:00 AM.

This morning we were given a knapsack, mess kit, tent flap, blanket roll etc. Guess what that signifies? A pleasant stroll is in store for us early Sunday morning --- something like a 20 mile hike. 9.3 miles to be exact. This is part of our training program to prepare us no doubt for our future living conditions. There won't be a special built camp to house "Navigators" and we might have to construct a pup tent for any emergency. I'm all set for a good heavy rain to make things interesting. I can still remember vividly the red clay of North Carolina and a letter I wrote that had an ___ signed in red clay. Mental telepathy was in its infancy — remember!

I received your wonderful invitation this morning and it was thoughtful of you to send me one. I sure owe plenty to good ole St John — why, if it hadn't been for one of their gunt affairs --- if a certain nurse

178

This morning[,] we were given a knapsack, mess kit, [t]ent flap, blanket roll[,] etc. Guess what that signifies? A pleasant stroll is in store for us early Sunday morning - - - something like a 10[-]mile hike. [Nine and three-tenths] miles to be exact. This is part of our training program to prepare us[,] no doubt[,] for our future living conditions. There won't be a special[ly] built camp to house "[n]avigators[,]" and we might have to construct a tent for any emergency. I'm all set for a good heavy rain to make things interesting. I can still remember vividly the red clay of North Carolina[,] and a letter I wrote that had an – signed in red clay. Mental telepathy was in its infancy—remember?

I received your wonderful invitation this morning[,] and it was thoughtful of you to send me one. I sure owe plenty to good 'ole [*sic*] St[.] John—why if it hadn't been for one of their great affairs - - - if a certain nurse [3*] wasn't training there, look where I would be and what an opportunity I would have missed.[98] I'd

---

[98] According to family lore, even though Anthony Mazza may have met Sylvia Jacobs through her brother, George Jacobs, when Anthony and George were high school classmates, Anthony and Sylvia did not start dating until Sylvia had to find a date for a women's choice dance affiliated with St. John's School of Nursing, where she had enrolled after high school. Sylvia decided to call the Mazza home, thinking that there were three bachelor brothers living there at the time who could be possible dates. Her plan was to invite to the dance the brother who answered the telephone. Anthony happened to pick up the telephone when she called, so she asked him to the dance, and he accepted. They enjoyed the dance and began seeing each other afterward. The dance was the Silver Ball, a fundraiser for St. John's General Hospital, held on Friday, November 20, 1942, at the Roosevelt Hotel in Pittsburgh, Pennsylvania. "Silver Ball," *Pittsburgh Sun-Telegraph*, November 18, 1942; "Silver Ball to Finance Blood Bank," *Pittsburgh Post-Gazette*, November 18, 1942; "Hospital Auxiliary to Sponsor Benefit to Raise Funds for Needed Equipment," *Pittsburgh Press*, November 9, 1942.

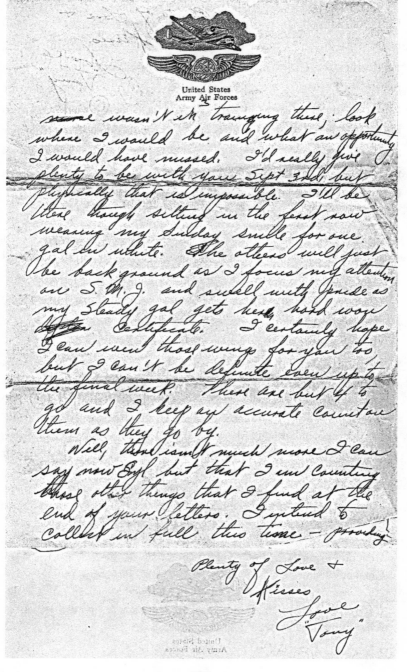

~~more~~ wasn't in training there; look where I would be and what an opportunity I would have missed. I'd really give plenty ~~to be with you~~ Sept 3rd, but physically that is impossible. I'll be there though sitting in the front row wearing my Sunday smile for one gal in white. The others will just be back ground as I focus my attention on S. M. J. and swell with pride as my steady gal gets her hard won ~~fly-in~~ certificate. I certainly hope I can win those wings for you too, but I can't be definite even up to the final week. There are but 4 to go and I keep an accurate count on them as they go by.

Well, there isn't much more I can say now Eryl but that I am counting ~~those~~ other things that I find at the end of your letters. I intend to collect in full this time – proudly!

Plenty of Love &
Kisses
Love
"Tony"

really give plenty to be with you Sept[.] 3rd, but physically that is impossible. I'll be there[,] though[,] sitting in the first row[,] wearing my Sunday smile for one gal in white. The others will just be background as I focus my attention on S.M.J. and swell with pride as my steady gal gets her hard[-]won certificate. I certainly hope I can earn those wings for you[,] too, but I can't be definite even up to the final week. There are but 4 to go[,] and I keep an accurate count on them as they go by.

Well, there isn't much more I can say now[,] Syl[,] but that I am counting those other things that I find at the end of your letters. I intend to collect in full this time—providing!

Plenty of Love +

Kisses

Love[,]

"Tony"

United States
Army Air Forces

Aug 28, 1944

Dearest Sylvia:

I don't know where to begin in stating the events that happened the past few days, but most of it has been centered around our bivouac this past week-end. Late Saturday evening about the time that the "Navigators" do their navigating in San Antonio, Austin and San Marcos; Class 44-12-6 clad in fatigues, helmets, full pack with blanket roll and shelter halves, canteen and mess equipment, plus 2 days worth of C ration, were trudging in a long narrow column to ~~our~~ destination 10 miles away. Just one year ago to date, I was doing the same and identical thing at Greensboro, N.C. Certainly have been getting up in the world, haven't I or shall I say further down since Texas is South of North Carolina?? Need 2 tell you the weather conditions?? My predication was perfect and I can sit back with a soft smile and casually

August 28, 1944

From: A./C. Mazza, A.S.
             44-12-6 S.M.A.A.F.N.S.
             San Marcos, Texas

To: Miss Sylvia M. Jacobs
             2334 Atmore Street
             N.S. Pittsburgh, Pa

Postmark: 4:30 PM
             August 29, 1944
             San Marcos, Texas

Letterhead: United States
             Army Air Forces

[1*]   Aug[.] 28, 1944

Dearest Sylvia:

I don't know where to begin in stating the events that happened the past few days, but most of it has been centered around our bivouac this past week-end [*sic*]. Late Saturday evening[,] about the time that the "[n]avigators" do their navigating in San Antonio, Austin[,] and San Marcos[,] class 44-12-6[,] clad in fatigues, helmets, full pack with blanket roll and shelter halves, canteen[,] and mess equipment, plus 2[-]days worth of C ration, were trudging in a long[,] narrow column to [our] destination 10 miles away. Just one year ago to date, I was doing the same and identicle [*sic*] thing in Greensboro, N.C. Certainly have been

remark: "I told you so." IT RAINED!!

It started with a slight sprinkle as we were marching to our bivouac area, but increased in tempo as we approached the vicinity where we were to pitch our tents. The ground was wet and damp to begin with, but soon "pup tents" began to sprout from all corners of the field. Ours was a "dandy", even if I say so myself . . . . Old Infantry Man Mazza, they called me in those days. I then demonstrated to the gang how to build a trench around the tent to prevent water from getting inside. I suggested a bit the conditions at Greensboro and dug my drainage system 1 ft deep. I certainly appreciated that drainage system last night though, when a literal deluge broke loose. Tents collapsed and shouting could be heard in the middle of the night. A thud, thud, thud of some-one working furiously with a pick. Two buddies engaged in conversation similar to this: "Now I told you not to put the tent up here" "But where in the *¢&!! did you want me to put it." and so on

getting up in the world, haven't I[,] or shall I say further down[,] since Texas is [s]outh of North Carolina?? Need I tell you the weather conditions?? My prediction was perfect[,] and I can sit back with a soft smile and casually [1R*] remark: "I told you so." IT RAINED!!

It started with a slight sprinkle as we were marching to our bivouac area, but [it] increased in tempo as we approached the vicinity where we were to pitch our tents. The ground was wet and damp to begin with, but soon "pup tents" began to sprout from all corners of the field. Ours was a "dandy," even if I say so myself - - - - Old Infantry Man Mazza, they called me in those days. I then demonstrated to the gang how to build a trench around the tent to prevent water from getting inside. I exaggerated a bit the conditions at Greensboro and dug my drainage system 1 ft[.] deep. I certainly appreciated that drainage system last night[,] though, when a literal deluge broke loose. Tents collapsed[,] and shouting could be heard in the middle of the night. A thud, thud, thud of some-one [sic] working furiously with a pick. Two buddies engaged in conversation similar to this: "Now I told you not to put the tent up here[.]" "But where in the [symbols denoting swearing]!! did you want me to put it[?]" and so on [2*] into the night.

United States
Army Air Forces

2

into the night.

Sunday morning we fired the "Carbine" for familiarization only, since the weather could not permit constant fire and totaling of qualification scores. The rest of the day we had to ourselves.... so we thought. We had to prepare our own meals (intended) from the C. ration tin. We built small camp fires to warm the canned Vegetable stew and prepare Coffee, G.I. style. What a cook, I am! After a while, I decided it was best to eat the food cold and throw the coffee out. The "hard tack" "dog biscuit" was horrible and I lived on ——.

Just took it easy thinking of '———' and wondering what she was doing then. Probably preparing the family's noon meal with a Can-Opener.?? What ugly rumors Guy must have spread of my Pie making abilities. Imagine how sour you'd get eating (always) Lemon Pies. I won't feel sorry for myself

Sunday morning[,] we fired the "Carbine"[99] for familiarization only, since the weather could not permit constant fire and totaling of qualification scores. The rest of the day we had to ourselves - - - - - so we thought. We had to prepare our own individual meals from the C[-]ration tin.[100] We built small camp fires to warm the canned [v]egetable stew and prepare coffee, G.I. style. What a cook, I am. After a while, I decided it was best to eat the food cold and throw the coffee out. The hard tack [*sic*] "dog biscuit" was horrible[,] and I lived on - - - -. Just took it easy thinking of ' ' and wondering what she was doing then. Probably preparing the family noon meal with a Can-Opener [*sic*]??? What ugly rumors Greg must have spread of my [p]ie[-]making abilities. Imagine how sour you'd get always eating [l]emon pies. I won't feel sorry for myself [2R*] one bit with you[r] cooking such a meal as fried

---

[99] The M1 Carbine was a standard firearm for the U.S. military during World War II. Mark Keefe, "The M1 Carbine: 10 Little Known Facts," *American Rifleman*, May 14, 2020, https://www.americanrifleman.org/articles/2020/5/14/the-m1-carbine-10-little-known-facts/.

[100] "U.S. Army Field Rations," Modeling the U.S. Army in WWII, accessed June 20, 2020, http://www.usarmymodels.com/ARTICLES/Rations/crations.html.

one but with your cooking such a meal as fried potatoes & steak with onions... The way to man's heart via stomach. However, I believe I could live on love for a long long time. — Who's a Wolf???

Last night we had a midnight hike for about 5 miles in the Texas bog. I lived very close to "Mudder" earth these past two days and came in this morning plastered from head to foot with the gooey, slimey, muck. They may call this a Training Course in bivouac; but I call it the Civie Corps Appreciation program and am thankful that I haven't as yet had to live completely in these conditions.

So we're having trouble with Lois's curiosity. Tell her if she don't behave, one of these days will get even with her... and how!!

It wouldn't be my luck to have all the lights go out while I was ~~with~~ with you. ~~then~~ what an opportunity though. Mother told me of the lights going out in her last letter. My little brother Julius seemed to be a victim of circumstantial evidence. He went upstairs and brought down the small radio to play it in the kitchen. Dad, mother and

potatoes, steak with onions - - - The way to [a] man's heart via stomach. However, I believe I could live on love for a long[,] long time. –Who's a wolf???

Last night we had a midnight hike for about 5 miles in the Texas bog. I lived very close to "Mudder" [E]arth these past two days and came in this morning plastered from head to foot with the gooey, slimey [sic], muck. They may call this a training course in bivouac, but I call it the Air Corps Appreciation [P]rogram and am thankful that I haven't as yet had to live completely in these conditions.

So we're having trouble with Lois's[101] curiosity. Tell her if she don't [sic] behave, one of these days[,] we'll get even with her - - - - and how!!

It wouldn't be my luck to have all the lights go out while I was with you. Hm[,] what an opportunity[,] though. Mother told me of the lights going out in her last letter. My little brother[,] Julius[,][102] seemed to be a victim of circumstantial evidence. He went upstairs and brought down the small radio to play it in the kitchen. Dad, [M]other[,] and [3*] and [sic] the rest of the family

---

[101] Lois Jacobs Talotta Droney (b. June 4, 1931) is Sylvia Jacobs' youngest sister.

[102] Julius Mazza (b. August 26, 1929; d. August 1, 2010) was Anthony Mazza's youngest brother.

United States
Army Air Forces

3

and the rest of the family watched him plug in the cord. At that moment the lights went out and the family spent quite a time scouting for fuses and trying several before they discovered that our neighbor's lights were out too.

I sure hope that furlough will be the real thing one of these days but you'll have to choose a better subject than A.S.M. to discuss. S.M.J. would be my preference. Maybe we can compromise. ??

I guess by the time you receive this letter you will be quite engrossed in your graduation activities. Again I am caught flat footed without the opportunity to get a little something as a remembrance to you from me of this great occasion in your life. I'll have it though and hand it to you in person I hope very soon. Gosh! but I'll miss the little party held in your honor but I'd probably be in the way and couldn't

190

watched him plug in the cord. At that moment[,] the lights went out[,] and the family spent quite a time scouting for fuses and trying several before they discovered that our neighbors' lights were out[,] too.

Sure hope that furlough will be the real thing one of these days[,] but you'll have to choose a better subject than A.S.M. to discuss. S.M.J. would be my preference. Maybe we can compromise??

I guess by the time you receive this letter[,] you will be quite engrossed in your graduation activities. Again[,] I am caught flat-footed without the opportunity to get a little something as a remembrance to you from me of this great occasion in your life. I'll have it[,] though[,] and hand it to you in person[,] I hope[,] very soon. Gosh! [B]ut I'll miss the little party held in your honor[,] but I'd probably be in the way and couldn't [3R*] operate successfully

operate successfully in public. I'll see
that at the exercises though and will have
a hand in pinning that little pin on
your dress. ----- My specialty though
is pinning wings.

I agree with your "funny" theory
a bit and sometimes conclude that
what is meant to be is meant.

Since you cleared the mystery
in your last letter, it does help
plenty. More or less confirms my
own hypothesis. I'll let you in on
that one of these days.

I just got a letter from Greg and
he is in New England preparing for
shipment. It seems quite evident that
he will participate in the European Theater
of Operations.

Well it is getting late and
another of these "rare" letters of mine
is concluded. I hope you will understand the situation now and that I am
doing my best to have you hear from
me often. I'll really catch up one of
these day ---- then it will be your turn
to stall   Loads of Love & Kisses
P.S. would like to been hand when "Tony"
you are in one of those moods.

192

in public. I'll see you[103] at at the exercises[,] though[,] and will have a hand in pinning that little pin on your dress. - - - - - - My specialty[,] though[,] is pinning wings.

I agree with your "funny" theory a bit and sometimes conclude that what is meant to be is meant.[104]

Since you cleared the mystery in your last letter, it does help plenty. More or less confirms my own hypothesis. I'll let you in on that[,] one of these days.

Just got a letter from Greg[,] and he is in New England[,] preparing for shipment. It seems quite evident that he will participate in the European Theater of Operations.

Well[,] it is getting late and another of these "rare" letters of mine is concluded. I hope you will under-stand the situation now and that I am doing my best to have you hear from me often. I'll really catch up one of these days - - - - then it will be your turn to stall[.] Loads of Love + Kisses[,][105]

P.S. Would like to be on hand when   "Tony"
you are in one of those moods.

---

[103] The word "you" is inscribed without ink, and the first "at" is crossed out in a similar manner.

[104] The second meant in this sentence may be mean't (i.e., mean it).

[105] An *x* serves as the dot for the *i* in "Kisses."

NAVIGATION SCHOOL BR.

SAN MARCOS, TEXAS
AUG 29
4:30PM
1944

Miss Sylvia M. Jacobs
2334 Atmore St.
N.S. Pittsburgh, Pa

a/c Mazza, A.S.
44-13-6   S.M.A.A.F.N.S.
San Marcos, Texas

194

September 3, 1944 (Received Invitation)

The Board of Directors and
Sisters of Divine Providence of
Saint John's General Hospital
School of Nursing

request your presence at the

Commencement Exercises

Sunday afternoon, September third
Nineteen hundred and forty-four
at three o'clock

School of Nursing Auditorium
Pittsburgh, Pennsylvania

14.3 ✓
7.9 ✓

P R O G R A M M E)

Commencement Exercises

September 3, 1944

ST. JOHN'S GENERAL HOSPITAL
SCHOOL OF NURSING

PROCESSIONAL...................St. Basil's Orchestra

INVOCATION............Reverend Bernardine Pendl, O.S.B.
Chaplain, St. John's General Hospital

PRESIDING.....................James A. Lindsay, M.D.
President, Medical Staff

ADDRESS.....................Rev. Thomas J. Quigley
Diocesan Superintendent of Schools

SELECTION......................St. Basil's Orchestra

PRESENTATION OF DIPLOMAS.......Charles F. Boucek, M.D.
Treasurer, Medical Staff

BENEDICTION.....................Rev. Ralph Young
Assistant, St. Paul's Church

ALMA MATER

RECESSIONAL....................St. Basil's Orchestra

ST. JOSEPH'S PROTECTORY PRINT, PITTSBURGH, PA.

197

United States
Army Air Forces

Sept 3, 1944

Dearest Sylvia:

I am just sitting back this evening after quite another active week, thinking of that certain "gal" back home who by now is really in the climax of her big day. Could she be thinking of a certain lad deep in the heart of Texas? He certainly has her uppermost in his mind at this moment and every moment that his conscious and sub-conscious mind will permit. Ah! I can see you for the first time in an all white uniform quite proud of the reward of 3 long hard years of work. Your one goal has been achieved but mine still lies ahead of me. What is your next goal??? I've already started my plans in the direction of a second goal." Back to the "party" at the Jacobs home --- Do I get the first dance? I naturally would have my bid in for that a long long time ago. Naturally too that first will be a Waltz!

198

September 3, 1944 (Letter)

Postmark: [The envelope is missing.]

Letterhead: United States
              Army Air Forces

[1*]   Sept[.] 3, 1944

Dearest Sylvia:

I am just sitting back this evening after quite another active week, thinking of that certain "gal" back home who by now is really in the climax of her big day. Could she be thinking of a certain lad deep in the heart of Texas? He certainly has her uppermost in his mind at this moment and every moment that his conscious and sub-conscious [*sic*] mind will permit. Ah! I can see you for the first time in an all[-] white uniform[,] quite proud of the reward of 3 long hard years of work. Your one goal has been achieved[,] but mine still lies ahead of me. What is your next goal??? I've already started my plans in the direction of a second goal?? Back to the "party" at the Jacobs['] home - - - Do I get the first dance? I naturally would have my bid in for that a long[,] long time ago. Naturally[,] too[,] that first will be a [w]altz.

The stroll you mentioned in the last letter was perfect and I grant that it will become authentic the first opportunity that presents itself to us. Over hill, over dale we will hit the dusty trail — up knolls, across brooks, down lanes --- and talk! You will have quite a time trying to match one word to my two or are the odds greater than that! Since you pick such wonderful subjects --- namely me --- I have a little edge on you as to the familiarity of the proposed topics.———. or do my letters give me away completely or can you see through me more than I can see through myself? Could be??

This past week found yours truely looking at the overcast above San Marcos wondering when the skies would clear to let our eschelon up into the blue. Occasionally an opening would present itself in the sky and we would dash madly to the flight line with plotting equipment, maps, sextant, brief case loaded with almanacs, parachute and rain coat. We had one flight planned to Glendale, Cal. but bad weather set in there too and the openings in the cloud closed.

200

[1R*] The stroll you mentioned in the last letter was perfect[,] and I grant that it will become authentic the first opportunity that presents itself to us. Over hill, over dale we will hit the dusty trail[106]—up hills, across brooks, down lanes - - - and talk! You will have quite a time trying to match one word to my two[,] or are the odds greater than that? Since you pick such wonderful subjects - - - namely me - - - I have a little edge on you as to the familiarity of the proposed topics. - - - or do my letters give me away completely[,] or can you see through me more than I can see through myself?? Could be??

This week found yours truely [sic] looking at the overcast above San Marcos[,] wondering when the skies would clear to let our eschelon [sic] up into the blue. Occasionally an opening would present itself in the sky[,] and we would dash madly to the flight line with plotting equipment, maps, sextant, brief case [sic] loaded with [a]lmanacs, parachute[,] and rain coat [sic]. We had one flight planned to Glendale, Cal.[,] but bad weather set in there[,] too. The openings in the cloud closed.

---

[106] The words are a slight adaptation of the first line to "The Army Goes Rolling Along," a song written in 1908 by Edmund Louis Gruber (i.e., "Over hill, over dale/As we hit the dusty trail . . . ."). The Army designated "The Army Goes Rolling Along" as its official song in 1956. "The Army Goes Rolling Along," Library of Congress, accessed June 20, 2020, https://www.loc.gov/item/ihas.200000019/.

We finally flew Thursday + Friday 16 hours out of 48. Our destination on both occasions was Kansas. Thursday it was to Winfield Kansas + back. Friday we went to Chanute Field from there to Coffeyville Army Air Field. It was here that Greg had his basic pilot training and it was here that Greg reached the peak of his army flying career, and it was here too that Greg wrote me the sad notice of his eyes being below qualifications for flying. It seems that I follow Greg all over the country but don't get to contact him.

Yesterday and today I was out doing an awful boring job to me. Selecting odd parts to make up my "future" uniforms. I need shoes, trench coat, summer uniforms, caps, gloves belt etc. The stores are all so crowded and swarms of cadets go in and out practically tearing the

[2*] We finally flew Thursday + Friday 16 hours out of 48. Our destination on both occasions was Kansas. Thursday[,] it was to Winfield[,] Kansas[,] and back; Friday[,] we went to Chanute Field[107] [and] from there to Coffeyville Army Air Field.[108] It was here that Greg had his basic pilot training[,] and it was here that Greg reached the peak of his Army flying [c]areer; and it was here[,] too[,] that Greg wrote me the sad note of his eyes being below qualifications for flying.[109] It seems that I follow Greg all over the country[,] but don't get to contact him.

Yesterday and today[,] I was out doing an awful[ly] boring job to me. Selecting odd parts to make up my "future" uniforms. I need shoes, trench coat, summer uniforms, caps, gloves, belt[,] etc. The stores are all so crowded[,] and swarms of cadets go in and out[,] practically tearing these [2R*] small[-]town stores apart.

---

[107] Chanute Air Force Base was a training facility near Rantoul, Illinois. "Chanute Air Force Base," Illinois Environmental Protection Agency, November 2013, https://www2.illinois.gov/epa/topics/community-relations/sites/chanute-afb/Pages/default.aspx.

[108] Coffeyville Army Air Field was in Southeastern Kansas. Paul Freeman, "Abandoned and Little-Known Airfields: Eastern Kansas," March 14, 2020, http://www.airfields-freeman.com/KS/Airfields_KS_E.htm#eda.

[109] Despite this referenced letter, Gregory Mazza went on to become a pilot in the Army Air Forces in World War II. See Letter from Anthony S. Mazza to Sylvia M. Jacobs (March 20, 1945); Gregory E. Mazza, "The Day after V-E Day," *Pittsburgh Post-Gazette,* May 6, 1995.

small town stores apart. Sept 14th we are to turn in our O.D. issue so thus we must get these summer uniforms as soon as possible. Our Credit is extremely good in these parts and all we do is walk into a store and "Charge" it. Uniforms may make some men but I'm not one to be fitted into that category.

We have but two remaining flights to go and both will be up this week. I sure hope Lady Luck will have a big smile for me...... I know that you can help her do just that.

Well I must close now and still wished I could have spent this day with you. A letter is a poor substitute but should suggest my sentiments. I wish you plenty of luck & success in your Career as a nurse and hope you can get the assignment you desire. I send plenty of love to you Syl.

Love "Tony"

P.S. Saw a movie this afternoon named "Bride by Mistake" The heroine was named "Sylvia" - The hero (Believe it or not) was named "Tony" - Coincidental

Sept[.] 14th we are to turn in our G.I. issue[,] so thus we must get these summer uniforms as soon as possible. Our credit is extremely good in these parts[,] and all we do is walk in a store and "charge" it. Uniforms may make some men, but I'm not one to be fitted into that category.

We have but two remaining flights to go[,] and both will be up this week. I sure hope Lady Luck will have a big smile for me. – – – I know that you can help her do just that.

Well[,] I must close now and still wished [sic] I could have spent this day with you. A letter is a poor substitute but should suggest my sentiments. I wish you plenty of luck and success in your career as a nurse and hope you can get the assignment you desire. I send plenty of love to you[,] Syl.

Love[,]
"Tony"

P.S. Saw a movie this afternoon named "Bride by Mistake[.]"[110] The heroine was named "Sylvia"—the hero ([b]elieve it or not) was named "Tony[.]"—Coincidental

---

[110] *Bride by Mistake*, directed by Richard Wallace, featuring Alan Marshal and Laraine Day (RKO Radio Pictures, 1944).

United States
Army Air Forces

Sept 10, 1944

Dearest Sylvia:

I'll bet you are wondering what that fellow must be doing down there in Texas that he can't write more than one letter per week. All I can say to that is that the past week was rough and I expect the next two weeks to be rougher + tougher. Tried to recuperate a bit today, but found it necessary to continue my shopping tour even today, Sunday. Hats, belts, ties etc are still items I need, but I am hard to please and usually end up with something that isn't worth the time and money involved anyway. I am rather at a disadvantage though, for wouldn't it be perfect if you could be down here to help me select the things that will increase the sparkle in your eyes. I'll bet I sure would look trim with your selections. After the clothing would be bought and

September 10, 1944

From: A./C. Mazza, A.S.
            44-12-6 SMAAFNS
            San Marcos, Texas

To: Miss Sylvia Jacobs
            2334 Atmore St[.]
            N.S. Pittsburgh, Pa[.]

Postmark: 11:00 AM
            September 11, 1944
            San Marcos, Texas

Letterhead: United States
            Army Air Forces

[1*]   Sept[.] 10, 1944

Dearest Sylvia:

I'll bet you are wondering what that fellow must be doing down there in Texas that he can't write more than one letter per week. All I can say to that is that the past week was rough[,] and I expect the next two weeks to be rougher + tougher. Tried to recuperate a bit[,] but found it necessary to continue my shopping tour even today, Sunday. Hats, belts, ties[,] etc[.] are still items I need, but I am hard to please and usually end up with something

Something didn't please me later, I could put all the blame on you!" — Good grounds to begin a "friendly" argument.

How is my little nurse getting along these days? I still have that ailment in the organ above the abdomen, enclosed by the ribs, covered by the lungs. Need any more clues? Need a graduate nurse now as complications are setting in and it takes a lass with plenty of tact and gentleness to handle the case --- meaning --- ---. You certainly will have a tough assignment ahead of you.

As usual, I must tell you of the places I have seen this past week and our flights across the country. We had our final graduation hop and began Wednesday afternoon with but a few minutes notice. We rushed to the flight line and took off to Tulsa Oklahoma by way of Shreveport. After eating a bite at the Tulsa Municiple Airport we flew a night celestial mission to Denver Colorado arriving there about 3 AM Thursday morning. With but 4 hours of sleep, we were awakened early for breakfast at Buckley Field Basic Training

208

that isn't worth the time and money involved[,] anyway. I am rather at a dis-advantage[,] though, for wouldn't it be perfect if you could be down here to help me select the things that will increase the sparkle in your eyes[?] I'll bet I sure would look trim with your selections. After the clothing would be bought and [1R*] something didn't please me later, I could put all the blame on you!! Good grounds to begin a "friendly" argument.

How is my little nurse getting along these days? I still have that ailment in the organ above the abdomen, enclosed by the ribs, covered by the lungs. Need anymore [sic] clues? Also need a graduate nurse now as complications are setting in[,] and it takes a lass with plenty of tact and gentleness to handle the case - - - - meaning - - -. You certainly will have a tough assign-ment ahead of you.

As usual, I must tell you of the places I have seen this past week and of our flights across the country. We had our final graduation hop and began Wednesday afternoon with but a few minutes['] notice. We rushed to the flight line and took off to Tulsa[,] Oklahoma[,] by way of Shreveport. After eating a bite at the Tulsa Municiple [sic] Airport[,] we flew a night celestial mission to Denver[,] Colorado[,] arriving there about 3[:00] AM Thursday morning. With but 4 hours of sleep, we were awakened early for breakfast at Buckley Field Basic Training

United States
Army Air Forces

2

center, that reminded me of the first dark
dismal days at Greensboro. Most of the poor
rookies saluted us; for we were the first
cadets they had seen. I returned the salute
in a manner as though I expected them to do
just that, thus saving both of us embarrassment.

Later Thursday morning after a critique session,
where the instructors went over the results
of the first leg of our flight, we headed East
again landing at Topeka Kansas the Capitol
of that state. Again we ate in mass but
this time at the Officer's mess hall. A few
moments later it was back to Denver, Col
again this time landing at Lowery Field,
a permanent army camp where the buildings
are of brick. We slept in a huge building
3 stories high but plenty long and wide. I
It reminded us of a hotel and soon enough
was "dubbed" by us the "R. I." Hotel.

Early Friday morning we could see

210

[2*] Center[;][111] that reminded me of the first dark[,] dismal days at Greensboro. Most of the poor rookies saluted us, for we were the first cadets they had seen. I returned the salute in a manner as though I expected them to do just that, thus saving both of us embarrassment.

Later Thursday morning, after a critique session, where the instructors went over the results of the first leg of our flight, we headed [e]ast[,] landing in Topeka, Kansas[,] the Capitol [*sic*] of that state. Again[,] we ate in mass[,] but this time at the [o]fficers' mess hall. A few moments later[,] it was back to Denver, Col[.], this time landing at Lowery Field,[112] a permanent [A]rmy camp where the buildings are of brick. We slept in a huge building 3 stories high but plenty long and wide. It reminded us of a hotel and soon enough was "dubbed" the "G.I." Hotel.

[111] Buckley Field is near Denver, Colorado. Christopher McCune, "Buckley Field in World War II: Part 1," Buckley Air Force Base, June 29, 2017, https://www.buckley.af.mil/News/Article-Display/Article/1233614/buckley-filed-world-war-ii-part-i/.

[112] Lowry Field is in Aurora, Colorado, which is also near Denver. "Lowry AFB: The History," The Lowry Foundation, April 4, 2020, http://www.lowryfoundation.org/lowryafb/index.htm.

the rockies in the background and the famed Pikes Peak Covered with snow in the distance. --- Sure but there is plenty of romance in them thar hills. The moon that night resembled a large bonfire as it lifted over the mountain tops, a huge bright red disc. Plenty of inspiration for two people like ourselves and it wouldn't take long to develop a definite mood. Who's a wolf ??

Our next destination Friday morning was ----. I know you've guessed it by now. --- TOPEKA, Kansas. Getting a little monotonous isn't it. Well, we thought so too and by that time could practically identify each ranch house on this so-called "milk run". Friday night we headed back for San Marcos one weary tired group and retired to the "sack" in a semi stupor or practically unconscious state.

What could be waiting for us on Saturday ---- nothing much except that the Physical Training department decided that we must have a

212

Early Friday morning[,] we could see [2R*] the [R]ockies in the background and the famed Pikes Peak covered with snow in the distance. - - - Sure bet there is plenty of romance in them thar hills. The moon [at] night resembled a large bonfire as it lifted over the mountain tops [*sic*], a huge[,] bright red disc. Plenty of inspiration for two people like ourselves[,] and it wouldn't take long to develop a definite mood. Who's a wolf??

Our next destination Friday morning was - - - - - I know you've guessed it by now. - - - TOPEKA, Kansas. Getting a little monotonous, isn't it[?] Well, we thought so[,] too[,] and by that time could practically identify each ranch house on the so-called "milk run." Friday night we headed back for San Marcos[,] one weary[,] tired group[,] and retired to the "sack" in a semi[-]stupor or practically unconscious state.

What could be waiting for us on Saturday - - - - nothing much except that the Physical Training [D]epartment decided that we must have a [3*] physical fitness rating and thus forced

United States
Army Air Forces

3

physical fitness rating and thus forced us to go the limit of endurance in sit-ups, pull-ups and race time in the 300 yd. shuttle run. The boys including myself, dragged our weary bones to the barracks a few moments later. The moment Open Post was granted out we all rushed to Austin, San Marcos, Seguin, New Braunfels, San Antonio, Lulling, Bestrop, and surrounding towns. Plenty of variety here and aching muscles were soon forgot as the lads continued their study of "Heavenly Bodies".

Rather an amusing situation occurred this afternoon at San Marcos. All the Catholic boys had to attend a Mexican chapel high on a hill on the outskirts of the town as our chaplin is having himself a "furlough". We decided to have lunch at San Marcos and began at one end of the street to find the best possible place that could be found. A sign stood prominently before our eyes "Little Pappas Cafe". The

214

us to go to the limit of endurance in sit[-]ups, pull-ups[,] and race time in the 300[-]yd. shuttle run. The boys, including myself, dragged our weary bones to the barracks a few hours later. The moment [o]pen [p]ost was granted out[,] we all rushed to Austin, San Marcos, Sequin, New Braunfels, San Antonio, Lulling, Bestrop [*sic*], and surrounding towns. Plenty of variety here[,] and aching muscles were soon forgot as the lads continued their study of "[h]eavenly [b]odies."

Rather an amusing situation occurred this afternoon at San Marcos. All the Catholic boys had to attend a Mexican chapel high on a hill on the outskirts of the town[,] as our chaplain's having himself a "furlough." We decided to have lunch at San Marcos and began at one end of the [s]treet to find the best possible place that could be found. A sign stood prominently before our eyes[,] "Little Pappas Cafe." The [3R*] place seemed dark + dismal[,] so

place seemed dark & dismal so on we went up the street to find another Sign "Pappas Cafe". This didn't please us much until a bit further up the street almost evenly spaced was another sign "Big Pappas Cafe". I guess before long "middle size Pappas", "Tiny Pappas" and "Giant Pappas" will have their restaurants added to the list. We settled it all by flipping a coin and ate a T-Bone steak dinner at just plain "Pappas Cafe". I see where you mentioned having "Brunch". Just what is Brunch? A buffet lunch, or a battle of tongues in gossip combined with lunch?

Mother told me of the wonderful gathering that you had at your home after the graduation and of the many gifts that were presented to you. Hmm, I can see many ways that these can benefit me too. You can't have all of them only to yourself. I had some hand in inspiring you to graduate. — It's not so — but sounds good any

on we went up the street to another sign[,] "Pappas Cafe." This didn't phase [sic] us much until a bit further up the street[,] almost evenly spaced[,] was another sign[,] "Big Pappas Cafe." I guess before long "[M]iddle[-]size Pappas," a "Tiny Pappas[,]" and ["]Giant Pappas["]] will have there [sic] restaurants added to the list. We settled it all by flipping a coin and ate a T-[b]one steak dinner at just plain "Pappas Cafe." I see where you mentioned having "[b]runch." Just what is [b]runch? A buffet lunch or a battle of tongues in gossip combined with lunch?

Mother told me of the wonderful gathering that you had at your home after the graduation and of the many gifts that were presented to you. Hmm, I can see many ways that these can benefit me[,] too. You can't have all of them only to yourself. I had some hand in inspiring you to graduate. —It's not so—but sounds good [4*] any way. Take the rosary beads - - - - they should add to

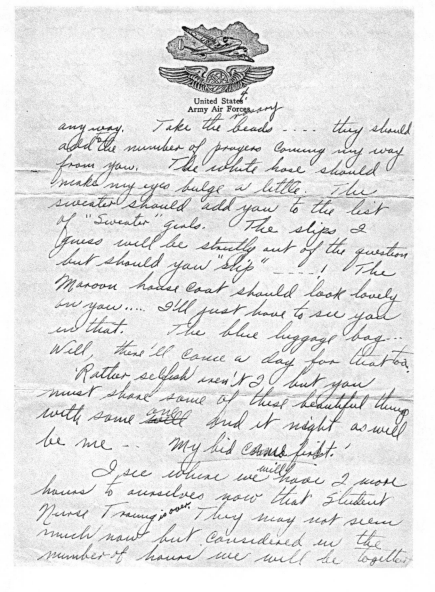

United States
Army Air Forces

anyway. Take the beads . . . . they should
add the number of prayers coming my way
from you. The white hose should
make my eyes bulge a little. The
sweater should add you to the list
of "Sweater" girls. The slips I
guess will be strictly out of the question
but should you "slip" _ _ _ _! The
Maroon house coat should look lovely
on you . . . . . I'll just have to see you
in that. The blue luggage bag . . .
Well, there'll come a day for that too.

'Rather selfish aren't I but you
must share some of these beautiful things
with some one And it might as well
be me - - My kid comes first.'

I see where we will have 2 more
hours to ourselves now that Student
Nurse Training is over. They may not seem
much now but considered in the
number of hours we will be together

the number of prayers coming my way from you. The white hose should make eyes bulge a little. The sweater should add you to the list of "[s]weater" girls.[113] The slips[,] I guess[,] will be strictly out of the question[,] but should you "slip" - - - -! The [m]aroon house coat [*sic*] should look lovely on you - - - - - I'll just have to see you in that. The blue luggage bag - - - Well, there'll come a day for that[,] too.

'Rather selfish aren't I[,] but you must share some of these beautiful things with some one [*sic*][,] and it might as well be me - - my bid comes first.'

I see where we will have 2 more hours to ourselves now that [s]tudent [n]urse [t]raining is over. They may not seem much now[,] but considered in the number of hours we will be together [*4R] in the next year, those few hours will be greatly appreciated.

---

[113] Sex-symbol starlets of the 1940s who wore tight-fitting sweaters were known as sweater girls. "The History of the Sweater Girl," The Sweater Girl Society, accessed June 20, 2020, https://sweatergirlsociety.org/history-of-sweater-girls.php.

in the next year, those few hours will be greatly appreciated.

I hope that you like the work that you are doing. The first thing that a person must have to enjoy life and its many freedoms is to do the things they like to do best when they like to do them, providing no one else is hurt in ~~that~~ their trying to follow that policy. One never realizes how much that opportunity means to them, until after ~~they~~ it has been taken from him.

Well I see where I have been rather ambiguous tonight and probably could write many pages more. I mustn't spoil you too much and have you tired of these rantings of mine. I too will make an end to the scribbling now and close with plenty of love and kisses and hope too that soon the first song on the hit parade will come true for us and that I can say
"I'll be seeing you"
Love
"Tony"

I hope that you like the work that you are doing. The first thing that a person must have to enjoy life and its many freedoms is to do the things they like to do best when they like to do them, providing no one else is hurt in their trying to follow that policy. One never realizes how much that opportunity means to them[,] until after it has been taken from him.

Well[,] I see where I have been rather ambiguous [*sic*] tonight and probably could write many pages more. I musn't [*sic*] spoil you too much and have you tired of these rantings of mine. I[,] too[,] will make an end to the scribbling now and close with plenty of love and kisses and hope[,] too[,] that soon the first song on the hit parade[114] will come true for us and I can say[,] "I'll be seeing you[.]"[115]

Love[,]
"Tony"

---

[114] "Your Hit Parade" was a radio program that broadcast every Saturday night from 1935 to 1953, featuring the most popular songs in the U.S. that week and always ending with the top three songs. "Your Hit Parade," Radio Hall of Fame, accessed June 20, 2020, http://www.radiohalloffame.com/your-hit-parade.

[115] See *supra* note 75.

Free

NAVIGATION SCHOOL B[

SAN MARCOS, TEXAS
SEP 11-AM
1944

Miss Sylvia Jacobs
2334 Atmore St
N.S. Pittsburgh, Pa

A/C Meggs A.S.
44-13-6 SMAAFS
San Marcos, Texas

United States
Army Air Forces

Sept 19, 1944

Dearest Sylvia:

I have some rather disappointing news to tell you, in that I shall not be home around the 25th of September. It is quite a long story so I'll have to start from the beginning. I told you in my last letter that I was recuperating from the long graduation hop but I apparently didn't think the head cold, and stuffed feeling I had would amount to much. We had left on that flight in such a hurry that I failed to bring my "life preserver". (That sweater you gave me last Christmas) and flying up north on high altitudes where the temperatures are from 0 to 9°C, I was chilled to the bone. I tried my best to take it easy last week-end but the extensive shopping tour didn't help my condition one bit. Monday the 11th, I staggered into class feeling miserable and failed to attract any attention until later in the morning I was called to recite and "Croaked" in a voice

224

September 19, 1944

Postmark: [The envelope is missing.]

Letterhead: United States
              Army Air Forces

[1*]   Sept[.] 19, 1944

Dearest Sylvia:

   I have some rather disappointing news to tell you, in that
I shall not be home around the 25th of September. It is quite a
long story[,] so I'll have to start from the beginning. I told you in
my last letter that I was recuperating from the long graduation
hop[,] but I apparently didn't think the head cold, and stuffed
feeling I had[,] would amount to much. We had left on that flight
in such a hurry that I failed to bring my "life preserver[,]" ([t]he
sweater you gave me last Christmas)[,] and flying up north in high
altitudes where the temperatures are from 0 to 9° C, I was chilled
to the bone. I tried my best to take it easy last week-end [*sic*][,]
but the extensive shopping tour didn't help my condition one bit.
Monday[,] the 11th, I staggered into class feeling miserable and
failed to attract any attention until later in the morning[.] I was
called to recite and "cracked" in a voice [1R*] not much above

225

not much above a whisper. The eschelon Comander asked me to go to the hospital to get some medicine to relieve my condition and when I hesitated, he reminded me that his word was a Command.

A few moments later I found myself at the Hospital, some-one jabbed a thermometer down my throat and few minutes later there I was in Ward 23 Sent I in "Solitary Confinement" with 19 empty beds + myself. The Doc said that I'd stay but a couple of days but he kept giving me sulfa tablets and had me lieing down as much as possible. It really was boresome not having anything to do for a change and I'll bet I read every magazine they had in the post Hospital library. The "fever" soon left me after the 2nd day but for 6 remaining days I really had it soft taking sun baths, and parading up and down from one ward to another. I was finally released yesterday morning only to hear the sad news that I may not graduate with my class.

The C.O. said that a Post regulation specifies that anyman having missed 5 consecutive days with a legal excuse is to be moved back one class. He said he'd try to do something for me as an

a whisper. The eschelon [*sic*] commander asked me to go to the hospital to get some medicine to relieve my condition[,] and when I hesitated, he reminded me that his word was a command.

A few moments later[,] I found myself at the hospital, some–one [*sic*] jabbed a thermometer down my throat[,] and [a] few minutes later[,] there I was in Ward 23 Sect[.] 2 in "Solitary Confinement" with 19 empty beds + myself. The [d]oc said that I'd stay but a couple of days[,] but he kept giving me sulfa tablets and had me lieing [*sic*] down as much as possible[.] It really was lonesome not having anything to do for a change[,] and I'll bet I read every magazine they had in the post [h]ospital library. The "fever" soon left me after the 2nd day[,] but for 6 remaining days[,] I really had it soft[,] taking sun baths [*sic*], and parading up and down from one ward to another. I was finally released yesterday morning only to hear the sad news that I may not graduate with my class.

The C.O. said that a [p]ost regulation specifies that any man having missed 5 consecutive days with a legal excuse is to be moved back one class. He said he'd try to do something for me as

United States
Army Air Forces

individual but individuals as such are
given very little consideration by the Army.
Since I completed all my missions in
fine style, the C.O. said he may get me
into an experimental group that are being
tested with new methods of Navigation and
I will be able to get the thing I missed too.

In the short period of 6 class days
I missed Polar navigation, Calibration of
several important instruments, and long
range navigation containing many of the
basic principals of Radar. If I get into
that select group I'll know more about
navigation — particularly long range
celestial navigation than the rest of the
class that have had only the regular course.

If I am held back I shall regret
very much the fact that all my
buddies will be gone and again I must
start all over making new friends
and acquaintances. The worst part

an [2*] individual[,] but individuals as such are given very little consideration by the [A]rmy. Since I completed all my missions in fine style, the C.O. said he may get me into an experimental group that [is] being tested with new methods of [n]avigation[,] and I will be able to get the things I missed[,] too.

In the short period of 6 days[,] I missed [p]olar navigation, [c]alibration of several important instruments, and long[-]range navigation containing many of the basic principals [*sic*] of [r]adar. If I get into that select group[,] I'll know more about navigation – – – particularly long[-]range celestial navigation[,] than the rest of the class that had only the regular course.

If I am held back[,] I shall regret very much the fact that all my buddies will be gone[,] and again[,] I must start all over making new friends and acquaintances. The worst part [2R*] will be that I can[']t see you as soon as I wanted[,] but fate can't be conquered[,] and perhaps all of this is, as S.M.J. would say, "really for the best."

will be that I cant see you as soon as I wanted but fate cant be conquered and perhaps all of this is, as S. M. G. would say, "really for the best."

4 weeks or more from now we will be in the middle of Indian Summer. Autumn will be at its heighth and there'll be many things we can do over again as we did one year ago. Football games, dancing (of course a Halloween Dance at the Colonial) dining out and strolling through the great out-doors. I know a beautiful lane through Riverview Park that would be wonderful to walk on a Sunday afternoon. Leaves ankle deep and long winding paths that lead up hill and down. Small bridges and little creeks that flow steadily beneath them. Trees that have stood for centuries in the hills — — from shining maple to the Red Oak; poplar to pine. We'll have a regular biology session trying to identify leaves, birds, and plant life. It used to take me an hour to go through it myself but for the two of us I'm sure it would take the greater part of

230

[Four] weeks or more from now[,] we will be in the middle of Indian [s]ummer. Autumn will be at its heighth [sic][,] and there'll be many things we can do over again as we did one year ago. Football games, dancing (of course[,] a Halloween [d]ance at the Colonial)[,][116] [d]ining out and strolling through the great out-doors [sic]. I know a beautiful lane through Riverview Park that would be wonderful to walk on a Sunday after-noon. Leaves, ankle deep[,] and long winding paths that lead up hill [sic] and down. Small bridges and little creeks that flow steadily beneath them. Trees that have stood for centuries in the hills – – – – from shining maple to the [r]ed [o]ak[,] poplar[,] and pine. We'll have a regular biology session trying to identify leaves, birds, and plant life. It used to take me an hour to go through it myself[,] but for the two of us[,] I'm sure it would take the greater part of [3*] an afternoon.

[116] The Colonial was a "dance palace" on Ohio River Boulevard, ten minutes from downtown Pittsburgh. "Summer Season to Get Under Way at Colonial," *Pittsburgh Post-Gazette*, June 27, 1941.

United States
Army Air Forces

3

an afternoon.

The movies and stage plays will be
at their heighth this time of year. The
evenings long -- but they sure melt away
ever so quickly when we are together.

I imagine that you are getting all
that tan at the Sea-shore by now and it
is too bad that it will fade away again
by the time I get a chance to see it......
or are you just one mess of freckles.

Maybe it is a good thing my stay
will be prolonged for I'm sure you'll
still be quite tired from the long trip
and excitement that prevailed at Atlantic City.
Now you'll really have time to recuperate
until I get back.

I am celebrating with the boys, however
and we have two beer parties and two
dances coming up this week. My beer
quota is still one bottle and the dances
are dedicated to you --- they always
have been.

The movies and stage plays will be at their heighth [*sic*] this time of year. The evenings long - - - - but they sure melt away ever so quickly when we are together.

I imagine that you are getting all that tan at the Sea-shore [*sic*] by now[,] and it is too bad that it will fade away again by the time I get a chance to see it - - - - - - or are you just one mess of freckles[?]

Maybe it is a good thing my stay will be prolonged[,] for I'm sure you'll still be quite tired from the long trip and excitement that prevailed at Atlantic City. Now you'll really have time to recuperate until I get back.

I am celebrating with the boys, however, and we have two beer parties and two dances coming up this week. My beer quota is still one bottle[,] and the dances are dedicated to you - - - they always have been.

I haven't heard from Greg since he left for overseas. I'm glad that Lois met Antoinette & Lucille. Antoinette will surely "hail" her every time she is within hearing distance, which is approximately the length of one of Oliver's Corridors.

My prayers for your Final State Board were very plentiful since I had plenty of time on my hands. There was plenty of quality ~~behind them~~ too so you shouldn't have have very much trouble at all.

Well Sylvia I must close now since we are having our final star check tonight. How Could I miss when I see you in every one of them? Goodnight and Plenty of Love.

Love

"Tony"

[3*] I haven't heard from Greg since he left for overseas. I'm glad that Lois met Antoinette + Lucille.[117] Antoinette will surely "hail" her every time she is within hearing distance, which is approximately the length of Oliver's [c]orridors.[118]

My prayers for your [f]inal [s]tate [b]oard were very plentiful since I had plenty of time on my hands. There was plenty of quality behind them[,] too[,] so you shouldn't have have [sic] much trouble at all.

Well[,] Sylvia[,] I must close now since we are having our final star check tonight. How could I miss when I see you in every one of them? Goodnight [sic] and [p]lenty of [l]ove.

Love[,]
"Tony"

---

[117] Lois is Sylvia Jacobs' youngest sister; Antoinette and Lucille were Anthony Mazza's younger sisters. See Appendix B.

[118] The reference is to David B. Oliver High School in Pittsburgh, Pennsylvania, where both Anthony Mazza and Sylvia Jacobs went to high school.

United States
Army Air Forces

Dearest Sylvia: Sept 24, 1944

            Well, here I am all set to start
in tomorrow morning at about the same spot
I was ~~in~~ four weeks ago. Class 44-12-6 will
have their graduation exercises tomorrow morning
and will leave immediately afterwards to their
10 days of furlough while yours truely moves
back one class designated ~~now~~ as 44-43N-14.
(The 43 marks the week I should graduate....
providing something else don't happen in the
mean time.) I may sound a little bitter
or provoked over the matter but again the
4 weeks means that I am in the states that
much longer and that the war is nearer
to its end by just 4 wks! The hard
part, as I mentioned before, is to realize that
I could be through with this course as the
boys who are graduating tomorrow and I can't
help but wish that I was moving out
with them. Saturday I met my new
commander and instructor ~~and~~. they seem like
regular guys to me. Most of Saturday
morning and this afternoon, I have been

September 24, 1944

From: Anthony S. Mazza

To: Sylvia M. Jacobs

Postmark: [The envelope is missing.]

Letterhead: United States
             Army Air Forces

[1*]   Sept[.] 24, 1944

Dearest Sylvia:

Well, here I am all set to start in tomorrow morning at about the same spot I was four weeks ago. Class 44-12-6 will have their graduation exercises tomorrow morning and will leave immediately afterwards to their 10 days of furlough while yours truly moves back one class[,] designated now as 44-43N-14. (The 43 marks the week I should graduate - - - - providing something else don't [sic] happen in the mean time [sic].) I may sound a little bitter or provoked over the matter[,] but again[,] the 4 weeks means [sic] that I am in the [S]tates that much longer and that the war is nearer to its end by just 4 wks. The hard part, as I mentioned before, is to realize that I could be through with this course as the boys who are graduating tomorrow[,] and I can't help but wish that I were moving out with them. Saturday[,] I met my new commander and instructor; they seem like regular guys to me.

moving my belongings from the old echelon to the new.

This past week all of our evenings were free and thus I went to town every opportunity I had. We did have our beer parties and a jolly get together among ourselves and the instructors. We had a ball game one afternoon of Instructors vs Cadets. - - - - We lost. 12 to 6.

Tuesday evening last Week was really the big night for it was then we had our graduation ball. All of us wore our officers uniforms for the first time and the girls their evening gowns since this was a formal affair. The dance was held at the Officers Club and the dance floor was out-doors. The sky was clear that night and at the center of the floor was a beautifully lit water fountain. The band played soft, soft music out a pavillion at one end of the floor. Tables were set on the outskirts of the dance floor and were also out-doors. The main beverage was "punch" but it certainly packed a wallop for it was saturated with rum. A buffet lunch was served that contained many fine dainty foods from deviled eggs to shrimps.

238

Most of Saturday morning and this afternoon, I have been [1R*] moving my belongings from the old eschelon [sic] to the new.

This past week[,] all of our evenings were free[,] and thus I went to town every opportunity I had. We did have our beer parties and a jolly get[-]together among ourselves and the instructors. We had a ball-game [sic] one afternoon of Instructors vs[.] Cadets. - - - - - We lost. 10 to 6.

Tuesday evening last [w]eek was really the big night[,] for it was then we had our graduation ball. All of us wore our officers uniforms for the first time[,] and the girls their evening gowns[,] since this was a formal affair. The dance was held at the Officers Club and the dance floor was out-doors [sic]. The sky was clear that night[,] and at the center of the floor[,] was a beautifully lit water fountain. The band played swift, soft music on a pavilion at one end of the floor. Tables were set on the outskirts of the dance floor and were also out-doors [sic]. The main beverage was "punch," but it certainly packed a wallop[,] for it was saturated with rum. A buffet lunch was served that contained many fine[,] dainty foods from deviled eggs to shrimps.

[2*] My buddies had "fixed" me up with a blind date from Austin. She turned out to be a fiery red-head [sic], but I managed to get through the evening and say a couple of sentences. She could out-talk [sic] any two other people I have ever known and was probably a natural[-]born jitter-bug [sic]. However, you can feel quite flattered, if you so desire, that I was thinking of you every minute and sincerely wishing you could have been here beside me to share that evening. Songs such as "Bessamé [sic] Mucho[,"][119]

---

[119] Consuelo Velázquez wrote "Bésame Mucho" in 1941. Margalit Fox, "Consuelo Velázquez Dies; Wrote 'Bésame Mucho,'" *New York Times*, January 30, 2005. Jimmy Dorsey and his orchestra released a recording

United States
Army Air Forces

2.

My buddies had "fixed" me up with a blind date from Austin. She turned out to be a finy red-head, but I managed to get through the evening and say a couple of sentences. She could out-talk any two other people I have ever known and was probably a natural born jitter-bug. However you can feel quite flattered, if you so desire, that I was thinking of you every minute, and sincerely wishing you could have been here beside me to share the evening. Songs such as "Bessame Mucho", "I'll be seeing you", "I'll Walk alone" etc just don't sound the same with-out you.

Saturday night we were given over-night passes so I thought I'd visit San-Antonio for the first time. It is really a beautiful city to be placed in this southern wilderness. Most of its buildings are new and consist of many stories in height. Night clubs "galore" and places to dine and dance scattered all over the area. Two Carnivals right within the city are to be had for added attractions. The

240

"I'll [B]e [S]eeing [Y]ou[,"][120] "I'll Walk [A]lone[,"][121] etc. just don't sound the same with-out [sic] you.

Saturday night we were given over-night [sic] passes[,] so I thought I'd visit San-Antonio [sic] for the first time. It is really a beautiful city to be placed in this southern wilderness. Most of its buildings are new and consist of many stories in heighth [sic]. Night clubs "galore" and places to dine and dance [are] scattered all over the area. Two carnivales [sic] right within the city are to be had for an added attraction. The [2R*] whole Air Corp[s] it seems [is] turned

---

of the song that was popular in 1944. Jimmy Dorsey and His Orchestra with Bob Eberly and Kitty Kallen, vocalists, "Bésame Mucho," music by Consuelo Velázquez and English lyrics by Sunny Skylar, released January 15, 1944, Decca, No. 18574B; "1944 Radio (Top 80 Playlist)," playback.fm, accessed June 20, 2020, https://playbackfm/year/1944.

[120] See *supra* note 75.

[121] The 1944 film *Follow the Boys* featured the song "I'll Walk Alone." *Follow the Boys*, directed by A. Edward Sutherland, featuring George Raft and Vera Zorina (Universal Pictures, 1944). In 1944, Dinah Shore's version of the song was the most popular one. *Dinah Shore*, vocalist, "I'll Walk Alone," by Jule Styne and Sammy Cahn, released August 12, 1944, Victor, No. 20-1586-A; Whitburn, 124; "1944 Radio (Top 80 Playlist)," playback. fm, accessed June 20, 2020, https://playbackfm/year/1944.

whole Air Corp it seems are turned loose on that poor city on Saturday night. Pilots, Navigators, Bombardiers, Cadets, Wacs, Waves, Gunners, Mechanics - anyone that can handle an air craft is bound to be found in San Antone. Felt quite at home in the town of my name's sake and even had Italian Spaghetti at St. Anthony's grill. A small clean clear cut stream flows through the center of the city at night along paved walks and large buildings. At certain sections there is a lover's haven where the grass is green on both banks of the stream and trees and bushes give young people a chance to sit and sigh, and still be out of the public eye. Naturally I couldn't help but think of the many times, perhaps, that Greg had been at the same places I had just visited. I just received a letter from Greg on Saturday saying that he has finally arrived at his destination - - - - -somewhere in Italy. - - - all of San Antonio was so crowded that the best way I could describe the thoroughfare up main street would be to say: I had to wait in line to get my turn to walk up. street. *

It certainly had been a long time since

loose on that poor city on Saturday night. Pilots, [n]avigators, [b]ombardiers, [c]adets, W[AC]s, W[AVES],[122] [g]unners, [m]echanics—anyone that can handle air craft [*sic*] is bound to be found in San Antone. Felt quite at home in the town of my name's sake [*sic*] and even had Italian [s]paghetti at St. Anthony's grill. A small[,] clean[,] clear[-]cut stream flows through the center of the city right along paved walks and large buildings. At certain sections[,] there is a lover[s'] haven where the grass is green on both banks of the stream[,] and trees and bushes give young people a chance to sit and sigh[,] and still be out of the public eye. Naturally[,] I couldn't help but think of the many times, perhaps, that Greg had been at the same place I just visited. I just received a letter from Greg on Saturday saying that he has finally arrived at his destination - - - - - - somewhere in Italy - - - - All of San Antonio was so crowded that the best way I could describe the thoroughfare up main street would be to say: "I had to wait in line to get my turn to walk up [the] street."

---

[122] Women Accepted for Volunteer Emergency Service (WAVES) was the women's branch of the U.S. Naval Reserve during World War II. Regina T. Akers, "The WAVES' 75th Birthday," Naval History and Heritage Command, May 10, 2019, https://www.history.navy.mil/browse-by-topic/wars-conflicts-and-operations/world-war-ii/1942/manning-the-us-navy/waves_75th.html.

United States
Army Air Forces

3

I received any word from you and I understood the circumstances quite well.---- particularly the study needed for an exam of the caliber of your State board and too the excitement that preceded your trip to Atlantic City. Say! what does Atlantic City have to attract your gals. First Edna, now Sylvia. Well anyway you'll be able to describe that place to me one of these days --- maybe in person to person conversation, I hope. Since the Aircorps is particularly interested in the weather and the phenomena of weather conditions all over the world, we as navigators and aerial observers knew and traced the path of the Hurricane that wrecked such havoc on the Eastern Sea board. See, If you had left one week or so earlier you might have been swept off your feet.... Wait a minute! I'm the only one that is permitted to do that and I crave no competition by either animate or in-animate objects.

New that you have been to that

244

It certainly has been a long time since [3*] I received any word from you[,] and I understood the circumstances quite well – – – – particularly the study needed for an exam of the caliber of your [s]tate [b]oard and[,] too[,] the excitement that preceeded [*sic*] your trip to Atlantic City. Say! What does Atlantic City have to attract you gals[?] First Edna. [N]ow Sylvia. Well[,] anyway[,] you'll be able to describe that place to me one of these days – – – – maybe in person[-]to[-]person conversation, I hope. Since the Aircorps [*sic*] is particularly interested in the weather and the phenomena of weather conditions all over the world, we as navigators and arial [*sic*] observers knew and traced the path of the [h]urricane that wrecked [*sic*] such havoc on the Eastern Sea board [*sic*]. See, [i]f you had left one week or so earlier[,] you might have been swept off your feet – – – – – Wait a minute! I'm the only one that is permitted to do that[,] and I crave no competition by either animate or in-animate [*sic*] objects.

famous resort, there will be one request that I shall make right now. How about sending me the picture that you took or had taken in a bathing suit? If you certainly must have one _ _ _ it wouldn't be proper to go all the way to New Jersey and miss such a golden opportunity to have your figure captured by the Photo-lens and the majestic back ground of the sandy beach and Ocean. Did you learn how to ride the waves or did you parade up and down the beach _ _ _ just for the fun of it??? I am very much convinced that you were a real good girl particularly if mama Jacobs and Uncle Bill were on hand. I hope you did have a great time and that you will tell me all about it when I do get home!!

So you think your smart registering to vote? I have quite the edge on you this year, since I have already mailed my ballot 3 weeks ago. I sure hope I picked the right men and that I used good judgment. Sincerely though I felt not that I was selecting the man I wanted but more or less trying to differentiate the lesser of two evils.

Now that you have been to that [3R*] famous resort, there will be one request that I shall make right now. How about sending me the picture that you took or had taken in a bathing suit? You certainly must have one[,] for it wouldn't be proper to go all the way to New Jersey and miss such a golden opportunity to have your figure captured by the Photo-lens [sic] and include the majestic back ground [sic] of the sandy beach and the ocean. Did you learn how to ride the waves[,] or did you parade up and down the beach - - - - - - just for the fun of it??? I am very much convinced that you were a real[ly] good girl[,] particularly if [M]ama Jacobs[123] and Uncle Bill[124] were on hand. I hope you did have a great time and that you will tell me all about it when I do get home!!

So you think your [sic] smart registering to vote?[125] I have quite the edge on you this year, since I have already mailed my ballot 3 weeks ago. I sure hope I picked the right men and that I used good judgement [sic]. Sincerely though[,] I felt not that I was selecting the man I wanted[,] but more or less trying to differentiate the lesser of two evils.

---

[123] Anna Kopcie Jacobs (b. April 7, 1887; d. October 24, 1980).

[124] William J. Stroyne (b. March 2, 1893; d. April 3, 1967) married Anna Kopcie Jacobs' younger sister Mary Kopcie Stroyne (b. June 2, 1894; d. February 14, 1978).

[125] Election day was November 7, 1944. The presidential candidates were the Democratic incumbent, President Franklin D. Roosevelt, and the Republican nominee, Governor Thomas E. Dewey of New York.

United States
Army Air Forces

N 4.

Sorry I could not have you pin the wings on tomorrow but will give that opportunity 4 weeks from date providing I do get them and too that little spark is still the same with you as when I left. Sure wished you could have had your vacation down here at San Marcos instead of Atlantic City. My, what you could have done to one certain Cadet. Say, the cartoons at the end of that last letter certainly were good. You are really developing talent as a cartoonist. See if you can get the after effects of an S.M.I. big healthy ---- on A.I.M. in your next sketch. So long for now Sylvia and I hope that I can hear regularly from you within the next few weeks. You will from me. I'd better close and send you muchos besoso y amor.

much   kisses   love

Love,

"Tony"

[4*] Sorry I could not have you pin the wings on tomorrow but will give you that opportunity 4 weeks from date[,] providing I do get them and[,] too[,] that the little spark is still the same with you as when I left. Sure wished you could have had your vacation down here at San Marcos instead of Atlantic City. My, what you could have done to one certain cadet. Say, the cartoons at the end of the last letter certainly were good. You are really developing talent as a cartoonist.

See if you can get the after[-]effects of an S.M.J. big healthy - - - - on A.S.M. in your next sketch. So long for now[,] Sylvia[,] and I hope that I can hear regularly from you within the next few weeks. You will from me. I'd better close and send you *muchos bessos* [*sic*] *y* [*a*]*mor.*

[M]uch kisses + love

Love,

"Tony"

Sept 27, 1944

Dearest Sylvia:

It has been rather gloomy here the past two days as a soled overcast hides the sunlight, while rain continues in a steady drizzle from dawn to dusk. Seems rather odd compared to the good old sun shiny days we have had all summer. The season is definitly changing at last but the ~~climate~~ temperatures and still very warm.

Little time has been wasted in my new class and all the work I had done the past three weeks has been more or less disregarded. I'll have to fly every mission with the new class even though I had flown that type of flight before. On Monday night we started with a bang flying to Jackson Mississippi, crossing the noted towns of Monroe Louisiana and Vicksburg. After but 4 hours sleep we flew back via Monroe, Shreveport, Dallas, Waco, Austin to S.MAAF. The weather conditions were rugged and a thin overcast hid the stars from view above while a thick undercast

September 27, 1944

From: A./C. Mazza, A.S.
               44-43N-14 S.M.A.A.F.N.S.
               San Marcos, Texas

To: Miss Sylvia M. Jacobs
               2334 Atmore St[.]
               N.S. Pittsburgh, Pa[.]

Postmark: 12:30 PM
               September 28, 1944
               San Marcos, Texas

Letterhead: United States
               Army Air Forces

[1*]   Sept[.] 27, 1944

Dearest Sylvia:

It has been rather gloomy here the past two days as a solid overcast hides the sunlight, while rain continues in a steady drizzle from dawn to dusk. Seems rather odd compared to the good old sun shiney [*sic*] days we have had all summer. The season is definitely changing at last[,] but the temperatures are still very warm.

Little time has been wasted in my new class[,] and all the work I had done the past three weeks has been more or less disregarded. I'll have to fly every mission with the new class[,]

hid the ground.   We flew between these layers of clouds for a couple of hours and it is really here that a navigator must prove his worth.   I had fair results but the turbulence and wind shifts prevents the results from being as good as I would like to have them.   I brought the ship in within a couple of miles of destination and breathed a sigh of relief after a hard nights of "sweating it out."   A couple dozen more missions like that one and I'll be a bundle of nerves before it is all over.

One thing about my new echelon is that night classes are found unnecessary for me and I am required but a couple of 3 star fixes which take only an hour of my time. The rest of the evening is free to write letters, see the popular post movies, and dream of you.   Still haven't heard from you since your vacation but I realize that you didn't expect to receive merely letters from me and that you were anticipating the "real being" this week.....At least I hope that was foremost in your thought.

Already I have made many new acquaintances and one of the boys is from Homewood. He shared his Pgh Press with me, although it is several days old

even though I had flown that type of flight before. On Monday night[,] I started with a bang[,] flying to Jackson[,] Mississippi, crossing the noted towns of Monroe[,] Louisiana[,] and Vicksburg. After but 4[-]hours sleep[,] we flew back via Monroe, Shreveport, Dallas, Waco, [and] Austin to S.M[.]A[.]A[.]F.[126] The weather conditions were rugged[,] and a thin overcast hid the stars from view above while a thick undercast [1R*] hid the ground. We flew between these layers of clouds for a couple of hours[,] and it is really here that a navigator must prove his worth. I had fair results[,] but the turbulence and wind shifts prevents [sic] the results from being as good as I would like to have them. I brought the ship in within a couple of miles of destination and breathed a sigh of relief after a hard night of "sweating it out." A couple dozen more missions like that one and I'll be a bundle of nerves before it is all over.

One thing about my new eschelon [sic] is that night classes are found unnecessary for me[,] and I am required but a couple of 3[-]star fixes[,] which take only an hour of my time. The rest of the evening is free to write letters, see the popular post movies, and dream of you. Still haven't heard from you since your vacation[,] but I realize that you didn't expect to receive merely letters from me and that you were anticipating the "real being" this week - - - - - At least I hope that was foremost in your thoughts.

Already I have made many new acquaintances[,] and one of the boys is from Homewood.[127] He shared his [*Pittsburgh Press*]

---

[126] San Marcos Army Air Forces.

[127] Homewood is a neighborhood in Pittsburgh, Pennsylvania.

253

United States
Army Air Forces

before we get it. I still see Clyde
Knight and his Orchestra playing at the
Aragon and naturally visualize the many
happy hours we spent at that dance-floor.
Even the intermissions upstairs in the
balcony!!

A very exciting poker game is in
progress in the barracks at this moment
but I still don't indulge. I like to
play cards but I know when I can and
when I can't. "Poker Games" are the time
I can't afford to play, not only for financial
reasons, but I never could win a hand
with some of these "experts" who know
every trick of the game.

Received another letter from Greg
today and imagine it took only 8 days from
Italy. I'll bet there are some of the letters
that I have sent from Texas to Pgh that
took almost as long to get to you. He
is rather disgusted with the living conditions
he found in Italy and Africa. He hasn't
much to say for the people either-except

254

with me, although it is several days old [2*] before we get it. I still see Clyde Knight and his [o]rchestra playing at the Aragon and naturally visualize the many happy hours we spent at that dancefloor [sic].[128] Even the intermissions upstairs in the balcony!!

A very exciting poker game is in progress in the barracks at this moment[,] but I still don't indulge. I like to play cards[,] but I know when I can and when I can't. "Poker [g]ames" are the time I can't afford to play, not only for financial reasons, but I never could win a hand with some of these "experts[,]" who know every trick of the game.

Received another letter from Greg today[,] and imagine, it took only 8 days from Italy. I'll bet there are some of the letters that I have sent from Texas to Pgh that took almost as long to get to you. He is rather disgusted with the living conditions he found in Italy and Africa. He hasn't much to say for the people

---

[128] The Aragon Ballroom was located at 628 Penn Avenue in Pittsburgh, Pennsylvania. Charles "Teenie" Harris, *Billy Eckstine Orchestra with Lucky Thompson, Dizzy Gillespie, Charlie Parker, and Billy Eckstine Performing in the Aragon Ballroom at 628 Penn Avenue*, August 1944, black and white film photograph, 4 x 5 in., Carnegie Museum of Art, Pittsburgh, Pennsylvania, https://collection.cmoa.org/objects/e208f006-3b57-4977-bddd-190126e46c30; Dick Fortune, "Bright Spots," *Pittsburgh Press*, September 8, 1942. The Clyde Knight Orchestra was a popular band in Pittsburgh, often playing on the radio and at local ballrooms. "Aragon Ballroom" and "West View Park," *Pittsburgh Post-Gazette*, September 3, 1945; "Memorial Day Commemorated in Network and Local Broadcasts Today," *Pittsburgh Post-Gazette*, May 30, 1941.

that they are responsible for their own plight and that we are fools for giving them any sympathy or relief from their condition. He quotes the high prices they are forced to pay for articles that could be had for a few cents in the U.S.A. One light bulb cost him $6.50 and that irritated him no end. Everyone has the "jimmies" so he says, and the even little "brats" practicly demand candy, chewing gum, and cigarettes. I guess Greg just can't understand the comparison of their standards of living to ours and the effects war has on some people. We can't judge all people by a few for even here in the states there are many who make minor fortunes exploiting from the armed services.

I wish you could be here this Saturday for I am sure the two of us would have a dandy time at the Football game at Austin where the University of Texas plays South Western. I'll be there with bells on and will pretend you are sitting beside me.... I can still dream Can't I. I must close now and send you all my love.

Love,
Tony

either[,] except [2R*] that they are responsible for their own plight and that we are fools for giving them any sympathy or relief from their condition. He quotes the high prices they are forced to pay for articles that could be had for a few cents in the U.S.A. One light bulb cost him $6.50 and that irritated him [to] no end. Every-one has the "gimm[i]es[,]" so he says, and even little "brats" practicly [sic] demand candy, chewing gum, and cigarettes[.] I guess Greg just can't understand the comparison to their standards of living to ours and the effects war has on some people. We can't judge all people by a few[,] for even here in the [S]tates[,] there are many who make minor fortunes exploiting from the armed services.

Sure wished you could be here this Saturday[,] for I am sure the two of us would have a dandy time at the [f]ootball game at Austin[,] where the University of Texas plays South Western [sic]. I'll be there with bells on and will pretend you are sitting beside me – – – – I can still dream[,] can't I[?] I must close now and send you all my love.

Love[,]
"Tony"

A/C Mezga, A.S.
44-45N-14 S.M.A.A.F.N.S.
San Marcos, Texas

Miss Sylvia M. Jackson
2334 Atmore Ct.
N.S. Pittsburgh, Pa.

258

United States
Army Air Forces

Oct 1, 1944

Dearest Sylvia:

It is late Sunday afternoon and I am setting in the quiet of my class-room penning this letter to you. Sundays are always very quiet at San Marcos, particularly the few hours before parade time. Most of the fellows seem to need this period to recuperate from the fast, furious, violent Saturday night that had just gone by.

I attended the football game at Austin and saw the Texas team defeat Southwestern 20 to 0. Naturally I rooted for the other team and a mere 20 points is an improvement over some of the teams I've backed. The loyal texas fans nearly threw my buddies and I from the stands, as we howled for good old Southwestern. I just happened to notice the newspapers a few minutes ago and note with much regret Pitt- 0; Notre Dame 58. Now had I gotten home on time, we'd have seen that game together and with our staunch loyal

October 1, 1944

Postmark: [The envelope is missing.]

Letterhead: United States
               Army Air Forces

[1*]   Oct[.] 1, 1944

Dearest Sylvia:

It is late Sunday afternoon[,] and I am sitting in the quiet of my class-room [*sic*][,] penning this letter to you. Sundays are always very quiet at San Marcos, particularly the few hours before parade time. Most of the fellows seem to need this period to recup-erate from the fast, furious, violent Saturday night that had just gone by.

I attended the football game at Austin and saw the Texas team defeat Southwestern 20 to 0. Naturally[,] I rooted for the other team[,] and a mere 20 points is an improvement over some of the teams I've backed. The loyal Texas fans nearly threw my buddies and I [*sic*] from the stands, as we howled for good old Southwestern. I just happened to notice the newspapers a few minutes ago and note with much regret Pitt-0; Notre Dame[-]58. Now had I gotten home on time, we'd have seen that game together[,] and with our staunch[,] loyal [1R*] support[,] the score might have been Pitt-0[;] Notre Dame[-]57. Well, maybe we'll see it the following year together[,] since your relation-ship to me never seems to change[,] and as far as I know[,] it never will. The rest of Saturday night I had the usual steak dinner and [went] later to the movie.

support the score might have been Pitt-0 Notre Dame 57. Well, maybe we'll see it the following year together since your relationship to me never seems to change and as far as I know it never will. The rest of Saturday night I had the usual steak dinner and later to the movie. This time I saw the "Eve of St. Mark". I don't know if you have even seen that picture or not but the two leading characters seemed so much like us in the struggle vs time and emotions. Why, even the leading character was referred to as the "Silent Job" or 15%.

It wasn't very late when I did get back to camp about 11:30 PM, but was surprised to have a call from the boy who bunks right across from me. His folks were passing thru Austin and he wanted to see them, yet an overnight pass was entirely out of the question on such a short notice. He didn't want to get in trouble or go A.W.O.L. and so consulted with us to see if we could suggest something. We told him not to worry and that we'd take care of everything. Immediately a hustling rushing bunch of fellows split his clothes among ours. Hid his blankets sheets

This time[,] I saw the "Eve of St. Mark[."][129] I don't know if you have even seen that picture or not, but the two leading characters seemed so much like us in the struggle vs[.] time and emotions. Why, even the leading character was referred to as the "Silent Job" or 15%.

It wasn't very late when I did get back to camp[,] about 11:30 PM, but was surprised to have a call from the boy who bunks right across from me. His folks were passing thru [*sic*] Austin[,] and he wanted to see them, yet an overnight pass was entirely out of the question on such short notice. He didn't want to get in trouble or go A.W.O.L.[130] and so consulted with us to see if we could suggest something. We told him not to worry and that we'd take care of everything. Immediately[,] a hustling[,] rushing bunch of fellows split his clothes among ours. Hid his blankets, sheets[,]

---

[129] The film is an adaptation of Maxwell Anderson's play with the same title. *Eve of St. Mark*, directed by John M. Stahl, featuring Anne Baxter, Harry Morgan, and Vincent Price (20th Century Fox, 1944).

[130] Away Without Leave.

United States
Army Air Forces

2.

pillow case and dragged his bed to an
empty barracks about ½ block down. We
then moved all the beds up evenly to fill the
gap left by the bed we had moved out and
removed all trace of that fellow ever living
in our barracks. At bed check, the O.C. just
went right down the line flashing his light
and looking for empty beds. Lucky for
us he didn't stop to count heads, but
went right out the other door. We called
it the "Perfect Crime" but now that poor
boy is subject to all of our slightest "whims"
and has been reduced to a slave status
to pay the debt he owes us for our
troubles.

Friday night last week we had
a riotous stage play performed by some of
the boys at the other end of the field. The
show was enacted much in the same
manner as the hit Comedy "Hellzapoppin"
a couple years back. Many odd parts
were played by grown men, from babies

[2*] pillow case [sic] and dragged his bed to an empty barracks about ½ block down. We then moved all the beds up evenly to fill the gap left by the bed we had moved out and removed all trace of that fellow ever living in our barracks. At bed check, the O.C[.][131] just went right down the line[,] flashing his light and looking for empty beds. Lucky for us[,] he didn't stop to count heads[] but went right out the other door. We called it the "[p]erfect [c]rime[,]" but now that poor boy is subject to all of our slightest "whims" and has been reduced to slave status to pay the debt he owes us for our troubles.

Friday night last week[,] we had a riotous stage play performed by some of the boys at the other end of the field. The show was enacted much in the same manner as the hit comedy "Hellza Poppin" [sic][132] a couple years back. Many odd parts were played by

---

[131] Officer Commanding.

[132] "Hellzapoppin'" was originally a successful comedy revue, written by John "Ole" Olson and Harold "Chic" Johnson with music and lyrics by Sammy Fain and Charles Tobias, which ran on Broadway from September 22, 1938, to December 17, 1941. "Hellzapoppin: The Screamlined Revue (Designed for Laughing)," IBDB, accessed June 20, 2020, https://www.ibdb.com/broadway-production/hellzapoppin-12378. Universal Pictures adapted the revue for the screen. *Hellzapoppin'*, directed by H.C. Potter, featuring Ole Olson, Chic Johnson, and Martha Raye (Universal Pictures, 1941).

with diapers to well "developed" young ladies. They even had a "swoon" Crooner that mimiced Frank Sinatra. His make-up had him as white as this sheet of paper and two fellows would hold him up to the micro-phone for fearing he would drop over in the middle of a high note.

Received your letter from Atlantic City only yesterday. - - - - the one where the telephone call indicated you were slipping. That isn't so and I guess you will realize by now the reason why. I must say as yet, those same three wishes I made with you at St. Gabriels are made at every new church I visit and are renewed every Sunday even in the regular chapel. If those you make are also the same, and I believe they are, why gosh! I don't see how we could ever do anything wrong or just without a good reason behind it.

Lately and I guess I should tell you, since my last class graduated, I've been in the "dumps," feeling pretty low more than once and at times even my work began to slip, but now I believe everything will work out O.K. This coming week is again another crisis and will determine whether or not I shall make the grade.

grown men[,] from babies [2R*] with diapers to well[-]"developed" young ladies. They even had a "swoon" crooner that mimiced [*sic*] Frank Sinatra. His make-up [*sic*] had him as white as this sheet of paper[,] and two fellows would hold him up to the micro-phone [*sic*][,] fearing he would drop over in the middle of a high note.

Received your letter from Atlantic City only yesterday - - - - - the one where the telephone call indicated you were slipping. That isn't so[,] and I guess you will realize by now the reason why. I must say, as yet, those same three wishes I made with you at St. Gabriel[']s[133] are made at every new church I visit and are renewed every Sunday even in the regular chapel.[134] If those you make are also the same, and I believe they are, why gosh! I don't see how we could ever do anything wrong or do just anything without there being a good reason behind it.

Lately[,] and I guess I should tell you, since my last class graduated, I've been in the "dumps," feeling pretty low more than once[,] and at times[,] even my work began to slip, but now I believe everything will work out O.K. This coming week is again another crisis and will determine whether or not I shall make

---

[133] Built in 1906, St. Gabriel Archangel Roman Catholic Church, 2459 California Avenue, North Side, Pittsburgh, was the home parish of Sylvia Jacobs' family. "Prospective 'Recruits' Discuss Plans for New Girl Scout Troop," *Pittsburgh Press*, March 12, 1937 (referring to Sylvia Jacobs' joining a Girl Scout Troop sponsored by her parish). The church was demolished in the early 1970s in the wake of highway construction. A new church was built nearby in 1972; however, the Roman Catholic Diocese of Pittsburgh later merged the dwindling congregation into neighboring parishes in 1993. Chuck Moody, "Building's New Shine Reflects Risen Lord Parish Revitalization," *Pittsburgh Catholic*, January 17, 2003.

[134] On visiting a new church, a common Catholic custom at the time in certain communities was to incorporate into one's prayers three wishes or intentions.

United States
Army Air Forces

3.

One such Crisis is enough but two of them is a little more than enough. A little prayer from you and I'm sure things will really turn out for the best at least I'll know and the instructors will know, that I've put up quite a bit of fight 'ere I leave San Marcos as either a pvt, F/o or 2nd Lt.

Well, Sylvia I guess there isn't much more I can tell you now except as always, I still

"Love"

"Tony"

Sylvia (bashful)

the grade. [3*] One such crisis is enough[,] but two of them is a little more than enough. A little prayer from you and I'm sure things will really turn out for the best[;] at least I'll know[,] and the instructors will know, that I've put up quite a bit of fight ere I leave San Marcos as either a pv't, F/O[135] or 2nd Lt.

Well, Sylvia[,] I guess there isn't much more I can tell you now except[,] as always[,] I still

Love Sylvia (bashful)[,]

"Tony"

---

[135] Flight Officer.

United States
Army Air Forces

October 8, 1944

Dearest Sylvia:

Another Sunday afternoon to reminisce in the quiet atmosphere of the classroom. Have just computed a couple of celestial fixes and am reviewing my work in order to prepare for the week to come. Just wondering what you could be doing on an afternoon such as this with the sky crystal clear and the sun as brilliant as a day in July. Also wondering exactly what we would do, both of us together under such blissful conditions. Would we sit and sigh? Play games? Walk and talk? Drink in the charm of each others presence? - - - - You "darn betcha" we would! Maybe I'd better start reviewing how to act and talk after not seeing you for so long a period of time but Alas! I haven't changed one bit and will always be just simply "Tony".

Today, you and I (had you been at San Marcos) would have taken one of those much talked of but often sought for strolls

270

October 8, 1944

From: A./C. Mazza, A.S.
            44-43N-14 S.M.A.A.F.N.S.
            San Marcos, Texas

To: Miss Sylvia Jacobs
            2334 Atmore St[.]
            N.S. Pittsburgh[,] Pa.

Postmark: 4:30 PM
            October 9, 1944
            San Marcos, Texas

Letterhead: United States
            Army Air Forces

[1*]   October 8, 1944

Dearest Sylvia:

Another Sunday afternoon to reminisce in the quiet atmosphere of the classroom. Have just computed a couple of celestial fixes and am reviewing my work in order to prepare for the week to come. Just wondering what you could be doing on an afternoon such as this with the sky crystal clear and the sun as brilliant as a day in July[,] alas[,] wondering exactly what we would do, both of us together under such blissful conditions. Would we sit and sigh? Play games? Walk and talk? Drink in the charm of each other[']s presence? - - - - You "darn betcha" we would! Maybe I'd better

that brings mother nature close to youth or visa
Versa. We would walk hand in hand breath
the trees talking to each other by them words, smiles, and
eyes, (they are the most important.) through the outskirts
of the town eyes to the banks of the San Marcos River.
A few hundred yards from the edge of the town,
the river has been damned and a quiet pool
lies almost hidden from View. Boats, Canoes,
and Fishing Poles are rented by the hour. Can
you visualize me paddling along with deft
swift strokes along the rivers edge where
tall Magnolia trees hug the shore and yourself
setting comfortably and facing me with alarm to learn
that it is about all I can do to steer the
Canoe to where I so desire. Splash!!

It is still rather warm down here
in Texas and as yet we are in our summer
uniforms. Even the nights have been warm.
Very few of the trees have shed their leaves
and only a rate of one or two per day. The grass is
still green and not a sign to signifie this
is almost the midde of October; It seems
rather more like the last two weeks of
August.

Yes by now my old class are at their
new stations and their leave has been completed
I have yet to look forward to mine and

272

start reviewing how to act and talk to you after not seeing you for so long a period of time[,] but [a]las! I haven't changed one bit and will always be just simply "Tony."

Today, you and I (had you been at San Marcos) would have taken one of those much[-]talked[-]of but often[-]sought[-]for strolls [1R*] that brings [sic] [M]other [N]ature close to youth or visa [sic] [v]ersa. We would walk hand in hand beneath the trees[,] talking to each other thru [sic] words, smiles, and eyes (they[136] are the most important) through the outskirts of the town to the banks of the San Marcos River. A few hundred yards from the edge of town, the river has been dammed and a quiet pool lies almost hidden from [v]iew. Boats, [c]anoes, and [f]ishing [p]oles are rented by the hour[.] Can you visualize me paddling with deft[,] swift strokes along the river[']s edge where tall [m]agnolia trees hug the shore and yourself sitting comfortably and facing me with alarm to learn that it is about all I can do to steer the canoe to where I so desire? Splash!!

It is still rather warm down here in Texas[,] and as yet[,] we are in our summer uniforms. Even the nights have been warm. Very few of the trees have shed their leaves[,] and only at a rate of one or two per day. The grass is still green and not a sign to signifie [sic] this is almost the middle of October; [i]t seems rather more like the last two weeks of August.

Yes[,] by now my old class[mates] are at their new stations[,] and their leave has been completed. I have yet to look forward to

---

[136] A small arrow attached to the word "eyes" appears below the line, pointing to the word "they."

find myself adopting your pessimistic altitude
of "if" and "or but." Maybe I'll get better
results this way..... It worth the try.

  I have completed a little article of
some note to navigators a few minutes ago.
Probably you have read it since it was in
N.E. another. Anyway it seems that a
Chinese crew was flying a B-25 on a
raid on one of the Jap held Islands. On
the way back they crossed the mainland of
China and could see several villages below.
The navigator was asked for his position
and to give the direction home. All he
could say was $\frac{?}{?}$ (meaning ....
I'm Lost!) The plane circled aimlessly
for about one hour without a good
clue to their position so the crew became
disgusted. They huddled together and
came out with a super-plan. The
poor Navigator was cornered and told

mine and [2*] find myself adopting your pessimistic attitude of "if[,"] "and[,]" or "but." Maybe I'll get better results this way - - - - - It[']s worth the try.

I have completed a little article of some note to navigators a few minutes ago. Probably you have read it since it has an N.E. author. Anyway[,] it seems that a Chinese [c]rew was flying a B-25 on a raid on one of the Jap[anese-]held Islands. On the way back[,] they crossed the mainland of China and could see several villages below. The navigator was asked for his position and to give the direction home. All he could say was [scribbles indicating swear words] (meaning I'm [l]ost!)[.] This plane circled aimlessly for about one hour without a good clue to their position so the crew became disgusted. They huddled together and came out with a super-plan [sic]. The poor [n]avigator was cornered and told to "bail out" and upon landing had was to get the direction to his base from the village Natives and in turn draw a huge arrow on the ground pointing that direction to the plane above. He in turn, was left to walk back and to meditate on his errors. We Navigators it seems are only given attention when something goes wrong. Anyway I imagine the Chinese Navigator got several of his figures slanted the opposite direction and unlike Confuscious, he was Confused.

Well I guess I'd better run along now as the Sunday afternoon Parade will be in session within a few minutes. Good Afternoon Syl.

Love

Tony

[2R*] to "bail out" and upon landing had to get the direction to his base from the village [n]atives and[,] in town[,] draw a huge arrow on the ground[,] pointing that direction to the plane above. He, in turn, was left to walk back and to meditate on his errors. We [n]avigators[,] it seems[,] are only given attention when something goes wrong. - - - - Anyway[,] I imagine the Chinese [n]avigator got several of his figures slanted [in] the opposite direction and unlike Confuscious [sic], he was confused.

Well[,] I guess I'd better run along now as the Sunday afternoon [p]arade will be in session within a few minutes. Good [a]fternoon[,] Syl.

Love[,]
"Tony"

Free

NAVIGATION SCHOOL BR.

SAN MARCOS, TEXAS
OCT 9
4:30PM
1944

Miss Sylvia Jacobs
2334 Amore St
N.S. Pittsburgh Pa.

a/c Mega, a.s.
44-43-N-14 S.M.A.A.F.N.S.
San Marcos, Texas

Oct 15, 1944

Dearest Sylvia:

I can picture you now tearing this letter open and glancing thru these first few lines wondering what the delay could have been this time. But deep down in your heart I'm sure you know the real reason. "He's' been quite busy these past few days and naturally couldn't have the opportunity to open his mind and heart in a few lines to me." See! all very simple and you've answered your own question thru me. This is a "round-about way" of telling you what you already know but anyway it is a bit ---- different.

The last week was a crucial one but through hard work, hard prayers, fingers crossed, toes crossed, voodoo charms and black magic yours truly will graduate soon as a Navigator. Now all you have to do is pick out the night dress

October 15, 1944

From: A/C Anthony S. Mazza
             44-43N-14 S.M.A.A.F.N.S
             San Marcos, Texas

To: Miss Sylvia Jacobs
             2334 Atmore St.
             N.S. Pittsburgh, Pa.

Postmark: 12:30 PM
             October 16, 1944
             San Marcos, Texas
             ["Air Mail!!" handwritten on the envelope]

Letterhead: Army Air Forces Navigation School
             Cadet Club
             San Marcos Army Air Field
             San Marcos, Texas

[1*]   Oct[.] 15, 1944

Dearest Sylvia:

    I can picture you now[,] tearing this letter open and glancing thru [*sic*] these first few lines[,] wondering what the delay could have been this time. But deep down in your heart[,] I'm sure you know the real reason. "He['s] been quite busy these past few days and naturally couldn't have the opportunity to open his mind and

to which the "wings" should be attached. The object of my aim has been attained and it certainly feels great to be able to accomplish something that is limited to a selected few. There probably will be one disappointment but only a slight one, since I expect to be a Flight Officer instead of a 2nd Lt. What is the difference? I really don't know exactly and my surmises would take many a page of paper and many an hour in time. I'll do my best to explain that to you in person if and when I get home. I mean every word that being a Flight Officer will be only a slight disappointment because the sole object of being an Officer in the service was not my goal. Rank in the flying game has its place and I'm quite sure I'll have my fill of it ere this war is over.

We flew three Cross Country flights on 3 consecutive days to El Paso, Little Rock, and Memphis. It was on these missions that I came out of my slight slump and crawled back up to the 90 bracket where I

heart in a few lines to me." See! [A]ll very simple[,] and you've answered your own question than me. This is a "round-about way" of telling you what you already know[,] but anyway[,] it is a bit - - - - different.

The last week was a crucial one[,] but through hard work, hard prayers, fingers crossed, toes crossed, voodoo charms[,] and black magic[,] yours truly will graduate soon as a [n]avigator. Now all you have to do is pick out the right dress [R1*] to which the wings should be attached. The object of my aim has been attained[,] and it certainly feels great to be able to accomplish something that is limited to a select few. There probably will be one disappointment[,] but only a slight one, since I expect to be a [f]light [o]fficer instead of a 2nd Lt. What is the difference? I really don't know exactly[,] and my surmises would take many a page of paper and many an hour in time. I'll do my best to explain that to you in person if and when I get home. I mean every word that being a [f]light [o]fficer will be only a slight disappointment because the sole object of being an [o]fficer in the service was not my goal. Rank in the flying game has its place[,] and I'm quite sure I'll have my fill of it 'ere [*sic*] this war is over.

We flew three cross[-]country flights on 3 consecutive days to El Paso, Little Rock, and Memphis. It was on these missions that I came out of my slight slump and crawled back up to the

usually belong. Now the prayers are concentrated on a leave and I hope it will be a substantial one; particularly to include one of those exclusive free Sundays I saw recorded in one of your letters. I expect a maximum of 5 days however, and a minimum of 0. So our few moments together will have to be compact.

The graduation date hasn't been set as yet, but should be any time between the 21st to 25th of October. Yesterday I went to San Antonio again, but this time to get all the information I needed for travel from Texas to Penna in the quickest possible method via Rail Road. It will take all of 2 days or more to make the trip providing connections are good and the schedule properly maintained.

At present I am involved in

90 bracket where I [2*] usually belong. Now the prayers are concentrated on a leave[,] and I hope it will be a substantial one, particularly to include one of those exclusive free Sundays I saw recorded in one of your letters. I expect a maximum of 5 days[,] however, and a minimum of 0. So our few moments together will have to be compact.

The graduation date hasn't been set as yet, but should be any time between the 21st and 25th of October. Yesterday[,] I went to San Antonio again, but this time to get all the information I needed for travel from Texas to Penna[.] in the quickest possible method via Rail Road [*sic*]. It will take all of 2 days or more to make the trip[,] providing connections are good and the schedule properly maintained.

signing "hundreds" of papers for my appointment. One of them included a discharge from the Army as an enlisted man & Cadet, another, enlisting back in again. For a few hours this week I'll be officially a Civilian then Zoom! back into the service once more.

I tried my hand at bowling again last night and it seems I improve with age. I broke my record of 75 and now sport the handsome sum of 113. I'll be a champion bowler yet.

I've been hearing from my old pals who are now stationed at Lincoln, Nebraska and they advise me to get an overcoat because of the weather up there. I've been hunting all over for one here and at San Antonio but couldn't find a good fit. I'll probably buy mine when I get up north. The prices charged here are something short of scandalous while material and

At present[,] I am involved in [2R*] [the] signing of "hundreds" of papers for my appointment. One of them included a discharge from the Army as an enlisted man + cadet. Another, enlisting back in again. For a few hours this week[,] I'll be officially a civilian[,] then Zoom! back into the service once more.

I tried my hand at bowling again last night[,] and it seems I improve with age. I broke my record of 75 and now sport the handsome sum of 113. I'll be a champion bowler yet.

I've been hearing from my old pals who are now stationed at Lincoln, Nebraska[,] and they advise me to get an overcoat because of the weather up there. I've been hunting all over for one here and at San Antonio but couldn't find a good fit. I'll probably buy mine when I get up [N]orth. The prices charged here are something

3

workmanship is of inferior quality. I've learned more about clothes, sizes, and prices these past few weeks than all the rest of the knowledge I acquired the past 21 yrs.

I am writing this letter, as you have already noticed, from our exquisite Cadet Club. Many improvements have been made since I first came to this field. We know have 4 pool tables instead of 1; 3 ping pong tables instead of two, a shuffle board, their new stationary, beer every Saturday night and Cadet-burgers (Hamburgers) sold from 5:00 PM on every evening, beside the usual quota of soft drinks, cookies, candy etc. We have a hostess that "supervise" the reception of Cadet wives, sweet-hearts and relatives a ——— nights during the wk.

short of scandalous while material and [3*] workmanship is of inferior quality. I've learned more about clothes, and sizes, and prices these past few weeks than all the rest of the knowledge I acquired the past 22 yrs.

I am writing this letter, as you have already noticed, from our exquisite Cadet Club. Many improvements have been made in it since I first came to this field. We know [sic] have 4 pool tables instead of 1[,] 3 ping[-]pong tables instead of two, a shuffle board [sic], this new stationary [sic], beer every Saturday night[,] and Cadet-burgers ([h]amburgers) sold from 5:00 PM on at every evening, beside the usual quota of soft drinks, cookies, candy[,] etc. We have a hostess that "supervises" the reception of cadet wives, sweet-hearts [sic], and relatives - - - during the wk.

(meaning Friday nights only ... The rest of the time the boys are in class.

Well ~~most~~ of the work the next few days will be mostly concentrated reviews, while some of the classes will be held only as a matter of formality. My thoughts will be as for away as they usually are, about 500 miles or so, and I ~~hope~~ they meet yours at the 750 Mile Mark.

I hope that you will excuse the sloppy writing and the pencil but I had the time right now and not the pen... but since both are used only to express the same thing; the result you have already seen. Get out the Raspberry flavor and keep adding those "extra prayers" this way.

Love
Tony

P.S. WISHED THE ST. JOHNS HOSPITAL DANCE COULD BE MOVED UP A COUPLE OF WEEKS.

P.S. HOPE TO SCARE YOU ON HALLOWEEN.

[3R*] (meaning Friday nights only) - - - [t]he rest of the time[,] the boys are in class.

Well[,] the work the next few days will be mostly concentrated review while some of the classes will be held only as a matter of formality. My thoughts will be as far away as they usually are[,] about 1500 miles or so[,] and hope they meet yours at the 700[-m]ile [m]ark.

I hope that you will excuse the sloppy writing and the pencil[,] but I had the time right now and not the pen - - - but since both are used only to express the same thing[,] the result you have already seen. Get out the [r]aspberry flavor[137] and keep adding those "extra prayers" this way.

Love[,]

Tony

P.S. Wished the St. John[']s Hospital dance could be moved up a couple of weeks.[138]

P.S. Hope to scare you on Halloween.

---

[137] The reference is most likely to lipstick. See *supra* page 135 (Letter from Anthony S. Mazza to Sylvia M. Jacobs (July 22, 1944)).

[138] See *supra* note 98.

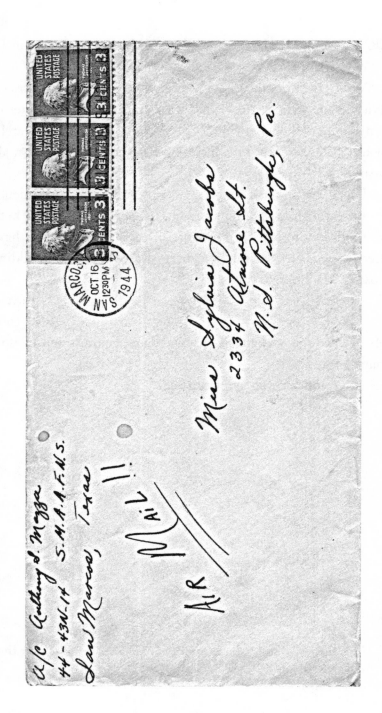

A/C Anthony J. Mizza
44-430-14 S.M.A.A.F.N.S.
San Marcos, Texas

AiR MaiL !!

Miss Sylvia Jacobs
2334 Atmore St.
N.S. Pittsburgh, Pa.

292

Nov 1, 1944

Dearest Sylvia:

"Back to the Army Routine" seems to fit descriptively the adjustment I am undergoing at present. A beautiful dream faded into oblivion and stark realization of what lies ahead are what confronts me now. The pleasant memories that we shared together will never be forgotten and the hope of further and continued happiness are foremost in my thoughts. Just being together alone, you and I, seemed to be the thing I wanted most during my leave, yet it seemed to be most difficult of problems. As I summarize my actions the past 7 days at home, perhaps I was too serious, too moody, or too demanding, but in all I had some of the most wonderful experiences ever. That last night will always be a climax in our affair, since it turned out to be nigh perfect in every respect to that I longed for so many months before.

I arrived at Lincoln on schedule at 10:10 AM yesterday morning. The Pennsylvania train was 40 minutes late at Chicago but the lapse of time to my next train was such that I had little to worry about, other than

294

November 1, 1944

From: F./O. Anthony S. Mazza
             Prov. Sq. B.
             L.A.A.B. Lincoln, Nebraska

To: Miss Sylvia M. Jacobs
             2334 Atmore St.
             N.S. Pittsburgh, Pa.

Postmark: 7:30 PM
             November 1, 1944
             Lincoln, Nebraska

Letterhead: [None]

[1*]   Nov[.] 1, 1944

Dearest Sylvia:

"Back to the Army Routine" seems to fit descriptively the adjustment I am undergoing at present. A beautiful dream faded into oblivion[,] and stark realization of what lies ahead [is] what confronts me now. The pleasant memories that we shared together will never be forgotten[,] and the hope of further and continued happiness are foremost in my thoughts. Just being together alone, you and I, seemed to be the thing I wanted most during my leave, yet it seemed to be [the] most difficult of problems. As I summarize my actions the past 7 days at home, perhaps I was too serious, too moody, or too demanding, but in all[,] I had some of the most wonderful experiences ever. That last night will always

an excursion through the City of Chicago would be ~~and~~ improbable ~~big~~. All I saw of Chicago was the depot. Nothing more. On arrival at my new base I called by phone for transportation since Taxies are not permitted on the field. At 11:00 AM a staff car drove yours truly to post headquarters where he was given assignment and quarters. A short time later after shower and shave I left the post to investigate the wonders of a Mid-western town. The bus situation is something short of marvelous and continues every 15 minutes, 24 hours per day. The base is about 7 miles from the town and is spread out over a wide area. Some remote corners of the field are so far that inter-camp bus service is refused.

By 2:00 PM I was in the heart of Lincoln stunned by its modern qualities and cleanliness. The streets are wide, almost 3 times the width of an average Pittsburgh road. The names of the streets are not difficult to remember and any location no matter how complex is simple to find since the streets are lettered by Alphabet and numericle number starting with A, B, C, etc and intersected ~~by~~ by streets perpendicular numbered 1, 2, 3, 4 etc.

be a climax in our affair, since it turned out to be nigh perfect in every respect to that I longed for many months before.

I arrived at Lincoln on schedule at 10:10 AM yesterday morning. The Pennsylvania train was 40 minutes late at Chicago[,] but the lapse of time to my next train was such that I had little to worry about[,] other than [1R*] an excursion through the City of Chicago would be improbable. All I saw of Chicago was the depot[,] nothing more. On arrival at my new base[,] I called by phone for transportation[,] since taxis are not permitted on the field. At 11:00 AM[,] a staff car drove yours truly to post headquarters[,] where he was given assignment and quarters. A short time later[,] after shower and shave[,] I left the post to investigate the wonders of a Mid-western [sic] town. The bus situation is something short of marvelous and continues every 15 minutes, 24 hours per day. The base is about 7 miles from the town and is spread out over a wide area. Some remote corners of the field are so far that inter-camp [sic] bus service is required.

By 2:00 PM[,] I was in the heart of Lincoln[,] stunned by its modern qualities and cleanliness. The streets are wide, almost 3 times the width of an average Pittsburgh road. The names of the streets are not difficult to remember[,] and any location, no matter how complex, is simple to find since the streets are lettered by [a]lphabet and numericle [sic] number[,] starting with A, B, C, etc[.] and intersected by streets perpendicular[,] numbered 1, 2, 3, 4[,] etc.

All of the buildings are of modern design with clean cut lines and indirect lighting. The Capitol building on the outskirts of the city is the beautifulest edifice I have seen yet, other than our own Capitol at Washington. Since this is the corn belt of the nation, many of the farming features and names connected with farming are prominent in their public buildings and even private enterprise. The statue at the top of the Capitol dome has the "Sower". The largest hotel is called the "Cornhusker" and a huge drinking bar at one section is known as the "Korn Kob".

The air out here has the northern "twang" without the excess soot and coal odor connected with the heavy industries.

Living is not too expensive when for instance yesterday afternoon a meal consisting of breaded Veal, diced vegetables, mashed potatoes, coffee, rolls and corn-bread topped with ice-cream cost but 45¢. $1.05 to $1.35 for the identical meal in Texas. The University of Nebraska is on the other side of town and have open invitations to us to attend their dramas, concerts

[2*] All of the buildings are of modern design with clean[-] cut lines and indirect lighting. The [c]apitol building on the outskirts of the city is the beautifulest [sic] edifice I have seen yet, other than our own Capitol at Washington. Since this is the corn belt of the nation, many of the farming features and names connected with farming are prominent in their public buildings and even private enterprise. The statue at the top of the [c]apitol dome [is] the "Sower." The largest hotel is called the "Cornhusker[,]" and a huge drinking bar at one section is known as the "Korn Kob[."]

The air out here has the northern "twang" without excess soot and coal odor connected with the heavy industries.

Living is not too expensive when[,] for instance[,] yesterday afternoon[,] a meal consisting of breaded veal, diced vegetables, mashed potatoes, coffee, rolls[,] and corn-bread [sic] topped with ice-cream [sic] cost but 45¢. [It was] $1.05 to $1.35 for the identicle [sic] meal in Texas. The University of Nebraska is on the other side of the town and have [sic] open invitations to us to attend their art exhibits??, and other social functions. Blonds, brunettes and red-heads are furnished for the Officers dance on Friday and Sunday. Saturday night the traditional square dance has chief priority over all else.

The Y.M.C.A. had wonderful facilities open to all of us and the Officers club at the Lincoln Hotel can comfort our idle moments. Night soon fell and I didn'N get to see all the things I wanted. Particularly I had to get to bed early to report 7:30 this morning for processing. Up in the sky Vega, deneb, and Altair shone as they have the many centuries past and even in Nebraska I was quite sure another mortal back in Penna almost lost her balance as her neck was straining and eyes focused in those heavenly bodies. Still another of our great friends rose in all his glory but with a chilled frosty look for the man in the moon knew he couldn'N provide the same warmth that existed when you and I were "Together".

dramas, concerts [2R*][,] art exhibits??, and other social functions. Blonds [sic], brunettes and red-heads [sic] are furnished for the [o]fficers['] dance on Friday and Sunday. Saturday night[,] the traditional square dance has chief priority over all else.

The Y.M.C.A. had wonderful facilities open to all of us[,] and the Officers Club at the Lincoln Hotel can comfort our idle moments. Night soon fell[,] and I didn't get to see all the things I wanted. Particularly, I had to get to bed early to report [at] 7:30 this morning for processing. Up in the sky[,] Vega, [D]eneb, and Altair shone as they have the many centuries past[,] and even in Nebraska[,] I was quite sure another mortal back in Penna[.] almost lost her balance as her neck was straining and eyes focused in those heavenly bodies. Still another of our great friends rose in all his glory[,] but with a chilled[,] frosty look[,] for the [M]an in the [M]oon knew he couldn't provide the same warmth that existed when you and I were "[t]ogether."

This morning by 9:40 processing was completed and it seems that I may be here an average of 10 days. Where to from here? I still haven't the slightest idea except to know that I should remain in the 2nd Air Force. Not only did you break a record with your last series of letters but you also broke a record of sending letters to me at my new base. One of those letters was at the Post Office waiting for me as I arrived yesterday morning. It was all about calling your beauty sleep to withstand "rugged treatment." I'm sure the treatment has been "rugged" and it will take all winter to catch up on the beauty sleep. Note was also made of shivering with a warm heart and sweating with a cold heart. Mysteries I cannot understand at present but hope to some day.

This afternoon I have a lecture at 4:15 PM on Medical Indoctrination and that will conclude a "strenuous" day. Two, two hour lectures tomorrow will be all that is scheduled so maybe I'll break a couple records myself. Would you mind?

[3*] This morning by 9:40[,] processing was completed[,] and it seems that I may be here an average of 10 days. Where to from here? I still haven't the slightest idea except to know that I should remain in the 2nd Air Force. Not only did you break a record with your last series of letters[,] but you also broke a record of sending letters to me at my new base. One of those letters was at the [p]ost [o]ffice[,] waiting for me as I arrived yesterday morning. It has all about your catching your beauty sleep to withstand "rugged treatment." I'm sure the treatment has been "rugged[,]" and it will take all winter to catch up on the beauty sleep. Note was also made of shivering with a warm heart and sweating with a cold heart. Mysteries I cannot understand at present but hope to some day [sic].

This afternoon[,] I have a lecture at 4:15 PM on [m]edical [i]ndoctrination[,] and that will conclude a "strenuous" day. Two two[-]hour lectures tomorrow will be all that is [sic] scheduled[,] so maybe I'll break a couple of records myself— would you mind?

I regret deeply that I hadn't the opportunity to say good-bye to your family. I hope they will understand the predicament I was in, and that I intended to call on them before leaving.

I also want to thank you for the picture and the signature. I'm sure I missed expressing my gratitude for them. See the wonderful inspiration it can have when it indirectly is responsible for this accumulation of worthless matter. I can see you smiling at it, even my salty jokes.

I see where I must close now and prepare for that 4:15 p.m. class. Too much dessert will not be appreciated and thus must be withheld in small invariable driblets: Philosophy of S.M.J. now confirmed by A.S.M.J.

Love +

Kisses

Tony

P.S. The C.O.D. policy was a treat.

[3R*] I regret deeply that I hadn't the opportunity to say good bye [*sic*] to your family. I hope they will understand the predicament I was in and that I intended to call on them before leaving.

I also want to thank you for the picture and the signature.[139] I'm sure I missed expressing my gratitude for them. See the wonderful inspiration it can have when it indirectly is responsible for this accumulation of written matter. I can see you smiling at it[,] even my salty jokes.

I see where I must close now and prepare for that 4:15 PM class. "Too much dessert will not be appreciated and must be with-held in small[,] invariable driblets." Philosophy of S.M.J.[,] now confirmed by A.S.M.

Love +

Kisses[,]

Tony

P.S. The C.O.D.[140] policy was a treat.

---

[139] See *supra* page 9 (Photograph of Sylvia M. Jacobs).
[140] Cash On Delivery.

Free

LINCOLN
NOV 1
1944
PM
NEBR.

From J. O. Maggon.
Prov. Sq. B.
L.A.A.B. Lincoln, Nebraska

Miss Sylvia M. Jacobs
2334 Atmore St.
N.S. Pittsburgh, Pa.

Nov. 3, 1944

Dearest Sylvia:-

It is quite early Friday morning, yet
here I am at the Officer's Club on my own time.
This morning I had the toughest work out when
I had to report at the ungodly hour of 9:00 A.M.,
listen to a series of names that did not include
mine for shipment, then stroll back to my
barracks with nothing to do but report again
tomorrow at 9:00 A.M. "At this rate, I'll be
worn down to a "frazzle". Can't help but
wish that a certain Miss Jacobs were on hand
to help me "recuperate".

With all this free time allotted, don't
think for one moment that I am idle. I'd
have a nervous breakdown if I did try to keep
still for a few hours. Already this morning
I bought a new pair of low cut shoes to alternate
with the ones I already have so that I could
save them for dress purposes only. I also
received my baggage from San Marcos and
began to arrange things to my own taste. I
got a much needed hair cut and bought
a pair of O.D. trousers (like George's) through
quartermasters for $5.67 which will prove
worthy for service wear around the field
this time of year.

November 3, 1944 (Letter and Postcard)

From: F./O. Anthony S. Mazza
Prov. Sqd. "B" L.A.A.B.
Lincoln, Nebraska

To: Miss Sylvia M. Jacobs
2334 Atmore St.
N.S. Pittsburgh, Pa.

Letter Postmark:
8:00 PM
November 3, 1944
Lincoln, Nebraska

Letterhead: Army Air Forces

[1*]   Nov. 3, 1944

Dearest Sylvia:

It is quite early Friday morning, yet here I am at the Officer's [sic] Club on my own time. This morning I had the toughest work out [sic] when I had to report at the ungodly hour of 9:00 AM, listen to a series of names that did not include mine for shipment, then stroll back to my barracks with nothing to do but report again tomorrow at 9:00 AM. At this rate, I'll be worn down to a "frazzle[."] Can't help but wish that a certain Miss Jacobs were on hand to help me "recuperate[."]

309

I stopped at the P.X. for a few minor toilet articles I needed and also included this writing material and ink. I also had to have one inch taken from the O.D. trousers so deposited them at the Tailors and they will be ready for me by 3:00 P.M.

I met a few moments ago, here inside this club, I met an old buddy of mine who left Pittsburgh the same time I did that August day in 1943. We were at Greensboro, St. Vincent, & Nashville together in the same squadrons, but at different squadrons at the same time at Maxwell. His name was Tom Rogers, a husky former All American football tackle of Bucknell University. For almost one hour we talked of old times and old pals wondering what they were doing now. Every now and then I confront one of my former pals at unexpected times and unexpected places. I was told that old Bud Neil my room-mate at St. Vincent had been eliminated as a pilot, but was in training as a gunner some-where south.

A group of Nurses are looking for men to complete their dance program for tonight. Since you are thoroughly familiar with nurses, I wonder if you think I did the wise thing by accepting their invitation.

310

With all this free time allotted, don't think for one moment that I am idle. I'd have a nervous breakdown if I did try to keep still for a few hours. Already this morning[,] I bought a new pair of low cut [*sic*] shoes to alternate with the ones I already have so that I could save them for dress purposes only. I also received my baggage from San Marcos and began to arrange things to my own taste. I got a much[-]needed hair cut [*sic*] and bought a pair of O.D.[141] trousers (like George's) through [the] quartermasters [*sic*] for $5.67[,] which will prove worthy for service wear around the field this time of year. [1R*] I stopped at the P.X. for a few minor toilet articles I needed and also included this writing material and ink. I also had to have one inch taken from the O.D. trousers[,] so [I] deposited them at the [t]ailors [*sic*][,] and they will be ready for me by 3:00 PM.

Just a few moments ago, here inside this club, I met an old buddy of mine who left Pittsburgh the same time I did that August day in 1943. We were at Greensboro, St. Vincent, + Nashville together in the same squadrons, but at different squadrons at the same time at Maxwell.[142] His name was Tom Rogers, a husky former All[-]American football tackle of Bucknell University. For almost one hour we talked of old times and old pals[,] wondering what they were doing now. Every now and then[,] I confront one of my former pals at unexpected times and unexpected places. I was told that old Bud Neil[,] my room-mate [*sic*] at St. Vincent[,] had been eliminated as a pilot, but was in training as a gunner some-where [*sic*] south.

---

[141] Olive Drab.

[142] Maxwell Air Force Base is near Montgomery, Alabama. "About Maxwell AFB," Maxwell Air Force Base, accessed June 20, 2020, https://www.maxwell.af.mil/About-Us/.

I still am quite loyal to that grand bunch of gals and owe a lot to one of them in particular.

This Officers Club is some lay-out and is very large with all up to date design and equipment. Two bars at two ends of the building quenches the thirst of all the much deprived Officers, while slot machines which I call ("One armed bandits") scoop away many a 5 and 10¢ piece per second. Pin ball machines are another added attraction to test the Coordination, skill, and will Power of these born leaders of men.

At the center of two long wings of this building are conveniently located Card tables that can seat a maximum of 6. Poker chips support the game that should be and is played from morning to night by our young eager enthusiasts of arm chair recreation. Huge clouds of Smoke Camouflage this section of the building as the players get rid of their nervous tension in that manner.

This life of an Officer Syl, has been worth every bit of the long hours of hard work and struggle. There is a certain air of freedom connected with it that almost makes me feel like a Civilian again. To come and go as one pleases with few or no questions asked is a reward all in itself.

A group of [n]urses are looking for men to complete their dance program for tonight. Since you are thoroughly familiar with nurses, I wonder if you think I did the wise thing by accepting their invitation. [2*] I still am quite loyal to that grand bunch of gals and owe a lot to one of them in particular.

This Officers Club is some lay-out [*sic*] and is very large with all up[-]to[-]date design and equipment. Two bars at two ends of the building quenches [*sic*] the thirst of much[-]deprived officers, while slot machines[,] which I call [. . .] "[o]ne[-] armed bandits[,"] scoop away many a 5 and 10¢ piece per second. Pin ball [*sic*] machines are another added attraction to test the coordination, skill[,] and will-Power [*sic*] of these born leaders of men.

At the center of the two long wings of this building are conveniently located card tables that can seat a maximum of 6. Poker chips suggest the game that should be and is played from morning to night by our young[,] eager enthusiasts of arm-chair [*sic*] recreation. Huge clouds of smoke camouflage this section of the building as the players get rid of their nervous tension in that manner.

This life of an [o]fficer[,] Syl, has been worth every bit of the long hours of hard work and struggle. There is a certain air of freedom connected with it that almost makes me feel like a civilian again. To come and go as one pleases with few or no questions asked is a reward all in itself. [2R*] Should an [o]fficer fail to

Should an Officer fail to report at 9:00 in the morning, the only form of discipline here is to assign him to be in charge of Military Police for the day. My bunk-mate seems to be what is commonly known here as a "Big Time Operator". He comes in bright and early at 10 minutes before 9:00 A.M., reports to see if he has been "alerted" and "Kerplunk" into bed he goes for the rest of the day. At 6:00 P.M., he get dressed in his finest and disappears only to be seen at the usual 8:50 A.M. the following morning. Our conversation has been limited to "hello", "good-bye" and "good-night." Needless to say, he is a married man with two beautiful children but that doesn't seem to cramp his ways or habits of life one bit.

I'm really thankful I got my short coat in Pittsburgh when I did. There is a shortage of them here and the prices are outrageously high. Some sell for $65 and they aren't near the quality of the one I have. Coats are a necessity at night where temperatures are in the 40's. I don't remember if you saw the leather jacket Greg sent me, but anyway it seems to be the handiest and most used garment I have here.

Incidently, Greg wrote a letter from

314

report a[t] 9:00 in the morning, the only form of discipline here is to assign him to be in charge of Military Police for the day. My bunk-mate [*sic*] seems to be what is commonly known here as a "[b]ig[-][t]ime [o]perator." He comes in bright and early at 10 minutes before 9:00 AM, reports to see if he has been "alerted[,]" and "[k]erplunk[,]" into bed he goes for the rest of the day. At 5:00 PM, he gets dressed in his finest and dis-appears only to be seen at the usual 8:50 AM the following morning. Our conversation has been limited to "hello[,"] "good-bye [*sic*][,]" and "good night." Needless to say, he is a married man with two beautiful children[,] but that doesn't seem to cramp his ways or habits of life one bit.

I'm really thankful I got my short [c]oat in Pittsburgh when I did. There is a shortage of them here[,] and the prices are outrageously high. Some sell for $65[,] and they aren't near the quality of the one I have. Coats are a necessity at night[,] where temperatures are in the 40's [*sic*]. I don't remember if you saw the leather jacket Greg sent me, but anyway[,] it seems to be the handiest and most used garment I have here.

Incidently [*sic*], Greg wrote a letter from [3*] France[,] which I received only yesterday. He claims to have been there on a special secret mission of which he couldn't say much[,] but he did rave at the warm reception he got from the liberated French [t]own. They just couldn't seem to do enough for the fliers and had a dinner and dance in their honor while [c]ognac + wines flowed freely.

Still can't help but think of the wonder-ful times I had with you last week. They went so fast that even now I can hardly be sure that it was real and not one of those wishful thoughts stored in that cranium of mine. Next time[,] I'll have to rope that gremlin

France which I received only yesterday. He claims to have been there on a special secret mission of which he couldn't say much but he did rave at the warm reception he got from the liberated French Town. They just couldn't seem to do enough for the fliers and had a dinner and dance in their honor while Cognac & wines flowed freely.

I still can't help but think of the wonderful times I had with you last week. They went so fast that even now I can hardly be sure that it was real and not one of those wishful thoughts stored in that cranium of mine. Next time I'll have to rope that gremlin who keeps pushing the clock around so fast when we are together and I am not looking, it will be up to you to keep one eye on him, the other on me. I'll keep both eyes on you!! One thing I must ask and require a frank answer from you. — Have I changed in any way?? If so, in what manner? So long for now

All my love

"Tony"

who keeps pushing the clock around so fast when we are together and I am not looking[;] it will be up to you to keep one eye on him, the other on me. I'll keep both eyes on you!! One thing I must ask and require a frank answer from you. Have I changed in any way?? If so, in what manner? So long for now[.]

All my love[,]

"Tony"

x[143]

Postcard Postmark:

> 8:00 PM
> November 3, 1944
> Lincoln, Nebraska

> [The postcard (made by Curt Teich & Co., Inc., Chicago, U.S.A. D-3247), addressed to "Miss Sylvia M. Jacobs, 2334 Atmore St., N.S. Pittsburgh, Pa.," includes an accordion foldout with nine color prints of the Nebraska State Capitol. The sole inscription under the interior tab, which completes the printed introductory phrase, "Greetings from," is "'Anthony' with love to Sylvie"].

---

[143] The x is inscribed in the tail of the y in "Tony."

Free

F/o. Anthony J. Meggas 7/36614
Provisional Sqd. "B" L.A.A.B.
Lincoln, Nebraska

LINCOLN
NOV 3
8 PM
1944
NEBR.

Miss Sylvia M. Jacobs
2334 Atmore St.
N.S. Pittsburgh, Pa.

318

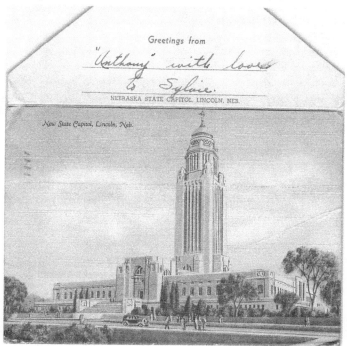

319

Nov. 5, 1944

Dearest Sylvia:

Sunday does not interrupt our work day schedule at Lincoln so, this morning bright and early we commenced our class sessions which consisted of a series of lectures on what our training will be like during the remainder of our stay with the 2nd Air Force. It seems that the free periods and time of laxity which exists now will not continue long and it wont be long before I will be again engrossed with plenty to do both night and day. From 12:30 PM to 1:00 PM, I had my Oxygen mask fitted and after a few moments was given this day to spend freely.

A cold steady all day rain is cutting through this Nebraska plain, while most of us lay close to the old Coal stove & changing "tall tales," "hitting the sack" or wishing that he were in the parlor with his "favorite" feminine companion many miles away. Need I mention who I'd prefer my feminine companion to be?? It seems rather strange that it was only today one week ago that we last saw each other. I still regret that we couldn't have had more of that afternoon together yet wouldn't give up that evening for any sum. (Still selfish, I guess)

I had rather a quiet evening yesterday and was slated for a Square Dance but this weather exhausted my enthusiasm for anything of that sort.

November 5, 1944

Postmark: [The envelope is missing.]

Letterhead: [No Letterhead]

[1*]   Nov[.] 5, 1944

Dearest Sylvia:

Sunday does not interrupt our work day [*sic*] schedule at Lincoln[,] so[] this morning[,] bright and early[,] we commenced our class sessions[,] which consisted of a series of lectures on what our training will be like during the remainder of our stay with the 2nd Air Force. It seems that the free periods and time of laxity[,] which exists [*sic*] now[,] will not continue long[,] and it won['']t be long before I will be again engrossed with plenty to do both night and day. From 12:30 PM to 1:00 PM, I had my oxygen mask fitted[,] and after a few moments[,] was given this day to spend freely.

A cold[,] steady[,] all[-]day rain is cutting through this Nebraska plain, while most of us hug close to the old coal stove[,] exchanging tales, "hitting the sack," or wishing that he were in the parlor with his 'favorite' feminine companion many miles away. Need I mention who I'd prefer my feminine companion to be?? It seems rather strange that it was only today one week ago that we last saw each other. I still regret that we couldn't have had more of that afternoon together[,] yet wouldn't give up that evening for any sum. (Still selfish, I guess[.])

2

So I turned on the hit parade but what did I hear.!! I heard the old political bla-bla filled as usual with many words, little facts, many promises, little explanations, many jokes, plenty of slander, while political machines were determined to sway people to their way of thinking and lead them blindly as usual to their sorrow (the people's, Naturally)

It is happening again! The boys are comparing hats to see whose is the rankiest. One lad seems to have taken all the honors. He claims to have walked into a store and priced many of these famous headgears. Suddenly he placed $15 on the counter for the best in the house. He guards that precious package as one would guard priceless gems. No one is allowed to even bump against that article that enlightens the soul of its proud possessor. Slowly he takes it from the bag and gloams with pride as he places it on the table for another examination. A frown develops on his face as he examines that most prized possession. Suddenly with a quick jerk of the arm he hurls the hat to a corner, runs to that spot and jumps on the hat 3 or 4 times, then over the grommet. Quickly he places it on his head and steps into the nearby shower. After passing said hat through a wringer and sleeping over it for one full week, his hat was given the

I had rather a quiet evening yesterday and was slated for a [s]quare [d]ance[,] but this weather exhausted my enthusiasm for anything of that sort. [2*] So I turned on the hit parade[,] but what did I hear!! I heard the old political bla[h]-bla[h]—filled as usual with many words, little facts, many promises, little explanations, many jokes, plenty of slander, as political machines were determined to sway people to their way of thinking and lead them blindly[,] as usual[,] to their sorrow (the people's, [n]aturally)[.]

It is happening again! The boys are comparing hats to see whose is the raunchiest. One lad seems to have taken all the honors. He claims to have walked into a store and priced many of these famous head-gears. Suddenly[,] he placed $15 on the counter for the best in the house. He guards that precious package as one would guard priceless gems. No one is allowed to even bump against that article that enlightens the soul of its proud possessor. Slowly he takes it from the bag and gleams with pride as he places it on the table for another examination. A frown developes [*sic*] on his face as he examins [*sic*] that most prized of possessions. Suddenly[,] with a quick jerk of the arm[,] he hurls the hat to a corner, runs to that spot[,] and jumps on the hat 3 or 4 times and removes the graumet [*sic*]. Quickly he places it on his head and steps into the nearby shower. After passing said hat through a wringer and sleeping over it for one full week, his hat

3

most sought title of the Squadron, "The Rumchiest."

Talking of awards and decorations the one "wise" guy at the corner of the barracks claims that Adam was the first man to be awarded the Oak Leaf Cluster. This poor boy was soon deluged with shoes and pillows and swiftly put out of his misery.

Adding to the list of corny names found here at Lincoln, the center of the corn belt, is the noted radio station of these parts with the call letters K.O.R.N.

André Kostelanez is now on the air playing those many melodious melodies that always include a you and me.

At this instant I have received word that I am "altered". This means that I have a day or so more or less to remain at this station and that it won't be long 'ere you shall hear from me at another address.

Quite a commotion is in progress at the reception of these tidings so thus I had better close this letter still sending you

Love + Kisses

"Tony"

324

was given the [3*] most[-]sought title of the [s]quadron, "The Raunchiest."

Talking of words and decorations[,] the one "wise" guy at the corner of the barracks claims that Adam was the first man to be awarded the [o]ak [l]eaf [c]luster.[144] This poor boy was soon deluged with shoes and pillows and swiftly put out of his misery.

Adding to the list of corney [*sic*] names found here at Lincoln, the center of the corn belt, is the noted radio station of these parts with the call letters K.O.R.N.

André Kostelonez [*sic*][145] is now on the air[,] playing those many melodious melodies that always include a you and me.

At this instant[,] I have received word that I am "altered[."] This means that I have a day or so more or less to remain at this station and that it won't be long 'ere [*sic*] you shall hear from me at another address.

Quite a commotion is in progress at the reception of these tidings[,] so thus I had better close this letter[,] still sending you

Love + Kisses[,]

"Tony"

---

[144] An oak leaf cluster is a military decoration that denotes "a second or subsequent entitlement of awards." "Air Force Awards and Decorations," AFH 1 and Enlisted Study Guides, accessed June 20, 2020, https://www. studyguides.af.mil/Portals/15/documents/rank_ribbons/Devices.pdf.

[145] The reference is most likely to Andre Kostelanetz (b. December 22, 1901; d. January 13, 1980), a Russian-American popular music conductor. "Andre Kostelanetz Collection," Library of Congress, accessed June 20, 2020, https://www.loc.gov/collections/andre-kostelanetz-collection/ about-this-collection/.

ARMY AIR FORCES

Nov. 9, 1944

Dearest Sylvia:

Within the next hour or so I shall
be well on my way toward my new destination.
I can't tell you where that will be now but
can say that it is further west. For the
past couple of days, we have been restricted
to the barracks area and there really isn't
much new that I can tell you. We occupied
the time by playing cards, following closely the
election returns, reading magazines and books,
and denouncing Bombardiers and Pilots. They
put up many stiff arguments and the debate
at present is at a standstill. The Bombardiers
have a slight edge, however, when they were
given an additional 11 day leave starting tomorrow.

From the looks of things, I will be
assigned as Navigator in a B-24. I missed
the B-17 shipment by one name on the shipping
roster.

As yet, I have not received one letter
from home or from you. I checked the
situation this morning and found that as
soon as I had been alerted my mail
was forwarded to my next base. I hope

November 9, 1944

From: F./O. A.S. Mazza T-136514
                    SqB L.A.A.B.
                    Lincoln, Nebraska

To: Miss Sylvia Jacobs
                    2334 Atmore St.
                    N.S. Pittsburgh, Pa.

Postmark: 7:30 PM
                    November 9, 1944
                    Lincoln, Nebraska

Letterhead: Army Air Forces

[1*]   Nov. 9, 1944

Dearest Sylvia:

Within the next hour or so[,] I shall be well on my way toward my new destination. I can't tell you where that will be now but can say that it is further west. For the past couple of days, we have been restricted to the barracks area[,] and there really isn't much new that I can tell you. We occuppied [*sic*] the time by playing cards, following closely the election returns, reading magazines and books, and denouncing [b]ombardiers and [p]ilots. They put up many stiff arguments[,] and the debate at present is at a standstill. The [b]ombardiers have a slight edge, however, when they were given an additional 11[-]day leave starting to-morrow.

it will be waiting for me when I get there.

The weather here is cold and crisp even though the sun is shining as bright as possible and not one cloud rests in the sky. The three coal stoves in this barracks are just about ample to provide enough warmth to keep things comfortable.

I have already shipped out my foot locker and baggage so now have only my B-4 bag and small handbag to arrange in order, so that I can carry them next to me personally. We will travel individually on Pullman Cars with only the orders to arrive at our new base on a specific time and date. If it were the least bit possible (time allotting) I would make the journey via Pittsburgh but that now is entirely out of the question.

Must close now and as I leave will be thinking of you always.

Love

"Tony"

From the looks of things, I will be assigned as [n]avigator on a B-24. I missed the B-17 shipment by one name on the shipping roster.

As yet, I have not received one letter direct from home or from you. I checked the situation this morning and found that as soon as I had been alerted[,] my mail was forwarded to my next base. I hope [2*] it will be waiting for me when I get there.

The weather here is cold and crisp[,] even though the sun is shining as bright[ly] as possible[,] and not one cloud rests in the sky. The three coal stoves in the barracks are just about ample to provide enough warmth to keep things comfortable.

I have already shipped out my foot locker [*sic*] and baggage[,] so now have only my B-4 bag[146] and small handbag to arrange in order, so that I can carry them next to me personally. We will travel individually on Pullman [c]ars with only the orders to arrive at our new base on a specific time and date. If it were the least bit possible (time allotting)[,] I would make the journey via Pittsburgh[,] but that now is entirely out of the question.

Must close now[,] and as I leave[,] will be thinking of you always.

Love[,]
"Tony"

---

[146] The B-4 bag was a popular military-issued, two-suiter garment bag.

Free

F/o. a.s. Mugga T-136514
3g B L. a. a. B.
Lincoln, Nebraska

Miss Sylvia Jacobs
2334 Atmore st.
N.s. Pittsburgh, Pa.

ARMY AIR FORCES

Nov 11, 1944

Dearest Sylvia,

Finally arrived at this station of Pueblo Colorado, near the base of the rockies, last night. The journey was uneventful with the old steam engine churning over the tracks from Lincoln to Denver then south through Colorado Springs to Pueblo. We traveled by Pullman having one car entirely to ourselves and were as comfortable as one could be at any time traveling by rail. We invaded other parts of the train, however, and soon filled the reading cars, club cars, and the dining car. This traveling as an Officer is certainly the thing for not only did the Gov't provide the Pullman car but we expect to be compensated $30 or more for subsistency, rental, and few more such claims. We traveled thru the Western Plains from Nebraska and couldn't see anything of scenic beauty to contrast the well kept farms. At Denver, immediately the mountains grasped our attention and snow covered peaks loomed across the horizon. Acres of grazing land at the

332

November 11, 1944 (Letter and Postcard)

Postmark: [The envelope is missing.]

Letterhead: Army Air Forces

[1*]   Nov[.] 11, 1944

Dearest Sylvia,

Finally arrived at this station of Pueblo, Colorado[,] near the base of the [R]ockies, last night. The journey was unevent-ful with the old steam engine churning over the tracks from Lincoln to Denver then south through Colorado Springs to Pueblo. We traveled by Pullman[,] having one car entirely to ourselves[,] and were as comfortable as one could be at any time traveling by rail. We invaded other parts of the train, however, and soon filled the reading cars, club cars, and the dining car. This traveling as an [o]fficer is certainly the thing[,] for not only did the [g]ov't provide the Pullman [c]ar[,] but we expect to be compensated $30 or more for subsistency [*sic*], rental, and [a] few more such claims. We traveled thru [*sic*] the Western Plains from Nebraska and couldn't see anything of scenic beauty to contrast [with] the well[-]kept farms. At Denver, immediately the mountains grasped our attention[,] and snow[-]covered peeks [*sic*] loomed across the horizon. Acres of grazing land at the [2*] foot of the mountains were such to have one realize why this can [be] and is a center for sheep raising. It isn't too far from Denver to Pueblo[,] almost [a] 3½[-]hrs[.] train ride. Should I get an overnight pass at any time

2

foot of the mountains were such to have one realize why this can and is a center for sheep raising. It isn't too far from Denver to Pueblo; almost 3½ hrs train ride. Should I get an overnight pass at any time or if I'm not scheduled to fly on a particular day, I may hike up that way and look the town over from the ground.

Staff cars were waiting for us at Pueblo last night. They were these long station wagons that can seat 15 or so. We are housed in 2 story barracks, since the Bachelor's Officers Quarters burned down a few nights ago. Many a man lost his complete outfit and some, who have been in the service for quite some time are filing claims, that will be paid to them eventually, ranging from $500 to $800. We had to get our things arranged the rest of the night and with specific orders to proceed at 8:00 AM the next morning.

What a processing that was too. It included, personal affairs, Oxygen mask fitting, a complete '64 medical exam with 2 more cholera and typus shots given by a man who was doing it for the first time, Dental check, Clothing check, Pay Vouchers, Allotments, and complete issue of flying clothes with an individual back pack parachute.

334

or [i]f I'm not scheduled to fly on a particular day, I may hike up that way and look the town over from the ground.

Staff cars were waiting for us at Pueblo last night. They were these long station wagons that can seat 15 or so. We are housed in 2[-]story barracks, since the [b]achelor's [*sic*] [o]fficers['] [q]uarters burned down a few nights ago. Many a man lost his complete outfit[,] and some, who have been in the service for quite some time[,] are filing claims[] that will be paid to them eventually[,] ranging from $500 to $800. We had to get our things arranged the rest of the night and with specific orders to process at 8:00 AM the next morning.

What a processing that was[,] too. It included[] personal affairs, [o]xygen mask fitting, a complete 64 [M]edical [E]xam with 2 more cholera and typus [*sic*] shots given by a man who was doing it for the first time, [d]ental [c]heck, [c]lothing [c]heck, [p]ay [v]ouchers, [a]llotments, and [a] complete issue of flying clothes with an individual back pack [*sic*] parachute. [3*] This afternoon[,] several lectures were given to familiarize us with what to expect and orders to report tomorrow morning at 5:45 AM for [p]re-flight briefing prior to take-off [*sic*]. You can readily see that they mean business here[,] although I don't believe things will be so rough before I become accustomed to the layout. I am more or less anxious to meet my crew[,] whom I shall see for the first time tomorrow. They have already been flying one week together and are probably as anxious to know what their [n]avigator will look like. I hope they won't be disappointed.

I wish you were here tonight to look up at the top of my shelf. There[,] beside my raunchy hat on one side and my alarm clock on the other[,] sits "Sylvie[,"] and as usual[,] all in smiles.[147] She looks

---

[147] See *supra* page 9 (Photograph of Sylvia M. Jacobs).

This afternoon several lectures were given to familiarize us with what to expect and orders to report tomorrow morning at 5:45 AM for Pre-flight briefing prior to take-off. You can readily see that they mean business here although I don't believe things will be so rough before I become accustomed to the layout. I am more or less anxious to meet my crew whom I shall see for the first time tomorrow. They have already been flying for one week together and are probably as anxious to know what their Navigator will look like. I hope they won't be too disappointed.

I wish you were here tonight to look up at the top of my shelf. There beside my raunchy hat on one side and my alarm clock on the other sets "Sylvie"; and as usual all in smiles. She looks prettier than ever tonight particularly since I bought her the most beautiful blue gown that is just too becoming. I've got her a new leather frame that has really streamlined things considerably. It is a folding frame done up in blue with the Air Corps wings on the front and a few planes skirting around the borders. A thin airplane paper will present the

prettier than ever tonight[,] particularly since I bought her the most beautiful blue gown that is just too becoming. I've got her a new leather frame that has really streamlined things considerably. It is a folding frame done up in blue with the Air Corps wings on the front and a few planes skirting around the borders. A thin cellophane paper will prevent the [4*] soot and dust particles from falling on her nose and preserve those good looks for quite some time to come. Really[,] the size is just perfect and is the standard used by other fellows. Incidently [*sic*][,] an 8 x 10 frame is just perfect. Speaking in terms of the 'gang buster' [*sic*] slang[, "]you can't get away[;] I've got you [']framed.["'] I'll include the picture of the gal you displaced.[148] That certainly ought to help your ego along a little.

Again[,] I received the pleasant surprise to have a letter from you waiting for me. I will congratulate you in print[,] but I knew all along, and was sure of myself, that R.N. would be registered beside your name. Didn't I include it in a particular wish with you one particular day not too long ago? See! Yes, both of us have been extremely fortunate to have attained our goals. I certainly am proud of your achievement and know[,] too, fate permitting[,] that if but a fraction of the effort we have placed in our past goal is directed to yet another and more important goal, it[,] too[,] will become a matter of realization.

It is but 8:00 PM Mountain [T]ime[,] [5*] and we are two hours behind your time. The hit parade has just concluded[,] and some-how [*sic*] I believe that a little lass is back in the Western Penna[.] Section[,] around the N.S. of Pittsburgh[,] listening to the same program and perhaps even writing a few lines to me. Songs

---

[148] The reference is presumably to the sample commercial photograph of a woman that was in the frame when purchased.

soot and dust particles from falling on her
nose and preserve those good looks for quite
some time to come. Really the size is
just perfect and is the standard used by the
other fellows. Incidently an 8x10 frame
is just perfect. Speaking in terms of
the 'gang buster' slang. 'You can't get away
I've got you "framed." I'll include the
picture of the gal you displaced. That
certainly aught to help your ego along a little.

Again I received the pleasant surprise
to have a letter from you waiting for me. I
will congratulate you in point but I knew
all along, and was sure of myself, that
R.N. would be registered beside your
name. Didn't I include it in a particular
wish with you one particular day not too
long ago? See! Yes, both of us have
been extremely fortunate to have attained our
goals. I certainly am proud of your achievement
and know too, fate permitting, that if but
a fraction of the effort we have placed in
our past goal is directed to yet another
and more important goal, it too will become
a matter of realization.

It is but 8:00 PM Mountain time

such as ["]Always[,"][149] ["]Make Believe[,"][150] and "I['ll] Walk [A]lone[,"][151] just to mention a few, can't help but reflect a bit of you to me[,] and I hope it is also visa [*sic*] versa in reflecting me to thee. Gee!

I haven't seen all of the beautiful country listed in the post card [*sic*] I sent, but intend to see every bit as much as I can when

---

[149] Irving Berlin wrote "Always" in 1926, and George Olson and Vincent Lopez each released versions of the song the same year. George Olson and His Music with Fran Frey, Bob Rice, and Edward Joyce, vocalists, "Always," by Irving Berlin, recorded February 5, 1926, Victor, No. 19955-A; Vincent Lopez and His Casa Lopez Orchestra, "Always," by Irving Berlin, released 1926, OKeh, No. 40567-A; "Songs from Year 1926," TSORT, accessed June 20, 2020, https://tsort.info/music/yr1926.htm. In 1944, the film *Christmas Holiday* featured the song "Always." *Christmas Holiday*, directed by Robert Siodmak, featuring Gene Kelly and Deanna Durbin (Universal Pictures, 1944). Although there were other popular recordings of "Always" released in December of 1944, the recording referenced here may be either to the earlier versions of the song or to the recording released in November of 1944 by Paul Lavalle. Paul Lavalle and His String Orchestra, "Always," by Irving Berlin, released November 11, 1944, Musicraft, No. 297A; "Song Title 8—Always," TSORT, accessed June 20, 2020, https://tsort.info/music/tyqmrb.htm; "Paul Lavalle and His String Orchestra—Always/Let Me Call You Sweetheart," discogs.com, accessed June 20, 2020, https://www.discogs.com/Paul-Lavalle-And-His-String-Orchestra-Always-Let-Me-Call-You-Sweetheart/release/5794133.

[150] The reference is most likely to the song "I'm Making Believe," written by Mack Gordon and James V. Monaco in 1944. The Ink Spots and Ella Fitzgerald released a popular version of the song in the same year. The Ink Spots and Ella Fitzgerald, vocalists, "I'm Making Believe," by Mack Gordon and James V. Monaco, released November 4, 1944, Decca, No. 23356A; "Top 80 Pop Songs in 1944" playback.fm, accessed June 20, 2020, https://playback.fm/charts/top-100-songs/1944; "I'm Making Believe," Second Hand Songs, accessed June 20, 2020, https://secondhandsongs.com/work/82782/versions.

[151] See *supra* note 121.

and we are two hours behind your time.
The hit parade has just concluded and
some-how I believe that a little lass is
back in the Western Penna. Section around the
N.S. of Pittsburgh listening to the same program
and perhaps even writing a few lines to me.
Songs such as 'Always', 'Make Believe',
and 'I Walk alone' just to mention a
few, can't help but reflect a bit of you
to me and I hope it is also vice versa
in reflecting me to thee. Gee!

I haven't seen all of the beautiful
country listed in the post card I sent, but
intend to see every bit as much as I can
when the opportunity permits. Only wished
that you were here to share these wonderful feasts of Natural beauty.

I'd better close now and with
a super quota of Love + Kisses bid thee
Goodnight.

Love
"Tony"

P.S. Hope I am the first to use your title by
letter and the first too to be placed under
your custody as a "difficult case."

340

the opportunity permits. Only wished that you were here to share these wonder-ful feasts of [n]atural beauty.

I'd better close now [and][,] with a super quota of [l]ove + [k]isses[,] bid thee [g]oodnight [*sic*].

Love[,]

"Tony"

P.S. Hope I am the first to use your title by letter and the first[,] too[,] to be placed under your custody as a "difficult case."

Postcard Postmark:

[Time undecipherable]
November 12, 1944
Pueblo, Colorado

Postcard:

[The postcard, "made by Curt Teich & Co., Chicago, U.S.A. D-2075," consists of an accordion foldout of printed color pictures of Southern Colorado, including San Luis Valley, San Isabel National Forest, Raton Pass, and Stonewall. The inside tab has the following return address:

F./O. A.S. Mazza T-136514
215 CCS Box 3323
1-26 P.A.A.B.
Pueblo, Col.

The inside tab of the postcard has the printing, "Greetings from," which is completed in handwriting as follows: "Tony Wish we were here 'Together.'"

SOUTHERN COLORADO

SAN LUIS VALLEY · SAN ISABEL NATIONAL FOREST
RATON PASS · STONEWALL

Miss Sylvia Jacobs
2334 Atmore St
N.S. Pittsburgh 14, Pa.

F/O. A.S. MAZZA   T-136514
215 CCS   BOX 3323
1-26   P.A.A.B.
Pueblo, Col. Greetings from

Tony

Wish we were here "Together."

Historic Spanish Peaks

343

ARMY AIR FORCES

Nov. 16, 1944

Dearest Sylvia:

Of the past 72 hrs., I have been in the air more than 24 hours. The rest of the week will contain ground school subjects only, and finally I may have a bit more time to myself. My first mission was Sunday morning, but the second day at this field. We were at the briefing room at 5:45 AM, while the sky was still dark. Here I met the crew to whom I shall be a very distinct part during the months to come. They are a likeable lot and we should get along amiably together. The rest of the officers are alright, but the crew is superb. They'd do just anything to please my tiniest wish and I would go just as far for them. Since probably I will be referring to my crew-mates quite often in days to come, I may as well introduce you to them.

The Pilot and captain of the team, is Lt. Alcibiades Skalamanos. Quite a name isn't it? And quite a flyer that boy is too. He is from Greek parentage, as the name plainly suggests

344

November 16, 1944

From: F./O. A. S. Mazza T-136514
            25th CCS 1-26 Box 3323
            P.A.A.B. Pueblo, Col.

To: Miss Sylvia M. Jacobs
            2334 Atmore St.
            N.S. Pittsburgh 12, Pa[.]

Postmark: 5:00 PM
            November 16, 1944
            Pueblo, Colorado

Letterhead: Army Air Forces

[1*]   Nov. 16, 1944

Dearest Sylvia:

Of the past 72 hrs[.], I have been in the air more than 24 hours. The rest of the week will contain ground school subjects only, and finally[,] I may have a bit more time to myself. My first mission was Sunday morning, on but the second day at this field. We were at the briefing room at 5:45 AM, while the sky was still dark. Here I met the crew to whom I shall be a very distinct part during the months to come. They are a likeable lot[,] and we should get along amiably together. The rest of the [o]fficers are alright [*sic*], but the crew is superb. They'd do just anything to please my tiniest wish[,] and I would go just as far for them. Since probably

he is
and quite set in his ways. He is over
27 yrs old, medium build and height, married
having a child 9 mo. old. He speaks very
seldom, almost only when necessary. He
strikes me as being a cool, confident, man
who is sure of his every move. I doubt
if we'll have any trouble whatsoever working
together.

The Right Halfback on the team is
our Co-Pilot. F/o. John Gilmore. He
too has a quiet reserve personality. He
is much too busy to spend much time
with us outside of flying hours, and
he was married but two weeks ago and
is deeply involved in the secret complications
of married life. A very likable chap.

Half Back Walter Brooks, a short
stocky guy from New York is the Bombardier.
He can talk the arm off of anyone but knows
his job thoroughly. Incidentally, he knocked
the "smithereens" out of our target yesterday. We
are quite chummy and already have gone
to Pueblo together, but only for a few hours to
get some clothing cleaned and pressed. He
and I will have plenty of work to do together
and I will have to learn how to Bomb
from him. Never a dull moment with

346

I will be refering [sic] to my crew-mates [sic] quite often in days to come[,] I may as well introduce you to them.

The [p]ilot and captain of the team is Lt. Alcibiades Skalamanos [sic].[152] Quite a name isn't it? And quite a flyer that boy is[,] too. He is from Greek parentage, as the name plainly suggests[,] [1R*] and he is quite set in his ways. He is over 27 yrs[.] old, medium build and height, married[,] having a child 9 mo[s]. old. He speaks very seldom, almost only when necessary. He strikes me as being a cool, confident[] man who is sure of his every move. I doubt if we'll have any trouble whatever working together.

The [r]ight [h]alfback on the team is our [c]o-[p]ilot[,] F./O. John Gilmore.[153] He[,] to[o,] has a quiet[,] reserve[d], personality. He is much too busy to spend much time with us outside of flying hours, since he was married but two weeks ago and is deeply involved in the secret complications of married life[, a] very likable chap.

Half Back [sic] Walter Brooks, a short[,] stocky guy from New York[,] is the [b]ombardier. He can talk the arm off of anyone but knows his job thoroughly. Incidently [sic][,] he knocked the "smithereens" out of our target today. We are quite chummy and already have gone to Pueblo together, but only for a few hours to get some clothing cleaned and pressed. He and I will have plenty

---

[152] The pilot's name was Alcibiades Skalomenos. "Skalomenos - #136," 461 Bombardment Group (H), accessed June 20, 2020, https://461st.org/Crews/764th%20Crews/skalomenos.htm.

[153] The name of John T. Gilmore appears on the roster for the 764th Squadron of the 461st Bombardment Group (H) as the co-pilot for Alcibiades Skalomenos. "764th Roster," 461st Bombardment Group (H), accessed June 20, 2020, https://461st.org/Roster/Roster%20764th.htm.

him about.

Quarterback and Navigator is the jerk from Pittsburgh who believes he can be placed in the air blindfolded, carried to the middle of nowhere, and yet, find his way back. Would like most to Navigate to the arms of L. M. J. if she'd have him do so. He is a very moody person that gets peeved when things don't go just as he would have them. Is determined to understand the personality of a certain young lady or know the reason why not. He does not have much faith in "mysteries", that perhaps being the reason why he makes things hard for himself. Operates in spells; sometimes talking without even time for breath, while other times he sits in a very quiet pensive mood deeply involved in solving that one word - (why?)

The Engineer is the Center for our team and I do mean he is the center of all activity in the plane. He is Wm. William Kenny a chap with a constant smile. It would be hard for anyone to argue with a personality of this sort for it doesn't take long for you to realize that this boy knows what its all about and

of work to do together[,] and I will have to learn how to [b]omb from him. Never a dull moment with [2*] him about.

Quarterback and [n]avigator is the [j]erk from Pittsburgh[,] who believes he can be placed in the air blindfolded, carried to the middle of nowhere, and yet, find his way back. Would like most to [n]avigate to the arms of S.M.J.[,] if she'd have him do so. He is a very moody person that gets 'peeved' when things don't go just as he would have them. Is determined to understand the personality of a certain young lady or know the reason why not. He does not have much faith in "mysteries[,"] that perhaps being the reason why he makes things hard for himself. Operates in spells[,] sometimes talking without even time for breath, while other times he sits in a vey quiet[,] passive mood[,] deeply involved in solving the one word - - - (why?)[.]

The [e]ngineer is the center for our team[,] and I do mean he is the center of all activity in the plane. He is Cpl[.] William Kenny [sic][,] a chap with a constant smile.[154] It would be hard for anyone to argue with a personality of this sort[,] for it doesn't take long for you to realize that this boy knows what it[']s all

---

[154] The name of William A. Kenney appears on the roster for the 764th Squadron of the 461st Bombardment Group (H) as the engineer and gunner for the crew of Alcibiades Skalomenos. "764th Roster."

that you don't mind placing yourself under his judgement. He knows about all there is to know on what makes those engines tick. I sometimes envy that knowledge and wished I could know the meaning of every wire and bolt that keeps the iron bird high in the sky with its rolling, chugging, but steady engine hums. When Kenny says the bird can fly, we know he is right. When he says it can't, not one of us would dare crawl inside the plane.

Left End, in the Tail Gunner position, is a boy from the lone star state. The only southerner on the crew but a likeable one at that. He is a product of a different era, one where the cow boy ruled supreme. Texas Billy Akines is a bow legged ex cowboy who has a clean cut blue eyed stare, blond hair, ruddy complexion from the out-doors, tall with firm lips and steady hand. He is not the oldest man of our crew but his 31 yrs gives us plenty of respect for his decisions. He is one of the best shots on the field and I'd hate to be in the plane that would ever come within the sights and range of his guns.

Right End, in the Nose turret guns, we have a young eager lad of no more than 18 or 19. He seems to be fresh out of high school but a hard worker

about and [2R*] that you don't mind placing yourself under his judgement [*sic*]. He knows about all there is to know on what makes those engines tick. I sometimes envy that knowledge and wished I could know the meaning of every wire and bolt that keeps the iron bird high in the sky with its rolling, chugging, but steady [e]ngine hum. When Kenny [*sic*] says the bird can fly, we know he is right. When he says it can't, not one of us would dare crawl inside the plane.

Left [e]nd, in the [t]ail [g]unner position, is a boy from the [L]one [S]tar [S]tate. The only [S]outherner on the crew but a likeable one at that. He is a product of a different era, one where the cow boy [*sic*] ruled supreme. Texas Sgt[.] Billy Shires is a bow legged [*sic*] ex[-]cowboy[,] who has a clean[-]cut[,] blue[-]eyed stare, blond hair, ruddy complexion from the out-doors [*sic*], tall with firm lips and steady hand.[155] He is not the oldest man of our crew[,] but his 31 yrs[.] gives [*sic*] us plenty of respect for his decisions. He is one of the best shots on the field[,] and I'd hate to be in the plane that would ever come within the sights and range of his guns.

Right [e]nd, in the [n]ose[-]turret guns, we have a young[,] eager lad of no more than 18 or 19. He seems to be fresh out

---

[155] The name of Ruben W. Shires appears on the roster for the 764th Squadron of the 461st Bombardment Group (H) as a gunner for the crew of Alcibiades Skalomenos. "764th Roster."

3.

determined to prove his worth. He is
the Cassanova of the lot is P.F.C. Harold Rich
He, according to his chums, with his soft
talk and baby faced features, has the Pueblo
gals in a "jitter". He frequents the Ballroom
here known as the Arcadia where from 9 to 12
he is but a confused mass of twisted torso,
arms and legs projecting this way and that as
he teaches these ~~Pueblo~~ gals his Boston Mass.
technique in the art of jive.

Our right guard and what a !
guardian of the air waves that boy is !
From our own town of Pittsburgh on its
east side, we have build Billy Deegan.
A tall solid built boy who seems to be
a reserved quiet ~~lad~~ but one who
can tear a radio apart and put it together
almost blindfolded. His sheer enjoyment
is to make as many contacts as he can
with varied stations on the ground and
other planes in the air. His first remark
was "With the Navigator from Pittsburgh, I'm
the Allegheny County Airport here we conce."
"I sure would like to make that statement
come true", ~~~~ my reply. That alone
has knitted the two us firmly together

352

of high school but a hard worker[,] [3*] determined to prove his worth. He is the Cassanova [*sic*] of the lot [. . . ,] P.F.C. Harold Rich[.][156] He, according to his chums, with his soft talk and baby faced [*sic*] features, has the Pueblo gals in a "jitter." He frequents the [b]allroom here known as the Arcadio[,][157] where from 9[] to 12 he is but a confused mass of twisted torso, arms[,] and legs projecting this way and that as he teaches these gals his Boston[,] Mass.[, t]echnique in the art of jive.

Our right guard[,] and what a guardian of the air waves that boy is[,] [f]rom our own town of Pittsburgh on its east side, we have wild Billy Deegan.[158] A tall[,] solid[-]built boy[,] who seems to be a reserved[,] quiet lad but one who can tear a radio apart and put it together almost blindfolded. His sheer enjoyment is to make as many contacts as he can with varied stations on the ground and other planes in the air. His first remark was[,] "With the [n]avigator from Pittsburgh, Allegheny County Airport here we come!" "I sure would like to make that statement come true," was my reply. That alone has knitted the two [of] us firmly together[,] [3R*] and it won[']t be long 'ere [*sic*] he and I have special radio sessions with me teaching him

---

[156] The name of Harold A. Rich appears on the roster for the 764th Squadron of the 461st Bombardment Group (H) as a gunner for the crew of Alcibiades Skalomenos. "764th Roster."

[157] The Arcadio Ballroom in Pueblo, Colorado, once located on 5th Street, no longer exists; it was a popular dancehall for World War II servicemen. "Mary Babnick Brown," Pueblo County, Colorado, accessed June 20, 2020, https://www.kmitch.com/Pueblo/bios0094.html (citing *Colorado Springs Gazette Telegraph*, June 8, 1987; *Colorado Springs Gazette*, November 11, 1990).

[158] The name of William E. Deegan appears on the roster for the 764th Squadron of the 461st Bombardment Group (H) as a radio operator and gunner for the crew of Alcibiades Skalomenos. "764th Roster."

and it wont be long 'ere he and I have special radio sessions with me teaching him how to find his position by radio, and he letting me in on the fundamentals of radio.

Our left guard is a tall lean lanky man from the Tri-state Area. From West Virginia and the city of Wheeling is Elmer Lloyd. A man who takes great pride in his youthfulness is readily brought out when he asked "Guess my age"? Sizing him up and down, looking at his teeth, eyes, wrinkles, hair and hands I calmly said 27. With a satisfactory smile, he with I thought so attitude, gave the modest reply "I'm only 36." and have been married 14 years." His job is to handle the Master upper turret guns and to help the Bombardier load the bombs in their correct position in the bomb-bay. Since he has been married so long and with several children to his credit, I'm almost more than certain we shall be well guarded from that upper turret position. Lloyd always is in charge of the sandwiches and hot coffee and never fails to crawl up in the nose to see that I get my share. He puts his head over my shoulder and

354

how to find his position by radio, and he letting me in on the fundamentals of radio.

Our left guard is a tall[,] lean[,] lanky man from [t]he [t]ri-[s]tate [a]rea. From West Virginia and the City of Wheeling is Elmer Lloyd.[159] A man who takes great pride in his youthfulness is readily brought out when he asked[,] "Guess my age[?"] Sizing him up and down, looking at his teeth, eyes, wrinkles, hair[,] and hands[,] I calmly said 27. With a satisfactory smile, he[,] with [an] I[-]thought[-]so attitude, gave the modest reply[,] "I'm only 36 and have been married 14 years." His job is to handle the Martin upper[-]turret guns and to help the [b]ombardier load the bombs in their correct position in the bomb-bay [*sic*]. Since he has been married so long and with several children to his credit, I'm almost more than certain we shall be well guarded from that upper[-]turret position. Lloyd always is in charge of the sandwiches and hot coffee and never fails to crawl up in the nose to see that I get my share. He pokes his head over my shoulder[,]

---

[159] The name of Elmer J. Lloyd appears on the roster for the 764th Squadron of the 461st Bombardment Group (H) as a gunner for the crew of Alcibiades Skalomenos. "764th Roster."

4

when he sees I know what I'm doing
and where we are to the nearest mile, he
leaves with an air of satisfaction and
there is no need to tell by words that
he has been impressed by the Navigators Worth.

Our left tackle and only tackle since
ours is but a ten man team is P.F.C. Jeremiah
Crowley
from Manhatten New York. It is a pleasure
to watch him tackle my old buddy, the
lower Sperry Ball turret. Round and round
that turret twists and rolls and within
a few seconds out climbs Crowley. He is
much like the nose gunner in build
and features. Another lad just out of
highschool to take his place among the
others to fight for the things he has
never had a chance to enjoy ~~under his~~
~~first admission~~ but with the aspiration
that he may have them later in life.
A happy go lucky G.I. Joe who mixes
fun with work and is a dare devil
who fears nothing. He will follow
those who show him but not those
who will only tell him. He has plenty

and [4*] when he sees I know what I'm doing and where we are to the nearest mile, he leaves with an air of satisfaction[,] and there is no need to tell by words that he has been impressed by the [n]avigator[']s [w]orth.

Our left tackle and only tackle[,] since ours is but a ten[-]man team[,] is P.F.C. Jeremiah Crowley from Manhatten [*sic*], New York.[160] It is a pleasure to watch him tackle my old buddy, the lower Sperry [b]all turret. Round and round that turret twists and rolls[,] and within a few seconds[,] out climbs Crowley. He is much like the nose gunner in build and features. Another lad just out of highschool [*sic*] to take his place among the others to fight for the things he has never had a chance to enjoy but with the aspiration that he may have them later in life. A happy[-]go[-] lucky G.I. Joe who mixes fun with work and is a dare devil [*sic*] who fears nothing. He will follow those who show him but not those who will only tell him. He has plenty [4R*] of respect for

---

[160] The name of Jeremiah C. Crowley appears on the roster for the 764th Squadron of the 461st Bombardment Group (H) as a gunner for the crew of Alcibiades Skalomenos. "764th Roster."

of respect for we flying Officers but is in
constant trouble with his ground Officials for
neglect or lack of Military Discipline yet he
does the work of two men in our preparations
for flight and like our Tail Gunner is a
top notch shot. Between the two of them, they
have Promised to teach me a few tricks at
the guns any time I so desire it. I told
them I would take advantage of that offer
and they would regret having made it. But I
know quite different that they would break their
necks to teach me all they know and more, so
long as they know some one on the plane realizes
they are there and are of importance to the
rest of us, We will have, I am sure, the
best Crew ever. I hope I haven't bored
you to death with my analysis of the
team which I think is a winning combination
no matter what. With the necessary practice
from fundamental to Complicated plays and
passes, ours is a team that should be
right there among the Champions!

What I wouldn't have given to be
there with you at the Silver Ball to see
Sylvia once more as I first saw her almost
two years ago. There in that evening dress
beaming with fresh loveliness, I guess I
really didn't have much of a chance

358

we [*sic*] flying [o]fficers but is in constant trouble with his ground [o]fficials for neglect or lack of [m]ilitary [d]iscipline[,] yet he does the work of two men in our preparation for flight and[,] like our [t]ail [g]unner[,] is a top notch [*sic*] shot. Between the two of them, they have promised to teach me a few tricks at the guns any time I so desire it. I told them I would take advantage of that offer[,] and they would regret having made it. But I know quite different[ly] that they would break their necks to teach me all they know and more, as long as they know some one [*sic*] on the plane realizes they are there and are of importance to the rest of us. We will have, I am sure, the best crew ever. I hope I haven't bored you to death with my analysis of the team[,] which I think is a winning combination no matter what. With the necessary practice from fundamental to complicated plays and passes, ours is a team that should be right there among the champions.

What I wouldn't have given to be there with you at the Silver Ball to see Sylvia once more as I first saw her almost two years ago.[161] There in that evening dress[,] beaming with fresh

---

[161] See *supra* note 98.

5.

that night or any other night since. My
total resistance collapsed completely as you
know quite well these past two years. Still
Can't help laughing at my silly dancing first
5 paces apart and yet closer as the evening wore
on. White Christmas will live forever in my
mind with a particular meaning as I shall
always remember that night over night but
two years ago. So long, yet the details are
never lacking in my memory. How could
I forget, the the great dance that was the
object that brought our personalities together?
How could I forget the smallest trivial happening
when yours truly saw the light and was
blinded all that Charm? I must thank you
for the dance ---- perhaps I never did but you
can be sure I was glad that I received that
call one month ahead of time. Will be
looking forward to that snapshot of you in
your new exquisite dress. I'm sure you
will make the dress look lovely instead
of the and give it plenty of radiance as
it drapes the 'shape'.

Well its finally about time I close
this letter with all my ambiguous patter
and within the next couple of hours be
aloft from 8 to 10 hours with freezing temperatures and mouth stuffed shut with an

360

lovliness [*sic*], I guess I really didn't have much of a chance [5*] that night or any other night since. My total resistance collapsed completely as you know quite well these past two years. Still can't help laughing at my silly dancing[,] first 5 paces apart and yet closer as the evening wore on. ["]White Christmas["] will live forever in my mind with a particular meaning[,] as I shall always remember that night[,] our night[,] but two years ago. So long ago, yet the details are never lacking in my memory. How could I forget, the great dance that was the object that brought our personalities together? How could I forget the smallest trivial happening when yours truly saw the light and was blinded by all that charm? I must thank you for the dance – – – – perhaps I never did[,] but you can be sure I was glad that I received that call one month ahead of time. Will be looking forward to that snapshot of you in your new exquisite dress. I'm sure you will make the dress look lovely and give it plenty of radiance as it drapes the ["]shape[."]

oxygen mask. Send

Love & Kisses

"Tony"

Well[,] it[']s finally about time I close this letter with all my ambiguous [*sic*] patter[,] and within the next couple of hours[, I'll] be aloft from 8 to 10 hours with freezing temper-atures and [a] mouth stuffed shut with an [5*] oxygen mask. Send

Love + Kisses[,]

"Tony"

Free

PUEBLO
NOV 16
3 PM
1944
COLO.

Miss Sylvia M. Jacobs
2334 Athena St.
N.S. Pittsburgh 12, Pa

T-136514
21st OCS. 1-26 Box 3323
P.A.A.B. Pueblo, Col.

364

Nov, 19, 1944

Dearest Sylvia:

'Tis early Sunday morning and the atmosphere is dull. Low hanging clouds cling to the mountain side, while another layer of this stratus prevents the penetrating, piercing rays of the Colorado sun on the east side, to liven up this rather cold wintry morning. It certainly is a shame that I could not be in these parts "When its spring time in the Rockies." All is rather quiet too, since perhaps the tired and weary lads exhausted themselves considerably at the dance held here in the Officers club for them yesterday. Even as I am writing in this comfortable Writing Room, the Orderlies are still cleaning up the mess from last nights 'frolics'. There is need to tell you how much I wished that the two of us were together to have found that "hilarity" last night. However, since I had no lady friend acquaintance in these parts, I took up the gentle art of roller skating at the town of Pueblo. The name of the place -- "Skatemore". After last night,

366

November 19, 1944

From: F./O. A.S. Mazza T-136514
215 C.C.S. 1-26 Box 3323
P.A.A.B. Pueblo, Colorado

To: Miss Sylvia M. Jacobs
2334 Atmore St.
N.S. Pittsburgh 12, Pa.

Postmark: 6:30 PM
November 19, 1944
Pueblo, Colorado

Letterhead: Officers Mess Club[162]
Army Air Base
Pueblo, Colorado

[1*]   Nov. 19, 1944

Dearest Sylvia:

'Tis early Sunday morning[,] and the atmosphere is dull. Low[-]hanging clouds cling to the mountain side [*sic*], while another layer of thin stratus prevents the penetrating, piercing rays of the Colorado sun on the east side, to liven up this rather cold[,] wintry morning. It certainly is a shame that I could not be in these parts

---

[162] The word "Mess" appears stricken out in ink, replaced with the handwritten word "Club."

I can only grimly smile and think "I wonder??"
Skating has been one sport, almost like
tennis, that the both of us have never indulged.
It probably was my fault that we didn't
and perhaps I wasn't insistant enough.
Anyway, there I was last night going
round, round, and round. At one particular
time, the ground came up and spanked me
in my 'nether' region, but I didn't mind
that so much as I did the fact that an
Officer loses much dignity in the prone
position. I am quite sure had I continued
longer the floor would be much cleaner
at the "Skatarena", while my trousers would
perhaps be a bit thinner too. I still insist
though that Ice Skating is my sport and
will give it a fling my first visit to Colorado
Springs. Come to think of it, I bowl about
as well as I roller skate, so your 71 perhaps
would put me to shame at tennis. My
average is around 75, so it wouldn't take much
practice or effort on your part to top that.
We have a bowling alley for Officers but
two doors down from my barracks and
as yet I have not even gone inside to
see what the place looks like. I'll
make a special effort to get there at
least once before this next week is over.

368

"When it[']s Spring time [*sic*] in the Rockies."[163] All is rather quiet[,] too, since perhaps the tired and weary lads exhausted themselves considerably at the dance held here in the Officers Club for them yesterday. Even as I am writing in this [c]omfortable [w]riting [r]oom, the [o]rderlies are still cleaning up the mess from last night[']s ["]fracus [*sic*][."] There is need to tell you how much I wished that the two of us were together to have joined that "hilarity" last night. However, since I had no lady friend acquaintance in these parts, I took up the gentle art of roller skating at the town of Pueblo. The name of the place - - - "Skatemore[.]" After last night, [1R*] I can only grimly smile and think[,] "I wonder??" Skating is one sport, almost like tennis, that the both of us have never indulged. I[t] probably was my fault that we didn't[,] and perhaps I wasn't insistant [*sic*] enough. Anyway, there I was last night[,] going round, round, and round. At one particular time, the ground came up and spanked me in my 'nether' region, but I didn't mind that so much as I did the fact that an

---

[163] The reference is to a popular song "When It's Springtime in the Rockies," written in 1929 by Robert Sauer and Mary Hale Woolsey. "When It's Springtime in the Rockies," Second Hand Songs, accessed June 20, 2020, https://secondhandsongs.com/work/138137/all. Two films, one released in 1937 and the other in 1942, featured the song. The 1937 film was a Western, starring Gene Autry, who also released a recording of the song. *Springtime in the Rockies*, directed by Joseph Kane, featuring Gene Autry and Smiley Burnette (Republic Pictures, 1937); Gene Autry, volcalist, "When It's Springtime in the Rockies," by Robert Sauer and Mary Hale Woolsey, recorded October 18, 1937, Vocalion, Perfect Record No. 8-03-51. The 1942 film was a musical comedy. *Springtime in the Rockies*, directed by Irving Cummings, featuring Betty Grable, John Payne, Carmen Miranda, and Cesar Romero (20th Century Fox, 1942).

Gosh! Here I go again with a change of
ink. My pen seems to run out at the most
embarrassing moments, but these two toned
affairs should at least provide variety and
perhaps too, a change of pace.

I was delighted to hear that you enjoyed
Alice Faye's picture, but I wouldn't worry too
much, if I were you, about that keen competition.
One of these days when I get up enough
courage to face the situation (camera), I may
have a photo portrait of myself made. If
you are insistent enough, I may let you have
one, but only if you are insistent. Got to
give you a taste of your own medicine now.
Hmm! wouldn't I look sweet up in your
room with all those women! What is your
opinion on the pose I should strike? Would
you care for a plain ordinary smile, a poker
face, a laugh, a frown, the peeved silent job,
the thinker, or the 11:45 PM approach?

Glad to find out that I was the first to
attach the title RN to my gal. Hope to keep
adding many "firsts" to S.M.I. in the future
too. I still insist that writing is not a
"knack" particularly if the source of the material
comes from within. There are many people
to whom I could barely fill the side of

370

[o]fficer loses much dignity in the prone position. I am quite sure[,] had I continued longer[,] the floor would be much cleaner at the "Skatemore," while my trousers would perhaps be a bit thinner[,] too. I still insist[,] though[,] that [i]ce [s]kating is my sport and will give it a fling my first visit to Colorado Springs. Come to think of it, I bowl about as well as I roller skate, so your 71 perhaps would put me to shame at times. My average is around 75, so it wouldn't take much practice or effort on your part to top that. We have a bowling alley for [o]fficers but two doors down from my barracks[,] and as yet[,] I have not even gone inside to see what the place looks like. I'll make a special effort to get there at least once before this next week is over. [2*] Gosh! Here I go again with a change of ink. My pen seems to runout [*sic*] at the most embarrassing moments, but these two[-]toned affairs should at least provide variety and perhaps[,] too[,] a change of pace.

I was delighted to hear that you enjoyed Alice Faye's picture, but I wouldn't worry too much, if I were you, about that keen competition. One of these days[,] when I get up enough courage to face the situation (camera), I may have a photo portrait of myself made. If you are insistant [*sic*] enough, I may let you have one, but only if you are insistant [*sic*]. Got to give you a taste of your own medicine now. Hmm! [W]ouldn't I look sweet up in your room with all those women![164] What is your opinion on the pose I should strike? Would you care for a plain[,] ordinary smile[;] a poker face[;] a laugh[;] a frown[;] the peeved[,] silent job[;] the thinker[;] or the 11:45 PM approach?

---

[164] At the time, Sylvia Jacobs was living at home with her parents and her single sisters, Gertrude, Irene, Elizabeth, and Lois.

one sheet of paper. Yet I could continue on and on while writing to you. See how you rate!

Thanksgiving day this week will find me high above the clouds. Instead of eating the bird, I'll be a destructive part of one. A little tough perhaps with all its heavy construction, but a dependable one at that. Tomo As long as Sylvie will be thinking of me that day, why she can celebrate for the both of us.

I still can never forget St. Vincent's dance one year ago. It really seems a century since that great event 12 months back. You remember that night? How well I remember it too but particularly the month that followed. I still have plenty to learn!

This afternoon My crew & I are slated to fly from 1:15 PM until 11:00 PM tonight. Quite a bit to do in that long stretch so I had better go back and prepare a few briefing notes. I shall close now with a Cheerio. Good-Day.

Love
Tony

372

Glad to find out that I was the first to attach the little RN to my gal. Hope to keep adding many "firsts" to S.M.J. in the future[,] too. I still insist that writing is not a "knack[,]" particularly if the source of the material comes from within. There are many people to whom I could barely fill the side of [2R*] one sheet of paper. Yet[,] I could continue on and on while writing to you. See how you rate!

Thanksgiving [D]ay this week will find me high above the clouds. Instead of eating the bird, I'll be a distinctive part of one. A little tough[,] perhaps[,] with all its heavy construction, but a dependable one at that. As long as Sylvie will be thinking of me that day, why she can celebrate for the both of us.

I still can never forget [the] St. Vincent dance one year ago.[165] It really seems a century since that great event 12 months back. You remember that night? How well I remember it[,] too[,] but particularly the month that followed. I still have plenty to learn.

This afternoon[,] my crew + I are slated to fly from 1:15 PM until 11:00 PM tonight. Quite a bit to do in that long stretch[,] so I had better go pack and prepare a few briefing notes. I shall close now with a cheerie [sic] [g]ood-[d]ay.

Love[,]
Tony

---

[165] See *supra* page 87 (Invitation from Anthony S. Mazza to Sylvia M. Jacobs (November 10, 1943)).

Free

PUEBLO
NOV 19
6:30 PM
1944
COLO.

Miss Sylvia Jacobs
2334 Atmore St.
N.S. Pittsburgh 12, Pa.

F/o. A.d. Mayer T-136514
215 C.C.S. 1-26 Box 3323
P.A.A.B. Pueblo, Colorado.

374

Nov 29, 1944

Dearest Sylvia:

It seems that I'm the one
that is getting about quite a bit in the
past few days. I'm certainly seeing
plenty of this world of ours right here in
the United States and for my part wouldn't
care to go any further. First of all, I
can say that thanksgiving day brought
back many happy memories of my past
home life. The meal here was excellant
and Turkey was had with all the trimmings,
However It didn't take me very long to
realize that it is not the meal that makes
Thanksgiving such a wonderful cherished
holiday. My thoughts were certainly of
you and of that other great woman in
my life, Mother. It couldn't have
been such a wonderful day at home
although there still was much to be
thankful for. Those 3 empty seats at
the dining table told a far different
story than they did several years ago
and I'm positive their emptiness was
not overlooked.

November 29, 1944 (Letter and Postcard)

From: F./O. A.S. Mazza T-136514
215 C.C.S. 1-26 Box 3323
P.A.A.B. Pueblo, Col.

To: Miss Sylvia M. Jacobs
2334 Atmore St[.]
Pittsburgh 12, Pa.

Letter Postmark:
1:00 PM
November 29, 1944
Pueblo, Colorado

Letterhead: Officers Mess
Army Air Base
Pueblo, Colorado

[1*]   Nov[.] 29, 1944

Dearest Sylvia:

It seems that I'm the one that is getting about quite a bit in the past few days. I'm certainly seeing plenty of this world of ours right here in the United States[,] and for my part[, I] wouldn't care to go any further. First of all, I can say that Thanksgiving [D]ay brought back many happy memories of my past home life. The meal here was excellent[,] and [t]urkey was had with all the

377

2.

About my travels the past couple days, I could perhaps fill a volume of print but I must say it was an eventful journey I shall never forget.

On Sunday, a trio of us went to Colorado Springs with the hope of climbing Pikes Peak. We were all set for that but postponed it to a later date because of the intense cold and heavy snow fall at the mountain top. In the course of the day we visited, "Garden of Gods", "Mountain Springs", Cave of Winds, Rampart Range Road, Cripple Creek Drive, Seven Falls, Will Rogers Memorial, Cheyenne Mountain, Helen Hunt Jackson's grave (author of "Ramona"), Broadmore Hotel, lake, and stadium, Antlers Hotel and even the zoo.

So delightful was this trip that no doubt in the course of later life when should ever the decision arrive to take a summer vacation at the mountains or sea shore my argument will be for the mountains every time.

I still can't get over Mr. Susuda's

378

trimmings[; h]owever[,] it didn't take me very long to realize that it is not the meal that makes Thanksgiving such a wonderful[,] cherished holiday. My thoughts were certainly of you and of that other great woman in my life, Mother. It couldn't have been such a wonderful day at home[,] although there was much to be thankful for. Those three empty seats at the dining table told a far different story than they did several years ago[,] and I'm positive their emptiness was not overlooked.[166]

[2*] About my travels the past couple of days, I could perhaps fill a volume of print[,] but I must say it was an eventful journey I shall never forget.

On Sunday[,] a trio of us went to Colorado Springs with the hope of climbing Pikes Peak. We were all set for that but postponed it to a later date because of the intense cold and heavy snow fall [sic] at the mountain top [sic]. In the course of the day[,] we visited[] "Garden of the Gods[;]" "Manitou Springs[;]" Cave of Winds[;] Rampart Range Road[;] Cripple Creek Drive[;] Seven [F]alls[;] Will Rogers Memorial[;] Cheyenne Mountain[;] Helen Hunt Jackson's grave (author of "Ramona")[;] Broadmore [sic] Hotel, lake[,] and stadium[;] Antlers Hotel[;] and even the zoo.

So delightful was this trip that no doubt in the course of later life when should ever the decision arrive to take a summer vacation at the mountains or Sea shore [sic][,] my argument will be for the mountains every time.

---

[166] In addition to Anthony Mazza, his brothers Greg and Joe were away from home, enlisted in the war effort at the time. See *infra* page 383 (Photograph of Brothers Gregory, Joseph, and Anthony Mazza).

3

sudden
death. The last time I saw him was that night he drove us as far as Marshall ave. Remember! that night I was sent home earlier than usual!! I did send Edna a note of sympathy which was all I could do from way out here in Colorado. They certainly have had about the toughest break possible and all so sudden.

You had better look at that picture in the Post Gazette twice for I can't ever remember posing for one to give newspapers. It must be a horrible picture at that, if it happens to be the one I think it is. I am only concerned if the fan mail is from one certain girl. Not much more to add except

Love
Tony

380

I still can't get over Mr. Surenda's [3*] sudden death. The last time I saw him was that night he drove us as far as Marshall Ave.[167] Remember! [T]hat night I was sent home earlier than usual!! I did send Edna a note of sympathy[,] which was all I could do from way out here in Colorado. They certainly have had about the toughest break possible[,] and all so sudden.

You had better look at that picture in the *Post Gazette*[168] twice[,] for I can't ever remember posing for one to give newspapers.[169] It must be a horrible picture at that, if it happens to be the one I think it is. I am only concerned if the fan mail is from one certain girl. Not much more to add except

Love[,]

Tony

Postcard Postmark:[170]

    9:30 AM

    November 29, 1944

    Pueblo, Colorado

Postcard: The postcard is an accordion foldout of color prints of "Scenic Colorado Springs," published by Sanborn

---

[167] Marshall Avenue is a main thoroughfare on the North Side of Pittsburgh.

[168] Italics added.

[169] A photograph of Anthony Mazza in uniform appeared in the *Pittsburgh Post-Gazette* with the following description: "Flight Officer Anthony Samuel Mazza, 23, of 817 Woods Run [A]venue, recently completed his training as an [A]rmy [A]ir [F]orces navigator at San Marcos, Tex. He is ready for transitional training." "With Our Fighting Forces," *Pittsburgh Post-Gazette*, November 21, 1944.

[170] The postmark is a mirror image.

F/O. A. L. Moyer T-136574
215 C.C.S. 126 BK 3323
P.A.A.B.
Pueblo, Col.

PUEBLO COLO
1 PM
NOV 29
1944

Miss Sylvia Jacobs
2334 Atmore St
Pittsburgh 12, Pa.

382

Brothers Gregory, Joseph, and Anthony Mazza
(date unknown)

Souvenir Company of Denver, Colorado. The prints contain handwritten comments and line drawings. In the picture depicting the summit at Pikes Peak are four handwritten drawings in pencil. From left to right, the first is a man climbing to the top of the mountain; the second is a rough stick figure; the third is a three-dimensional box; and the fourth appears to be a rough sketch of a horse or mule. In the picture of the Helen Hunt Falls in North Cheyenne Cañon, a handwritten ink arrow points to a bridge over the falls with the words "Made a wish over here." In the picture of Pikes Peak from Monument Valley Park, there is handwriting and three arrows; one points to a miniscule stick figure

on the top of the mountain, "me," and another arrow points to a similar figure beside it, "you." The third arrow, pointing to a ridge in the background, has the inscription "Rampart Range Road." In the picture of Colorado Springs, the handwritten addition is "Drove through Colorado Springs." The picture of Cheyenne Lodge has the notation "Didn't get this far." The picture of the Will Rogers Shrine, which is a stone tower, an arrow points to the top with the notation "[C]limbed up to this point." In the picture of the Broadmoor Hotel, an arrow points to the hotel, noting "Dined Here." On the picture of St. Peter's Dome is the inscription "Nature[']s Citadel." On the picture of the Dutch Wedding Rock, which depicts two natural stone pillars, one arrow points to the left pillar with the writing "Guess!" Another arrow points to the right pillar with the writing "Guess again!" The picture of the Antlers Hotel has an arrow pointing to the hotel with the words "Dined here." In the picture of the entrance to the Cave of the Winds is the inscription "Will go here next time." In the picture of Balance and Steamboat Rocks, the following writing appears in the center: "Helped balance Balance Rock." A small ink stick figure with arms raised appears to be holding up Balance Rock. In parenthesis, next to the figure, are the words "Hercules Mazza." The picture of Seven Falls shows hundreds of steps leading from the base of the falls to its top; an arrow points to the top of the stairs with the words "Walked! I'm tired!" The inside flap of the postcard has the printed words "From," completed by the handwritten words "Tony who still wished we were here 'together.'"

FROM *Tony who still wished we were here together!*

N

Municipal Auditorium

Modern Woodmen of America Sanatorium, near Colorado Springs

FROM *Tony who still wished we were here together.*

Union Printers' Home

Made a wish out here.

Helen Hunt Falls, North Cheyenne Cañon

387

SCENIC COLORADO SPRINGS, COLORADO

Pikes Peak from Monument Valley Park

Pikes Peak (Alt. 14,109 Ft.) from Pikes Peak Avenue, Colorado Springs, (Alt. 6,072 Ft.)

FROM *Tony who still wished we were here together!*

SCENIC COLORADO SPRINGS, COLORADO

Didn't get this far.

Cheyenne Lodge—Summit of Cheyenne Mountain, Broadmoor-Cheyenne Mountain Highway

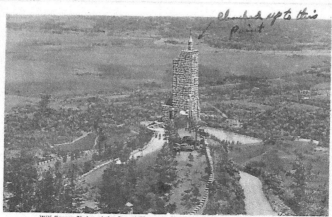

climbed up to this point

Will Rogers Shrine of the Sun of Cheyenne Mountain, Broadmoor-Cheyenne Highway

SCENIC COLORADO SPRINGS, COLORADO

DINED HERE

The Broadmoor Hotel Mirrored in the Lake

COLORADO SPRINGS is Colorado's most celebrated Tourist Resort. Many famous drives and attractions are centered about it. Among them the Seven Falls and South Cheyenne Cañon, the Garden of the Gods, the Pikes Peak Auto Highway, the Pikes Peak Cog Road, the Cave of the Winds, the Corley Mountain Highway, the Big Circle Trip thru the Cripple Creek Mining District and Phantom Cañon to Cañon City and the Royal Gorge and return, and the Broadmoor-Cheyenne Mountain Highway. It is also the center for a great many Sanatoriums and Health Resorts, notable among which are the Union Printers Home and the Modern Woodmen of America Sanatorium. A striking feature of the city is the splendid wide streets, many such as Pikes Peak Avenue being nearly double the usual width. Pikes Peak, perhaps the best known mountain of America, rears itself to an altitude of 14,109 feet directly west of Colorado Springs and its snow capped top is a guiding beacon over the plains to the East for over a hundred miles.

390

Scenic Colorado Springs

St. Peter's Dome, Gold Camp Highway

391

Dutch Wedding Rock, near Woodmen Sanatorium

The Antlers Hotel

Entrance to the Cave of the Winds, Manitou Springs

Streamline Cog Train at the Famous Old Summit House, Summit of Pikes Peak

Hidden Inn, Garden of the Gods

Pikes Peak, Alt. 14,110 Ft. from Platte Ave.

Balanced and Steamboat Rocks, Garden of the Gods

Seven Falls—Cheyenne Cañon

Dec 16, 1944

Dearest Sylvia:

In one of your letters,
just after I mailed that last one,
you stated quote " Probably by
now you are lucky you have
any morale left with the letters
I write. unquote That sentence
there is the key to what prompted
my last rather nasty letter.
Yep, believe it or not my morale
needs pepped up once in a while
too and your the only girl who
can do just that. I may have
exaggerated or over-rated some things
in that letter but I'm sure the
main and rather essential points
were not missed. Those thoughts
were foremost in my mind for
a while. I could have taken
the easy way out and forget
to mention anything to you but
that has never been or ever

December 16, 1944

From: F./O. A.S. Mazza T-136514
                 215 CCS 1-26 Box 3323
                 P.A.A.B. Pueblo, Colo.

To: Miss Sylvia M. Jacobs
                 2334 Atmore St.
                 Pittsburgh 12, Pa.

Postmark: 4:30 PM
                 December 16, 1944
                 Pueblo, Colorado
                 Air Mail

Letterhead: Air Mail

[1*]   Dec[.] 16, 1944

Dearest Sylvia:

In one of your letters, just after I mailed that last one, you stated[,] quote[,] "Probably by now you are lucky you have any morale left with the letters I write[,"] unquote[.] That sentence there is the key to what prompted my last rather nasty letter. Yep, believe it or not[,] my morale needs pepped up once in a while[,] too[,] and your [*sic*] the only girl who can do just that. I may have exaggerated or over-rated [*sic*] some things in that letter[,] but

will be my method
of doing things. I have found by
bitter experiences in the past to always
face foremost the ugly things first.
Hmm! from the results, 3 letters in
2 days, I'll have to dig up another
letter of that sort. Seriously though,
I did want to know how my girl
would stand up under fire and gosh!
she's a real trooper if there ever
was one. However, don't pat yourself
on the back too hard yet. You may
be under fire quite a few more times
before the Campaign is over. and even
after that.

Now, I don't want you to get
the impression that I want you to believe
as other girls do. Far be it from
that. You are different in so many
respects from them and in so many
ways for it is that reason that I
have become so attached to you.
I do, however, like to have you
express yourself now and then

I'm sure the main and rather essential points were not missed. Those thoughts were foremost in my mind for a while. I could have taken the easy way out and forget [*sic*] to mention anything to you[,] but that has never been [n]or ever [2*] will be my method of doing things. I have found by better experiences in the past to always face foremost the ugly things first. Hmm! [F]rom the results, 3 letters in 2 days, I'll have to dig up another letter of that sort. Seriously[,] though[,] I did want to know how my girl would stand up under fire and gosh! she's a real trooper[,] if there ever was one. However, don't pat yourself on the back too hard yet. You may be under fire quite a few more times before the [c]ampaign is over and even after that.

Now[,] I don't want you to get the impression that I want you to behave as other girls do. Far be it from that. You are different in so many respects from them and in so many ways[,] for it is the reason that I have become so attached to you. I do, however, like for it has the same effect on me perhaps as that ~~was~~ one word "assume" had on you not so very long ago.

I don't want you to go out of your way to write to me every day but I do want to hear from you at least every two or three days. Writing is the only means of contact we have. It is only through writing and by lack of writing that people so far apart by distance as we ~~are~~, can know and realize that the person on the other side feels the same or differently about them. All this I assumed you realized but then again I just must get away from assuming.

As for your sticking to your basic principles, ~~I want you to know~~ ~~that~~ that I am not only proud of you but admire you all the more for it.

to have you express yourself now and then[,] [3*] for it has the same effect on me perhaps as that one word "assume" had on you not so very long ago.

I don't want you to go out of your way to write to me every day[,] but I do want to hear from you at least every two or three days. Writing is the only means of contact we have. It is only through writing and by lack of writing that people so far apart by distance[,] as we [are,] can know and realize that the person on the other side feels the same or differently about them. All this I assumed you realized[,] but then again[,] I just must get away from assuming.

As for you sticking to your basic principles, I want you to know that I am not only proud of you but admire you all the more for it.

Gee! your right. December must be our out month. I'll have to remember that and get set for December next year. Just as Advent must preceed Christmas and Lent preceed Easter, our little difficulties just seem to come prior to the noted Holidays. It just can't be helped I guess but it is only them we have trouble straightning out the wing that has dipped a little in the wrong direction. I haven't much time to write all I can about the things I have been doing the past couple of weeks and yet get this letter out today. I'm sorry I didn't write immediately following that letter but I foolishly decided that I would have to hear your response first. There is much truth in that beautiful ballad "you always hurt the one you love."

[*4] Gee! [Y]our [*sic*] right. December must be our month. I'll have to remember that and get set for [D]ecember next year. Just as Advent must preceed [*sic*] Christmas[,] and Lent preceed [*sic*] Easter, our little difficulties just seem to come prior to the noted [h]olidays. It just can't be helped[,] I guess[,] but it is only then we have trouble straightening out the wing that has dipped a little in the wrong direction. I haven't much time to write all I can about the things I have been doing the past couple of weeks and yet get this letter out today. I'm sorry I didn't write immediately following that letter[,] but I foolishly decided that I would have to hear your response first. There is much truth in that beautiful ballad "You [A]lways [H]urt the [O]ne [Y]ou [L]ove."[171]

---

[171] The Mills Brothers, vocalists, "You Always Hurt the One You Love," by Allan Roberts and Doris Fisher, released June 3, 1944, Decca, No. 18599A.

Air Mail

5.

I hope I can cut that part to
a very bare minimum and close
now with those three noted words

I love you" - Sylvia
more "As time goes by".

Love
Tony

404

[5*] I hope I can cut that part to a very bare minimum and close now with those three noted words[,] "I love you"—Sylvia[,] more "As [T]ime [G]oes [B]y."[172]

Love[,]
'Tony'

---

[172] The song "As Time Goes By," written in 1931 by Herman Hupfield, became popular through the performance of Dooley Wilson in the 1942 film *Casablanca*. *Casablanca*, directed by Michael Curtiz, featuring Humphrey Bogart, Ingrid Bergman, Paul Henreid, and Claude Rains (Warner Bros. Pictures, 1942). The original recording by Rudy Vallée was rereleased with the screening of *Casablanca* and became a hit in 1943. Rudy Vallée and His Connecticut Yankees, "As Time Goes By," by Herman Hupfield, rereleased April 4, 1943, Victor, No. 20-1526-A; Whitburn, 136; "Top 80 Pop Songs in 1943," playback.fm, accessed June 20, 2020, https://playback.fm/year/1943.

AIR MAIL
UNITED STATES OF AMERICA
AIR 8 MAIL

Airmail

PUEBLO COLO.
DEC 16
4 36 PM
1944

F/o. U.S. Mazza T-136514
WS Ce5 1-26 Box 3323
P.A.A.B. Pueblo, Colo.

Miss Sylvia Jacobs
2334 Atmore St.
Pittsburgh 12, Pa.

Dec 17, 1944

Dearest Sylvia:

Wow! 4 letters now in the short span of 3 days. All of them master-pieces too. I've got them all laid out in front of me now and re-read the high-lights of each one just as eagerly as I did when I first got them. This first one is a honey; particularly where Sylvia Mary Grace Jacobs explodes. You've had the opportunity to see and observe my reactions but I haven't had that chance to see exactly how you reaction such an occasion. I hope though that I won't get many opportunities to view Sylvia's temper. I'll bet it is very well controlled, however.

I am certainly glad that you are thinking of our future. That is something worthy of note even though the future, due to present

December 17, 1944

Postmark: [The envelope is missing.]

Letterhead: Air Mail

[1*]   Dec[.] 17, 1944

Dearest Sylvia:

Wow! [Four] letters now in the short span of 3 days. All of them master-pieces [*sic*][,] too. I've got them all laid out in front of me now and re-read [*sic*] the high-lights [*sic*] of each one just as eagerly as I did when I first got them. This first one is a honey, particularly when Sylvia Mary Grace Jacobs <u>explodes</u>. You've had the opportunity to see and observe my reactions[,] but I haven't had the chance to see exactly how you react on such an occasion. I hope[,] though[,] that I won't get many opportunities to view Sylvia's temper; I'll bet it is very well controlled, however.

I am certainly glad that you are thinking of our future. That is something worthy of note[,] even though the future, due to political conditions, is still a bit hazy. It is good to know that you are "Hard to get", of that I am quite certain. Meantime I do want to assure you that in all my time in the services I have yet to pick up a "Pick. up". I have had a couple of dates, but that was necessary to put me on an even social keel with the rest of my companions; nothing more. The dates were made through formal introductions by some Officer or friend and there ~~has been~~ has never been a time that I took the same person out twice.

I'll bet you would have never guessed what play I saw the other night. There was something definitely missing this time in fact the main character. Guess who? I am enclosing the program and if you compare it with the one we got before. You will note quite a change in cast.

present [2*] political conditions, is still a bit hazy. It is good to know that you are "[h]ard to get[;"] of that I am quite certain. Meantime[,] I do want to assure you that in all my time in the services[,] I have yet to pick up a "[p]ick-up." I have had a couple of dates, but that was necessary to put me on an even social keel with the rest of my companions[,] nothing more. The dates were made through formal introductions by some [o]fficer or friend[,] and there has never been a time that I took the same person out twice.

I'll bet you would have never guessed what play I saw the other night. There was something definitely missing this time[,] in fact the main character. Guess who? I am enclosing the program[,] and if you compare it with the one we got before[,] you will note quite a change in cast.

3

The ballet queen So So this time was a long tall slender girl who reminded me of Olive Oil in the Popeye Comic. She did "toe dances" flat on her feet. She would whirl half way across the stage in two bounds and it was all I could do to keep from laughing every time she appeared in a scene.

A few days before I saw the Merry Widow, I attended a concert given by Anne Brown, noted Negro Soprano singer who rates second only to Marian Anderson. Her singing was superb but the selection of songs did not meet my fancy. I hope to see the "Gypsy Baron" ~~when~~ when it gets to Pueblo Jan 3rd.

Last night I saw the moving picture "Wilson". It had one scene that included this fair town of Pueblo. It was here that Woodrow Wilson collapsed with paralysis during the final months of his term of office as President.

[3*] The ballet queen[,] LoLo[,][173] this time was a long[,] tall[,] slender girl who reminded me of Olive Oil [*sic*] in the Popeye [c]omic[s]. She did "toe dances" flat on her feet. She would whirl halfway across the stage in two bounds[,] and it was all I could do to keep from laughing every time she appeared in a scene.

A few days before I saw [*T*]*he Merry Widow*, I attended a concert given by Anne Brown, noted Negro [s]oprano singer[,] who rates second only to Mirian [*sic*] Anderson.[174] Her singing was superb[,] but the selection of songs did not meet my fancy. I hope to see the "Gypsy Baron" when it gets to Pueblo Jan[.] 3rd.[175]

Last night[,] I saw the moving picture "Wilson[."]][176] It had one scene that included this fair town of Pueblo. It was here that

---

[173] The reference appears to be to LoLo, one of the grisettes (or perhaps, more accurately, the reference is to ZoZo, the principal grisette) in *The Merry Widow*, an operetta by Franz Lehár, which premiered in 1905. "The Merry Widow," The Guide to Musical Theater, accessed June 20, 2020, https://www.guidetomusicaltheatre.com/shows_m/merry_widow.htm. The subsequent reference to the operetta appears in italics.

[174] In 1935, Anne Brown (b. August 9, 1912; d. March 13, 2009) created the role of Bess in George Gershwin's *Porgy and Bess*. "Anne Brown," The Historymakers, accessed June 20, 2020, https://www.thehistorymakers. org/biography/anne-brown-41. Marian Anderson (b. February 27, 1897; d. April 8, 1993) was a well-known African American contralto, who famously sang at the steps of the Lincoln Memorial in Washington, DC, in 1939 after the Daughters of the American Revolution refused to let her perform at Constitution Hall. "Marian Anderson," Biography, January 3, 2020, https://www.biography.com/musician/marian-anderson.

[175] *The Gypsy Baron* is an operetta by Johann Straus II, which premiered in 1885. "The Gipsy Baron" The Guide to Musical Theater, accessed June 20, 2020, http://www.guidetomusicaltheatre.com/shows_g/gipsy_baron.htm.

[176] *Wilson*, directed by Henry King, featuring Charles Coburn, Alexander Knox, and Geraldine Fitzgerald (20th Century Fox, 1944).

4

You should have been with me Christmas Shopping this year. I believe one can hardly get into the spirit of the thing unless he goes from store to store selecting little gifts for those he loves back home. I had quite a time making the selections at odd places on odd occasions but nevertheless got it completed. My major problem turned out to be not the selection of the gifts, but the mailing of them and particularly how to wrap them so they would withstand the rough treatment usually given Christmas packages during the Christmas Rush. I won't keep you too much in suspense but will tell you that you were included in my list. Where I got your gift and why I bought it will be told only after you have received and know what they are. Will also let you know how I settled both Greg and my Christmas obligations when I write the next time.

Woodrow Wilson collapsed with paralysis during the final months of his term of office as [p]resident.

[4*] You should have been with me Christmas shopping this year. I believe one can hardly get into the spirit of the thing unless he goes from store to store selecting little gifts for those he loves back home. I had quite a time making the selections at odd places on odd occasions but nevertheless got it completed. My major problem turned out to be not the selection of the gifts, but the mailing of them and particularly how to wrap them so they would withstand the rough treatment usually given Christmas packages during the Christmas [r]ush. I won't keep you too much in suspense but will tell you that you were included in my list. Where I got your gift and why I bought it will be told only after you have received and know what they are. Will also let you know how I settled both Greg and my Christmas obligations when I write the next time.

Within about twenty minutes
I must attend the Physical Training
Program at the other end of the field.
They are rather nasty about such
minor trifles as "being on time". That
means that I must conclude this
letter sooner than I thought. I'm
~~and~~ sending you love & kisses also
closing with

Love

'Tony'

[5*] Within about twenty minutes[,] I must attend the Physical Training Program at the other end of the field. They are rather nasty about such minor trifles as "being on time." That means that I must conclude this letter sooner than I thought. I'm sending you love + kisses[,] also closing with

Love[,]
'Tony'

Dec 18, 1944

Dearest Sylvia:

It is almost 9:00 AM Monday morning and I have nothing scheduled until 1:15 this afternoon, when we shall undoubtedly fly a cross country flight to either Fort Worth, Kansas City, Lincoln or Minneapolis. I did go to bed rather early last night hence the reason why yours truly is not with the rest of the gang fast asleep in deep slumber at the barracks.

I was just at the Mess Hall a few moments ago and had my usual stand-by- 'Waffles' for breakfast. Seems as though I never get tired of them. The Officers Club is rather quiet this morning, in fact bare save for a Chinese Captain and myself. He has the radio going full blast and believe it or not shows great enthusiasm for our fast jitter bug rythms.

We had some snow last night but merely enough to be seen in patches on the grassy sections of the camp. It is amazing this Colorado climate for there is seldom a day that old 'sol' fails to

418

December 18, 1944

From: F./O. A.S. Mazza T-136514
215 CCS 1-26 Box 3323
P.A.A.B. Pueblo, Colo.

To: Miss Sylvia M. Jacobs
2334 Atmore St.
Pittsburgh 12, Pa.

Postmark: 9:30 PM
December 18, 1944
Pueblo, Colorado

Letterhead: Officers Mess
Army Air Base
Pueblo, Colorado

[1*]   Dec[.] 18, 1944

Dearest Sylvia:

It is almost 9:00 AM Monday morning[,] and I have nothing scheduled until 1:15 this afternoon when we shall undoubtedly fly a cross[-]country flight to either Fort Worth, Kansas City, Lincoln[,] or to Minneapolis. I did go to bed rather early last night[,] hence the reason why yours truly is not with the rest of the gang[,] fast asleep in deep slumber at the barracks.

show up on the horizon. No matter how cold
the temperature, which is incidently always below
freezing in the morning, those radiant rays of
the sun penetrates that cold to make every afternoon
so beautiful and comfortable to behold. No
fog, no smoke, no smog, no filthy ever
annoys or irks man out here. Sometimes
I sort of dread going back to Pittsburgh and the
Civilization of Industrialized mechanisms and
feel I would be more than content to invest
money in a wheat corn, or cattle ranch
out here where the west begins. These
ranchers and farmers have seem to have
an air of security that is always lacking
back home where all economy is based
soley alone on Industry. Where man is
a mere Cog of a Corporation confined to
basic routined life not often of his own choosing.
These men have the democratic air of inde-
pendence of which we have read and
idealized in our early days of schooling and
not the beaten and enslaved attitude most
men have in industrialized cities and
towns. It has been fun for me to

I was just at the [m]ess [h]all a few moments ago and had my usual stand-by [sic]—'[w]affles' for breakfast. Seems as though I never get tired of them. The Officers Club is rather quiet this morning, in fact bare[,] save for a Chinese [c]aptain and myself. He has the radio going full blast[,] and believe it or not[,] shows great enthusiasm for our fast[,] jitter[-]bug rhythms.

We had some snow last night[,] but merely enough to be seen in patches on the grassy sections of the camp. It is amazing this Colorado climate[,] for there is seldom a day that the old 'sol' fails to [2*] show up on the horizon. No matter how cold the temperature, which is incidently [sic] always below freezing in the morning, those radiant rays of the sun penetrates [sic] that cold to make every afternoon so beautiful and comfortable to behold. No fog, no smoke, no smog, no filth ever annoys or irks man out here. Sometimes I sort of dread going back to Pittsburgh and the civilization of [i]ndustrialized mechanisms and feel I would be more than content to invest money in a wheat, corn, or cattle ranch out here where the [W]est begins. These ranchers and farmers seem to have an air of serenity that is always lacking back home[,] where all economy is based solely [] on [i]ndustry, where man is a mere [c]og of a [c]orporation confined to basic[,] routined [sic] life not of his own choosing. These men have the democratic air of inde-pendence of which we have read and idealized in our early days of schooling and not the beaten and enslaved attitude most men have in industrialized cities and towns. It has been fun for me

study and contrast people, trying my best
to put them in specific categories, I may be
wrong in many of my classifications but nevertheless I enjoy it just the same.

Christmas is almost around the corner
and it is quite definite that I shall not get
home. We will be granted perhaps 3 days
but that would be hardly enough time for me
to get to the people I love. I may pick some
huge city or town nearby and spend that time
investigating, comparing, and classifying it
with the many others I have seen this past
year. I received my first Christmas present
yesterday; a box of shaving soap, talc and
after shave lotion sent by my brother Joe.
The box was marked Special Delivery that
is why I opened it ahead of time. Why he
sent it that way I cannot understand but
nevertheless it got here in very good shape.
No, come to think of it, his was not the
first Christmas present I got this year.
The Italian Lodge from Center Ave sent
me an overseas package which traveled to

to [3*] study and contrast people, tr[y]ing my best to put them in specific categories[;] I may be wrong in many of my classifications[;] but nevertheless[,] I enjoy it just the same.

Christmas is almost around the corner[,] and it is quite definite that I shall not get home. We will be granted perhaps 3 days[,] but that would be hardly enough time for me to get to the people I love. I may pick some huge [c]ity or town nearby and spend that time investigating, comparing, and classifying it with the many others I have seen this past year. I received my first Christmas present yesterday[, a] box of shaving soap, talc[,] and after[-]shave lotion sent by my brother Joe. The box was marked Special Delivery[;] that is why I opened it ahead of time. Why he sent it that way I cannot understand[,] but nevertheless[,] it got here in very good shape. No, [c]ome to think of it, his was not the first Christmas present I got this year. The Italian Lodge from Center Ave[.] sent me an overseas package[,] which

4.

San Marcos, Lincoln, and finally to Pueblo.
Never thought they would think of me yet.
The Contents were these: a Readers Digest for
December, 1 lb of peanuts, 1 lb box of butterscotch
Candy, 2 doz of dried figs, 1 lb fruit cake,
1 tube of Pebeco tooth past, 1 tube of Barbasol
shaving Cream, a box of razor blades, and
a deck of Playing Cards and a white linen
handkerchief. Gosh! if they sent a package
like that to all the boys in the neighborhood
they would have made many of them surprised
and happy this Yuletide.

Wonder just what Sylvia is doing
this morning? Lets see – I can see her
now all dressed in her spotless white uniform,
wearing her usual morning smile and fresh,
fresh as a daisy with a after a good
nights rest. There beside her is Sister
- - - - - sleeves all rolled up ready to
do another days work of Comforting, healing
both body and soul of patients who will
be sad victims of some-ones carelessness today.
Between rolls of gauze, bathing of cuts
and bruises, bandages, and the odor
of Iodine, some little R.N. should

traveled to [4*] San Marcos, Lincoln, and finally Pueblo. Never thought they would think of me yet. The contents were these: a *Reader[']s Digest*[177] for December, 1 lb[.] of peanuts, 1[-]lb[.] box of butterscotch candy, 2 doz[.] dried figs, 1 lb[.] fruit cake [*sic*][,] 1 tube of Peb[e]co toothpast[e], 1 tube of Barbasol shaving cream, a box of razor blades, a deck of [p]laying [c]ards[,] and a white linen handkerchief. Gosh! [I]f they sent a package like that to all the boys in the neighborhood[,] they would have made many of them surprised and happy at Yuletide.

Wonder just what Sylvia is doing this morning? Let[']s see—I can see her now[,] all dressed in her spotless[,] white uniform[,] wearing her usual morning smile and fresh, fresh as a daisy[,] after a good night[']s rest. There beside her is Sister - - - - - sleeves all rolled up ready to do another day[']s work of comforting, healing both body and soul of patients who will be sad victims of some-ones [*sic*] carelessness today. Between the rolls of gauze, bathing of cuts and bruises, bandages, and the odor of

---

[177] Italics added.

425

5

have her thoughts directed to that no-account Navigator who helps direct the "Heavies" deep in the heart of Colorado. Probably since she hasn't heard from him again in a period of 4, 5, or 6 days, today she is pouting, disgusted, and mad. She will be tying those bandages a little tighter than usual too. hmm! Will have to get sister to watch her today or some poor victim will suffer. — So long for now with the magic trio

Love

Tom

[i]odine, some little R.N. should [5*] have her thoughts directed to the no-account [n]avigator who helps direct the "Heavies"[178] deep in the heart of Colorado. Probably since she hasn't heard from him again in a period of 4, 5, or 6 days, today she is pouting, disgusted, and mad. She will be tying those bandages a little tighter than usual[,] too. [H]mm! We'll have to get [S]ister to watch her today or some poor victim will suffer.

So long for now

+

with the magic trio[179]

'Love[,]'

Tony

---

[178] The reference is to heavy bombers. For the Army Air Forces during World War II, heavy bombers included the Boeing B-17 Flying Fortress and the Consolidated B-24 Liberator. Simon Parkin, "7 Key Heavy Bomber Aircraft of World War Two," Historyhit, August 8, 2018, https://www.historyhit.com/key-heavy-bomber-aircraft-of-world-war-two/.

[179] The magic trio is "I love you."

Free

PUEBLO COLO.
DEC 18
9:30 PM

F/o. A.S. Morgan T-136614
21.C CCS 1-2c Box 3323
P.A.A.B. Pueblo, Colo.

Miss Sylvia Jacobs
2334 Atmore St.
Pittsburgh 12, Pa

428

Dec 19, 1944

Dearest Sylvia:

Today our work consisted totally of ground school classes. This work included a lecture on Oxygen masks and equipment to combat anoxia at high altitude, navigation for 2 hrs on calibration of several navigatory instruments, 1hr of Aircraft recognition plus an hour of gun camera analysis. After dinner 2 hrs on use of bomb sight followed by 2 more hours of physical training. The Last night our mission was to Fort Worth, Texas and I had little or no trouble finding that once upon a time milk run from San Marcos. I never got back until 2:30 AM this morning yet there was an 8.00 AM class scheduled which couldn't be disregarded. That is the way things are done here. Once a person seldom finds a moment to himself, then there are several days when he can relax completely with little or no work to haunt him. I sort of like it this way though for a person seems to be able to accomplish a lot more than he would otherwise.

I have just returned from our Officers bowling alley and find that I have

430

December 19, 1944

From: F./O. A.S. Mazza T-136514
215 C.C.S. 1-26 Box 3323
P.A.A.B. Pueblo, Colo.

To: Miss Sylvia M. Jacobs
2334 Atmore St.
Pittsburgh 12, Pa.

Postmark: 8:00 PM
December 20, 1944
Pueblo, Colorado

Letterhead: Officers Mess
Army Air Base
Pueblo, Colorado

[1*]   Dec[.] 19, 1944

Dearest Sylvia:

Today our work consisted totally of ground school classes. This work included a lecture on [o]xygen masks and equipment to combat anoxia at high altitude, navigation for 2 hrs[.] on calibration of several navigation instruments, 1 hr[.] of air craft [*sic*] recognition plus an hour of gun[-]camera analysis. After dinner[,] 2 hrs[.] on use of bomb sight[,] followed by 2 more hours of physical training. Last night[,] our mission was to Fort Worth, Texas[,]

2

finally graduate to the 3 digit score group.
Tonights scores were 106, and 149 respectively.
I must send you this pamphlet to show
you that the game can be rather scientific
and that by following some principles shown
there you will will be able to surpass
me by far. You may even get the chance
to surpass some of your friends not saying
what effect your score will have on yourself.
        I went to my mail box today and the cupboard
was not bare; a precious white envelope greeted
my glance. I don't know if I shall be able
to stand all this sudden 'prosperity' but
nevertheless it certainly does something to
my morale. I don't care what you write
about only as long as it includes you and
sometimes me. When you write often, after
a while you will find that there will always
be plenty to write about since the time lapse
will be so short to prevent you from forgetting
anything that happens. Little details often
prove much more interesting than generalities.
        Gee! I wished I could share
that cozy atmosphere with you cuddled
by the fire. I thought of that last
night as I watched from my plane

432

and I had little or no trouble finding that once[-]upon[-]a[-]time milk run from San Marcos. I never got back until 2:30 AM this morning[,] yet there was an 8:00 AM class scheduled[,] which couldn't be disregarded. That is the way things are done here. Once a person seldom finds a moment to himself then there are several days when he can relax completely with little or no work to haunt him. I sort of like it this way[,] though[,] for a person seems to be able to accomplish a lot more than he would otherwise.

I have just returned from our [o]fficers['] bowling alley and find that I have [2*] finally graduate[d] to the 3[-]digit score group. Tonight[']s scores were 106[] and 149 respectively. I must send you this pamphlet to show you that the game can be rather scientific and that by following some principles shown therein[,] you will be able to surpass me by far. You may even get the chance to surprise some of your friends[,] not saying what effect your score will have on yourself.

I went to my mail box [*sic*] today[,] and the cupboard was not bare; a precious white envelope greeted my glance. I don't know if I shall be able to stand all this sudden 'prosperity[,]' but nevertheless[,] it certainly does something to my morale. I don't care what you write about only as long as it includes you and sometimes me. When you write often, after a while[,] you will find that there will always be plenty to write about[,] since the time lapse will be so short to prevent you from forgetting anything that happens. Little details often prove much more interesting than generalities.

the most beautiful of planets Venus.[3] Remember
when I last showed her to you? Well last
night she was flirting with the man in
the moon. ☀☽ ASM = man in moon } now
SM♀ = Venus

just do a bit of substitution and there you
have a most wonderful of situations.

A big smile that stretched from ear to
ear could be seen on my face as I read the
one word "fudge". After 3 years I finally
may get another sample of Sylvias great
handiwork. I have often thought of suggesting
you try again and let me sample the efforts
but considering the sugar shortage and
having some regard for the Jacobs sugar
supply I refrained from making such a
suggestion. Surely! a half dozen batches
would be necessary to determine the
difference between caramel & fudge and the
Jacobs kitchen would be bustling with pots and pans
every night for a week. I can
picture poor Sylvia now dipping the boiling
chocolate sugar mixture in a glass
of water trying her darndest to determine

Gee! I wished I could share that cozy atmosphere with you cuddled by the fire. I thought of that last night as I watched from my plane [3*] the most beautiful of planets[,] Venus. Remember when I last showed her to you? Well[,] last night she was flirting with the [M]an in the [M]oon.[180]

ASM = [M]an in the [M]oon/now

SMJ = Venus

[J]ust do a bit of substitution[,] and there you have a most wonderful of situations.

A big smile that stretched from ear to ear could be seen on my face as I read the one word "fudge."[181] After 3 years[,] I finally may get another sample of Sylvia[']s great handiwork. I have often thought of suggesting you try again and let me sample the efforts[,] but considering the sugar shortage and having some regard for the Jacobs['] sugar supply[,] I refrained from making such a suggestion.[182] Surely! A half[-]dozen batches would be necessary to determine the difference between caramel + fudge[,]

---

[180] Following the sentence is a line drawing of a small star on the left and a crescent moon on the right.

[181] According to family lore, even though Anthony Mazza and Sylvia Jacobs could have met in high school, they did not initially meet until Anthony visited the Jacobs' home with his friend George Jacobs, Sylvia's brother. According to the letter, this was sometime in 1941. While Anthony was visiting George, Sylvia was in the kitchen attempting to make fudge. She was, however, having trouble with getting the fudge to set. She kept interrupting Anthony and George, soliciting their advice on what she should do. In the end, the fudge never did set, so she invited Anthony, George, and the others in the house at the time to eat her fudge with a spoon.

[182] See *supra* note 61.

if the "fudge" is done, also running in and
out with Caramel in a pan wondering if the
slightest temperature Change would have some
magic effect in the Conversion from Caramel to Fudge.
Good thing I'm not near by to have anything
thrown at me but now you'll have to prove
I'm wrong. Chuckle Chuckle.

Hmmm getting late and I'm on
Dawn Patrol manana. 5:45 AM. Briefing
means I must get in my beauty sleep
for tomorrows ordeal right now. Good
night I'll have the Pleasant dreams this
time and will share them with you.

Love from
Tony

P.S. WHITE IS BETTER THAN BLUE.

436

and the Jacobs['] kitchen would be bustling with pots and pans every night for a week. I can picture poor Sylvia now[,] dipping the boiling[,] chocolate[-]sugar mixture in a glass of water[,] trying her darndest to determine [4*] if the "fudge" is done[,] also running in and out with caramel in a pan[,] wondering if the slightest temperature change would have some magic effect in the conversion from caramel to FUDGE. Good thing I'm not nearby to have anything thrown at me[,] but now you'll have to prove I'm wrong. Chuckle Chuckle.

Hmm[,] getting late and I'm on [d]awn [p]atrol ma[ñ]ana. [A] 5:45 AM[b]riefing means I must get in my beauty sleep for tomorrow[']s ordeal right now. Good night[.] I'll have the [p]leasant dreams this time and will share them with you.

Love from
'Tony'

P.S. WHITE IS BETTER THAN BLUE.[183]

---

[183] The preference appears to be for sending correspondence in white rather than blue envelopes. See *infra* page 511 (Letter from Anthony S. Mazza to Sylvia M. Jacobs (January 3, 1945) (postscript)).

F/O. A.S. Meggus T-136514
2.15CCS 1-26 Box 3323
P.A.A.B. Pueblo, Colo.

PUEBLO
DEC 20
8 PM
1944
COLO

Miss Sylvia Jacobs
2334 Artmore St.
Pittsburgh 12, Pa.

438

Dec 21, 1944

Dearest Sylvia:

I received your christmas Card
last night just as I returned from my
flight. It really is beautiful but what
I like most about it are the words.
Had I been able to find a card identicle
to that, you can bet I would send it
to my 'Sweet-heart'. Some-how I couldn't
find a sweet-heart Card in the entire
Pueblo vicinity, at least not one that
I liked, so you shall be minus one
this year. I hope the other little things
I sent will express better than words or
cards what you mean to me.

I was just looking at the
christmas tree in the corner of my barracks.
Guess whose it is? Mine, of course, and
here is how I got it. About a week
ago a friend of mine Charles Mayes asked
me to go with him on a drive to see
the Royal gorge and the highest bridge
in the world. This we did going by
way of Canyon City, where I bought
one of your christmas gifts, and finally

440

December 21, 1944

From: F./O. A.S. Mazza T-136514
215 C.C.S. 1-26 Box 3323
P.A.A.B. Pueblo, Colo.

To: Miss Sylvia M. Jacobs
2334 Atmore St[.]
Pittsburgh 12, Pa[.]

Postmark: 5:00 PM
December 20, 1944
Pueblo, Colorado

Letterhead: Officers Mess
Army Air Base
Pueblo, Colorado

[1*]   Dec[.] 21, 1944

Dearest Sylvia:

I received your Christmas [c]ard last night just as I returned from my flight. It really is beautiful[,] but what I like most about it are the words. Had I been able to find a card identicle [*sic*] to that, you can bet I would send it to my 'Sweet-heart [*sic*][.'] Some how [*sic*] I couldn't find a sweet-heart [*sic*] card in the entire Pueblo vicinity, at least not one that I liked, so you shall be minus one this year. I hope the other little things I sent will express better than words or cards what you mean to me.

2.

past the skyline drive to top of the Gorge.
All was very picturesque and mother
nature looked her grandest to me that
day. We finally got back to Canyon City
with time to spare so we decided to drive
through the Country side to a Silver Mining
town of Victor, Colorado but 21 miles through
the Canyon. So on we went passing the real
Cow-boys, cattle ranches, and sheep ranches until
not a soul or house was in
sight. We followed a narrow twisting
road up-hill all the way through Phantom
Canyon for about one-half hour when
I spotted a beautiful pine tree about 3½ ft
tall and fell in love with it right on the
spot. I had Mayes stop the car and I
whittled it down with my knife and set
it in back of the car. On we went
until a sign faced us with the inscription
"road at your own risk". Since nothing
Can stop the Air Corps, we continued
ahead until the 21 miles were passed
yet no Victor in sight.

I was just looking at the Christmas tree in the corner of my barracks. Guess whose it is? Mine, of course, and here is how I got it. About a week ago[,] a friend of mine Charles Mayes asked me to go with him on a drive to see the Royal [G]orge and the highest bridge in the world. This we did, going by way of Canyon City, where I bought one of your Christmas gifts, and finally [2*] past the skyline drive to [the] top of the [g]orge. All was very picturesque[,] and [M]other [N]ature looked her grandest to me that day. We finally got back to Canyon City with time to spare[,] so we decided to drive through the [c]ountry side [*sic*] to [the] [s]ilver [m]ining town of Victor, Colorado[,] but 21 miles through the [c]anyon. So on we went[,] passing the real cow-boys [*sic*], cattle ranchers[,] and sheep ranchers until not a soul or house was in sight. We followed a narrow[,] twisting road up-hill [*sic*] all the way through Phantom Canyon for about one-half hour when I spotted a beautiful pine tree about 3½ ft[.] tall and fell in love with it right on the spot. I had Mayes stop the car[,] and I whittled it down with my knife and set it in [the] back of the car. On we went until a sign faced us with the inscription "Travel at your own risk." Since nothing can stop the Air Corps, we continued ahead until the 21 miles were passed[,] yet no Victor

3

our gas supply was low, no civilization in sight and nothing to indicate we were on the right road. 30, 35, 40 miles from Canyon City and still only mountains and canyons, the road still climbing upward. Visions of a lonely dark night, out of gas miles from anywhere, lost, and the worst of everything perhaps bad weather would leave us stranded for a couple of days. We couldn't help but laugh at our plight when a few buzzards circled above and an Eagle flew by disturbed by our chugging car. 45, 50, miles holding our breaths we finally glimpsed a huge mine ahead, a little further houses; still further people and finally black gold — gasoline.

The town was not Victor but the once world noted mid western gold town of Cripple Creek. Now almost everything was desolate and deserted. A ghost town if there ever was one. A couple of people lived on their past hopes and still dreaming

in sight. [3*] [O]ur gas supply was low[,] no civilization in sight[,] and nothing to indicate we were on the right road[—]30, 35, 40 miles from Canyon City and still only mountains and canyons, the road still climbing upward. [We had v]isions of a lonely dark night, out of gas[,] miles from anywhere, lost, and the worst of everything[;] perhaps bad weather would leave us stranded for a couple of days. We couldn't help but laugh at our plight when a few buzzards circled above and an [e]agle flew by[,] disturbed by our chugging car. [Forty-five], 50 miles, holding our breaths[,] we finally glimpsed at a huge mine ahead, a little further[,] houses, still further[,] people[,] and finally[,] black gold—gasoline.

The town was not Victor but the once world[-]noted mid western [*sic*] gold town of Cripple Creek. Now almost everything was desolate and deserted. A ghost town if there ever was one. A couple of people lived there on their past hopes and still

that this town will again rise to greatness.
All over the mountain side one could see
what looked like gopher holes or worse still
mole hills where greedy people once dug
frantically for the yellow ladened quartz.

We saw Cafes and saloons that
were just a token as to what the town
stood for. Nugget Cafe; Gold Ore Palace,
theatre house, Stage Coach Inn and etc were
they so typical of a gold town. I stopped at
a little novelty shop where an old gent
who was among the first to come to the
region told me of the town and what it
looked like there many years ago. He had
several cards that I bought and I am sending
them to you as souvenirs. I bought your
Indian bracelet here too which is hand-
made by an Indian tribe nearby. The
center is of turquois and this kind of
jewelry is extremely popular out these
parts. I've seen girls with as far as 7 or
8 on each arm.... That isn't fiction either.
The card with "burros" is of historic

446

dreaming [4*] that this town will again rise to greatness. All over the mountain side [*sic*][,] one could see what looked like gopher holes[,] or worse still[,] mole hills[,] where greedy people once dug frantically for the yellow[-]ladened quartz.

We saw cafes and saloons that were just a token as to what the town stood for. Nugget Cafe; Gold Ore Palace, the theater house[;] Stage Coach [*sic*] Inn[;] and etc. were so typical of a gold town. I stopped at a little novelty shop where an old gent[,] who was among the first to come to the region[,] told me of the town and what it looked like these many years ago. He had several cards that I bought[,] and I am sending them to you as a souvenir. I bought your Indian bracelet here[,] too[,] which is hand-made [*sic*] by an Indian tribe nearby. The center is of tourquois [*sic*][,] and this kind of jewelry is extremely popular out [in] these parts. I've seen girls with as [many] as 7 or 8 on each arm - - - - That isn't fiction

note since Geronimo was the leader of the Indians who banded together with the purpose of driving the white men from their lands. A charge by his braves always was one continuous yell of that word "Geronimo". It is of significance in this war since that battle cry has been adopted by our own Para-troopers. I did take a good look at the gold one and will recognize it should I ever stumble over some of it accidentally which of course is an improbability.

Well all this to tell you about a little tree. Anyway I brought the tree back to the barracks set it up in a can filled with dish sand and water. I put a sign up for the rest of the boys. "This is your tree help decorate it". It sure has been fun to watch them this week. One fellow bought a wreath, another tinsel, another bulbs, one fellow who lived in Denver brought back a couple set of electric lights all blue. Snow, miniature animals for the bottom, a manger, and other odds and ends are now attached. All packages that want be opened until Christmas are piled right along side of it. All this tribute which followed my picking that bit

either. The [c]ard with "Geronimo" is of historic [5*] note[,] since Geronimo was the leader of the Indians who banded together with the purpose of driving the white man from their lands.[184] A charge by his braves always was one contuous [*sic*] yell of that word[,] "Geronimo[."] It is of significance in this war[,] since the battle cry has been adopted by our own [p]ara-troopers [*sic*]. I did take a good look at the gold ore and will recognize it if I should ever stumble over some of it accidentally[,] which[,] of course[,] is an improbability.

Well[,] all this to tell you about a little tree. Anyway[,] I brought the tree back to the barracks[,] set it up in a can filled with dirt, sand[,] and water. I put a sign up for the rest of the boys[:] "This is your tree[;] help decorate it." It sure has been fun to watch them this week. One fellow bought a wreath, another tinsel, another bulbs[;] one fellow who lived in Denver brought back a couple set[s] of electric lights[,] all blue. Snow, minature [*sic*] animals for the bottom, a manger, and other odds and ends are now attached. All packages that won[']t be opened until Christmas are piled right along side [*sic*] it. All this tribute[,] which followed my picking

---

[184] Cecily Hilleary, "Geronimo: From America's Most Wanted to Tourist Attraction," Voice of America, November 13, 2017, https://www.voanews.com/usa/geronimo-americas-most-wanted-tourist-attraction.

6.

of spruce in "Phantom Canyon". Better get set again since I am to fly again this afternoon. Close with Love + Kisses+Hugs

"Tony"

that bit [6*] of spruce in "Phantom Canyon." Better get set again[,] since I am to fly again this afternoon. Close with Love + Kisses + Hugs[,]

"Tony"

Free

QUEBL
Q DEC 26
5 PM
1944
COLO

Miss Sylvia Jacobs
2334 Atmore St
Pittsburgh 12, Pa

F/o. A.S. Muga T-136614
W5ees 1-26   Box 3823
P.A.4.B.   Pueblo, Colo.

452

Dec 23, 1944

Dearest Sylvia:

Tis the day before the day before
Christmas and how the winds doth blow.
In all probability we shall have snow;
yes, as a matter of fact, the snow flakes
are beginning to fall fast and in clusters
eastward to whiten the entire country side.
This will be the first actual snow fall I
have seen since that night I was on C.Q
duty at Nashville, Tenn. I am scheduled
to fly this afternoon but if the weather continues thus, the blue will not claim us
today. That will not excuse us, however,
and no doubt the remainder of the afternoon,
and perhaps evening, will be spent listening
to dry lectures and viewing old restricted
films that we have seen over and over again.
The army believes in the policy that if you
hammer and drive a thing into a persons
mind he will finally grasp what is wanted
of him and do those things methodically without
taxing his mentality one bit.

I received your most cherished

454

December 23, 1944

Postmark: [The envelope is missing.]

Letterhead: Officers Club
              Army Air Base
              Pueblo, Colorado

[1*]   Dec[.] 23, 1944

Dearest Sylvia:

[']Tis the day before the day before Christmas[,] and how the winds doth blow. In all probability[,] we shall have snow. Yes, as a matter of fact, the snow flakes [*sic*] are beginning to fall fast and in clusters earthward to whiten the entire country side [*sic*]. This will be the first actual snow-fall [*sic*] I have seen since that night I was on C.Q. duty[185] at Nashville, Tenn. I am scheduled to fly this afternoon[,] but if the weather con-tinues thus, the blue will not claim us today. That will not excuse us, however, and no doubt the remainder of the afternoon, and perhaps evening, will be spent listening to dry lectures and viewing old[,] restricted films that we have seen over and over again. The [A]rmy believes in the policy that if you hammer and drive a thing into a person[']s mind[,] he will finally grasp what is wanted of him and do those things methodically without taxing his mentality one bit.

---

[185] Charge of Quarters (C.Q.) duty entails guarding the entrance to the barracks.

455

2

Christmas gift yesterday. I couldn't resist the temptation to open the package before Christmas day. so I already know and appreciate most sincerely its contents. The beautiful bow made from the red ribbon was well protected and so wonderful to behold. I wonder if Sylvia did the wrapping of that gift? If so, you've certainly got me beat on that score. I can't help but smile at the time I had wrapping and mailing your little gift. The socks, tie and handkerchiefs are extremely practical to a person like myself. I shall wear one of each on Christmas morn which should prove quite definite how your Christmas gift and especially how you rate with me.

I am happy that my gift reached you by now. It was bought by me at Canyon City Colo in a small novelty shop at one corner of a typical western Cow-boy town. It is not uncommon to see these men come tootling into town via horse back.

I received your most cherished [2*] Christmas gift yesterday. I couldn't resist the temptation to open the package before Christmas [D]ay[,] so I already know and appreciate most sincerely its contents. The beautiful bow made from the red ribbon was well protected and so wonderful to behold. I wonder if Sylvia did the wrapping of that gift? If so, you've certainly got me beat on that score. I can't help but smile at the time I had wrapping and mailing your little gift. The socks, tie[,] and handkerchieves are extremely practical to a person like myself. I shall wear one of each on Christmas morn[,] which should prove quite definite[ly] how your Christmas gift[s] and especially how you rate with me.

I am hoping that my gift reached you by now. It was bought by me at Canyon City[,] Colo[rado,] in a small novelty shop at one corner of a typical, [W]estern[, c]ow-boy [*sic*] town. It is not uncommon to see these men come trotting into town via horseback.

3

There in the remote corner of this shop I found the gift for you. An old music box whose wood finish did not rate it with some of the other more exclusive boxes I had seen but whose clear decisive tone had something all the others lacked. I wonder if that music box was wrapped secure enough so that the music producing qualities were not lost or broken in the Christmas mailing shuffle. "When Irish Eyes are Smiling". I did not buy that tune to signify anything typically Irish between us. Far be it from that for I'm quite sure I would never desire to exchange my heritage or culture for anything Irish and I believe neither would you. That tune will, I hope, tinkle out the little messages we ~~exchanged~~ signaled to each other at our last hand-holding session at the movie "When Irish Eyes are Smiling."

Gosh! I certainly would appreciate any baked goods sent by your mother and it little matters whether it is before or after Christmas just as long as it

[3*] There in the remote corner of the shop[,] I found the gift for you. An old music box whose wood finish did not rate it with some of the other more exclusive boxes I had seen but whose clear[,] decisive tone had something all the others lacked. I wonder if that music box was wrapped secure enough so that the music[-]producing qualities were not lost or broken in the Christmas mailing shuffle. "When Irish Eyes are Smiling."[186] I did not buy that tune to signify anything typically Irish between us. Far be it from that[,] for I'm quite sure I would never desire to exchange my heritage or culture for anything Irish[,] and I believe neither would you. That tune will[,] I hope, tinkle out the little messages we signaled to each other at our last hand-holding session at the movie "When Irish Eyes [A]re Smiling."[187]

Gosh! I certainly would appreciate any baked goods sent by your mother[,] and it little matters whether it is before or after Christmas[,] just as long as it [4*] it [sic] includes namely "nut roll."

---

[186] American songwriter Ernest R. Ball (b. July 22, 1878; d. May 3, 1927) composed the music to the popular song "When Irish Eyes Are Smiling" in 1912. "Ernest Ball," Songwriters Hall of Fame, accessed June 20, 2020, https://www.songhall.org/profile/Ernest_Ball. The reference here appears to be to the 1944 film about his life, which featured the song. *Irish Eyes Are Smiling*, directed by Gregory Ratoff, featuring Monty Woolley, June Haver, and Dick Haymes (20th Century Fox, 1944).

[187] Above the word "Irish" in superscript are the words "Sylvia + Tony's."

p. 4.

It includes namely "nut roll". Be sure however this time that it is your mother's baking so I can compliment the right person!

The Christmas song I shall never forget and which has a particular meaning each time it is played is now being rendered over the air: "I'm dreaming of a White Christmas." So odd that no matter how my thoughts stray that melody takes me back to the first and last dance of the "Silver Ball". So long for a while with Love A'plenty.

Love,

"Tony"

460

Be sure[,] however[,] this time that it is your mother's baking[,] so I can compliment the right person.

The Christmas song I shall never forget and which has a particular meaning each time it is played is now being rendered over the air. "I'm [D]reaming of a [W]hite Christmas."[188] So odd that no matter how my thoughts stray[,] that melody takes me back to the first and last dance of the "Silver Ball."[189] So long for a while with Love A'plenty [*sic*].

Love[,]
"Tony"

---

[188] See *supra* note 60.
[189] See *supra* note 98.

Dec 25, 1944

Merry Christmas to
    My Sweetheart Sylvia:

            I have just returned from our
Christmas day feast which contained almost
all of the good foods known to man. I
could describe all of them but I thought I'd
inclose the menu which has all of that
already written up in fine style. We have
a typical White Christmas today with snow
covered ground and snow ladened atmosphere
as the flakes keep dancing merrily to the
ground. I only wished you were here
with me this afternoon so I could snow-
ball you and roll you thru the snow. - - -
Not saying what you would do to me and
what we wouldn't both do the remainder
of the afternoon??

            A slight 'hangover' is now throbbing
in the form of a headache on yours truly's
noggin as a result from too much last
night. Our entire crew was invited by
a friend of our Bombardier to spend Christmas
eve dining, dancing, and drinking with
them and their friends. The invitation

December 25, 1944

From: F./O. A.S. Mazza T-136514
215 CCS 1-26 Box 3323
P.A.A.B. Pueblo, Colo.

To: Miss Sylvia Jacobs
2334 Atmore St[.]
Pittsburgh 12, Pa.

Postmark: 2:30 PM
December 26, 1944
Pueblo, Colorado

Letterhead: Officers Mess
Army Air Base
Pueblo, Colorado

[1*]   Dec[.] 25, 1944
Merry Christmas to
    my [s]weetheart Sylvie:
    I have just returned from our Christmas [D]ay feast[,] which
contained all of the good foods known to man. I could describe
all of them[,] but I thought I'd enclose the menu[,] which has all
of that already written up in fine style. We have a typical White
Christmas today with snow[-]covered ground and snow[-]ladened
atmosphere as the flakes keep dancing merrily to the ground.
I only wished you were here with me this afternoon so I could
snow-ball you and roll you thru [*sic*] the snow - - - - Not saying
what you would do to me and what we wouldn't both do the
remainder of the afternoon??

2

came as a result of an incident which
occured about a month ago. My bombardier,
Walt Brooks and I happened to be walking thru
the fair city of Pueblo heading for a movie
when our conversation was abruptly haulted
by the shrill voice of a young lady waving
and shouting frantically to attract Walts attention
from a ~~passing window~~ of a trolley passing
right along side of us. Walt waved back
thinking nothing about the individual when
suddenly at the next car stop who should step
out but said young lady named Harriet.
An introduction plus talk; two is company
three is a crowd and before one can hardly
realize it I find myself alone for the evening
while Walt and Harriet silently disappear into
the night. Walt knew Harriet and her family
~~from~~ before the Army had called him thru
business ~~that~~ connections that his family had
had with them. I told Walt that the next
time he saw Harriet to tell her that I had
a little song I wanted to sing for the both
of them. This he did and thus the invitation

464

A slight 'hangover' is now throbbing in the form of a headache on yours truly[']s noggin as a result from too much last night. Our entire crew was invited by a friend of the [b]ombardier to spend Christmas [E]ve dining, dancing, and drinking with them and their friends. The invitation [2*] came as a result of an incident[,] which occured [sic] about a month ago. My bombardier, Walt Brooks[,] and I happened to be walking thru [sic] the fair City of Pueblo[,] heading for a movie when our conversation was abruptly haulted [sic] by the shrill voice of a young lady waving and shouting frantically to attract Walt[']s attention from a window of a trolley passing right along side [sic] us. Walt waved back[,] thinking nothing about the individual[,] when suddenly at the next car stop[,] who should step out but said young lady named Harriet. An introduction plus talk[—]two is company[;] three is a crowd[;] and before one can hardly realize it, I find myself alone for the evening while Walt and Harriet silently disappear into the night. Walt knew Harriet and her family before the Army had called him thru [sic] business connections that his family had had with them. I told Walt that the next time he saw Harriet to tell her that I had a little song I wanted to sing for the both of them. This he did[,]

for myself and later the whole crew. I
was only joking about the song but in the
middle of the party last night I was called
on for a solo. Yes I sang it: "Clang
Clang Clang went the Trolley." Harriet
was a bit embarrassed at least but thought it
pretty clever so before the evening was over
poor Harriet was subjected to a new nick name
"Clang-Clang" and the trolley incident was the
highlight of the evening for a while.

This family had everything for us
in the form of a 40 lb turkey, hams, nuts, fruit,
cakes and about all the delicatessents one can
think of. Wines, gin, rum, whiskey as
cocktail, highballs and the like flowed freely
all evening. Our crew had a remarkable time
drinking and toasting to our future together and
I couldn't be left out of any of those toasts.
I was extremely careful of quantity of drinks
but it was the combination of so much of it
that gave me this morning effects. About
11:45 the party dispersed and all the crew
was convinced by me to attend Mid-night

and thus the invitation [3*] for myself and later the whole crew. I was only joking about the song[,] but in the middle of the party last night[,] I was called on for a solo. Yes[,] I sang it: "Clang[,] [c]lang[,] [c]lang went the [t]rolley."[190] Harriet was a bit embarrassed at first but thought it pretty clever[,] so before the evening was over[,] poor Harriet was subjected to a new nick name [sic][,] "Clang-Clang[,]" and the trolley incident was the highlight of the evening for a-while [sic].

This family had everything for us in the form of a 40[-]lb. [t]urkey, ham, nuts, fruit, cakes and about all the dellicatessants [sic] one can think of. Wines, [g]in, [r]um, [w]hiskey as cocktail[s], highballs and the like flowed freely all evening. Our crew had a remarkable time drinking and toasting to our future together[,] and I couldn't be left out of any of those toasts. I was extremely careful of quantity of drink[,] but it was the combination of so much of it that gave me this morning[']s effects. About 11:45[,] the party dispersed[,] and all the crew was convinced by me to attend [m]id-night [sic] [M]ass[,] even though the [p]ilot and [b]ombardier

---

[190] The lyrics are from "The Trolley Song," by Hugh Martin and Ralph Bane, which Judy Garland sang in the film *Meet Me in St. Louis. Meet Me in St. Louis*, directed by Vincente Minnelli, featuring Judy Garland, Margaret O'Brien, and Mary Astor (Metro-Goldwyn-Mayer and Warner Bros., 1944); "The Trolley Song by Judy Garland," Songfacts, accessed June 20, 2020, https://www.songfacts.com/facts/judy-garland/the-trolley-song.

mass even though the Pilot and Bombardier were non-Catholics. We stopped in front of the Cathedral steps just as the procession went by. Little chow boys, alter boys, Knights of Columbus, and Celebrants of priests made up the procession. The Co-Pilot rubbed his eyes and could hardly believe what he saw. "Why that's a "Cardinal" he shouted; we _must_ see a mass sung by a Cardinal!" Gosh! That would be something to tell the folks I thought, so we entered the vestibule all set for Mid-night mass. A priest halted us and asked us for our "tickets." Tickets?? Tickets for a Catholic to go to church; to mass? What kind of a joke was this? Nope you must have Tickets or I can't let you in was his reply and he stuck by it. I really was extremely embarrassed before my non-Catholic Crew members but there was nothing I could do about that. I pleaded that we were strangers, didn't know of

were non-Catholics.[191] We stopped in front of the Cathedral steps just as the procession went by.[192] Little choir boys, alter [*sic*] boys, Knights of Columbus, [c]elebrants[,] and priests made up the procession. The [c]o-[p]ilot rubbed his eyes and could hardly believe what he saw. "Why that[']s a [c]ardinal[,"] he shouted[.] ["W]e must see a [M]ass sung by a [c]ardinal!" Gosh! That would be something to tell the folks[,] I thought, so we entered the vestibule[,] all set for [m]id–night [*sic*] [M]ass. A priest halted us and asked us for our "tickets." Tickets?? Tickets for a Catholic to go to [c]hurch, to [M]ass?? What kind of joke was this? Nope[.] ["Y]ou must have [t]ickets[,] or I can't let you in[,"] was his reply[,] and he stuck by it. I really was extremely embarrassed before my non-Catholic crew members[,] but there was nothing I could do about that. I pleaded that we were strangers, didn't know of [5*] such rules[;]

---

[191] See *supra* page 93 (Letter from Anthony S. Mazza to Sylvia M. Jacobs (December 24, 1943)).

[192] The Roman Catholic Cathedral of the Sacred Heart, built in 1910, is located at 414 West 11th Street, Pueblo, Colorado. "Cathedral History," Cathedral of the Sacred Heart, accessed June 20, 2020, http:/www.shcathedral.net/ cathedral-history.

5.

such rules, we were soldiers perhaps for our last Christmas in the states, we had never seen or had the opportunity to see a Bishop and Cardinal perform services. All this to us avail which reminded me of certain sisters I knew at St Johns when they made no exceptions for rules on a scrap of paper. I almost lost a little of my religion for a while but got over it this morning when I went to both Confession & Communion this morning clad in the tie, socks and Hankies that Sylvia sent me. I guess even Cardinals, priests and Bishops are human and make plenty of mistakes, however, I shall never forget this incident which has dropped them by a couple of steps from the pedestal I had once placed them.

Well Sylvia I guess I'd better close now and send loads of love this Christmas day to you. May the next one or two or three that follows find us at least part of the day together.

Love
"Tony"

470

we were soldiers[,] perhaps for our last Christmas in the [S]tates[;] we had never seen or had the opportunity to see a [b]ishop and [c]ardinal perform services. All this to no avail[,] which reminded me of certain sisters I knew at St. John[']s when they made no exceptions for rules on a scrap of paper. I almost lost a little of my religion for a while[,] but got over it this morning when I went to both confession + communion clad in the tie, socks[,] and [h]ankies that Sylvia sent me. I guess even [c]ardinals, priests[,] and [b]ishops are human and make plenty of mistakes[;] however, I shall never forget this incident[,] which has dropped them a couple of steps from the pedestal [on which] I had once placed them.

Well[,] Sylvia[,] I guess I'd better close now and send loads of love this Christmas [D]ay to you. May the next one or two or three that follows [*sic*] find us at least part of the day together.

Love[,]
'Tony'

[Enclosure: Christmas Program]

Officers Mess

Army Air · Base
PUEBLO, COLORADO

★

Merry Christmas

DECEMBER 25, 1944

Christmas Dinner

★

MENU

Turkey Noodle Soup

Roast Colorado Turkey

Oyster Dressing   Cranberry Sauce

Candied Yams   Snowflake Potatoes

Fresh Peas and Carrots

Combination Salad

Olives   Stuffed Celery

Home Made Hot Rolls

Mince Pie   Pumpkin Pie

Fruit Cake Louis

Coffee   Milk   Tea

LT. COL. WILLIS G. CARTER
Station Commander

LT. COL. JAMES A. MOORE
Deputy Station Commander

LT. COL. RALPH F. FRIEDENTHAL
Director of Administration and Services

LT. COL. THOMAS FOWLER
Director of Maintenance and Supply

LT. COL. HALEY W. AYCOCK
Director of Training

★

BOARD OF GOVERNORS

Lt. Col. Marvin C. Schleeter   Capt. Thomas G. Thigpin
Lt. Col. Henry C. Coles   Lt. Herman Hritdar
Major J. W. Schaaf   Lt. Ruby E. Chapman
Captain William Manning

★

2nd LT. ALLEN A. McMANAMY
Mess Officer

473

F/o. U.S. Mayga T-136614
215 CCS 1-26 Box 3323
P.A.A.B. Pueblo, Colo.

Miss Sylvia Jacobs
2334 Avenue St
Pittsburgh 12, Pa.

Dec 29, 1944

Dearest Sylvia:

Well it is fine to hear from you again after another short relapse. Let see! You must have given the Marines quite a time this week to cause this delay.??? No, I'm only foolin and know the reason and expected a delay after my not writing a letter for quite some period of time to _._._

Gee! I'm certainly glad to hear you received my little gifts and the picture. I don't know why all the fuss over the picture since I had quite a time deciding whether I should send that one or not. I thought surely after looking at it

December 29, 1944

From: F./O. A.S. Mazza T-136514
215 CCS 1-26 Box 3323
P.A.A.B. Pueblo, Colo.

To: Miss Sylvia Jacobs
2334 Atmore St.
Pittsburgh 12, Pa.

Postmark: 8:00 PM
December 29, 1944
Pueblo, Colorado

Letterhead: [The letter is on yellow stationery with a picture of
a cowboy lassoing a steer in the upper left corner.
On the first page, the cowboy is identified in small
print as "Tony."]

[1*]   Dec[.] 29, 1944

Dearest Sylvia:

Well[,] it is fine to hear from you again after another short relapse. Let[']s see! You must have given the Marines quite a time this week to cause this delay??? No, I'm only foolin' and know the reason and expected a delay after me not writing a letter for quite a period of time to - - -[.]

several times you would come to your
'senses' and realize that love is blind.
I wanted a pose with a smile but
Ugh! you should have seen the proofs---
on the contrary, I'm happy you didn't,
I even shudder now when I think of them.
So the 'natural' picture was the best
I could do, even though parts are blurred
but again I realize that Pueblo is not a
first class ~~titty~~ and that Tony too is
not a first class subject.

I wished I could have been
there to see you open the music box.
I know it would have fooled most
people, including myself. Its a wonder
you didn't drop it, or did you? I
had quite a time ~~with it~~ myself show-
ing it to all my buddies especially the
Irishmen. They would have given
plenty for it but that article was
not for sale.

Say, how do you like this

Gee! I'm certainly glad to hear you received my little gifts and the picture.[193] I don't know why all the fuss over the picture[,] since I had quite a time deciding whether I should send that one or not. I thought surely after looking at it [1R*] several times[,] you would come to your 'senses' and realize that love is blind. I wanted a pose with a smile[,] but [u]gh! You should have seen the proofs - - - on the contrary, I'm happy you didn't. I even shudder now when I think of them. So the 'natural' picture was the best I could do, even though parts are blurred[,] but again[,] I realize that Pueblo is not a first[-]class city and that Tony is not a first[-]class subject.

I wished I could have been there to see you open the music box. I know it would have fooled most people, including myself. It[']s a wonder you didn't drop it[,] or did you? I had quite a time myself show-ing it to all my buddies[,] especially the Irishmen. They would have given plenty for it[,] but that article was not for sale.

---

[193] See *supra* page 8 (Photograph of Anthony S. Mazza).

+elusive stationary. No, its not mine
but it does belong to my Co-Pilot Johnny
Gilmore. I had classes this morning
from 5 AM until 10:00 AM with nothing
more for the day. From 10 to 12 I went
to the Quatermaster Sales and bought a
couple more pair of "Long Johns" (winter
underwear.) They have proved their
"worth time and time again on these
cold winter mornings when we climb to
20,000 ft just as the sun pokes its nose
on the horizon. Ole J. T. Gilmore and
myself decided we'd leave camp merely
for a change of scenery than for any
other reason. Gilmore's wife "Toddy" had
gone to her folks during the season
holidays so we went by his home
to see if everything was in good order.
To our surprise, we found a fruit
Cake waiting for us from Grandmother

Say, how do you like [2*] this exclusive stationary [*sic*][?] No, it[']s not mine[,] but it does belong to my [c]o-[p]ilot[,] Johnny Gilmore. I had classes this morning from 5 AM until 10:00 AM with nothing more for the day. From 10 to 12[,] I went to the [q]uartermaster [s]ales and bought a couple more pair of "[l]ong [j]ohns" (winter underwear[).] They have proved their worth time and time again on these cold[,] wintry mornings when we climb to 20,000 ft[.] just as the sun pokes its nose on the horizon. Ole "J.T." Gilmore and myself decided we'd leave camp merely for a change of scenery than for any other reason. Gilmore[']s wife[,] "Toddy[,]" had gone to her folks during the season holidays[,] so we went by his home to see if everything was in good order. To our surprise, we found a fruit cake [*sic*] waiting for us from

Gilmore. A couple bottles of root-beer, fruit Cake, stationary, ink, Pen, sunshine, love, letter, girl and the results are plain to observe.

The last couple of days, that is, 2 out of the last 3, we flew twice. The rest of the time we slept since there isn't much time left to a 14 hour day that usual is the case when one includes pre-flying, flying and post flying time.

Last night however, Brooks, Gilmore and I had our weekly spaghetti dinner in town, then bleary eyed made our way back to camp to rise and shine early 5:00 AM this morning. Yesterday I had quite a thrill when my Bombardier Walt Brooks let me drop 11 bombs from high altitude on the targets below. Well, I didn't score a bull's eye every time but did as well as can be expected with so little practice. I still have plenty to learn since the Pilot has

Grandmother [2R*] Gilmore. A [c]ouple bottles of root-beer [*sic*], fruit cake [*sic*], stationary [*sic*], ink, [p]en, sunshine, love, letter, girl[,] and results are plain to observe.

The last couple of days, that is, 2 out of the last 3, we flew twice. The rest of the time[,] we slept[,] since there isn't much time left to a 14[-]hour day[—]that usual[ly] is the case when one includes pre-flying, flying[,] and post[-]flying time.

Last night, however, Brooks, Gilmore[,] and I had our weekly [s]paghetti dinner in town, then bleary[-]eyed made our way back to camp to rise and shine early 5:00 AM this morning. Yesterday[,] I had quite a thrill when my[b]ombardier[,] Walt Brooks[,] let me drop 11 bombs from high altitude on the targets below. Well[,] I didn't score a bull's[-]eye every time but did as well as can be expected with so little practice. I still have plenty to learn[,] since

3.

offered to teach me a bit about handling the plane. He also wants me to learn how to Copilot in Case of emergencies!

The Radio Operator & Engineer too are giving me lessons on their particular jobs which will take me quite a while to learn.

I received a letter from home today that told me that our Joe was home for Christmas and Caused quite a sensation in his new middie uniform. They also told me of your phone Call Christmas day which they appreciated very much --- so do I.

My Christmas gifts were not many but all were just what a person like myself would want on such an Occasion. Mother sent quite a huge box filled with "a bit of" everything. Fruit, nuts, candy, shaving materials, Cake, Cookies etc plus a beautiful

the [p]ilot has [3*] offered to teach me a bit about handling the plane.[194] He also wants me to learn how to [c]o[-]pilot in case of emergencies. The [r]adio [o]perator +[e]ngineer[,] too[,] are giving me lessons on their particular jobs[,] which will take me quite a while to learn.

I received a letter from home today that told me that our Joe was home for Christmas and caused quite a sensation in his new middie[195] uniform. They also told me of your phone call Christmas [D]ay[,] which they appreciated very much – – – so do I.

My Christmas gifts were not many[,] but all were just what a person like myself would want on such an occasion. Mother sent quite a huge box filled with a lot of everything. Fruit, nuts, candy, shaving materials, cake, cookies[,] etc[.] plus a beautiful

---

[194] At the top of page three, the stationery has a printed drawing of a woman dressed in Western riding clothes, riding a horse. Next to the image is the handwritten word "Syl."

[195] Midshipman.

pink wool scarf. My Uncle Grey also sent a package with an assortment of Italian pastries and more fruit, nuts cakes etc. My brother Joe sent the shaving set of talc, lotion, and shaving soap and Sylvia sent --- thats all. I was going to buy myself an expensive gift but just can't find it yet. It is a bit expensive but will be most practicle soon. It can't be found here at Pueblo but maybe they can be found in a larger city. What I wanted was a Portable Radio that has both battery and tubes and works on A.C. - D.C. Current. I have had myself quite a time slumming & shopping from Music stores, Hardware, Jewelry, 2nd hand, Pawnshops and repair shops with no results. I hope to have some success at Denver - (when I ever get there.) I could have gone this Sunday but we must be paid on that date

[3R*] pink wool scarf. My [u]ncle Greg[196] also sent a package with an assortment of Italian pastries and more fruit, nuts, cakes[,] etc. My brother Joe sent the s[h]aving set of talc, lotion, and shaving soap[,] and Sylvia sent - - - that[']s all. I was going to buy myself an exclusive gift[,] but just can't find it yet. It is a bit expensive[,] but will be most practicle [*sic*] soon. It can't be found here at Pueblo[,] but maybe they can be found in a larger city. What I wanted was a [p]ortable [r]adio that has both battery and tubes and works on A.C.-D.C. current. I have had myself quite a time slumming + shopping from [m]usic stores, [h]ardware, [j]ewelry, 2nd hand, [p]awnshops[,] and repair shops with no results. I hope to have some success at Denver—(when I ever get there[).] I could have

---

[196] Gregory (Gregorio) Mazza was the brother of Anthony Mazza's father, Louis (Luigi) Mazza. Both were born in Serrastretta, Italy, and emigrated to the United States in the 1910s. The two brothers married two sisters on June 18, 1920. Gregory married Angeline Guzzi Mazza, and Louis married Anthony's mother, Pauline (Pasqualina) Guzzi Mazza. "Brothers, Sisters—Wed Together—Observe 50th," *Pittsburgh Press*, June 14, 1970; see Appendix B.

4

or else skip a month. I am in no position
to argue so will meekly stand in line
early Sunday morning muttering to myself
about rules and regulations and what should
or should not be done about them. By now
poor Miss Christine at Denver will be
sad and broken hearted waiting for my
expected but never actual visit.

Gosh! I see where I've really
been at this letter hard and heavy and
too 'Johnny' is about to chase me out.
So I'll close sending oodles of love,
wishing I could be a real "hot Navigator"
on your hands for the New year Holiday
plus many many more days after that.

Happy New Year
Love
Tony

gone this Sunday[,] but we must be paid on that date [4*] or else skip a month. I am in no position to argue[,] so will meekly stand in line early Sunday morning[,] muttering to myself about rules and regulations and what should or should not be done about them. By now[,] poor Miss Christine at Denver will be sad and broken hearted [*sic*][,] waiting for my expected but never actual visit.

Gosh! I see where I've really been at this letter hard and heavy and[,] too[,] 'Johnny' is about to close me out. So I'll close sending oodles of love, wishing I could be a real "hot [n]avigator" on your hands for the New Year['s] [h]oliday plus many[,] many more days after that.

Happy New Year[!]
Love[,]
Tony

Free

P/o. U.S. M/yza 1-1345/4
21SCCS 1-26 Box 3323
P.A.A.B. Pueblo, Colo.

PUEBLO
COLO
DEC
8 PM
1944

Miss Sylvia Jacobs
2334 Atmore St.
Pittsburgh 13, Pa.

490

Dec 31, 1944

Dearest Sylvia:

Tonight, I sit quietly on my bunk staring at the image that smiles sweetly for me from the shelf above. It's New Years eve the last day of the year 1944 and usually the time for two people just as we to reflect all that took place between us in the short span of one year, 365 days to be exact. Gosh! last year like now I was at Nashville probably writing to Sylvia as I am at present. It is amazing the things that can happen in one year. Nashville, Maxwell, Tyndall, San Marcos, Lincoln and Pueblo. We certainly have operated under the severest of handicaps, the lack of each others company but some how I feel that we are much closer than we were this same period one year ago. I may have traveled in person to all the above named places alone but S. M. J. sure did come along tugging at my heart strings never causing one dull moment. Two short leaves in that period, although not the most pleasant of experiences, cleared so many things that stood between us. Both times it had to be for constant companion

492

December 31, 1944

From: F.O. A.S. Mazza T-136514
215 CCS 1-26 Box 3323
P.A.A.B. Pueblo, Colo.

To: Miss Sylvia M. Jacobs
2334 Atmore St.
Pittsburgh 12, Pa.

Postmark: 3:00 PM
January 1, 1945
Pueblo, Colorado

Letterhead: Officers Mess
Army Air Base
Pueblo, Colorado

[1*]   Dec[.] 31, 1944

Dearest Sylvia:

Tonight, I sit quietly on my bunk[,] staring at the image that smiles sweetly for me from the shelf above.[197] It's New Year['s] [E]ve[,] the last day of the year 1944[,] and usually the time for two people just as we [*sic*] to reflect [on] all that took place between us in the short span of one year, 365 days to be exact. Gosh! [L]ast year[,] like now[,] I was at Nashville[,] probably writing

---

[197] See *supra* pages 9 (Photograph of Sylvia M. Jacobs) and 305 (Letter from Anthony S. Mazza to Sylvia M. Jacobs (November 1, 1944)).

OFFICERS MESS
ARMY AIR BASE
PUEBLO, COLORADO

2.

ship was not our lot and we could never
find any other means than person to person
talks to settle the things deepest in our minds
and hearts. Our joyous moments were so
many and too numerous, perhaps to mention.
Riverview Park, Pictures, Martini, St Francis
Alcove, strolls, stores, dances, Conch,
movies, and dinners together. ~~Holidays~~ Illyenes
were Sylvia's infested finger and Tony's
bad cold at San Marcos. Highlights were
R.N. Jacobs and Navigator Mazza. Slight
disappointment F/o. instead of 2nd Lt. Our
most serious difference Letter writing
which ranks in the same spot it did
one year ago almost. Last years New
years resolution must be renewed with
greater determination this time, I hope.
        What's this? No, it can't be but
some how mental telepathy just now
took number one priority on the air ways
via BKS 375. There right in front
of "mine own eyes" Sylvia Mary Grace
Jacobs stepped right out of the Picture
frame and still in Nurses costume

494

to Sylvie as I am at present. It is amazing the things that can happen in one year. Nashville, Maxwell, Tyndall,[198] San Marcos, Lincoln[,] and Pueblo. We certainly have operated under the severest of handicaps, the lack of each other[']s company[,] but some-how [*sic*] I feel that we are much closer than we were this same period one year ago. I may have traveled in person to all the above[-]named places alone[,] but S.M.J. sure did come along[,] tugging at my heart-strings[,] never causing one dull moment. Two short leaves in that period, although not the most pleasant of experiences, cleared so many things that stood between us. Both times it had to be[,] for constant companion[-][2*]ship was not our lot[,] and we could never find any other means than person[-] to[-]person talks to settle the things deepest in our minds and hearts. Our joyous moments were so many and too numerous[,] perhaps[,] to mention. Riverview Park, [p]ictures, [m]artini, St. Francis Alcove, strolls, stars, dances, couch movies, and dinners together. Illnesses were Sylvia's infected finger and Tony's bad cold at San Marcos. Highlights were R.N. Jacobs and Navigator Mazza. Slight disappointment F./O. instead of 2nd Lt. Our most serious difference [was] [l]etter writing[,] which ranks in the same spot it did one year ago almost. Last year[']s New [Y]ear[']s resolution must be renewed with greater determination this time, I hope.

What[']s this? No, it can't be[,] but some how [*sic*] mental telepathy just now took number one priority on the air ways [*sic*]

---

[198] Tyndall Air Force Base is twelve miles from Panama City, Florida. "The History of Tyndall," Tyndall Air Force Base, accessed June 20, 2020, https://www.tyndall.af.mil/About/.

3.

stepped just so sweetly from the shelf to the floor. (Quite some step.) Gee! but you are radiant tonight with charm and personality plus. We shall spend New Years at the Officers Ball held at the Officers Club so we've got to find an exquisite evening gown for the occasion. By golly! the old picture frame just molded itself into a perfect fitting blue vivacious gown that will be the envy of all the Ladies there tonight. (All this thanks to Fairy God father" Tony's imagination). Hmmm! that dress sure does show up all those curves. Better we should stay at home?? Well, I promised, so off we go floating through air to the beautiful melodies played by an entire 100 piece orchestra. (Nothing but the best and it don't cost any more either.) All these boys know how to play (I saw to that) nice waltzes. Now I'm really in two-step heaven with the girl of my dreams.

via BKP[199] 375. There[,] right in front of "mine own eyes[,]" Sylvia Mary Grace Jacobs stepped right out of the [p]icture frame and still in [n]urse[']s costume [3*] stepped just so sweetly from the shelf to the floor. (Quite some step.) Gee! [B]ut you are radiant tonight with charm and personality plus. We shall spend New Year[']s at the Officers Ball held at the Officers Club[,] so we've got to find an exquisite evening gown for the occasion. By [g]olly! The old picture frame just molded itself into a perfect[-]fitting[,] blue[,] vivacious gown that will be the envy of all the [l]adies there tonight. (All this thanks to Fairy Godfather Tony's imagination[.)] Hmm! [T]hat dress sure does show up all those curves. Better we should stay at home?? Well, I promised, so off we go[,] floating through air to the beautiful melodies played by an entire 100[-]piece orchestra. (Nothing but the best[,] and it don't [*sic*] cost any more[,] either.) All that these boys know how to play (I saw to that) are waltzes. Now I'm really in two-step heaven with the girl of my dreams.

---

[199] The last letter is not clear. Perhaps this is a reference to a BC-375E, a liaison radio transmitter, which U.S. aircraft commonly used during World War II. Ronald Schultz, "What Constitutes a Radio on a WWII Era Bomber?" MAPS Air Museum, November 14, 2018, https://mapsairmuseum.org/what-constitutes-a-radio-on-a-wwii-era-bomber/.

4.

Champagne, for dance, Caviar, Turkey, served in buffet style plus everything one's heart desires. (might as well go the limit). I keep catching the smile from your eyes, our hands are quite blistered from such a long hand holding session, in fact a good case of 1st degree burn. The dance finally, as all good things do, ends at so quickly. We are quite tired but who wouldn't be dancing with a partner such as I. I decide to take you home early with "purposes" in mind and we finally arrive at 4:00 AM (Wait till Mama Jacobs hears about this!!) I leave early too at 7:00 AM counting my "just rewards" 55 hugs and 155 kisses; not bad for a 3 hour session. (Casanova Mazza.) Now to recuperate for 365 days to get set for the next year Swish! There goes Mental Telepathy as one of my pals grimly reminds me that the U.S.

498

[4*] [C]hampagne for drink, [c]aviar, [t]urkey, served in buffet style plus everything one's heart desires[...]might as well go to the limit. I keep catching the smile from your eyes[;] our hands are quite blistered from such a long hand holding [sic] session, in fact[,] a good case of 1st[-]degree burn. The dance finally[,] as all good things do[,] ends oh so quickly. We are quite tired[,] but who wouldn't be[,] dancing with a partner such as I. I decide to take you home early with "purposes" in mind[,] and we finally arrive at 4:00 AM[.] ([W]ait till Mama Jacobs hears about this!!) I leave early[,] too[,] at 7:00 AM[,] counting my just rewards[:] 55 hugs and 155 kisses, not bad for a 3[-]hour session. (Cassanova [sic] Mazza.) Now to rest and recuperate for 365 days to get set for the next year[.] Swish! There goes [m]ental [t]elepathy as one

Army requests my presence for flying at 4:45 A.M. tomorrow morning. Very considerate of them, I must say, to help me start the New year off right. I hope you enjoyed yourself at my Telepathy Two-step just as much as I did arranging it. My News Resolution is bigger and better x's + o's to Sylvie from Tony.

Love
Tony

Mental
Telepathy
Q
D (P.S.) The corsage was of orchids (Naturally!!).

of my pals grimly reminds me that the U.S. [5*] Army requests my presence for flying at 4:45 AM tomorrow morning. Very considerate of them, I must say, to help me start the New Year off right. I hope you enjoyed yourself at my Telepathy Two-Step just as much as I did arranging it. My [n]ew[r]esolution is bigger and better x's and o's to Sylvie from Tony.

Love[,]

Tony

Mental

Telepath [*sic*]

   Q

   (PS) The [c]orsage was of orchids

   (Naturally!!).

   D

Free

PUEBLO
JAN 1
3 PM
1945
COLO.

T/6. U.S. Mayya T-136674
2560E3 1-26 Bn 3323
P.A.B. Pueblo, Colo.

Miss Sylvia Jacobs
2334 Atmore St.
Pittsburgh 13, Pa.

1945

Jan 3, 1945

Dearest Sylvia:

Had a bit of excitement on
New years day flight when we
were headed for Abolene, Texas.
About half way there, our number
4 engine "cut out" and we were
flying on 3 engines. This isn't
anything to get worried about since
the sturdy old crate can fly on
one engine alone if such is
ultimately necessary but we
according to rules of the 2nd
Air force had to land as soon
as possible for repairs. I
immediately picked out an alternate
air port which happened to be
Amarillo, Texas right close to the
New Mexico border, and the Pilot
proved his worth with a perfect
landing even though the field
had crash wagons, fire trucks
and ambulances waiting for

January 3, 1945

From: F./O. A.S. Mazza T-136514
215 CCS 1-26 Box 3323
PAAB Pueblo, Colo.

To: Miss Sylvia Jacobs
2334 Atmore St.
Pittsburgh 12, Pa.

Postmark: 11:00 AM
January 4, 1945
Pueblo, Colorado
Air Mail

Letterhead: Air Mail

[1*]   Jan[.] 3, 1945

Dearest Sylvia:

Had a bit of excitement on New Year[']s [D]ay flight when we were headed for Abolene [*sic*], Texas. About halfway there, our number 4 engine "cut out[,]" and we were flying on 3 engines. This isn't anything to get worried about[,] since the sturdy old crate can fly on one engine alone[,] if such is ultimately necessary[,] but we[,] according to the rules of the 2nd Air [F]orce[,] had to land as soon as possible for repairs. I immediately picked out an

us. We stayed overnight but
I didn't bother going to town since
I had all my old clothes, G.I. shoes,
and heavy flying clothing which probably
would have had people staring for
fare. The next day our base
sent a plane down for us while
the one we had had to go through
entire over-hauling and replace-
ment of one engine.

I did listen to Sister Jacob's
sermon and you may rest assured
I shall never go back to the days
when I was an old soak (about the
age of 5 to be correct.) I discovered
that since that time I still suffer
the after affects of even the slightest
bit of drink and am not willing
to suffer even for society's sake.
My record of soberness remains intact
to that hectic day so many years
ago.

I would like to sing to
you one of these days

alternate air port [*sic*][,] which happened to be Amarillo, Texas[,] right close to the New Mexico border[,] and the [p]ilot proved his worth with a perfect landing[,] even though the field had crash wagons, fire trucks[,] and ambulences [*sic*] waiting for [2*] us. We stayed overnight[,] but I didn't bother going to town[,] since I had all my old clothes, G.I. shoes, and heavy flying clothing[,] which probably would have had people staring for[200] fare. The next day[,] our base sent a plane down for us while the one we had had to go through [an] entire over-hauling [*sic*] and [the] replace-ment of one engine.

I did listen to Sister Jacobs['] sermon[,] and you may rest assured I shall never go back to the days when I was an old soak (about the age of 5 to be correct[).][201] I discovered that since that time[,] I still suffer the after affects [*sic*] of even the slightest bit

---

[200] The word is not completely clear, and, of course, the phrase "for fare" does not make sense.

[201] According to family lore, when Anthony Mazza was a young boy, he and his brothers were great fans of cowboy movies. When they returned home from the cinema, they would often reenact the Western films they saw. One of the scenes they decided to reenact was of dusty cowboys riding into town and heading to the local saloon for a drink. At the time, Anthony's father made wine at home, stored in a wooden barrel. Anthony connected the wine to what cowboys drank, so he tapped into the barrel and served himself and his fellow "cowboys" "shots" of the wine. In the course of their play, the boys became unsteady on their feet and despondent. When Anthony's mother found her sons in this state, she urgently called the family doctor and asked him to make a house call. The doctor quickly arrived, examined the boys, and presented his professional assessment: "Mrs. Mazza, your sons are not sick. They are drunk!"

Air Mail

but it seems I'm always out of voice when you are near. You must certainly do something to the warbling I do, that singing is utterly impossible. Perhaps too I am so involved in looking at and studying S. M. J. that singing seems to pass into the darkness a far 3rd or 4th rate item. I'm not the 2nd Bing Crosby but the 1st Tony Mazza. Bing <u>croons</u>, Frankie has em <u>swoon</u> while Tony makes em aware of the <u>moon</u>???

One of the boys happened to take a picture of me at one of my lighter moments. There is a sun light leak at the lower left hand corner. You may keep this one but only on one condition. That I get the one you took in battery suit at Atlantic City last summer. Now if you don't I demand this

of drink and am not willing to suffer even for society's sake. My record of soberness remains intact to that hectic day so many years ago.

I would like to sing to you one of these days[,] [3*] but it seems I'm always out of voice when you are near. You must certainly do something to the warbling I do, [so] that singing is utterly impossible. Perhaps[,] too[,] I am so involved in looking at and studying S.M.J. that singing seems to pass into the darkness[,] a far 3rd[-] or 4th[-]rate item. I'm not the 2nd Bing Crosby[,][202] but the 1st Tony Mazza. Bing <u>croons</u>, Frankie has [']em <u>swoon</u>[,][203] while Tony makes [']em aware of the <u>moon</u>???

One of the boys happened to take a picture of me at one of my lighter moments. There is a sun light [*sic*] leak at the lower left hand [*sic*] corner. You may keep this one[,] but only on one condition. That I get the one you took in a bathing suit at Atlantic City last summer. Now if you don't[,] I demand this [4*] one be returned. I thought it quite a bit different from many others I have and much more informal. See! I can smile once in a while[,] too.

What I think about the [n]urses program in the [a]rmed [s]ervices will take a letter in itself. Then I'll preach to my heart[']s delight and pity poor you having to read all I write. Many adjectives I'll have to omit in order to maintain my gentlemanly status.

---

[202] Bing Crosby (b. May 3,1903; d. October 14, 1977) was a popular American entertainer known for his smooth singing style. See notes 37, 56, 60, 73-76, 253.

[203] Frank Sinatra (b. December 12, 1915; d. May 14, 1998) was an American entertainer, who has an enduring fan base who appreciates his singing of American standards. See *supra* pages 266-67 and notes 31 and 250.

4

one be returned. I thought it
quite a bit different from many
others I have and much more
informal. See! I can smile once
in a while too.

What I think about the Nurses program
inter-Armed Services will take a
letter in itself. Then I'll preach to
my heart's delight and pity poor you
having to read all I write. Many
adjectives I'll have to omit in order
to maintain my gentlemanly status.

Must close now and I do think
the mistletoe cartoon was extremely
clever. Imagine with a
motive such as that plus my
usual amativeness, then poor Sylvia
would have to think of more better
strategic defenses in order to even
survive.

Love
Tony

P.S. White envelopes are still the thing.

510

Must close now[,] and I do think the mistletoe cartoon was extremely clever. Imagine with a motive such as that plus my usual [undecipherable],[204] then poor Sylvia would have to think of more strategic defenses in order to even survive.

Love[,]
Tony

P.S. White envelopes are still the thing.

[204] The word may be "assertiveness."

AIR MAIL
8 CENTS
UNITED STATES OF AMERICA

Airmail

PUEBLO
JAN 4.
11 AM
1945
COLO.

C/o. A.S. Shaggn T-136514
USCES 1-26 Box 3523
PAAB Pueblo, Colo.

Miss Sylvia Jacobs
2334 Atwood st
Pittsburgh 13, Pa

512

OFFICERS MESS
ARMY AIR BASE
PUEBLO, COLORADO

Jan 6, 1945

Dearest Sylvia:

Received your most wonderful letter written on New years day today. Gosh! but it had everything in it I love to hear. Some day I hope that both of us can combine our dreams into the real thing. I too would prefer to be off the streets at the stroke of 12:00 with that certain some-one in my arms.

The last few days here at Pueblo have been really tightly filled with classes and flying. Even sleep is slowly being flattened into meager 4, 5 or six hour quotas. Yesterday, thanks to the "paddle-foots" (ground officers) we had to get up at 7:10 A.M., line up in formation, have roll call and even march to class. Instead of men, these ground officers think we are a bunch of kids or something in that order. They having nothing to do but think up these "clever" ideas! Its about time some of them realized who is fighting the war. They in their soft safe jobs back in the states or

514

January 6, 1945

From: F./O. A.S. Mazza T-136514
             215 CCS 1-26 Box 3323
             PAAB Pueblo, Colo.

To: Miss Sylvia Jacobs
             2334 Atmore St.
             Pittsburgh 12, Pa.

Postmark: 6:00 PM
             January 7, 1945
             Pueblo, Colorado

Letterhead: Officers Mess
             Army Air Base
             Pueblo, Colorado

[1*]   Jan[.] 6, 1945

Dearest Sylvia:

Received your most wonderful letter written on New Year[']s [D]ay today. Gosh! [B]ut it had everything in it I love to hear. Some day [sic] I hope that both of us can combine our dreams into the real thing; I[,] too[,] would prefer to be off the streets at the stroke of 12:00 with that certain some-one [sic] in my arms.

The last few days here at Pueblo have been really tightly filled with classes and flying. Even sleep is slowly being flattened into

2.

the boys that risk their necks on 4 engines here and most of all, over there in the heat of Combat. This kind of discipline they should realize died with the turn of the Century and is no longer useful in this modern era. It has the same effect as a single shot rifle used against a Giant Tank. All of it is good for showmanship but not for fighting men. We have no time for that useless kind of drill when most of us need time it in technical training where it will do the most good.

While I'm on the subject a bit I may as well tell you what I think about their nurse campaign. Yes, they need nurses and just so many of them. Where they shall go and what they shall do can be settled not upon enlistment but some time after that. All the top officials want is to fill a quota. You, Gloria, would be number 11,965 out of a proposed 25,000 or something to that effect. As an individual you would lose your complete identity as far as

516

meager 4[-], 5[-] or six[-]hour quotas. Yesterday, thanks to the "paddle-foots" (ground officers)[,] we had to get up at 7:10 AM, line up in formation, have roll call [*sic*][,] and even march to class. Instead of men, these ground officers think we are a bunch of kids or something in that order. They hav[e] nothing to do but think up these "clever" ideas. It[']s about time some of them realized who is fighting the war. They in their soft, safe jobs back in the [S]tates or [2*] the boys that risk their necks on 4 engines here and most of all, over there in the heat of combat[?] Their kind of discipline they should['ve] realized died with the turn of the century and is no longer useful in this modern era. It has the same effect as a single[-]shot rifle used against a Grant [t]ank. All of it is good for showmanship but not for fighting men. We have no time for that usless [*sic*] kind of drill when most of us need time in technical training[,] where it will do the most good.

While I'm on the subject a bit[,] I may as well tell you what I think about their nurse campaign. Yes, they need nurses and just so many of them. Where they shall go and what they shall do can be settled not upon enlistment but some time after that. All the top officials want is to fill a quota. You, Sylvia, would be number 11,965 out of a proposed 25,000 or something to that effect. As an individual[,] you would lose your complete identity as far as

3'

they would be concerned. A good example of
Army + Navy tactics can be viewed when
one just remembers the 35,000 blanket
wash outs of Cadets whose hopes were
thwarted by a letter from Higher Headquarters.
Yes, they had promises and many enlisted
on the faith of that promise. Today, they are
in the muddy battlefields of Europe as First
line Infantry men even though they are well
trained and intelligent, fit for duty such as
we are doing. Now early this week the
Navy again realizes a shortage; another quota
must be filled and hence another drive
plus advertisements. The Doc you mentioned
is exactly correct in his opinion and I
don't believe I'm too far off in mine. I
only wished that you could join and get
a good taste of it all; then quit when you
so desired. That is definitely out of the
question so you must be right before
you start. Deep down deep I know

[3*] they would be concerned. A good example of Army + Navy tactics can be viewed when one just remembers the 35,000 blanket wash outs [*sic*] of cadets[,] whose hopes were thwarted by a letter from [h]igher [h]eadquarters. Yes, they had promises[,] and many enlisted on the faith of that promise. Today, they are in the muddy battlefields of Europe as [f]irst[-]line [i]nfantry men [*sic*][,] even though they are well trained and intelligent, fit for duty such as we are doing. Now[,] only this week[,] the Navy[205] again realizes a shortage; another quota must be filled[,] and hence another drive plus advertisements. The [d]oc you mentioned is exactly correct in his opinion[,] and I don't believe I'm too far off in mine. I only wished that you could join and get a good taste of it all [and] then quit when you so desired. That is definitely out of the question[,] so you must be right before you start. Deep down deep I know

---

[205] The word is unclear.

4

that you know what is right about Army Nurse Corp and what is wrong about it too. and that that issue will be settled in your own mind before long. You do as much good to the war-effort by remaining on your job at the home front to relieve suffering and misery there.

I see where I must be making some headway in the right direction when S. M. J. doesn't care whether or not I pass with relatives. That is exactly how I feel about it too just so long as I pass with you. (Plenty of passes in that last play.) I see where your cousins musn't know you very well particularly if they think you ain't the type. Perhaps you're not the type they think you are but you are the type for me. (How's that for typing?)

Just wondering whether S. M. J. is realizing that she is not 15 or 16 anymore is either a good or bad sign for me??

I hope I am not putting you to any trouble about the next-roll. I only mentioned it for I thought there would be plenty

[4*] that you know what is right about [the] Army Nurse Corp[s] and what is wrong about it[,] too[,] and that that issue will be settled in your own mind before long. You can do as much good to the [w]ar effort by remaining on your job at the home front to relieve suffering and misery there.

I see where I must be making some headway in the right direction when S.M.J. doesn't care whether or not I pass with relatives. That is exactly how I feel about it[,] too[,] just as long as I pass with you. (Plenty of passes in that last play.) I see where your cousins musn't [sic] know you very well[,] particularly if they think you aren't the type. Perhaps you're not the type they think you are[,] but you are the type for me. (How[']s that for typing?)

Just wondering whether S.M.J.['s] realizing that she is not 15 or 16 anymore is either a good or bad sign for me??

I hope I am not putting you to any trouble about nut–roll [sic]. I only mentioned it[,] for I thought there would be plenty

5

around during Christmas time. Perhaps it is only in the Easter baking season that Nut Cake dominates? I really don't know but I really hope that I'm not making anyone go out of their way to please my little whim.

"Chuckle Chuckle!" Not one word do I hear about fudge! Sylvia must have failed again??? Or has she lost her nerve? Hmmm. (That ought to stir her up.)

Well, I had better run along now for it is getting late and I must hit the sack for tomorrows early classes. There is plenty of love in this letter from me to thee.

Love

"X"
Tang
XO

P.S. Still like these two almost ancient ballads
"What for me Mary"
"You'll never know"
"

XO

522

[5*] around during Christmas time [*sic*]. Perhaps it is only in the Easter baking season that [n]ut [c]ake dominates? I really don't know[,] but I really hope that I'm not making anyone go out of there [*sic*] way to please my little whim.

Chuckle [c]huckle!! Not one word do I hear about fudge! Sylvia must have failed again??? Or has she lost her nerve? Hmm. (That ought to stir her up.)

Well, I had better run along now[,] for it is getting late and I must hit the sack for tomorrow[']s early classes. There is plenty of love in this letter from me to thee.

Love[,]

x

"Tony"

P.S. Still like those two almost ancient ballads,
"W[ait] for [M]e[,] Mary"[206]
"You'll [N]ever [K]now"[207]

---

[206] See *supra* note 39.

[207] Dick Haymes and The Song Spinners, vocalists, "You'll Never Know," by Harry Warren and Mack Gordon, recorded May 27, 1943, Decca, No. 18556A; "Dick Haymes, (vocalist)," DAHR, accessed June 20, 2020, https:// adp.library.ucsb.edu/index.php/talent/detail/149417/Hames_Dick_vocalist; see also *supra* note 31.

Free

F/O. A.S. Megga T-136514
215AC5 1-26 Box 3323
PAAB Pueblo, Colo.

PUEBLO, COLO.
JAN 7
6 PM
1945

Miss Sophia Jacobs
2334 Atmore St.
Pittsburgh 12, Pa.

Jan 8, 1945

Dearest Sylvia :

I guess you have already
surmised by the color and type of station
ary that Tony is writing this letter
from Gilmore' apartment. Yes, here I
am tonight helping that poor Co-Pilot
transfer all his belongings from this
cozy place to the Main Hotel. Why?
Well it seems that 'Gil' has been 'blessed'
with in-law trouble. His wife went
home for the Christmas Holidays and
now tells him that she is bringing
her mother back to Pueblo and it is
up to him to find a place for her.
That has been utterly impossible because
of the housing shortage but to please
everyone and maintain his 'happy home'
he has found too room set-up at
the hotel Main. This room here has
cost him $23 per month which I

January 8, 1945

From: F./O. A.S. Mazza T-136514
        215 CCS 1-26 Box 3323
        P.A.A.B. Pueblo, Colo.

To: Miss Sylvia M. Jacobs
        2334 Atmore St.
        Pittsburgh 12, Pa.

Postmark: 1:00 PM
            January 9, 1945
            Pueblo, Colorado

Letterhead: [The letter is on yellow stationery with a picture in the upper left corner of two saddles hanging over a wooden rack, which consists of a horizontal pole supported on both sides by perpendicular poles. Under the left saddle is a handwritten letter *T* for Tony, and under the right saddle is a handwritten *S* for Sylvia. An arrow with a question mark points toward a jug resting next to the right perpendicular post.]

[1*]   Jan[.] 8, 1945

Dearest Sylvia:

I guess you have already surmised by the color and type of stationary [sic] that Tony is writing this letter from Gilmore's [a]partment. Yes, here I am tonight[,] helping that poor [c]o-[p]ilot

thought rather high rent for a single room with very few conveniences Now for two weeks it will cost him $40 and all his meals will of necessity be bought instead of prepared at home plus the inconveniences of "in-laws" just for the few remaining weeks he will be here. These Women???

Wonder how I would handle a situation such as this? I probably would put up a stiffer fight than he did but no doubt would succomb to the terrific verbal bombardment that women give men quite often. (Such is life!)

After the packing and moving we shall have our Spaghette dinner. It seems that "Gil" is a tremendous eater of that famed dish and could eat it every meal every day of the week. I like Spaghette but never to that extreme.

I couldn't help but smile at Carsanova Mazza's accomplishments on New Years Eve. Getting down to fine points at the rate of 55

transfer all his belongings from this cozy place to the Main Hotel. Why? Well[,] it seems that 'Gil' has been 'blessed' with in-law trouble. His wife went home for the Christmas [h]olidays and now tells him that she is bringing her mother back to Pueblo[,] and it is up to him to find a place for her. That has been utterly impossible because of the housing shortage[,] but to please everyone and maintain his 'happy home[,]' he has found a two[-]room set-up [sic] at the [H]otel Main. This room here has cost him $23 per month[,] which I [1R*] thought rather high rent for a single room with very few conveniences. Now for two weeks[,] it will cost him $40[,] and all his meals will of necessity be bought instead of prepared at home plus the inconveniences of an in-law just for the few remaining weeks he will be here. These [w]omen??? Wonder how I would handle a situation such as this? I probably would put up a stiffer fight than he did but no doubt would succomb [sic] to the terrific verbal bombardment that women give men quite often. (Such is life!)

After the packing and moving[,] we shall have our spaghetti dinner. It seems that 'Gil' is a tremendous eater of that famed dish and could eat it every meal every day of the week. I like spaghetti but never to that extreme.

I couldn't help but smile at Cassanova [sic] Mazza's accomplishments on New Year[']s Eve. Getting down to fine hugs in 3 hours. 2. we would

[marginal calculation: 55)180, 155, 250, 3.5]

have to clinch once every 3.5 minutes

[marginal calculation: 155)180, 155, 250, 166, 950, 930, 1.16]

and kiss once every 1.16 minutes.

(Quite a busy session if you
ask me?) It really would take one
year to recuperate from blisters & bruises,
and broken ribs. I guess I'll slow
down a bit and sure would settle for
5 of each. (With plenty of time for quality.)

Yes, I have a copy of the New
Testament and have read it at least
3 times. (The old testament too.) I like
the Old Testament better for reading because
there are so many things that are
hard to understand and that tax imagination
beyond even reason.

I looked all over the letter
you signed S.W.A.K.A.A.G.B.H.
for lip marks but not a trace
did I find of even one & you

points[,] at the rate of 55 [2*] hugs in 3 hours [dividing 180 by 55 to reach 3.5][,] we would have to clinch once every 3.5 minutes [dividing 180 by 155 to reach 1.16] and kiss once every 1.16 minutes ([q]uite a busy session if you ask me[).] It really would take one year to recuperate from blisters + bruises and broken ribs. I guess I'll slow down a bit and sure would settle for 5 of each. (With plenty of time for quality.)

Yes, I have a copy of the New Testament and have read it at least 3 times. (The [O]ld [T]estament[,] too.) I like the Old Testament better for reading because there are so many things that are hard to understand and that tax imagination beyond reason.

I looked all over the letter you signed S.W.A.K.A.A.G.B.H.[208] for lip marks[,] but not a trace did I find of even one. You

---

[208] The letters probably stand for sealed with a kiss and a great big hug.

531

must have cheated and merely filled in the letters. ('Taint' fair!)

Must run along now; we're all set for the moving. Suse insisted 2 were moving on a Causse of approximately 55° N.E. to Atmore St + Sylvie. Poor Syl wouldn't be able to get a minutes rest with me near by.

Love; Love; Love

Tony.

[2R*] must have cheated and merely filled in the letters.
(['Tain't] fair!)

Must run along now; we're all set for the morning. Sure wished I were moving on a course of approximately 55° N.E. to Atmore St[.] + Sylvie. Poor Syl wouldn't be able to get a minute[']s rest with me near by [*sic*].

Love; Love; Love[,]
Tony[209]

---

[209] One small *x* is inserted in the tail of the *y* in "Tony."

F/o. A.S. Mazza T-136514
215 CCS 1-26 Bar 3223
P.A.A.B. Pueblo, Colo.

PUEBLO
JAN 9
1 PM
1945
COLO.

FREE

Miss Sylvia M. Jacobs
2334 Atmore St.
Pittsburgh 13, Pa

534

Jan 9, 1945

Dearest Sylvia:

I'll have to be a little more careful when I open my letters now or I'll surely miss that inscription which increases heart beat tempo. You should see the way I mutilate the envelope; I never open a letter the same way twice. As a matter of fact maybe I'll inclose this one envelope to show you what I mean. Doesn't the ~~envelope~~ one itself not have a story to tell? I'll let Psychologist S.M.J. (R.N.) give me her diagnosis. (This ought to be good.)

What! you won't send me that picture in a bathing suit? I don't mind the other 2 beauties either, the more the merrier but I'll have quite a while to wait before Sylvia puts on another swimming suit and takes a snap-shot out doors. Particularly since she has always been an honorable member of the Lilly White Club. (Nix to tan.) + Her motto.

536

January 9, 1945

From: F./O. A.S. Mazza T-136514
                 215 CCS 1–26 Box 3323
                 P.A.A.B. Pueblo, Colo.

To: Miss Sylvia Jacobs
                 2334 Atmore St.
                 Pittsburgh 12, Pa.

Postmark: 3:30 PM
                 January 10, 1945
                 Pueblo, Colorado

Letterhead: Officers Mess
                 Army Air Base
                 Pueblo, Colorado

[1*]   Jan[.] 9, 1945

Dearest Sylvia:

I'll have to be a little more careful when I open my letters now[,] or I'll surely miss that inscription which increases heart beat [*sic*] tempo. You should see the way I mutilate the envelope; I never open a letter the same way twice. As a matter of fact[,] maybe I'll inclose [*sic*] this one envelope to show you what I mean. Doesn't the envelope in itself not have a story to tell? I'll let Psychologist S.M.J. (R.N.) give me her diagnosis. (This ought to be good.)

As for Competition, I'm sure you can hold your own so my request should be considered once more and I hope the results are favorable this time. If you have the "doozy" one or can have it made soon I'll also put in my order for one of those. (The pins are all set and just aching to be put to some use.)

Les Zalavy has had a tough break in life. It has been a long time since I saw him in person. In fact, I visited him at the Bedford Ave Hospital one day on my way back from early classes at Tech in the spring of '41. I thought that at least by now he would have fared better and would resume normal life. We have an air base at Tucson Arizona and I just missed going there by several names on a roster at Lincoln. Perhaps we would have met once more but such was not the case.

What! [Y]ou won't send me that picture in a bathing suit? I won't mind the other 2 beauties either; the more the merrier[,] but I'll have quite a while to wait before Sylvia puts on another swimming suit and takes a snap-shot [sic] out doors [sic]. Particularly since she has always[s] been an honorable member of the Lilly [sic] White Club. (Nix to tan.)—Her motto. [2*] As for competition, I'm sure you can hold your own[,] so my request should be considered once more[,] and I hope the results are favorable this time. If you have the "doozy" one[,] or can have it made soon[,] I'll also put in my order for one of those. (The pins are all set and just aching to be put to some use.)[210]

Leo Zilavy has had a tough break in life.[211] It has been a long time since I saw him in person. In fact, I visited him at the Bedford Ave. Hospital[212] one day on my way back from early classes at Tech in the [s]pring of '41. I thought that at least by now he would have fared better and would resume normal life. We have an air base at Tuscon [sic][,] Arizona[,] and I just missed going there by several names on a roster at Lincoln. Perhaps we would have met once more[,] but such was not the case.

---

[210] The reference here to pins may be to the ones used to affix a photograph to a wall or bulletin board. During World War II, posting images of glamorous actresses or models, known as "pin-up girls," was a mainstay of military life. "Pin-Ups," California State University Northridge Oviatt Library, February 21, 2017, https://library.csun.edu/SCA/Peek-in-the-Stacks/pin-ups.

[211] See *infra* note 213.

[212] The Tuberculosis Hospital of Pittsburgh was located on 2851 Bedford Avenue, Pittsburgh, Pennsylvania. Albert W. Bloom, "New Surge to Meet Mental Ills Forecast," *Pittsburgh Post-Gazette*, May 4, 1961.

3.

If Sylvia had been in my class at high school, I doubt very much if I would have been aware of her existence, particularly if I would have reacted towards her as I did towards the others of the class of June '39. Then again I believe it would have been all so different and I would have enjoyed her presence at least two to four years earlier than actually happened. All those dances we'd have had, all week-ends filled with fun + frolic, picnics, dates galore, proms, and every college social, skating, and even P.B.W. parties. (George wouldn't have liked that?) I know that some-where some-how you would have struck my fancy but no matter what, you did pick the right time and moment. (So did I.)

"Tea for two". How well I remember! I believe we missed it on my last leave but it will have to be on the "must" list should I ever get that chance again. You had better get plenty of practice in water boiling just to keep in trim for that special session. It wouldn't hurt either to be up on "toasting" bread.

[3*] If Sylvia had been in my class at high school, I doubt very much if I would have been aware of her existence[,] particularly if I would have reacted towards her as I did towards the other gals of the class of June '39. Then again[,] I believe it would have been all so different[,] and I would have enjoyed her presence at least two to four years earlier than has actually happened. All the dances we'd have had, all week-ends [sic] filled with fun + frolic, picnics, dates galore, proms, and every college social[,] skating, and even P.B.W. parties.[213] (George wouldn't have liked that??) I know that some-where [sic][,] some-how [sic] you would have struck my fancy[,] but no matter what, you did pick the right time and moment. (So did I.)

---

[213] In high school, Anthony Mazza and George Jacobs, Sylvia Jacobs' brother, were members of a social fraternity called the P.B.W. Society. The acronym intentionally hid the reference to the expression, "pitch a bit of woo." Pitching woo is an obsolete idiom for kissing, courting, or making love. "Pitch Woo," *The Free Dictionary*, accessed June 20, 2020, https://idioms. thefreedictionary.com/pitch+woo. According to *The Omicron*, Oliver High School's yearbook, the description of the fraternity was as follows:

> The P.B.W. Society consists of a group of boys who organized to carry out their high ideals of citizenship and morals. They stand for social, political, and economic betterment of Oliver High School from the students' view point. . . .
>
> To be eligible for admission to this organization, one must show academic ability and accomplishment, and an appreciation of the fine arts.

Members of the club included John Baltzer, John Fasso, George Jacobs, Anthony Mazza, Albert Miller, Robert Stroyne, Samuel Young, John Yount, and Leo Zelavy [also Zilavy]. *The Omicron* (June 1939), 69.

4.

Well, come to think of it, I was partially responsible for that too.

I have been writing this letter propped upon my cot, listening to the radio, looking at Sylvie, munching pecans and looking at Sylvie. One of the boys here has a pecan farm and at least a couple of bushel of pecans are on hand for us monthly. I am busy using up my quota plus several of the other fellows quota too.

Will soon drop off into dream land and Eutopia for two. Main ideology there is

Love.

signed
(The Dreamer)
Tony

"Tea for [T]wo[."]²¹⁴ How well I remember! I believe we missed it on my last leave[,] but it will have to be on the "must" list[,] should I ever get that chance again. You had better get plenty of practice in water boiling just to keep trim for that special session. It wouldn't hurt either to be up on "[t]oasting" bread. [4*] Well, come to think of it, I was partially responsible for that[,] too.

I have been writing this letter propped upon my cot, listening to the radio, looking at Sylvie, munching pecans[,] and looking at Sylvie. One of the boys here has a pecan farm[,] and at least a couple of bushel[s] of pecans are on hand for us monthly. I am busy using up my quota plus several of the other fellows['] quotas[,] too.

Will soon drop off into dream land [*sic*] and Eutopia for two. Main ideology there is

Love[,]
Signed
(The Dreamer)
Tony²¹⁵

---

²¹⁴ Vincent Youmans and Irving Caesar wrote the song "Tea for Two" for the 1924 Broadway musical *No, No Nanette*. "Tea for Two," Second Hand Songs, accessed June 20, 2020, https://secondhandsongs.com/work/40924. The reference here appears to be about actually sharing tea together rather than a reference to the song, a recording, a stage production, or a film.

²¹⁵ One small *x* appears in the tail of the *T*, and three *o*'s appear in the tail of the *y*.

Free

QUEBLO
COLO
JAN 10
3³⁰ PM
1945

F/o. A. J. Mazza T-136614
215 EES 1-26 Box 3323
P.A.A.B. Pueblo, Colo.

Miss Sylvia Jacobs
233t Athlone St.
Pittsburgh 12, Pa.

544

Jan 11, 1945

Dearest Sylvia:

I believe that you are extremely modest when you mention "writing ability." The last four letters have indicated quite definitely the _hidden_ talent that you have in that direction. You have never applied that gift which I know to definitely these; or else you have been as I have stated above "most. About the other gifts you have, well, I won't go into detail about those but there are many perhaps that you are not aware of, but I am!!

I too saw the movie "30 seconds over Tokyo" last week. The poor navigator, as usual, was lost in the glamour that draped those exclusive characters, the pilots. Some of the lads here have the real story of Capt Lawson's crash landing and it seems that the navigator had picked a spot further inland to land but the pilot refused to consider his judgement and used his own to crash land on the rough sea off the China Coast

January 11, 1945

From: F./O. A.S. Mazza T-136514
             215 CCS 1-26 Box 3323
             P.A.A.B. Pueblo, Colo.

To: Miss Sylvia Jacobs
             2334 Atmore St.
             Pittsburgh 12, Pa[.]

Postmark: 4:30 PM
             January 11, 1945
             Pueblo, Colorado

Letterhead: Officers Mess
             Army Air Base
             Pueblo, Colorado

[1*]   Jan[.] 11, 1945

Dearest Sylvia:

I believe that you are extremely modest when you mention your "writing ability." The last four letters have indicated quite definitely a <u>hidden</u> talent that you have in that direction. You have never applied the gift[,] which I know to definitely be there; or else you have been[,] as I have stated above[,] "modest." About the other gifts you have, [w]ell, I won't go into detail about those[,] but there are many[,] perhaps[,] that you are not aware of, but I <u>am</u>!!

547

Gosh! didn't know I could take Van Johnson's place in your dreams. It must have been oh so dramatic plus romantic. I'll have to see if I can picture Syl playing the role of Capt Lawson's wife. (I wonder how she'd handle that part.) Say, that was pretty close "the secret mission". Why only yesterday I was on one, in fact, a _complete_ movement. Yep, I had to move all my belongings from Barracks 375 to Barracks 601. The reason? "Army efficiency." That seems to be the only answer I can think of right now. I am rooming with a 'pal' who incidently is another Penn State Graduate. John H. Mendenhall of the Forestry Service. He has a radio; I an alarm clock; both of us are fresh air fiends and keep the windows wide open at night and neither of us smoke. We should get along very amiably together.

I[,] too[,] saw the movie "[Thirty S]econds over Tokyo"[216] last week. The poor navigator, as usual, was lost in the glamour that draped those exclusive characters, the pilots. Some of the lads here have the real story of Capt[.] Lawson's crash landing[,] and it seems that the navigator had picked a spot further inland to land[,] but the pilot refused to consider his judgement [sic] and used his own to crash[-]land on the rough sea off the China [c]oast. [2*] Gosh! [D]idn't know I could take Van Johnson's place in your dreams. It must have been oh so dramatic plus romantic. I'll have to see if I can picture Syl playing the role of Capt[.] Lawson's wife. (I wonder how she'd handle that part?) Say, that was pretty close [to] "the secret mission[."] Why only yesterday[,] I was on one, in fact, a complete <u>movement</u>. Yep, I had to move all my belongings from Barracks 375 to Barracks 601. The reason? Army efficiency? That seems to be the only answer I can think of right now. I am rooming with a pal, who incidently [sic] is another Penn State [g]raduate. John H. Mendenhall of the Forestry Service. He has a radio; I [have] an alarm clock; both of us are fresh[-]air fiends and keep the windows wide open at night[;] and neither of us smoke.

---

[216] *Thirty Seconds over Tokyo*, directed by Mervyn LeRoy, featuring Van Johnson, Robert Walker, and Spencer Tracy (Metro–Goldwyn–Mayer, 1944).

3.

By the way, do you sleep with your windows open? Do you snore or talk in your sleep? (Got to investigate!)

Mendenhall here seems to be quite a poet and I have just read some of his exclusive masterpieces; he doesn't do a bad job at all but some-how some place he mixes business with pleasure to include a lonesome pine-tree or a budding spruce etc.

If you are worried about milk shakes, I have lots more than that to worry about. I dare-not get near a scale for fear the results will not be too favorable. I imagine I must have gained back all those precious pounds I lost at San Marcos. These christmas fillings have indeed taken their toll, of that I am quite certain. We'll have to have a special built threshold if we continue at this rate. I wouldn't drop you over either but instead would bounce you over. (Ain't I mean!)

550

We should get along very amiably together. [3*] By the way, do you sleep with your windows open? Do you snore or talk in your sleep? (Got to investigate!)

Mendenhall here seems to be quite a poet[,] and I have just read some of his exclusive masterpieces; he doesn't do a bad job at all[,] but some-how [*sic*][,] some place[,] he mixes business with pleasure to include a lonesome pine-tree [*sic*] or a budding spruce[,] etc.

If you are worried about milk-shakes [*sic*], I have lots more than that to worry about. I dare-not [*sic*] get near a scale for fear the results will not be too favorable. I imagine I must have gained back all those precious pounds I lost at San Marcos. These Christmas fillings have indeed taken there [*sic*] toll, of that I am quite certain. We'll have to have a special built threshold if we continue at this rate. I wouldn't drop you over[,] either[,] but instead would bounce you over. ("Aren't" I mean!)

4.

I guess it must be kind of rough now to be losing all your old time friends. With Blanche Ball and Margret Hoffman gone, I imagine things will get a bit duller, but it won't be long before new friends and faces will substitute. It has always been that way with me in the army.

Little Paul & Sylvia must be growing up quite fast these days. Good thing I'm not about when Paul turns to my picture and calls me "Daddy". Yeow! wouldn't my face get red. I'd better sign off now and will close as little Paul would say.

Love to Sylvia

"Uncle" Tony.

[4*] I guess it must be kind of rough now to be losing all your old[-]time friends. With Blanche Ball and Margaret Hoffman gone, I imagine things will get a bit duller, but it won't be long before new friends and faces will substitute. It has always been that way with me in the [A]rmy.

Little Paul and Sylvia must be growing up quite fast these days.[217] Good thing I'm not about when Paul turns to my picture and calls me "Daddy." Yeow! [W]ouldn't my face get red. I'd better sign off now and will close as little Paul would say.

Love to Sylvia[,]

'Uncle' Tony.

---

[217] "Little Paul" and "Little Sylvia" are Sylvia Jacobs' nephew and niece. Little Paul, Paul Soltis (b. October 7, 1941; d. May 1, 2018), is the son of Sylvia Jacobs' older sister Alice Jacobs (b. February 9, 1911; d. April 21, 1999), who married in May of 1939 Emil S. Soltis (b. January 14, 1910; d. October 29, 1947). Little Sylvia, Sylvia A. Krey, née Ilcisin (b. November 5, 1941), is the daughter of Sylvia Jacobs' older sister Mathilda Jacobs (b. March 24, 1913; d. November 24, 1983), who married in September of 1940 John J. Ilcisin (b. September 18, 1913; d. January 16, 1963). See Appendix B. Both children at the time lived directly across the street from the Jacobs' Pittsburgh residence in adjoining townhouses. The Ilcisin family lived at 2335 Atmore Street, and the Soltis family lived at 2337 Atmore Street.

Free

PUEBLO COLO.
JAN 11
4:00 PM
1945

Sgt. R. S. Myers, F-136554
215 CCS 1-26 Box 3323
P.A.A.B. Pueblo, Colo.

Mrs. Sylvia Jacobs
2334 Atmore St.
Pittsburgh 12, Pa

Jan 14, 1945

Dearest Sylvia:

Had I known you were afraid of bugs
while I was in Texas I'd have sent you
a few of those noble specimens inclosed in
either a letter or carton. Many a time
at San Marcos we would pull our coats
from the hangers and shake the "little fellows"
out by the dozens. I'm beginning to realize
that I am now stationed at a camp north
of the Mason Dixon line (thank goodness) for
no longer am I haunted by pests of the sort
they had in the lone star state; not
even one roach have I seen while I've
been here.

I had planned to see "Gypsy Baron"
and "Sons of Fun" but on both nights the
Army made me realize that I am no
longer a free man and on both those
nights we flew the heavens and always
it seems into Texas. Can't get rid
of that state "no-how."

556

January 14, 1945

From: F./O. A.S. Mazza T-136514
215 CCS 1-26 Box 3323
P.A.A.B. Pueblo, Colo.

To: Miss Sylvia Jacobs
2334 Atmore St.
Pittsburgh 12, Pa[.]

Postmark: 6:30 PM
January 14, 1945
Pueblo, Colorado

Letterhead: Officers Mess
Army Air Base
Pueblo, Colorado

[1*]   Jan[.] 14, 1945

Dearest Sylvia:

    Had I known you were afraid of bugs while I was in Texas[,] I'd have sent you a few of those noble specimens inclosed [*sic*] in either a letter or a carton. Many a time at San Marcos[,] we would pull our coats from the hangers and shake the "little fellows" out by the dozens. I'm beginning to realize that I am now stationed at a camp north of the Mason[-]Dixon [L]ine

2.

I don't advise you to enlist in the Army
Nurse Corps now. That much I am sure
you gathered from one of my letters. Should,
however, a law be passed by Congress to
that effect, it wouldn't hurt to enlist in
the branch of service you would like best
and also to try and pick the best set-up that
would suit your personal interests. (and
that's my advice to you — Mr. _____.) Next Case.
Gossip of drafting spurs enlistments (a good
method of advertisement) Don't be fooled by it!
The Cadet Nurse Corps was for a purpose
and it would not have been passed had
they known that women could be drafted
and such a system prove effective.

The last couple of days we have
been as busy as we were any time in
the Cadet system. Work and sleep on a
24 hour basis with no free time in-
between. Yesterday, we started at 4:45 AM
and never got in until 8:00 PM last night.
I believe that this Wed we shall have

558

(thank goodness)[,] for no longer am I haunted by pests of the sort they had in the [L]one [S]tar [S]tate; not even one roach have I seen while I've been here.

I had planned to see the "Gypsy Baron" and "Sons of Fun[,]"[218] but on both nights[,] the Army made me realize that I am no longer a 'free' man[;] on both those nights[,] we flew the 'heavies[,]' and always it seems to Texas. Can't get rid of that state "no-how."

[2*] I don't advise you to enlist in the Army Nurse Corps now. That much I am sure you gathered from one of my letters. Should, however, a law be passed by Congress to that effect, it wouldn't hurt to enlist in the branch of service you would like best and also to try and pick the best set up [*sic*] that would suit your personal interests. ([A]nd that['] s my advice to you— Mr. Anthony.) Next [c]ase. Gossip of drafting spurs enlistments (a good method of advertisement)[.] Don't be fooled by it! The Cadet Nurse Corps was for a purpose[,] and it would not have been passed had they known that women could be drafted and such a system prove effective.

The last couple of days[,] we have been as busy as we were anytime in the [c]adet system. Work and sleep on a 24[-]hour basis with no free time in-between [*sic*]. Yesterday[,] we started at 4:45 AM and never got in until 8:00 PM last night. I believe that this Wed[.] we shall have [3*] our first free day since Christmas.

---

[218] *Sons o' Fun*, a Broadway musical, was apparently on tour in Colorado at the time. *Sons o' Fun*, music and lyrics by Jack Yellen and Sam E. Fain, directed by Edward Duryea Dowling, choreographed by Robert Alton, Winter Garden Theater and 46th Street Theater, New York, NY, December 1, 1941, to August 29, 1943. "Sons o' Fun," IBDB, accessed June 20, 2020, https://www.ibdb.com/broadway-production/sons-o-fun-1142.

our first free day since Christmas.

I sure wished you could be on hand to help me spend that time on Wed. Lets see what we'd do. Simple isn't it?? Why didn't I think of it before? Why I'd simply do nothing but watch Sylvia stir about. Lazy aren't I, but I'm sure it would be time well worth the "effort". Perhaps I'd let you prepare a couple of cups of coffee. (About time you graduated from the tea-kettle.) We'd play many an old record (no dancing though, thats too strenuous) and synchronize with the ~~rhythm~~ rhythm via finger tips. We'd go through the arm and shoulder movements while sitting on the couch and keep our feet firmly planted on the floor. This indeed would prove the old axiom that I once mentioned before that dancing is hugging put to music. Lets see! What other things can we do confined to the limits of one couch and one

Sure wished you could be on hand to help me spend that time on Wed. Let[']s see[,] what we'd do? Simple isn't it?? Why didn't I think of it before? Why I'd simply do nothing but watch Sylvia stir about. Lazy aren't I, but I'm sure it would be time well worth the "effort." Perhaps I'd let you prepare a couple of cups of coffee. (About time you graduated from the tea-kettle [*sic*].) We'd play many an old record (no dancing, though; that[']s too strenuous) and synchronize with the rhythm via finger tips [*sic*]. We'd go through the arm and shoulder movements while sitting on the couch and keep our feet firmly planted on the floor. This indeed would prove the old axiom that dancing is hugging to music. Let[']s see! What other things can we do confined to the limits of one

4

lazy tired character. Oh yes, wouldn't be
right if I didn't pull your nose a couple of
times; perhaps even rubnoses. Shucks!
since I got that far how could (I mean you)
escape without just one .. (If I made the
x in proportion to quality it wouldn't fit on this
sheet.)

    Gosh! that day sure went fast
didn't it though? I know I sure would
have regained all my vim vigor and
vitality with those ~~x~~
Syl-fun-illi-mine ~~doses~~.

        All my love,

          Tony —

P.S. Here is the old story on stars and
moon confined to a four word poem
using modern verse.

        Car;
        Star.
        moon;
        spoon.

couch and one [4*] lazy[,] tired character. O[h] yes, wouldn't be right if I didn't pull your nose a couple of times; perhaps even rub noses. Shucks! [S]ince I got that far[,] how could I (I mean you) escape without just one x. (If I made the x in proportion to quality[,] it wouldn't fit on this sheet.)

Gosh! [T]hat day sure went fast didn't it[,] though? I know I sure would have regained all my vim[,] vigor[,] and vitality with those Syl-fun-illi-mine doses.

All my love,
Tony

P.S. Here is the old story on stars and moon confined to a four[-] word poem using <u>modern</u> verse.

 Car;
 Star.
 Moon;
 Spoon.

Free

F/o. A. d. Mazza T-136514
2150085 1-26 Box 3323
P.A.A.B. Pueblo, Colo

PUEBLO COLO.
JAN 13
6:30 PM
1945

Mrs. Sylvia Jacobs
534 Atwood St.
Pittsburgh 13, Pa

Jan 18, 1945

Dearest Sylvia,

It is quite early Thursday morning and for the first time since I've been here there is a slight ground fog out-doors. Maybe I'll get the first chance to wear my Rain Coat in Colorado too, as an extremely thin drizzle can be seen from my window.

Yesterday, I thought I'd have my free day but instead it was moved up one day and today this is it. I don't know what to do first this morning for there are many little details that must be considered. I must turn my Laundry into town, buy little items of clothing, have a pair of shoes repaired, get a hair cut, collect my dry-cleaning, continue my search for one pr of pajamas which seem to be about the scarcest garment to find. It must rank a close second to Silk or Nylon hose yet I can see no immediate reason for their scarcity while I can understand the hose shortage.

566

January 18, 1945

From: F./O. A.S. Mazza T-136514
                215 CCS 1-26 Box 3323
                P.A.A.B. Pueblo, Colo.

To: Miss Sylvia M. Jacobs
                2334 Atmore St.
                Pittsburgh 12, Pa[.]

Postmark: 1:00 PM
                January 20, 1945
                Pueblo, Colorado

Letterhead: Officers Mess
                Army Air Base
                Pueblo, Colorado

[1*]   Jan[.] 18, 1945

Dearest Sylvia,

It is quite early Thursday morning[,] and for the first time since I've been here[,] there is a slight ground fog out-doors [*sic*]. Maybe I'll get the first chance to wear my Rain Coat [*sic*] in Colorado[,] too, as an extremely thin drizzle can be seen from my window.

Yesterday, I thought I'd have my free day[,] but instead[,] it was moved up one day[,] and today[,] this is it. I don't know what

2.

You see I have quite a busy afternoon ahead
of me. Tonight I shall attend the stag
dinner and party at the Officers Club. Plenty
of food, drinks, and entertainment is promised.

I should have gone to Denver last night
but was too tired to do so particularly after
spending 3 hours in a DR trainer and another
6 hrs in the Celestial Navigation Trainer on an
assimulated mission from Chicago to Los Angeles.
I barely crawled to bed at 10:00 PM last night
and slept myself completely out by 8:00 AM this
morning. My room-mate has gone to
Denver to Ski; he is quite some skier
too since he had been on the Penn State
Ski team for a number of years.

I see very little of my Co-pilot
these days now that his wife is in town
but the Bombardier and I have quite
a rowdy time together. He is really
full of fun and about as witty as

to do first this morning[,] for there are many little details that must be considered. I must turn my [l]aundry into town, buy little items of clothing, have a pair of shoes re-paired, get a hair cut [*sic*], collect my dry-cleaning [*sic*], continue my search for one pr[.] of pajamas[,] which seem to be about the scarcest garment to find. It must rank a close second to [s]ilk or [n]ylon hose[,] yet I can see no immediate reason for their scarcity[,] while I understand the hose shortage.[219]

[2*] You see[,] I have quite a busy afternoon ahead of me. Tonight I shall attend the stag dinner and party at the Officers Club. Plenty of food, drinks, and entertainment is promised.

I should have gone to Denver last night but was too tired to do so[,] particularly after spending 3 hours in a DR trainer[220] and another 6 hrs[.] in the [c]elestial [n]avigation [t]rainer on an assimulated [*sic*] mission from Chicago to Los Angeles. I barely crawled to bed at 11:00 PM last night and slept myself completely out by 8:00 AM this morning. My room-mate [*sic*] has gone to

---

[219] Silk stockings were in short supply during World War II because the sole source of silk for the American market was Japan, and by 1941, the supply was cut off. Moreover, the U.S. Government needed whatever raw silk stockpiles remained for the war effort (e.g., for making silk parachutes). DuPont introduced nylon in 1938, which quickly became a substitute for silk stockings; however, by 1942, the U.S. Government commandeered all of DuPont's nylon production for military purposes. Sarah Sundin, "Make It Do—Stocking Shortages in World War II," Sarah's Blog (blog), April 4, 2011, http://www.sarahsundin.com/ make-it-do-stocking-shortages-in-world-war-ii-2/.

[220] DR most likely refers to Dead Reckoning. "Dead reckoning determines the position of the airplane at any given time by keeping an account of the track and distance flown over the earth's surface from the point of departure or last known position." "World War II Navigators," World War II-Prisoners of War-Stalag Luft 1, accessed June 20, 2020, http://www.merkki.com/ navigators%20of%20usaaf%20in%20world%20war%20II.htm.

3

an individual can be. 'Clang-Clang' has promised to sing and play for us one of these nights. Fred Brooks says she has a marvelous voice and has been taking singing lessons for quite some time. That was one reason why she had been to California for the past two weeks. He has bought the piece of music "Chansonette" by Victor Herbert and I have one of my old favorites "Maligonia". What an evening that will be particularly if Walt & I add our two cents worth.

Must run along now in order to complete all the little 'ditties' I mentioned and in so doing close with

Love

Tony

Denver to [s]ki; he is quite some skier[,] too[,] since he had been on the Penn State [s]ki team for a number of years.

I see very little of my [c]o-pilot these days now that his wife is in town[,] but the [b]ombardier and I have quite a rowdy time together. He is really full of fun and about as whitty [*sic*] as [3*] an individual can be. 'Clang-Clang' has promised to sing and play for us one of these nights. Brooks says she has a marvelous voice and has been taking singing lessons for quite some time. That was one reason why she had been to California for the past two weeks. He has bought the piece of music, "Chaunconette" [*sic*]221 by Victor Herbert[,] and I have one of my old favorites, "Maligonia[."]222 What an evening that will be[,] particularly if Walt + I add our two cents['] worth.

Must run along now in order to complete all the little 'ditties' I mentioned and in so doing close with

Love[,]

Tony

---

221 "Chansonette" is the setting of Gus Kahn's English lyrics to Victor Herbert's piano composition "Punchinello," op. 38 (1910), for the film *Naughty Marrieta*. "Naughty Marrieta," CastAlbums, accessed June 20, 2020, http://castalbums.org/shows/Naughty-Marietta/1943/#covers; *Naughty Marietta*, directed by Robert Z. Leonard and W.S. Van Dyke, featuring Jeanette MacDonald and Nelson Eddy (Metro-Goldwyn-Mayer, 1935).

222 Perhaps the reference is to "Malagueña" by Ernesto Lecuona.

F/O. A.S. Mazza T-136514
215025 1-26 BM 3323
R.A.A.B. Pueblo, Colo.

PUEBLO
COLO.
JAN 18
1 PM
1945

Miss Sylvia M. Jacobs
2334 Atmore St.
Pittsburgh 13, Pa.

Jan 19, 1945

Dearest Sylvia:

My free day certainly did go
rather fast but I practically accomplished
all I set out to do. I hitched hiked
my way into town and was picked up
by a lady driver. (Honest, I didn't have
to wink once.) Walt and I were together
on this jaunt and so immediately on
our entrance to the gay city, I deposited
my laundry and also dropped the shoes
at a place called Jaggers' Shoe Repair with
their promise that they would be done by
6:30 PM.

Walt decided he wanted his
teeth cleaned so we went to the chamber
of Commerce building where about 10
dentists were located on the same floor.
Each of them had their appointments filled
except one. This dentist gave us one
of his ivory smiles and ~~with~~ assured the attitude
that he would do Walt a big favor

January 19, 1945

From: F./O. A.S. Mazza T-136514
215 CCS 1-26 Box 3323
P.A.A.B. Pueblo, Colo.

To: Miss Sylvia Jacobs
2334 Atmore St.
Pittsburgh 12, Pa[.]

Postmark: 1:30 PM
January 20, 1945
Pueblo, Colorado

Letterhead: Officers Mess
Army Air Base
Pueblo, Colorado

[1*]   Jan[.] 19, 1945

Dearest Sylvia:

My free day certainly did go rather fast[,] but I practically accomplished all I set out to do. I hitched hiked [*sic*] my way into town and was picked up by a lady driver. (Honest, I didn't have to wink once.) Walt and I were together on this jaunt[,] and so immediately on our entrance to the gay city, I deposited my laundry and also dropped the shoes at a place called 'Jaggers' Shoe Repair with their promise that they would be done by 6:30 PM.

575

OFFICERS MESS
ARMY AIR BASE
PUEBLO, COLORADO

2.

by letting him have a one hour appointment for 3:30 P.M. The price?? Only a minor matter of $7.50 Walts jaw dropped about 3 inches and the smile and vanished from his face. Swish! out the door we disappeared and breathlessly were settled on the side walk out-doors. Soon Walt was in rather a gay mood once more mumbling to himself that he had just saved $7.00 and wanted to treat me to a soda which I took him up on complied.

I hunted the pajamas with no success. I could have bought a pair of flannel ones that I didn't care for rayon and loud colored pairs that would have brought the barracks to its feet, but not one simple ordinary common cotton pair pajamas.

Then we decided to go to the movie. Listing the four movie houses in town, much to our disappointment we had seen three of the features. The only

Walt decided he wanted his teeth cleaned[,] so we went to the chamber of commerce building[,] where about 10 dentists were located on the same floor. Each of them had their appointments filled except one. This dentist gave us one of his wry smiles and assumed the attitude that he would do Walt a big favor [2*] by letting him have a one[-]hour appointment for 3:30 PM. The price?? Only a matter of $7.50[.] Walt[']s draw dropped about 3 inches[,] and the smile vanished from his face. Swish! [O]ut the door we disappeared and breathlessly were settled on the side walk [sic] out-doors [sic]. Soon Walt was in a rather gay mood once more[,] mumbling to himself that he had just saved $7.50 and wanted to treat me to a soda[,] to which I complied.

I hunted [for] the pajamas with no success. I could have bought a pair of flannel ones that I didn't care for, rayon and loud[-]colored[,] pairs that would have brought the barracks to its feet, but not one simple[,] ordinary[,] common cotton pajamas.

Then we decided to go to the movie. Listing the four movie houses in town, much to our disappointment[,] we had seen three

3.

feature we hadn't seen was a Mexican billing "Maria Elena flore del fuego" *flower of fire* One minor difficulty we would have to cope with was the Spanish language.

Quite an exhotic film that was with pearl hunters, singing Caballeros dances, romance, tragedy, schooners and 'to boot' even Amazon warriors. I soon discovered that my Spanish vocabulary was rather limited but enjoyed the contrast of technique between Mexican and American film producers. We saw a preview of the coming Mexican film "Caballeros de Terreor" with Dolores Del Rio as the leading lady. The preview lasted every bit of 20 minutes. The Mexican people attending the movie must have gotten quite a kick out of Walt and I seriously discussing what we thought the characters were saying. I could see by the many smiles on their faces that we weren't always correct in our of the features. The only [3*] feature we hadn't seen was a Mexican billing[,] "Maria Elena[,] flore [*sic*] del [*sic*] fuego[.]"[223] One minor difficulty we would have to cope with was the Spanish language.

Quite an exhotic [*sic*] film that was with pearl hunters, singing caballeros, dances, romance, tragedy, schooners[,] and to boot[,] even Amazon warriers [*sic*]. I soon discovered that my Spanish vocabulary was rather limited but enjoyed the contrast of technique between Mexican and American film producers. We saw a preview of the coming Mexican film "Caballeros de[l] [t]error" with Delores [d]el Rio as the leading lady.[224] The preview lasted every-bit [*sic*] of 20 minutes. The Mexican people attending the movie must have gotten a kick out of Walt and I [*sic*] seriously discussing what we thought the characters were saying. I could see by the many smiles on their faces that we weren't always correct in our [4*] hypotheses.

---

[223] Underneath the title are the words "flower of fire." *María Elena (Flor de Fuego)*, directed by Rafael J. Sevilla, featuring Carmen Guerrero and Adolfo Girón (Columbia Films, 1936).

[224] The filmography of Delores del Río does not include the title cited, even though she did return to Mexico from Hollywood to take leading film roles at the time. "Delores del Rio (1904-1883)" IMDb, accessed June 20, 2020, https://www.imdb.com/name/nm0003123/. Research of Mexican films provided no information for *Caballeros del terror*.

4.

hypotheses.

Later we attended the stag party,
had quite a gathering with all our buddies;
enjoyed the entertainment which was in
accordance with a 2nd Air Force Directive
that no Civilian licensiousness be permitted
within an Army Post. (strip teasing and the like.)
They would think of everything !!! As
the evening progressed I began to see that
the main purpose of the stag party was to
have everyone "stagger" so I retired
to the barracks.

This morning it was up into the
blue flying a tight formation for 6 hrs
and thirty minutes. Tonight, after dinner,
I stopped at the Officers club for a coke
and this scribbling was the aftermath.
"Maybe that coke was spiked ?? Good night
with
            Love
              Tony

Later[,] we attended the stag party, had quite a gathering with all our buddies, enjoined the entertainment[,] which was in accordance with a 2nd Air Force [d]irective that no civilian businesses be permitted within an Army [p]ost. (Strip teasing and the like.) They would think of everything!!! As the evening progressed[,] I began to see that the main purpose of the <u>stag</u> party was to have everyone "stagger[,]" so I returned to the barracks.

This morning[,] it was up into the blue[,] flying a tight formation for 6 hrs[.] and thirty minutes. Tonight, after dinner, I stopped at the Officers Club for a coke[,] and this scribbling was the aftermath. Maybe that coke was spiked?? Good night with

Love[,]

'Tony'

Free

PUEBLO JAN 20 1·30 PM 1945 COLO.

F/o. A. S. Maggu T-134514
415 CCS 1·26 Bm. 3323
P.A.A.B. Pueblo, Colo.

Miss Sylvia M. Jacobs
2334 Atmore St
Pittsburgh 12, Pa

Jan 21, 1945

Dearest Sylvia:

It is about 4:00 PM on a
rather quiet afternoon. The sun is out
in its usual brilliancy but the ground
is covered with soft fine velvet white
snow. The snow was the result of
24 hours of precipitation that stopped
only early this morning. If the weather-
map I saw was correct, Western Penna
is also getting some of this very same snow
storm, perhaps at this very moment even
while Sylvia is jotting a letter to some-
one in Southern Colorada (I hope.)

I have just returned from another
Celestial Navigation Trainer mission that
began at 8:00 AM this morning. This
time the assimilated mission was to Rapid
Falls, Minnesota. The results, as usual,
had me feeling rather proud of my
efforts.

From one of my pals across
the hall, I borrowed this phonographic

584

January 21, 1945

From: F./O. A.S. Mazza T-136514
            215 CCS 1-26 Box 3323
            P.A.A.B. Pueblo, Colo.

To: Miss Sylvia M. Jacobs
            2334 Atmore St.
            Pittsburgh 12, Pa[.]

Postmark: 1:00 PM
            January 23, 1945
            Pueblo, Colorado

Letterhead: [No Letterhead]

[1*]   Jan[.] 21, 1945

Dearest Sylvia:

It is about 4:00 PM on a rather quiet afternoon. The sun is out in its usual brilliancy[,] but the ground is covered with soft[,] fine[,] velvet[,] white snow. The snow was a result of 24 hours of precipitation that stopped only early this morning. If the weather-map [*sic*] I saw was correct, Western Penna[.] is also getting some of this very same snow storm [*sic*], perhaps at this very moment[,] even while Sylvia is jotting a letter to some-one [*sic*] in Southern Colorado (I hope[).]

set and records. You'd never guess the tune that is being played at present. Give up? "One Meat Ball"!

You certainly are getting to meet quite a number of my cousins. Tony Notaro is the sailor boys name and his mother happens to be Tony Nicoteri's sister. Mother told me that he was home on a short leave but the leaves the Navy gives, to her, seems rather many when compared to the Army Air Corps. She casually remarked "You should have joined the Navy."

I told you once that if I started to introduce you to all my cousins, it would take quite some time and there are many of them. The good part is that most of them are very close to our age group and once this old war is over many are the good times we should have together with them.

I wonder if Eleanor Slobodnick did me a good turn or not. If the picture you mentioned was some thing like the last one I had in the Post-Gazette,

I have just returned from another [c]elestial [n]avigation [t]rainer mission that began at 8:00 AM this morning. This time[,] the assimulated [*sic*] mission was to Rapid Falls, Minnesota. The results, as usual, had me feeling rather proud of my efforts.

From one of my pals across the hall, I borrowed a phonographic [1R*] set and records. You'd never guess the tune that is being played at present. Give up? "One Meat Ball[!"][225]

You certainly are getting to meet quite a number of my cousins. Tony Notaro is the sailor boy's name[,] and his mother happens to be Tony Nicotero's sister. Mother told me that he was home on a short leave[,] but the leaves the Navy gives, to her, seems [*sic*] rather many when compared to the Army Air Corps. She casually remarked[,] "You should have joined the Navy."

I told you once that if I started to introduce you to all my cousins, it would take quite some time[,] and there are many of them. The good part is that most of them are very close to our age group[,] and once this old war is over[,] many are the good times we should have together with them.

I wonder if Eleanor Slobodnick [*sic*][226] did me a good turn or not. If the picture you mentioned was some thing [*sic*] like the last

---

[225] Josh White, vocalist, "One Meat Ball," by Lou Singer and Hy Zaret, recorded 1944, track 2 on *Josh White Sings Easy*, Asch Records, No. 348-2B; "One Meat Ball by Josh White," Second Hand Songs, accessed June 20, 2020, https://secondhandsongs.com/performance/124450; "Josh White," Wirz' American Music, accessed June 20, 2020, https://www.wirz.de/music/whitejos.htm.

[226] Eleanor Slobodnik Sinagra (b. November 20, 1921; d. October 10, 2015) was Sylvia Jacobs' maternal first cousin. She was the daughter of John Slobodnik (b. June 24, 1896; d. January 6, 1963) and Lillian Kopcie Slobodnik (b. January 18, 1899; d. November 18, 1991). See Appendix B.

I'm quite sure she didn't. Gosh! all the pictures you've been getting lately, after the long famine now comes a deluge of them and you will have more than you know what to do with!!

Greg's last letter was dated Jan 10th, so up to that time everything is going along rather smooth for him. He is still in Italy and the heavy snow-falls there have kept them on the ground quite a bit. Joe is half-way thru his Mid-shipman's program and is at present sweating out mid-term xams. He believes that he will finish near the end of February, providing all goes well.

Say! I sure liked the proof on that last letter you sent. (This was one time I opened a letter casually.) From the print right here before my eyes, I can readily see that you didn't cheat on me this time. I wonder what kind of lip-stick you used?

one I had in the *Post-Gazette*,[227] [2*] I'm quite sure she didn't. Gosh! [A]ll the pictures you've been getting latley [*sic*]; after the long famine[,] now comes a deluge of them[,] and you will have more than you know what to do with!!

Greg's last letter was dated Jan[.] 10th, so up to that time[,] everything is going along rather smooth[ly] for him. He is still in Italy[,] and the heavy snow-falls [*sic*] there have kept them on the ground quite a bit. Joe is half-way [*sic*] thru [*sic*] his [m]id-shipman's program and is at present sweating out mid-term [*sic*] exams. He believes that he will finish near the end of February, providing all goes well.

Say! I sure like the 'proof' in that last letter you sent. (This was one time I opened a letter casually.) From the print right here before my eyes, I can readily see that you didn't cheat on me this time. I wonder what kind of lip-stick [*sic*] you used?

---

[227] Italics added. See *supra* note 169.

Come to think of it though, that piece of paper hardly removed any of the lip-stick and least not near as much as yours truly did when he had the chance.

As I am drawing this letter to a close "Tea for Two" fills in the background. This time the music was not Coincidental for I Litterally selected and played that piece on the phonograph; I hope you liked it.

Love

Tony

[2R*] Come to think of it[,] though[,] that piece of paper hardly removed any of the lip-stick [*sic*] and at least not near as much as yours truly did when he had the chance.

As I am drawing this letter to a close[,] "Tea for Two" fills in the background. This time[,] the music was not coincidental[,] for I deliberately selected and played that piece on the phonograph; I hope you liked it.

Love[,]
'Tony'

Free

PUEBLO
JAN 23
1 PM
1945
COLO.

F/o A.S. Mazza 7-36654
216 CCS 1-26 Box 3323
P.A.A.B. Pueblo, Colo.

Miss Sylvia Jacobs
2334 Atmore Dr.
Pittsburgh 13 Pa

592

THE SHIRLEY-SAVOY HOTEL ● DENVER, 2, COLORADO

Jan 25, 1945

Dearest Sylvia:

Have just spent a night at this hotel and am up bright & early at 10:00AM still looking for "Shirley". (No, I didn't find her.) We have had 3 days to ourselves with nothing scheduled at Pueblo, so I "took off". In fact I had quite a day of it yesterday. It all started at 2:00 PM when within 15 minutes I learned I was to be a "Best man". My Co-Pilot, John Gilmore, had married a non-Catholic and his family insisted that their marriage be made through the church. We saw the Chaplin, Father Haggerty, and the ceremonies commenced. Without either family present, without bridal vestments of any sort, without rice and the other little things that seem to take its place on such an occasion, the marriage, a great institution that happens once in the many life-time of an individual, looked rather drab and morbid. The words made sense and seemed sincere to Gil but the "wife"

594

January 25, 1945

Date: January 25, 1945

From: F./O. A.S. Mazza T-136514
               215 CCS 1-26 Box 3323
               P.A.A.B. Pueblo, Colo.

To: Miss Sylvia M. Jacobs
               2334 Atmore St[.]
               Pittsburgh 12, Pa[.]

Postmark: 12:30 PM
               January 25, 1945
               Pueblo, Colorado

Letterhead: The Shirley-Savoy Hotel
               Denver, 2, Colorado

[1*]   Jan[.] 25, 1945

Dearest Sylvia:

Have just spent a night at this hotel and am up bright + early
at 10:00 AM still looking for "Shirley[."][228] (No, I didn't find

---

[228] The Shirley Hotel opened in 1903, and the adjacent Savoy Hotel opened in
1904. The two Denver hotels, located at 17th Street and Broadway, merged
in 1919. The Shirley-Savoy Hotel was razed, however, in 1970. "Savoy
and Shirley Hotels, Denver," Denver Public Library Digital Collections,
accessed June 20, 2020, https://digital.denverlibrary.org/digital/collection/
p15330coll22/id/77734/.

seemed to me to be bored with it all. On the one part of the ceremonie the Priest got the names twisted and said: "Do you John Stuart take this woman to be your etc.) I quickly put in my two cents worth and presented perhaps for the first time the marriage of man to woman instead of woman to man. (our hero!) Poor 'Mel' would have walked out with his wife's last name instead of his own. In the process of it all, I was robbed, I never got to kiss the bride and the bridesmaid was a WaC who had been married herself for 24 years. (Darn it!) The first words the bride said as she got out of the chapel door was " I hope your family is satisfied". She must certainly have no regard for the religious angle and I don't see why she should have done something that she did not want to do in the first place. It all seemed too hypocritical to me and I'm sorry I had a part in it. We toasted to their future with milk-shakes and the Wac & I left them to their fate.

At 4:15 PM John Mendenhall, my room-mate, and I took the Pueblo to Denver bus and arrived here last night at 8:15 PM in a blinding snow-storm. Without even time out for supper we dashed to the City Auditorium and heard a concert given by the Denver Symphony Orchestra with the woman guest conductor Antonia Brico.

596

her.) We have had 3 days to ourselves with nothing scheduled at Pueblo, so I "took off[.")] In fact[,] I had quite a day of it yesterday. It all started at 2:00 PM when within 15 minutes[,] I learned I was to be a '[b]est man.' My [c]o-[p]ilot[,] John Gilmore, had married a non[-]Catholic[,] and his family insisted that their marriage be made through the church. We saw the chaplin [sic], Father Haggerty, and the ceremonies commenced. Without either family present, without bridal vestments of any sort, without rice and the other things that seem to take its place on such an occasion, the marriage, a great institution that happens once in the life-time [sic] of an individual, looked rather drab and morbid. The words made sense and seemed sincere to Gil[,] but the 'wife' [1R*] seemed to me to be bored with it all. On the one part of the ceremonie [sic], the [p]riest got the names twisted and said: "Do you[,] John <u>Stuart</u>[,] take this woman to be your etc.["]) I quickly put in my two cents['] worth and prevented[,] perhaps for the first time[,] the marriage of man to woman instead of women to men. ([O]ur hero!) Poor 'Gil' would have walked out with his wife's last name instead of his own. In the process of it all, I was robbed[;] I never got to kiss the bride[;] and the brides-maid [sic] was a WAC who had been married herself for 24 years. (Darn it!) The first words the bride said as she got out of the chapel door was[,] "I hope your family is satisfied[."] She must certainly have had no regard for the religious angle[,] and I don't see why she should have done something that she did not want to do in the first place. It all seemed too hypocritical to me[,] and I'm sorry I had a part in it.

THE SHIRLEY-SAVOY HOTEL • DENVER, 2, COLORADO

2.

They played 'Beethoven' all night and to tell you the truth this was one time I was really "bored to death". The music carried no melodies but consisted of a lot of itty bitty notes' that didn't make sense and to me described nothing. My interest was held by a girl who played the clarinet in the next to last row. She looked ever so much like S.M.J.; in fact enough to be her double. She also had on a black dress identical to the one that you wore with the flesh colored cloth near the neck. I went back stage when it was all over, but couldn't find hide nor hair of her. (Maybe it was my imagination but no I'm positive it wasn't.)

We left the Auditorium at 10:30 PM and were able to locate a room in this, the Shirley Savoy Hotel. A few moments later found us at the Algerian Club dining on Fried chicken, watching a floor show, and later listening to Lou Briggs' orchestra. I'd sure have given plenty to have had you there with me for even one single hour but I guess there

We toasted to their future with milk-shakes [*sic*], and the W[AC] + I left them to their fate.

At 4:15 PM, John Mendenhall, my room-mate [*sic*], and I took the Pueblo[-]to[-]Denver bus and arrived here last night at 8:15 PM in a blinding snow-storm [*sic*]. Without even time out for supper[,] we dashed to the City Auditorium[229] and heard a concert given by the Denver Symphony Orchestra[230] with the woman guest conductor Antonia Bric[o].[231] [2*] They played 'Beethoven' all night[,] and to tell you the truth[,] this was one time I was really bored to death! The music carried no melodies but consisted of a lot of 'itty[-]bitty notes' that didn't make sense and to me described nothing. My interest was held by a girl who played the clarinet in the next to last row. She looked ever so much like S.M.J., in fact[,] enough to be her double. She also had on a black dress identicle [*sic*] to the one that you wore with the flesh[-]colored cloth near the neck. I went back-stage [*sic*] when it was all over, but couldn't

---

[229] Designed by Denver architect Robert Willison, the Denver Municipal Auditorium at 1323 Champa Street, Denver, was constructed in 1908. "Denver Municipal Auditorium (Quigg Newton Denver Municipal Auditorium)," History Colorado, accessed June 20, 2020, https://www.historycolorado.org/location/denver-municipal-auditorium-quigg-newton-denver-municipal-auditorium.

[230] The Denver Symphony Orchestra, formed in 1934, disbanded in 1989, merging with the Colorado Symphony Association in 1990. "Denver Symphony Orchestra and Association Papers," Denver Public Library, accessed June 20, 2020, https://archives.denverlibrary.org/repositories/3/resources/8445.

[231] Antonia Brico (b. June 26, 1902; d. August 3, 1989) was a pioneering American conductor, who opened the Brico Music Studio in Denver in 1945. "Antonia Brico," Colorado Women Hall of Fame, accessed June 20, 2020, https://www.cogreatwomen.org/project/antonia-brico/.

isn't much I can do about that.

2:00 AM found us tucked away in dream land. Today, we shall take in more of the town, splurge at another hotel and possibly another night club for variety's sake and incidentally search for my pair of pajamas. Might look up Christine or whatever her that name may be. I know it sounds something like that I mentioned above, it all depends on what my buddie has planned for the day.

If you happen to see Mrs. gone give her my best regards and congratulations for the bouncing baby girl. I'm sure Greg won't mind you sending his letter to me; after all I remember on one occasion he sent one of your letters to me.

Sure hope that one day we can go to see the places pictured on this stationary and do the things shown here in the quiet but magnificent back ground of the Rockies.

So long for now and with more than enough love & kisses.

Love

find hide nor hair of her. (Maybe it was my imagination[,] but no[,] I'm positive it wasn't.)

We left the [a]uditorium at 10:30 PM and were able to locate a room in this, the Shirley[-]Savoy Hotel. A few moments later found us at the Algerian Club[232] dining on [f]ried chicken, watching a floor show, and later dancing to [the] Lou Briggs Orchestra. I sure would have given plenty to have had you there with me for even one single hour[,] but I guess there [2R*] isn't much I can do about that.

[Two] AM found us tucked away in dreamland. Today, we shall take in more of the town, splurge at another hotel and possibly another night club [sic] for varieties [sic] sake[,] and incidently [sic][,] search for my pair of pajamas. Might look up Christine or whatever her last name may be. I know it sounds something like that I mentioned above[;] it all depends on what my buddie [sic] has planned for the day.

If you happen to see Mrs[.] Jane[,][233] give her my best regards and congratulations for the bouncing baby girl. I'm sure Greg won't mind you sending his letter to me; after all[,] I remember on one occasion[,] he sent one of your letters to me.

---

[232] The nightclub is also referred to as the Club Algerian. See "Off the Cuff," *Billboard*, January 27, 1945, 21; "Profiles of Small Bands and Cocktail Attractions: Three Bits of Rhythm," *Billboard Music Year Book 1944*, 321-22; "Leading Cocktail Lounges," *Billboard Music Year Book 1944*, 324. The location of the club was on 17th Street near Tremont Place in downtown Denver. "Gallery: Brown Palace Turns 125: A Visual History of a Denver Icon," The Denver Chanel, accessed June 20, 2020, https://www.thedenverchannel.com/news/gallery-brown-palace-turns-125-a-visual-history-of-a-denver-icon#id2.

[233] Perhaps the word is "Jones."

THE SHIRLEY-SAVOY HOTEL • DENVER, COLORADO

DENVER
JAN 25
12:30 PM
1945
COLO.

Pfc. A. J. Mayer 7-136514
215 CCS 1-26 Pm 3323
F.A.A.B. Pueblo, Colo.

Miss Sylvia Jacobs
2334 Gehrue St
Pittsburgh 12, Pa.

602

Sure hope that one day we can go to see the places pictured on this stationary [*sic*]²³⁴ and do the things shown here in the quiet but magnificent back-ground [*sic*] of the [R]ockies.

So long for now and with more than enough love + kisses.

Love[,]

Tony

---

²³⁴ The upper quarter of the stationery has black-and-white photographs depicting a small flotilla of sailboats, horseback riding, snowcapped mountains bordering water, and a river with a man who is apparently fly fishing.

Jan 26, 1945

Dearest Sylvia:

Here I am back safe + sound at Pueblo after my Denver jaunt. After I wrote that last letter to you, Mendenhall and I went to visit the Denver state capitol, the dome of which is solid gold. From there to the Museum which contained the unique history of the Plains Indians and their struggle against our frontier expansion. Kit Carson and Bill Cody relics seemed to be the things of particular note capitalized by the Colorado state fathers. The municiple building was quite different from most from the architectural stand-point. By 1:00 PM, we were rather tired and hungry (no breakfast) so dined at Boggio's Parisienne Rotisserie. (Don't ask me what Rotisserie means, but it sounds important.) Here for the first time I dined on

604

January 26, 1945

From: F./O. A.S. Mazza T-136514
          215 CCS 1-26 Box 3323
          P.A.A.B. Pueblo, Colo.

To: Miss Sylvia M. Jacobs
          2334 Atmore St.
          Pittsburgh 12, Pa.

Postmark: 1:30 PM
          January 27, 1945
          Pueblo, Colorado
          Air Mail

Letterhead: Air Mail

[1*]   Jan[.] 26, 1945

Dearest Sylvia:

Here I am back safe + sound at Pueblo after my Denver [j]aunt. After I wrote that last letter to you, Mendenhall and I went to visit the Denver [S]tate Capitol, the dome of which is solid gold. From there to the [m]useum, which contained the unique history of the Plains Indians and their struggle against our frontier expansion. Kit Carson and Bill Cody relics seemed to be the things of particular note capitalized by the Colorado state fathers. The municiple [*sic*] building was quite different from most[,] from

2

broiled lobster.   Sounds so
funny to be so far in land to get my
first taste of such an exclusive sea-
food. It was quite a job to get
at the meat but since we weren't
in any particular hurry we took our
time and were out by 2:30 PM. We
then went direct to the Denver City
Park Zoo and to its Natural and
Historic Museum in the same
locality. By 5:00 PM, back to the
City of Denver hunting for Hotel Rooms.
We found one at the Ken-Mark
but one block from the center of things.
A quick bath and shave and by 6:00 PM
the movie 'Suspect' with Charles Laughton
and Ella Raines was flickering before
our eyes. Ella Raines also appeared
in person with a little speech soliciting
donations for the march of dimes.
Since Raines seemed the theme for
the day, the evening wound up
finding us at the Chez Paree
dining on another oddity of food

606

the architectural stand-point [*sic*]. By 1:00 PM, we were rather tired and hungry (no breakfast) so dined at Boggis's Parisienne Rotisserie. (Don't ask me what Rotisserie means, but it sounds important.) Here for the first time I dined on [2*] broiled lobster. Sounds so funny to be so far in land [*sic*] to get my first taste of such an exclusive sea-food. It was quite a job to get at the meat[,] but since we weren't in any particular hurry[,] we took our time and were out by 2:30 PM. We then went direct[ly] to the Denver City Park Zoo[235] and to its Natural and Historic Museum in the same locality.[236] By 5:00 PM, back to the City of Denver[,] hunting for [h]otel [r]ooms. We found one at the Ken-Mark [*sic*][,][237] but one block from the center of things. A quick bath and shave and by 6:00 PM the movie 'Suspect'[238] with Charles Laughton and Ella Raines was flickering before our [e]yes. Ella Raines also appeared in person with a little speech[,] soliciting donations for the [M]arch of [D]imes. Since Paris seemed the theme for the day,

---

[235] The Denver Zoo at 2300 Steele Street is located within the City Park of Denver. "History," Denver Zoo, accessed June 20, 2020, https://denverzoo. org/?s=History.

[236] The Denver Museum of Nature and Science at 2001 North Colorado Boulevard is located within the City Park of Denver. "About Us: Museum History," Denver Museum of Nature and Science, accessed June 20, 2020, https://www.dmns.org/about/about-us/.

[237] Built in 1910, the Kenmark Hotel, located at the corner of 17th and Welton Streets in Denver, was razed in 1995. Stuart Steers, "Rubble's Back in Town," *Westword*, January 3, 1996, http://www.westword.com/news/ rubbles-back-in-town-5055896.

[238] *The Suspect*, directed by Robert Siodmak, featuring Charles Laughton and Ella Raines (Universal Pictures, 1944).

Air Mail

gourmets, "Frog Legs". I didn't think I'd have the nerve to try them but since Howard ordered them I took a chance too. I was rather surprised when I found Frog legs to taste almost like Chicken with a sort of fishy taste and it turned out indeed to be a delicacy.

Early this morning we made our way back to Pueblo and arrived about 1:30 PM. The letter from you dated Jan 23 was sure a "humdinger"! I learned more about you than I have for quite some time. Lets see!: don't snore, don't talk in sleep, keeps window open, and even solves complicated in-law problems. Slick (clunk) Jake must be quite a gal. I reckon. Anyway I bet she pulls all the covers on her side of the bed and leaves her poor Sis shivering in the cold?? Me? Well, I haven't been able to hear myself talk or snore. I believe I'm about the lightest sort of

the evening wound up finding us at the Chez Paree[,] dining on another oddity of food [3*] gourmets, "[f]rog [l]egs." I didn't think I'd have the nerve to try them[,] but since Howard ordered them[,] I took a chance[,] too. I was rather surprised when I found [f]rog legs to taste almost like chicken with a sort of fishy taste[,] and it turned out indeed to be a delicacy.

Early this morning[,] we made our way back to Pueblo and arrived around 1:30 PM. The letter from you dated Jan[.] 23 was sure a 'humdinger.' I learned more about you than I have for quite some time. Let[']s see!: don't snore, don't talk in sleep, keeps window open, and even solves complicated in-law problems. Slick (chick) Jake must be quite a gal, I reckon. Anyway[,] I bet she pulls all the covers on her side of the bed and leaves her poor [s]is shivering in the cold?? Me? Well, I haven't been able to hear myself talk or snore. I believe I'm about the lightest sort of

4

sleeper that exists and even though deep in slumber can jump up awake at the drop of a pin. Windows wide open from top to bottom with plenty of covers on bed; fresh air to me is a necessity. There now you have all the dope on me. Do I still rate?

Sure wouldn't be difficult to play ½ of that title "Student Prince". All I can ever remember about my past can be summed in one word. - - student! I'll let you play the role of a Princess, (not Sleeping Beauty though!)

Phil's last letter to me stated that he hopes to be a married man by Easter. He sure has me licked by his fast pace but like the race between the Tortoise and the Hare, I hope to be the real winner at the finish line — including time as the all important

610

[4*] sleeper that exists[,] and even though deep in slumber[,] can jump up awake at the drop of a pin. Windows wide open from top to bottom with plenty of covers on bed; fresh air to me is a necessity. There[,] now you have all the dope on me. Do I still rate?

Sure wouldn't be difficult to play ½ of that title "Student Prince[."]²³⁹ All I can ever remember about my past can be summed up in one word - - - <u>student</u>! I'll let you play the role of [p]rincess, (not [S]leeping [B]eauty[,] though!)[.]

Phil[']s last letter to me stated that he hopes to be a married man by Easter. He sure has me licked by his fast pace, but like the race between the [t]ortoise and the [h]are, I hope to be the real winner at the finish line—excluding time as the all[-]important [5*] factor.

---

²³⁹ *The Student Prince* is a 1924 operetta by Sigmund Romberg. Kurt Gänzl, "The Student Prince: Musical Play in 2 Acts," *Encyclopedia of the Musical Theater*, Operetta Research Center, January 1, 2001, http://operetta-research-center.org/student-prince-heidelberg-musical-play-2-acts/.

5

factor.

Did not get a chance to see Christenson. Dancing, ice skating, and skiing are certainly the style out here now. I want mine along now thus closing with the Magic four.

L - O - V - E

'Tony'

Let's see! I'll have to try something new since boys can hardly SWAK and leave any impression of any sort. This letter is S.W.A.G.E.H. (See! What I did to this poor sheet of paper. (Came pretty close to breaking one rib that time) I'll have to be a bit more careful next time.

Did not get a chance to see Christenson. Dancing, ice skating, and skiing are certainly the style out here now. I must run along now[,] thus closing with the [m]agic four

L-O-V-E[,]

'Tony.'

Let[']s see! I'll have to try something new[,] since boys can hardly SWAK[240] and leave an impression of any sort. This letter is S.W.A.G.B.H.[241] []See! What I did to this poor sheet of paper.[242] (Came pretty close to breaking one rib that time[.]) I'll have to be a bit more careful next time.

Enclosure: [Whether the enclosure was originally included with the letter is unknown. The enclosure is a clipped newspaper cartoon by Pvt. Willard G. Levitas. The clipping has no information to identify the newspaper or the date of publication. The drawing shows military men with bashed-in hats surrounding a commanding officer, who is holding a crop and has a similarly altered hat. Only one of the men has a hat in perfect, unrumpled condition. The commanding officer addresses him, saying, "Let's bash that cap in, Lieutenant, or we may find ourself [sic] walking again."]

---

[240] Seal with a kiss.

[241] Sealed with a great big hug.

[242] The page is badly crinkled, suggesting that its appearance is the result of being hugged.

F/O A. L. Mayer F/36514
215 CCS 1-24 Box 3323
P.A.A.B. Pueblo, Colo.

PUEBLO
JAN 27
1:30 PM
1945
COLO.

Air Mail

Miss Sylvia Jacobs
2534 Webster St.
Pittsburgh 19, Pa.

614

"LET'S BASH THAT CAP IN, LIEUTENANT, OR WE MAY FIND OURSELF WALKING AGAIN."

—Pvt. Willard G. Levitas

Jan 29, 1945

Dearest Sylvia:

I know that you have been expecting my transfer from Pueblo especially after seeing that notice in the paper. The 1-26 must have meant something too, particularly if you took the clue I gave you while at San Marcos.

I couldn't get a leave of any sort that would see me home even for a few hours. We will get a couple of days here but again getting home will be an impossibility. Our stay at Topeka will be rather short; not much more than 10 days even if that long. This is either our last or next to last stop prior to overseas. We may go to a P.O.E. from here and again we may not.

January 29, 1945

From: F./O. A.S. Mazza T-136514
            PB 1-26 General Delivery
            c/o. Base Post Office
            T.A.A.F. Topeka, Kansas

To: Miss Sylvia M. Jacobs
            2334 Atmore St.
            Pittsburgh 12, Pa.

Postmark: 7:00 PM
            January 29, 1945
            Topeka, Kansas
            Air Mail

Letterhead: Air Mail

[1*]   Jan[.] 29, 1945

Dearest Sylvia:

I know that you have been expecting my transfer from Pueblo[,] especially after seeing that notice in the paper. The 1-26 must have meant something[,] too, particularly if you took the clue I gave you while at San Marcos.

I couldn't get a leave of any sort that would see me home even for a few hours. We will get a couple of days here[,] but again[,] getting home will be an impossibility. Our stay at Topeka will be rather short[,] not much more than 10 days[,] even if that long.

A shiney brand new plane is awaiting us at the flight line. We don't know our destination and if we did, we couldn't tell.

My duties have been doubled now since we left our Bombardier Walt Brooks at Pueblo. I have a new title Bombo - Navigator. and my responsibilities are ~~many~~ much more than they were before.

I am rather disappointed that I couldn't get even a short leave to spend some time with you. I had planned quite a time for the both of us had I gotten to Atmore street; but that we shall do sometime at a later date than I planned originally.

This stop here is but the last leg of a long, long, journey and you can be

This is either our last or next[-]to[-]last stop prior to overseas. We may go to a P.O.E.[243] from here[,] and again[,] we may not.

[2*] A Shiney [sic][,] brand[-]new plane is awaiting us at the flight line. We don't know our destination[,] and if we did, we couldn't tell.

My duties have been doubled now[,] since we left our [b]ombardier[,] Walt Brooks[,] at Pueblo. I have a new title[, b]ombo-[n]avigator[,] and my responsibilities are much more than they were before.

I am rather disappointed that I couldn't get even a short leave to spend some time with you. I had planned quite a time for the both of us[,] had I gotten to Atmore [S]treet; but that we shall do sometime at a later date than I planned originally.

---

[243] Point of Embarkation.

3

assured that you ~~will~~ follow
me every bit of the way, if only
in my dreams.

Love

'Tony'

620

This stop here is but the last leg of a long, long[] journey[,] and you can be [3*] assured that you will follow me every bit of the way, if only in my dreams.

Love[,]
'Tony'

Feb 3, 1945

Dearest Sylvia:

It has been rather a long while since I last heard from you but that, of course, has been due to the mail mix-up that usually follows a transfer. Your letters will probably have some trip following me across this cock-eyed world.

The past couple of days found us busy both night and day checking and calibrating all instruments, going over every rivet, nut, and bolt. Some ship we have too! with all the most modern up to date equipment. I have been working on the nose of the plane and now have it rigged up like a private office—even with a sign: Navigation Office : Keep Out!   You should see the flying equipment; all the latest design in what a well dressed airman should wear and each garment practically form fitted. Quite a contrast to what I have been used to up till now.

February 3, 1945

From: F./O. A.S. Mazza T-136514
PB 1-26 General Delivery
Topeka Army Air Field
Topeka, Kansas

To: Miss Sylvia M. Jacobs
2334 Atmore St[.]
Pittsburgh 12, Pa[.]

Postmark: 7:00 PM
February 3, 1945
Topeka, Kansas
Air Mail

Letterhead: Officers Mess
Topeka Army Air Field
Topeka, Kansas

[1*]   Feb[.] 3, 1945

Dearest Sylvia:

It has been rather a long while since I last heard from you[,] but that, of course, has been due to the mail mix-up that usually follows a transfer. Your letters will probably have some trip following me across the cock-eyed [*sic*] world.

2.

All my navigation equipment is brand new worth several thousand dollars and I can hardly wait to get a chance to use them.

I did not expect to be here this long for we have been all set to leave at a moments notice. Only the weather with a snow storm and low but thick cloud layer covering the greater portion of the U.S. is the thing that has prevented our movement. Even now the low ceiling makes everything here look rather dismal in contrast to the sunny Colorado region.

Everything in Topeka is or has same connection to the word "Jayhawk". We have the Jay Hawk movie, hotel, bowling alley, dance hall, Candy Co, and even to the Paint of Jay Hawk Coal not to mention the many other uses for that name.

Topeka as a dry town in a dry state. At 7:00PM the sidewalks are pulled in and all the Puritan Fathers rest quite peaceful in the quiet atmosphere they have created for themselves.

626

The past couple of days found us busy both night and day[,] checking and calibrating all instruments[,] going over every rivet, nut, and bolt. Some ship we have[,] too[,] with all the most modern, up[-]to[-]date equipment[!] I have been working on the nose of the plane and now have it rigged up like a private office[,] even with a sign: Navigation Office: Keep Out! [Y]ou should see the flying equipment[,] all the latest design in what a [w]ell[-]dressed airman should wear[,] and each garment practically form[-]fitted. Quite a contrast to what I have been used to up 'till [*sic*] now.

[2*] All my navigation equipment is brand new[,] worth several thousand dollars[,] and I can hardly wait to get a chance to use them [*sic*].

I did not expect to be here this long[,] for we have been all set to leave at a moment[']s notice. Only the weather with a snow storm [*sic*] and low but thick cloud layer covering the greater portion of the U.S. is the thing that has prevented our movement. Even now[,] the low ceiling makes everything here look rather dismal in contrast to the [s]unny Colorado region.

Every thing [*sic*] in Topeka is or has some connection to the word "Jayhawk."[244] We have the Jay[h]awk movie, hotel, bowling alley, dance hall, [c]andy [c]o[.], and even to the point of Jay[h]awk Coal[,] not to mention the many other uses for that name.

Topeka is a dry town in a dry state. At 7:00 PM[,] the sidewalks are pulled in[,] and all the Puritan [f]athers rest quite peaceful in the quiet atmosphere they have created for themselves.

---

[244] The term "Jayhawk" derives from a mythical bird of Kansas. The Jayhawk is not only the mascot for the University of Kansas in Lawrence, Kansas, but it has also come to designate anyone from the state. "Kansas Jayhawkers—Terror in the Civil War," Legends of America, accessed June 20, 2020, https://legendsofamerica.com/kansas-jayhawkers/.

3.

Transportation is a horrible problem with one bus going to and from camp every hour. Each bus is so loaded that many fail to find even standing room and must twiddle their thumbs for a second hour.

Two dance halls are on the outskirts of the town. The Egyptian is usually packed with old people who maintain their folk and square dances from a different era. The White Lakes is jam packed with soldiers and the wildest she devils this side of hell. Many of them mere minors smoking cigarettes over a high-balls and wearing enough rouge and paint to out do the most savage of Indian tribes this land has ever seen. It was about all I could do to control myself the other night from giving some of them my honest frank opinion and a sound spanking that a good many of them I thought richly deserved.

We have a good officers club here with many forms of entertainment and it is here I intend to remain

[3*] Transportation is a horrible problem[,] with one bus going to and from camp every hour. Each bus is so loaded that many fail to find even standing room and must twiddle their thumbs for a second hour.

Two dance halls are on the outskirts of the town. The Egyptian is usually packed with old people who maintain their folk and square dances from a different era; The White Lakes is jam packed [sic] with soldiers and the wildest she[-]devils this side of hell. Many of them were minors smoking cigarettes over a highball [sic] and wearing enough rouge and paint to out do [sic] the most savage of Indian tribes this land has ever seen. It was about all I could do to control myself the other night from giving some of them my honest[,] frank opinion and a sound spanking that a good many of them[,] I thought[,] so richly deserved.

We have a good Officers Club here with many forms of entertainment[,] and it is here I intend to remain [4*] prior to take-off [sic].

4.

prior to take-off.

I sure wished you were down here
to spend the hours with me chatting at the
Lounge just outside this writing room; to
hold your hand in mine, to see your
pleasant smile, to watch the twinkle in
your eyes and just to note the blending
of your personality with mine. I would
ask for nothing more right this moment,
but all this I shall hope to have sometime in the future; with proper faith
and fortitude it will be so.

All my love

Tony.

Sure wished you were down here to spend the hours with me chatting at the [l]ounge just outside this writing room[,] to hold your hand in mine, to see your pleasant smile, to watch the twinkle in your eyes[,] and just note the blending of your personality with mine. I would ask for nothing more right this moment[,] but all this I shall hope to have some-time [*sic*] in the future; with proper faith and fortitude[,] it will be so.

All my love[,]
'Tony'

C/o. A. S. Magee T-136514
PE 126 Officers Mess General Delivery
TOPEKA ARMY AIR FIELD
TOPEKA, KANSAS

TOPEKA
7 PM
FEB 3
1945
KANS.

Miss Sylvia Jacobs
2334 Atmore St
Pittsburgh 10, Pa

Air Mail

Feb 6, 1945

Dearest Sylvia,

I had the most pleasant surprise
today for my birth-day. It all happened
when I casually strolled by the mail room
nonchalantly but wishing I could hear just
a few lines from my girl back in Pgh.
When there on the shelf, I found all the accumulated
mail from Pueblo and all the letters that have
been addressed to Topeka plus several packages.
I couldn't have received anything better than
that for a Birth day present. So, I began
to read all the letters in chronological order
enjoying them just as much, if not more, had
I received them when I should have just a
couple of days after they were written. The
kisses on the inside flap of the envelope
were extremely alluring and I took a little
lipstick from all of them! Don Juan has
at last found one useful form for lip
stick, but nevertheless I wished I could
be near Sylvia and have the stuff smeared
all over me. (+ her too)

February 6, 1945

From: F./O. A.S. Mazza T-136514
PB 1-26 General Delivery
c/o Base Post Office
T.A.A.F. Topeka, Kansas

To: Miss Sylvia Jacobs
2334 Atmore St.
Pittsburgh 12, Pa[.]

Postmark: 7:30 PM
February 8, 1945
Topeka, Kansas
Air Mail

Letterhead: Officers Mess
Topeka Army Air Field
Topeka, Kansas

[1*]   Feb[.] 6, 1945

Dearest Sylvia,

I had the most pleasant surprise today for my birth-day [*sic*]. It all happened when I casually strolled by the mail room [*sic*] nonchalantly but wishing I could hear just a few lines from my girl back in Pgh. When there on the shelf, I found all the accumulated mail from Pueblo and all the letters that have been addressed to

OFFICERS MESS

TOPEKA ARMY AIR FIELD
TOPEKA, KANSAS

2.

Gosh! I don't know how to thank you for the wonderful gifts. I couldn't have received anything that I wished for more than the items you sent. Those Pajamas are really the thing but I'm wondering who was the victim of a bump over the head and the loss of 1 museum exhibit item. Rare is no name for it, so I'll treasure the set you gave me more than ever. You should see me in them; they show all the contours of my shapley "figure"···· Perhaps its best that you can't! The nut rolls were delicious; note I used passed tense, since within the past couple of hours my Pilot, Co-pilot and myself devoured over 3/4 of it. There'll be enough for me to have in the morning just before breakfast. I hope I didn't cause too much of an inconvenience in satisfying my whim, but if I did, the nut rolls were worth every bit of that effort. They were quite fresh in the neat package and wrappings and arrived whole and in perfect condition! Some lofty life I shall lead after

636

Topeka plus several packages. I couldn't have received anything better than that for a [b]irthday present. So, I began to read all the letters in chronological order[,] enjoying them just as much, if not more, had I received them when I should have[,] just a couple of days after they were written. The kisses on the inside flap of the envelope were extremely alluring[,] and I 'took a little lipstick from all of them.' Don Juan has at last found one useful form for lip stick [sic], but nevertheless[,] I wished I could be near Sylvia to have the stuff smeared all over me. (+her[,] too) [2*] Gosh! I don't know how to thank you for the wonderful gifts. I couldn't have received anything that I wished for more than the items you sent. Those [p]ajamas are really the thing[,] but I'm wondering who was the victim of a bump over the head and the loss of 1 museum exhibit item. Rare is no name for it, so I'll treasure the set you gave me more than ever. You should see me in them; they show all the contours of my shapley [sic] "figure" - - - - Perhaps it[']s best that you can't! The nut rolls were delicious; note I used passed [sic] tense, since within the past couple of hours[,] my [c]o-pilot and myself devoured over ¾ of it. There'll be enough for me to have in the morning just before breakfast. I hope I didn't cause too much of an inconvenience in satisfying my whim, but if I did, the nut rolls were worth every bit of that effort. They were quite fresh in the neat package + wrappings and arrived whole and in perfect condition.

OFFICERS MESS
TOPEKA ARMY AIR FIELD
TOPEKA, KANSAS

3.

this war is over! My meals will
consist of spaghetti with meat balls, tea
and nut rolls for dessert. Fudge for in-
between meals and Sylvia's Charming
Company all the time. Say! remember
those Chairs in the St. Francis Alcove.
Well, it wouldn't take long to over lap
them at the pace I mentioned above, would
it.?? Oh! Well, it wouldn't be a dull
life at that, I'm sure. I can see
Sylvia now all flustered and in an uproar
trying to subdue another of my many bright &
'absurd' ideas.

Quite a Contrast can be found in
Comparing Sylvia's sugar notes of Dec &
Jan. One heap reminds you of a
distinct sugar shortage, while the other
although in some quarters would be called
a surplass; but there could never be
such a term applied to Sylvia's letters to
me. (I simply can't get enough of 'em).
The trying times in our Correspondence
is yet to come. It is one thing to write

Some hefty life I shall lead after [3*] this war is over. My meals will consist of [s]paghetti with meat balls [*sic*], tea[,] and nut rolls for dessert. Fudge for in-between [*sic*] and Sylvia's charming company all the time. Say! [R]emember those chairs in the St. Francis Alcove[?] Well, it wouldn't take long to over lap [*sic*] them at the pace I mentioned above, would it?? Oh! Well, it wouldn't be a dull life at that, I'm sure. I can see Sylvia now all fustered and in an uproar[,] trying to subdue another of my many bright + 'absurd' ideas.

Quite a contrast can be found in comparing Sylvia's sugar notes of Dec[.] + Jan. One heap reminds you of a distant sugar shortage, while the other[,] although in the same quarters[,] would never be such a term applied [to] Sylvia's letters to me. (I simply can't get enough of 'em). The trying times in our correspondence

4

and know that you will get an answer
within a few days but again it is
something completely different to write
knowing that you may get a letter
acknowledging your letter of several
months perhaps after it was written.
To write on and on The mood to write
will wear away after little or no response
and it will take grit plus a lot of that
thing called love to keep you going. I
hope and some-how I know that we
both have what it takes to withstand
such a crisis.

Tonight even Tomorrow night
weather permitting of course, our crew is
destined to fly to our Port of Embarkation.
We don't know how long we will be
there and it will be impossible to even
tell you where it is. I will send
you my A.P.O. address as soon as
we get set to depart from here. The
APO I give you will be temporary
and will change when I arrive at

is yet to come. It is one thing to write [4*] and know that you will get an answer within a few days[,] but again[,] it is something completely different to write knowing that you may get a letter acknowledging your letter several months[,] perhaps[,] after it was written. The mood to write will wear away after little or no response[,] and it will take grit plus a lot of that thing called love to keep you going. I hope[,] and some–how [sic] I know[,] that we both have what it takes to with–stand [sic] such a crisis.

Tonight or even [t]omorrow night[,] weather permitting[,] of course[,] our crew is destined to fly to our Port of Embarkation. We don't know how long we will be there[,] and it will be impossible to even tell you where it is. I will send you my A.P.O.[245] address as soon as we get set to depart from here. The A[.]P[.]O[.] I give

---

[245] Army Post Office.

5

my destination.

The Birthday Card too was very sweet and sweeter still was the little message found 'neath the pink ribbon. It will be some day when I can collect "Love & Kisses"! Poor Sylvia! is all I can say looking ahead to the future fulfillment of that phrase.

Greg's letter was typical of him and it was thoughtful of you to send that note to me. I would give plenty today if all of us could be at that same table celebrating my birthday as we did but two years back. Seems a long long time, doesn't it?

Am at present munching on the chewing gum you sent. I would have enclosed a whole stick of Peppermint gum but I have that packed in my foot-locker which will be shipped to me later. We have limited luggage on the airplane and don't want to exceed its load capacity. I miss your smiling face before me each evening since your picture was included in the locker that is to follow.

you will be temporary and will change when I arrive at [5*] my destination.[246]

The [b]irthday card[,] too[,] was very sweet[,] and sweeter still was the little message found 'neath the pink ribbon. It will be some day when I can collect 'Love + Kisses!['] Greg's letter was typical of him[,] and it was thoughtful of you to send that note to me. I would give plenty today if all of us could be at that same table celebrating my birthday as we did but two years back. Seems a long[,] long time, doesn't it?

Am at present munching on the chewing gum you sent. I would have enclosed a whole stick of [p]eppermint gum[,] but I have that packed in my foot-locker [sic][,] which will be shipped to me later. We have limited baggage on the airplane and don't want to exceed its load capacity. I miss your smiling face before me each evening since your picture was included in the locker that is to follow.[247]

---

[246] Anthony Mazza sent a postcard with a Notice of Change of Address, postmarked 7:30 PM on February 8, 1945, Topeka, Kansas, to Sylvia Jacobs at 2334 Atmore St., Pittsburgh 12, Pa., notifying her that as of February 7, 1945, his A.P.O. No. was 19043–BT-15 c/o Postmaster New York, N.Y.

[247] See *supra* page 9 (Photograph of Sylvia M. Jacobs).

OFFICERS MESS
TOPEKA ARMY AIR FIELD
TOPEKA, KANSAS

6.

I hope you have had success in the attempt for a raise. No truer words were ever spoken in the sentence "Ask and you shall receive." The quiet passive person is stepped on by all who are a bit bolder than he. There is no truth in the phrase 'The meek shall inherit the land'. It is the meek person's land that is always invaded. Lesson #1 in Philosophy by A.S.M.

Enjoyed the President's Ball with you in my arms, my dancing doesn't improve but who cares. It is quite a job to keep the feet in rythem to the music and in step with our heart beats at one and the same time.

Must close now and will start the old job of packing again. I shall close with this song in my heart: "I dream of you".

Love always
Tony

P.S. Definition of a X
contraction of lips to express
enlargement of heart.

[6*] I hope you have had success in the attempt for a raise. No truer words were ever spoken in the sentence, "Ask and you shall receive."[248] The quiet[,] passive person is stepped on by all who are a bit bolder than he. There is no truth in the phrase[,] 'The meek shall inherit the land.'[249] It is the meek person's land that is always invaded. Lesson #1 in Philosophy of A[.]S[.]M.

Enjoyed the President[']s Ball with you in my arms; my dancing doesn't improve[,] but who cares[?] It is quite a job to keep the feet in rhythm to the music and in step with our heart beats [*sic*] at one and the same time.

Must close now and will start the old job of packing again. I shall close with this song in my heart: "I dream of you."[250]

Love always[,]

Tony

P.S. Definition of a X

Contraction of lips to express enlargement of heart.

---

[248] Mt 7:7–8.

[249] Ibid., 5:5.

[250] Frank Sinatra, vocalist, "I Dream of You (More Than You Dream I Do)," by Marjorie Goetschius and Edna Osser, released January 27, 1945, Columbia, No. 36762.

F/o. A.d. Moyya F-136514
PBI-26 Second Delivery
% Base Post Office
T.A.A.F. Topeka, Kansas.

Miss Sylvia Jacob
2334 Atmore St.
Pittsburgh 12, Pa.

AIR MAIL

Feb 11, 1945

Dearest Sylvia:

I cannot send any mail since our APO address; but that doesn't prevent me from writing regularly and then sending the accumulated messages of love to you. I am still at Topeka, as you can note from the letter head. I'll try to describe my day as it has been almost the past week. Nothing to do up to 12:00 AM, so yours truly hits the deck at 9:00 AM and strays lazily over to the Club. There, I sit and chat with some of my few remaining buddies until my Pilot & Co-Pilot drag their 'carcasses' from the sack, which usually occurs about 11:00 or 11:30 AM. Then, we play a vigorous game of pool followed by several sessions of ping-pong. After that comes our Breakfast-Dinner Combination. I have had breakfast but once since I've been here and probably won't again,

February 11, 1945

Postmark: [The envelope is missing.]

Letterhead: Officers Mess
              Topeka Army Air Field
              Topeka, Kansas

[1*]   Feb[.] 11, 1945

Dearest Sylvia:

I cannot send any mail since our A[.]P[.]O[.] address [has changed], but that doesn't pre-vent me from writing regularly and then sending the accumulated messages of love to you. I am still at Topeka, as you can note from the letter head [*sic*]. I'll try to describe my day as it has been almost the past week. Nothing to do up to 12:00 [P]M, so yours truly hits the deck at 9:00 AM and strays lazily over to the [c]lub. There, I sit and chat with some of my few remaining buddies until my [p]ilot + [c]o-[p]ilot drag their 'carcasses' from the sack, which usually occurs about 11:00 or 11:30 AM. Then, we play a vigorous game of pool followed by several sessions of ping-pong. After that, comes our [b]reakfast-[d]inner [c]ombination[.] I have had breakfast but once since I've been here and probably won't again. [1R*] The meals here are extremely good and rich[,] with the best of foods well prepared. At 1:00 PM, we go back to our barracks and give the bulletin board

The meals here are extremely good and rich with the best of foods well prepared. At 1:00 PM, we go back to our barracks and give the bulletin board the once over. It usually has the message "Load Airplanes and prepare to leave tonight!" Hastily, we get our belongings together and call a truck from the motor pool to carry our luggage and that of our men to the plane. We get the plane all loaded and return to our barracks awaiting further notices. About 5:00 PM comes the repeated story "Fly Away Canceled for tonight!" Rather than have our boys stand guard all night, we again get the truck and unload the plane. About 7:00 or 8:00 PM we are finished with that task, and with much disgust the men go to town to get drunk for the night. My Co-pilot goes to his wife who is with him here in Topeka, while the Pilot and I usually go to a picture show or to some dance hall. ~~for the night.~~

We either get in at 11:00 PM or

the once over. It usually has the message 'Load Airplanes and prepare to leave tonight.' Hastily, we get our belongings together and call a truck from the motor pool to carry our luggage and that of our men to the plane. We get the plane all loaded and return to our barracks[,] awaiting further notices. About 5:00 PM[,] comes the repeated story 'Fly Aways Canceled for tonight.' Rather than have our boys stand guard all night, we again get the truck and unload the plane. About 7:00 or 8:00 PM we are finished with that task, and with much disgust[,] the men go to town to get drunk for the night. My [c]o-pilot goes to his wife[,] who is with him here in Topeka, while the [p]ilot and I usually go to a picture show or to some dance hall.

We either get in at 11:00 PM or [2*] at 1:30 AM the next morning[,] and that sequence goes on and on and on. At first[,]

2.

at 1:30 AM the next morning and that sequence goes on and on and on. At first the weather was the cause of this delay but now it must be something different since I checked all weather maps and could find nothing to hamper our flight.

The day before yesterday my pilot got completely disgusted with the entire set-up and has 'disappeared'. I haven't seen him for the past two days but last night received a telegram that he'll be back on the 12th. He will probably be fined and perhaps we may even lose our brand new plane because of his sudden outburst but there isn't a thing I can do about that. Waiting is a particular thing to expect of Army life and by now I am becoming quite accustomed to it.

I received your letter written on my birthday and enjoyed our dancing session at the William Penn. Had I been

the weather was the cause of this delay[,] but now it must be something different[,] since I checked all weather maps and could find nothing to hamper our flight.

The day before yesterday[,] my pilot got completely disgusted with the entire set-up [*sic*] and has disappeared! I haven't seen him for the past two days but last night received a telegram that he'll be back on the 12th. He will probably be fined[,] and perhaps we may even lose our brand[-]new plane because of his sudden outburst, but there isn't a thing I can do about that. Waiting is a particular thing to expect of Army life[,] and by now[,] I am becoming quite accustomed to it.

I received your letter written on my birthday and enjoyed our dancing session at the William Penn.[251] Had I been [2R*] at home,

---

[251] Sylvia also practiced the art of mental telepathy. To bridge the distance between them, she apparently wrote that she had invited Anthony to celebrate his birthday with her at an imagined dance at the William Penn Hotel. Built in 1916, the William Penn Hotel, now the Omni William Penn Hotel, located at 30 William Penn Place in downtown Pittsburgh, continues to be one of the City of Pittsburgh's premier hotels. "Omni William Penn Hotel," Omni Hotels and Resorts, accessed June 20, 2020, https://www.omnihotels.com/hotels/pittsburgh-william-penn.

at home, we would either have gone there or to the Skenely Hotel. I liked our little discussion on 'Weather,' but wouldn't it be more appropriate ~~worded~~ to use that other word Whether. Whether or not Tony will kiss S.M.J. now or later.?? You would have to be 'On Guard'. all night.

Again I cannot help but wish that you were here with me to use up all of this valuable time I have on my hands. Waste would never exist when I would spend each one of these minutes and seconds with you.

Adieu to you,- right now with love a' plenty.

Love

'Tony'

we would either have gone there or to the Schenely [*sic*] Hotel.[252]
I liked our little discussion on '[w]eather,' but wouldn't it be more
appropriate to use that other word [']whether[?'] Whether or not
Tony will kiss S[.]M[.]J. now or later?? You would have to be '[o]n
[g]uard' all night.

Again[,] I cannot help but wish that you were here with me to
use up all of this valuable time I have on my hands. Waste would
never exist when I would spend each one of these minutes and
seconds with you.

Adieu to you, right now with love a'plenty [*sic*].

Love[,]
'Tony'

---

[252] The Schenley Park Hotel, built in 1898, located at Bigelow Boulevard
at Forbes and Fifth Avenues in Pittsburgh, Pennsylvania, was one of
Pittsburgh's leading hotels. It closed in the 1950s but reopened in 1983 as
the Student Union of the University of Pittsburgh. "Schenley Park Hotel,"
Historic Pittsburgh, accessed June 20, 2020, https://historicpittsburgh.
org/islandora/object/pitt:MSP285.B002.F36.102.

Feb 13, 1945

Dearest Sylvia:

On the night of Feb 11th and early morning of Feb 12th, we were all set to fly to our P.O.E. I went to bed at 7:00 PM and slept up to 1:00 AM in order to be alert for the long trip ahead. I went to my Pilots room to see if he had returned, but Al was nowhere to be seen. A few minutes later my Engineer came over to find out if the Pilot had arrived and whether or not he and the rest of the crew should turn in their bedding. I told them to turn it in and have everything set just in case he would show up in the last minute. The huge trucks arrived on the hour and carried us and the few belongings to the flight line. We assembled in the briefing room listening to all the data for the flight every once in a while scanning and straining our necks to see if Al would be in on time. Alas Alack! briefing came and went and the time to start engines was past, so we reported to the capt in charge that it would hardly be possible to get the plane aloft without the Pilot.

February 13, 1945

Postmark: [The envelope is missing.]

Letterhead: Officers Mess
              Topeka Army Air Base
              Topeka, Kansas
[1*]   Feb[.] 13, 1945

Dearest Sylvia:

On the night of Feb[.] 11th and early morning Feb[.] 12th, we were all set to fly to our P.O.E. I went to bed at 7:00 PM and slept up to 1:00 AM in order to be alert for the long trip ahead. I went to my [p]ilot[']s room to see if he had returned, but Al was no where [*sic*] to be seen. A few minutes later[,] my [e]ngineer came over to find out if the [p]ilot had arrived and whether or not he and the rest of the crew should turn in their bedding I told them to turn it in and have everything set[,] just in case he would show up in the last minute. The huge trucks arrived on the hour and carried us and the few belongings to the flight line. We assembled in the briefing room[,] listening to all the data for the flight [and] every once in a while[,] straining our necks to see if Al would be in on time. Alas[,] [a]lack! [B]riefing came and went[,] and the time to start engines was past, so we reported to the capt. in charge that it would hardly be possible to get the plane aloft without the

We were ordered back to our quarters and told to give our Pilot the message that he was to see the Colonel immediately upon arrival.

About 8:00 AM I was awakened by the light steps of Al who by now must have been wondering exactly what the score was since he hadn't been to the base in 3 days. He went to the Colonel and told him his excuse: "He had none." A few minutes later the Co-Pilot, Myself and the Engineer were called before the Major of our section. He wanted to know what we thought of our Pilot as a flyer and as a man. He said that he had let us down as a crew and that our records proved that we rated in the Superior bracket and it wouldn't be fair to us that we should fly with some-one who had broken a severe military disciplinary measure A.W.O.L. and who possibly may let us down again. Of one accord, we told him that Al was the best flyer on the field and that since he had been in the Army a long time and intends to make it his career, he must have known what he was doing; that his stepping out of line was strictly out of character, and we still believed he had a good enough reason for his action.

The Major then told us that was all

658

[p]ilot. [1R*] We were ordered back to our quarters and told to give our [p]ilot the message that he was to see the [c]olonel immediately on arrival.

About 8:00 AM[,] I was awakened by the light steps of Al, who by now must have been wondering exactly what the score was[,] since he hadn't been to the base in 3 days. He went to the [c]olonel and told him his excuse: "He had none [!"] A few minutes later[,] the [c]o-[p]ilot, [m]yself[,] and the [e]ngineer were called before the [m]ajor of our section. He wanted to know what we thought of our [p]ilot as a flyer and as a man. He said that he [i.e., the pilot] had let us down as a crew and that our records proved that we rated in the [s]uperior bracket[,] and it wouldn't be fair to us that we should fly with some-one [sic] who had broken a severe military disciplinary measure[,] A.W.O.L.[,] and who possibly may let us down again. Of one accord[,] we told him that Al was the best flyer on the field and since he had been in the Army a long time[,] and intends to make it his career[,] he must have known what he was doing[,] that his stepping out of line was strictly out of character[,] and we still believed he had a good enough reason for his action.

2.

he wanted to know. He could have given
Al a "General Court Martial" but in order not
to lose a complete crew, he just gave him
a severe reprimanding and a heavy fine of
$100. Had we testified against him, we could
have grounded him permanently and our crew
would have been broken up and we would have
to go through transitional training all over again.
Later I found out from Al the reason
for his A.W.O.L. His little girl back at Pueblo
would neither eat or sleep since her daddy had
left. The mother could do nothing for her so
the Pilot asked for a 3 day pass. It wasn't
granted on the grounds "Insufficient Reason"!
Al did what I probably would have done under
the same circumstances and simply "took-off".
So in the meantime I keep waiting
for orders to leave. I don't know if my
P.O.E. has been changed or not but I do
know that I can send this letter

The [m]ajor then told us that was all [2*] he wanted to know. He could have [g]iven Al a '[g]eneral [c]ourt [m]artial,' but in order not to lose a complete crew, he just gave him a severe reprimanding and a heavy fine of $100. Had we testified against him, we could have grounded him permenantly [sic][,] and our crew would have been broken up[,] and we would have to go through transitional training all over again.

Later[,] I found out from Al the reason for his A.W.O.L. His little girl back at Pueblo would neither eat [n]or sleep since her daddy had left. The mother could do nothing for her[,] so the [p]ilot asked for a 3[-]day pass. It wasn't granted on the grounds [of] 'Insufficient Reason[!'] Al did what I probably would have done under the same circumstances and simply 'took-off.'

So in the meantime[,] I keep waiting for orders to leave. I don't know if my P.O.E. has been changed or not[,] but I do know that I can send this letter[,] [2R*] and the one I had written before this.

and the one I had written before this.

I can too tell you that I love you still, but nothing much more. So thus I close and as I always must.

I send plenty of Love

To Sylvie from

Tony

I can[,] too[,] tell you that I love you still, but nothing much more. So thus I close[,] and as I always must[,]

I send plenty of Love[,]

To

Sylvie from

'Tony'

February 14, 1945 (Valentine)

Valentine's Day brings
special thoughts
Of how much you mean to me
Of how very near and dear you are—
How dear you'll always be ~
And I'm sending you a loving wish
That all the whole year through
Life will be filled
with all that's good
Especially for you ~

"Love"
"Tony"

OFFICERS MESS

TOPEKA ARMY AIR FIELD

TOPEKA, KANSAS

Feb 15, 1945

Dearest Sylvie:

I am still here at Topeka waiting for further orders as I have been for the past 2½ weeks. Right now the weather seems to be again the deciding factor and as soon as it clears, our plane will soar into the heavens and point its nose onward to our destination. However, we must also wait for a telegram from higher headquarters confirming the fine placed on Al, since this particular office alone is capable of placing a fine on an officer in the 2nd Air Force.

Last night I finally caught up with the movie that I have been chasing halfway across the continent. Have you already guessed the name of that picture? Yes indeed, I saw "Going my Way." It was every bit as good as you said it would be and even then some. Barry Fitzgerald was the actor that held my utmost attention through-out the whole film and it was he, I thought, that made

February 15, 1945

From: F./O. A.S. Mazza T-136514
               PB 1-26 General Delivery
               Topeka Army Air Field
               Topeka, Kansas

To: Miss Sylvia M. Jacobs
               2334 Atmore St[.]
               Pittsburgh 12, Pa[.]

Postmark: 7:00 PM
               February 16, 1945
               Topeka, Kansas

Letterhead: Officers Mess
               Topeka Army Air Field
               Topeka, Kansas

[1*]   Feb[.] 15, 1945

Dearest Sylvie:

I am still here at Topeka waiting for further orders as I have
been for the past 2½ weeks. Right now[,] the weather seems
to be again the deciding factor[,] and as soon as it clears, our
plane will soar into the heavens and point its nose on-ward to
our destination. However, we must also wait for a telegram from

"Going my Way" such a sensational hit. He
reminded me of my old pastor long ago
when I was but a tiny tot learning my
P's + Q's at St Peter & Pauls Parish on
Farmer Ave in the East End district. Father
Casimir Schuler was his name and he had
one of the roughest exteriors that any person
could have but a heart that was warm,
soft and as good as gold. One moment he'd
scare the living daylights out of us, yet the
very next moment we would be gathered around
him anxious to hear another of his many
wonderful stories.

Well, Our ship has finally got a
name so now our long search for names
of all sorts is terminated. We have called
it "Dianalee" after one of the cutest girls
we have ever met. She has the most
pleasant smile and beaming personality that
certainly does attract. Its about all one
can do to refrain himself from picking
her up in his arms and hug her. She
has long black tresses that become her
and adds so much to her charm, while
her shiney bright black eyes seem to

higher headquarters confirming the fine placed on Al, since this particular office alone is capable of placing a fine on an [o]fficer in the 2nd Air Force.

Last night[,] I finally caught up with the movie that I have been chasing half-way across the continent. Have you already guessed the name of that picture? Yes[,] indeed, I saw "Going [M]y Way."[253] It was every bit as good as you said it would be and even then some. Barry Fitzgerald was the actor that held my ut-most attention through-out [sic] the whole film[,] and it was he, I thought, that made [2*] "Going [M]y Way" such a sensational hit. He reminded me of my old pastor long ago[,] when I was but a tiny tot learning my [p]'s + [q]'s at SS[.] Peter + Paul Parish on Larimer Ave. in the East End district.[254] Father Cassimir [sic] Schuler was his name[,] and he had one of the roughest exteriors that any person could have but a heart that was warm, soft[,] and as good as gold. One moment he'd scare the living daylights out of us, yet the very next moment we would be gathered around him[,] anxious to hear another of his many wonderful stories.

Well, [o]ur ship has finally got a name[,] so now our long search for names of all sorts is terminated. We have called it "Dianalee"

---

[253] *Going My Way*, directed by Leo McCarey, featuring Bing Crosby and Barry Fitzgerald (Paramount Pictures, 1944).

[254] Constructed in 1891, Saints Peter and Paul Roman Catholic Church, 130 Larimer Avenue, Pittsburgh, Pennsylvania, was closed by the Diocese of Pittsburgh in 1992. Community organizations have been trying to find a use for the damaged historical landmark. Charles Rosenblum, "Will East Liberty Resident Feedback Save Saints Peter and Paul Church?" *Pittsburgh City Paper*, May 1, 2019, https://www.pghcitypaper.com/pittsburgh/will-east-liberty-resident-feedback-save-saints-peter-and-paul-church/Content?oid=14874420.

3.

penetrate to the very depths of her pure
white soul. She has very tiny like body
features and soft white skin with extremely
fine texture with the rosiest cheeks ever.
All the boys would go to extremes to please
her every little wish; that includes me
too. Yes, Dianalee, our Pilots little
girl, who caused quite a bit of Military
Mix up and who was responsible partially
for our present delay, has a whole big
B-24 m Liberator Bomber named for her. If
I had but a single engined plane and did
not have to consider other peoples interests
my plane would probably be called
"Sweet Syl" after guess who?

Will check the weather in a
few minutes to find out whether??
So long for now.
and you know how

Why with plenty of love
From,
Tony

670

after one of the cutest girls we have ever met. She has the most pleasant smile and beaming personality that certainly does attract. It[’]s about all one can do to refrain himself from picking her up in his arms and hug[ging] her. She has long black tresses that become her and adds so much to her charm, while her shiney [*sic*] black eyes seem to [3*] penetrate to the very depths of her pure white soul. She has very tiny[-]like body features and soft white skin of extremely fine texture with the rosiest cheeks ever. All the boys would go to extremes to please her every little wish; that includes me[,] too. Yes, Dianalee, our [p]ilot[’]s little girl, who caused quite a bit of [m]ilitary [m]ix-up and who was responsible partially for our present delay, has a whole big B-24M Liberator Bomber named for her. If I had but a single[-engine] plane and did not have to consider other people[’]s interests[,] my plane would probably be called "Sweet Syl" after guess who?

Will check the weather in a few minutes to find out whether??

So long for now, and you know how

Why with plenty of love[,]

From

'Tony'

F/o. A. J. Mezza 7-136514
PB1st OFFICERS MESS General Delivery
TOPEKA ARMY AIR FIELD
TOPEKA, KANSAS

Free

TOPEKA
1 PM
FEB 15
1945
2
KANS

Miss Sylvia Jacobs
2334 Avenue St
Pittsburgh 12, Pa

672

Feb 18, 1945

Dearest Sylvia:

It happened rather sudden just as I expected it would and within a few hours I found myself many miles from Topeka, Kansas & deep in New England territory. I am stopping over at Grenier Field, New Hampshire an air field just on the outskirts of the city of Manchester.

Our trip was rather uneventful except for low lying clouds most of the way that forced us to resort mostly to radio and instruments. These clouds also prevented me from seeing many noted cities even from a birds eye view, but anyway I can truthfully say I had been over them.

The scenery is extremely

February 18, 1945

From: F./O. A.S. Mazza T-136514
A.P.O. 19043 BT-15
c/o P.M. New York City, N.Y.

To: Miss Sylvia M. Jacobs
2334 Atmore St[.]
Pittsburgh 12, Pa[.]

Postmark: 4:30 PM
February 20, 1945
Manchester, New Hampshire

Letterhead: [No Letterhead]

[1*]   Feb[.] 18, 1945

Dearest Sylvia:

It happened rather sudden[ly,] just as I expected it would[,] and within a few hours[,] I found myself many miles from Topeka, Kansas + deep in New England territory. I am stopping over at Grenier Field, New Hampshire[,] an air field [*sic*] just on the outskirts of the City of Manchester.

Our trip was rather uneventful[,] except for low[-]lying clouds most of the way that forced us to resort mostly to radio and instruments. These clouds also prevented me from seeing many noted cities even from a bird[']s eye view, but anyway[,] I can truthfully say I had been over them.

beautiful as the snow is an average of 2 to 3 ft deep; some drifts are way over ones head. I can picture the fun that the two of us could have if we could bob-sled and toboggan down this snow laden slopes together.

It is rather quiet here this Sunday afternoon and I in a few moments will add to the stillness. The effects of the flight are beginning to tell and I find myself getting the comfortable lazy feeling that predicts sleep.

Will be leaving the good old Y.L.A. snow but my doing so will have left my heart with a certain young lady who I hold very dear to me. Must run along now and close with

All my love
'Tony'

The scenery is extremely [2*] beautiful as the snow is an average of 2 to 3 ft[.] deep; some drifts are way over one[']s head. I can picture the fun that the two of us could have if we could bob-sled [*sic*] and toboggan down th[ese] snow[-]ladened slopes together.

It is rather quiet here this Sunday afternoon[,] and I in a few moments will add to the stillness. The effects of the flight are beginning to tell[,] and I find myself getting the comfortable[,] lazy feeling that predicts sleep.

Will be leaving the good old U.S.A. soon[,] but upon doing so, will have left my heart with a certain young lady who[m] I hold very dear to me. Must run along now and close with

All my love[,]
'Tony'

Free

Feb 291.

F/o A.S. Meyer F-136514
A.P.O. 17043 BT-16
P.M. New York City, N.J.

ANCHESTER
FEB 20
4³⁰ PM
1945
N.H.

Miss Sylvia Jacobs
2334 Adams St
Pittsburgh 12, Pa

678

Feb 21, 1945

Dearest Sylvia:

I am at present in the middle of no-where on one of many stop-overs prior to reaching my ultimate destination. I can't say much due to strict censorship enroute but I believe I can tell you that I am outside the continental limits of the good old U.S.A.

It has been a rather long time since I last heard from you but I imagine all that was due to the mail mix-up that usually follows transfers such as I have made in the past month. A couple of letters from Sylvie would indeed be an extremely welcomed treat right now.

Navigation has been extremely fun for me. It is wonderful to pick out all the places I have

February 21, 1945

From: F./O. A.S. Mazza T-136514
                A.P.O. 19043 BT-15
                c/o P.M. New York City, N.Y.
                /s/ Anthony S. Mazza

To: Miss Sylvia Jacobs
                2334 Atmore St.
                Pittsburgh 12, Pa.
                U.S.A.

Postmark: P.M.
                February 22, 1945
                U.S. Army Postal Service A.P.O.

Letterhead: [No Letterhead]

[1*]   Feb[.] 21, 1945

Dearest Sylvia:

I am at present in the middle of no-where [*sic*] on one of many stop-overs [*sic*] prior to reaching my ultimate destination. I can't say much due to strict censorship enroute [*sic*][,] but I believe I can tell you that I am outside the continental limits of the good old U.S.A.

It has been a rather long time since I last heard from you[,] but I imagine all that was due to the mail mix[-]up that usually

2.

been; to note all the strange cities and towns, rivers and lakes and natural boundaries that were at one time mere names in a geography or history book. Come to think of it, I should have little trouble deciding where I want to spend my future vacations when the war is over! (On Atmore St.!)

It is rather cozy here in this barracks where the officer members of each crew are stationed in a single room, with all the conveniences of showers and wash rooms; the 6 enlisted men on each crew also are together at the Enlisted mens barracks not far from here.

Can't say much more except that I must rest up for my next long hop and that, of course and always, with emphasis I send

LOVE

'Tony'.

follows transfers such as I have made in the past month. A couple of letters from Sylvia would indeed be an extremely welcomed treat right now.

Navigation has been extremely fun for me. It is wonderful to pick out all the places I have [2*] been[,] to note all the strange cities and towns, rivers and lakes[,] and natural boundaries that were at one time mere names in a geography or history book. Come to think of it, I should have little trouble deciding where I want to spend my future vacations when the war is over! (On Atmore St[.]!)

It is rather cozy here in the barracks where the [o]fficer members of each crew are stationed in a single room + with all the conveniences of showers and washrooms; the 6 enlisted men on each crew also are together at the [e]nlisted men[']s barracks not far from here.

Can't say much more except that I must rest up for my next long hop and that, of course and always, with emphasis I send

LOVE[,][255]

'Tony'

---

[255] The *o* in "Love" is in the shape of a heart.

F/o. a. J. ??? T-136514
A.P.O. 19043 BT-15
c/o P.M. New York City, N.Y.

Miss Sylvia Jacobs
2334 Avenue St.
Pittsburgh 12, Pa.
U. S. A.

Feb 24, 1945

Dearest Sylvia:

Things are rather quiet today for a change even though it is late evening, and We are trying our best to rest up once more before we get "Dianalee's" engines and our own primed for another extensive flight.

I wished I could go into detail to describe this place but again I must leave that to some later date when both you and I are together alone; it would be more fun that way too when we both can look back to see what each of us did at about the same time.

Again I must resort to my own resources as a wash-woman. I took count of my laundry to-day and noted regretfully that tonight I must apply soap & water plus plenty of muscle to my many

February 24, 1945

From: F./O. A.S. Mazza T-136514
A.P.O. 19043 BT-15 c/o P.M.
New York City, New York.
/s/ Anthony S. Mazza

To: Miss Sylvia Jacobs
2334 Atmore St.
Pittsburgh 12, Pa.
U.S.A.

Postmark: [Time and Location Undecipherable]
February 27, 1945
U.S. Army Postal Service A.P.O.

Letterhead: [No Letterhead]

[1*]   Feb[.] 24, 1945

Dearest Sylvia:

Things are rather quiet today for a change[,] even though it is late evening. We are trying our best to rest up once more before we get "Dianalee's" engines and our 'own' primed for another extreme flight. I wished I could go into detail to describe this place[,] but again[,] I must leave that to some later date when both

undergarments that need a vigorous
rub-down. With lighter fluid as
a cleaning agent, I also must do a
bit of dry cleaning to remove grease
spots and stains from my pinks. I
sure hate the assignment I have
set out for myself but its got to be
done and I'm the only one that will
do it.

I wonder how Sylvie is getting
along these days with the Emergency
room and gauze bandages. Busier
than ever I'll bet, sure wished I
could peek through the key hole and
watch her at work. I'd have to
control myself though and stay away
at a distance of several yards or
she wouldn't get a single thing
done because I'd surely demand
all of her attention???

I wonder if she still makes
those Tuesday night excursions
down to the church on Beaver

you and I are together alone; it would be more fun that way[,] too[,] when we both can look back to see what each of us did at about the same time.

Again[,] I must resort to my own resources + initiative as a wash-woman [sic]. I took count of my laundry to-day [sic] and noted regretfully that tonight I must apply soap + water plus plenty of muscle to my many [2*] undergarments that need a vigorous rub-down [sic]. With lighter fluid as a cleaning agent, I also must do a bit of dry cleaning to remove grease spots and stains from my pinks.[256] I sure hate the assignment I have set out for myself[,] but it[']s got to be done[,] and I'm the only one that will do it.

I wonder how Sylvia is getting along these days with the [e]mergency room and gauze bandages. Busier than ever I'll bet; sure wished I could peek through the key hole [sic] and watch her at work. I'd have to control myself[,] though[,] and stay away at a distance of several yards[,] or she wouldn't get a single thing done because I'd surely demand all of her attention???

I wonder if [s]he still makes those Tuesday night excursions down to the [c]hurch on Beaver [3*] Ave. and if there still are

---

[256] The officers' service uniform in the Army Air Forces during World War II was known as the "pinks and greens." The jackets were the "greens," and the trousers were the "pinks." The khaki trousers had a slight pink cast, which gave them their name. "Trousers, Service, Officer, United States Army Air Forces," Smithsonian National Air and Space Museum, accessed June 20, 2020, https://airandspace.si.edu/collection-objects/trousers-service-officer-united-states-army-air-forces/nasm_A19610010001.

3.

Ave. and if there still are St Anthony devotions being offered for us. I wonder too how often that Phantom A.S.M. enters her thoughts and just what kind of commotion is caused when he is some-how dug up from the depths of the sub-conscious to the conscious mind of Sylvia. Plenty of fuss, no doubt???

I wonder what she is doing tonight exactly at this moment as I write thousands of miles away from her on a typical Saturday night late in the month of February. I'm almost sure I'd know what she would be doing if a certain lad, namely me, were on hand in the Pittsburgh district. I'm quite sure that a person to person exchange of love and kisses would far surpass these cold letters and that in itself is plenty to look forward to. Goodnight Syl., with

"Love"

Tony

690

St. Anthony [d]evotions being offered for us.[257] I wonder[,] too[,] how often that [p]hantom A.S.M. enters her thoughts and just what kind of commotion is caused when he is some-how [sic] dug up from the depths of the sub-conscious [sic] to the conscious mind of Sylvia. Plenty of fuss, no doubt??? I wonder what she is doing tonight exactly at this moment[,] as I write thousands of miles away from her[,] on a typical Saturday night late in the month of February. I'm almost sure I'd know what she would be doing if a certain lad, namely me, were on hand in the Pittsburgh district. I'm quite sure[,] though[,] that a person[-]to[-]person exchange of love and kisses would far surpass these cold letters and that in itself is plenty to look forward to. Goodnight [sic][,] Syl, with

Love[,]

"Tony"

---

[257] The church may be St. Andrew Roman Catholic Church on Beaver Avenue in Pittsburgh. The parish, founded in 1863, built its second church in 1872. The Diocese of Pittsburgh suppressed the parish in 1962 and sold the church building to the Urban Development Authority, which then razed the structure. Mary Ann Knochel, *Roman Catholic Diocese of Pittsburgh: Images of America* (Charleston, SC: Arcadia, 2007), 36-37; "Final Mass on Tuesday at Old St. Andrew's: Historic R.C. Church to be Razed to Make Way for Urban Program," *Pittsburgh Post-Gazette*, September 1, 1962. Among the memorabilia that Sylvia Jacobs kept along with the wartime letters from Anthony Mazza was a holy card depicting St. Anthony of Padua with a small piece of brown cloth sewn to the card, which is identified as a relic, as it was "touched to the Holy Relics of the Saint." The Toner Institute on Castlegate Avenue in Pittsburgh, Pennsylvania, published the card.

F/o. A. J. Mazza T-136514
A.P.O. 19043 BTG 70 P.M.
New York City, New York.

Miss Sylvia Jacobs
2334 Atmore St.
Pittsburgh 13, Pa.
U.S.A.

Anthony L. Mazza

692

Feb 28, 1945

Dearest Sylvia:

As I sit on my bunk writing this very quiet evening in February, flickering through my thoughts are many of the happy, radiant moments that you and I had not so very long ago. Not so very long ago? It seems ages since we last parted that night of Oct 29, 1944 but in terms of months only 4 months ago, to the very day!!

On Oct 28th, I believe, (since I have no calendar to check on; nothing except memory which isn't the best thing to rely on) I had made a date with the girl of my dreams. Gee! It doesn't seem too long ago now as I recall my expected entrance at the Jacobs home (about an hour ahead of the schedule.) Sylvia, as usual, was upstairs putting in those finishing touches which always have been able to fascinate me. In a few moments, I found myself involved in a couple of doctor books reading George's case history of a patient that seemed to have no symptoms whatsoever. (By the way, how did George come out on diagnosis).

694

February 28, 1945

From: F./O. A.S. Mazza T-136514
             A.P.O. 19043 BT-15 c/o P.M.
             New York City; New York.
             /s/ Anthony S. Mazza

To: Miss Sylvia M. Jacobs
             2334 Atmore St.
             Pittsburgh 12, Pa.
             U.S.A.

Postmark: P.M.
             March 3, 1945
             U.S. Army Postal Service A.P.O.
             Air Mail

Letterhead: [No Letterhead]

[1*]   Feb[.] 28, 1945

Dearest Sylvia:

    As I sit on my bunk writing this very quiet evening in February, flickering through my thoughts are many of the happy[,] radiant moments that you and I had not so very long ago[.] It seems ages since we last parted that night of October 29, 1944, but in terms of months[,] only 4 months ago almost to the very day!!

Then, down she came all spruced up with that certain gleam in her eye, and too, with a searching look that met my appraising eyes.

A moment later we were undecided (supposedly) as to whether we should go to the Colonial or to a dance where Eliz + George were headed. The (We want to be alone) won over all and we were soon found entering the Colonial. A dance band composed of high school kids blared away all the jazz they could think of plus a few then some, but it wasn't long 'ere we succumbed to a couple of beautiful slow pieces. We sat by the window over looking the Ohio River and could see the distant lights of the city far away. We talked a bit about nothing, then seriously only for a few moments, then followed by a palm reading session. The time just oozed out of our grasp and slipped away ever so fast. We didn't say too much but again that at times is not absolutely necessary. This black out dance came and went, but due to the fact that a complete black-out

On October 28th, I believe, (since I have no calendar to check on; nothing except memory[,] which isn't the best thing to rely on) I had made a date with the girl of my dreams. Gee! [I]t doesn't seem too long ago now as I recall my expected entrance at the Jacobs['] home (about an hour ahead of the schedule). Sylvia, as usual, was upstairs putting on those finishing touches[,] which always have been able to fascinate me. In a few moments, I found myself involved in a couple of doctor books[,] reading George[']s case history of a [p]atient that seemed to have no symptoms whatsoever. (By the way, how did George come out on [the] diagnosis[?)] [1R*] Then, down she came[,] all spruced up with that certain gleam in her eye and[,] too[,] with a searching look that met my appraising eyes.

A moment later[,] we were undecided (supposedly) as to whether we should go to the Colonial or to a dance, where Eliz.[258] + George were headed. The ([w]e want to be alone)[259] won over all[,] and we were soon found entering the Colonial.[260] A dance band composed of high school kids blared away all the jazz[] they could think of plus even then some, but it wasn't long 'ere [*sic*] we succombed [*sic*] to a couple of beautiful slow pieces. We sat by the window over-looking [*sic*] the Ohio River and could see the distant lights of the city far away. We talked a bit about nothing, then seriously only for a few moments, then that followed by a palm[-]reading session. The time just oozed out of our grasp and slipped away ever so fast. We didn't say too much[,] but again[,]

---

[258] Elizabeth Jacobs was Sylvia Jacobs' older sister. See Appendix B.

[259] The phrase echoes the famous line of the film actress Greta Garbo: "I want to be alone." "The 'I Want to Be Alone' Quote," Garbo Forever, accessed June 20, 2020, http://www.garboforever.com/I_want_to_be_alone.htm.

[260] See *supra* note 116.

2.

never actually occured, yours truely
was gypped out of a bit of Dan Juan's
specialty. Yet to Elizabeth totured and more
looking skyward and hand in hand we
were making the usual dash to be in on
time even though we had a few hours more grace
than usual. After a couple of S.M.J.'s
specials, of which I never seem to get enough,
I find myself staggering back home in the
wee hours of early morn.

Gee! I have plenty of time on my
hands at present and I'll bet there isn't
a single moment I've had with you that
I couldn't remember almost the most
minute detail and it wouldn't take me
long to recreate by pen every bit of it.
I wonder if our moments together have
had that same effect on you? I believe
it has, but can't be too certain.

For the past several days we
have remained at this one particular
base, unable to proceed forward
to our destination. We are restricted
to the area of the field, but even
if we weren't it would make

698

that at times is not absolutely necessary. The blackout dance came and went, but due to the fact that a complete black-out [*sic*] [2*] never actually occurred, yours truly was 'gipped' out of a bit of Don Juan's specialty. Up to Elizabeth Street once more[,] looking skyward and hand in hand[,] we were making the usual dash to be in on time[,] even though we had a few hours more grace than usual. After a couple of S.M.J.'s specials, of which I never seem to get enough, I find myself staggering back home in the wee hours of early morn.

See! I have plenty of time on my hands at present[,] and I'll bet there isn't a single moment I've had with you that I couldn't remember almost the most minute detail[,] and it wouldn't take me long to recreate by pen every bit of it. I wonder if our moments together have had the same effect on you?? I believe it has, but can't be too certain.

For the past several days[,] we have remained at the one particular base, unable to proceed forward to our destination. We are restricted to the [a]rea of the field, but even if we weren't[,] it would make [2R*] no difference to us out here surrounded by no civilization and plenty of nothing.

By the way, I've started for myself a 'Short Snorter[.']261 Perhaps you have never heard of the term[,] but it is common among airmen. Each time a person comes in contact with foreign soil[,] he tacks on a dollar of that particular foreign currency to the ones he already has. As time goes by[,] each collection is often the

---

261 A short snorter is a banknote that people traveling together sign. The tradition began with bush pilots in Alaska in the 1920s and was popular among the U.S. military in World War II. The consequence of not producing the signed banknote on demand was to cover the cost of a "short snort" or drink. "What is a Short Snorter?" The Short Snorter Project, accessed June 16, 2020, http://shortsnorter.org/.

no difference to us out here surrounded by no civilization and plenty of nothing.

By the way, I've started for myself a "Short Snorter". Perhaps you have never heard of the term but it is common among Armies. Each time a person comes in contact with foreign soil he tacks on a dollar of foreign currency to the ones he already has. As time goes by each collection is often the subject of wide discussion and interest. The "Short Snorter" must be carried at all times and when not presented on demand the individual must treat to either drinks, sodas, candy bars etc. We have plenty of fun already among our own particular crew over that issue.

Tex, our tail gunner, has started to raise a moustache and has talked a couple other boys in our crew to join him. Do you think I ought to try it? Think of what effects a tickling sensation under the nose would have upon one of those S.M.g. specials???

Good night with

LOVE

"Tony"

subject of wide discussion and interest. The 'Short Snorter' must be carried at all times[,] and when not presented on demand[,] the individual must treat to either drinks, sodas, candy bars[,] etc. We have plenty of fun already among our own particular crew over that issue.

Tex, our tail gunner, has started to raise a moustache and has talked a couple other boys in our crew to join him. Do you think I ought to try it? Think of what effects a tickling sensation under the nose would have upon one of those S.M.J. specials?? Good night with

LOVE,[262]
'Tony'

---

[262] The *O* in "LOVE" is in the shape of a heart.

Miss Sylvia Jacobs
2334 Atmore St.
Pittsburgh 12, Pa.
U.S.A.

F/o. A.J. Meggs T-186514
A.P.O. 19043 BT-15 %P.M.
New York City; New York.

AIR MAIL

Anthony J. Meggs

702

March 4, 1945

Dearest Sylvia:

Today, I am just one step further along my route at a strange place with strange people. I had imagined that the things I found here would be as is, but reality is just a bit different from imagination. All the land blossoms forth with fertility and green vegetation of divisions shades and are pleasant to behold. The climate is rather mild and the damp moist air from the sea causes it to be rather humid. We, as usual, are not allowed to visit the nearby villages but are restricted only to the limits of our base; that, naturally, spoils a good deal of the trip for me since I can have only a one sided distorted view of the conditions and the people that exhist here.

All around the field, are farms that are managed by poor peasants with the aid of their oxen. Every square inch of land is not wasted but fenced in by neatly arrayed stone hedges. The people all are most of the time in

704

March 4, 1945

From: F./O. A.S. Mazza T-136514
A.P.O. 19043 CCS BT-15 c/o P.M.
New York City; N.Y.
/s/ Anthony S. Mazza

To: Miss Sylvia M. Jacobs
2334 Atmore St.
Pittsburgh 12, Pa.
U.S.A.

Postmark: [No Time Indication]
March 5, 1945
U.S. Army Postal Service A.P.O.
Opened by U.S. Army Examiner

Letterhead: [No Letterhead]

[1*]   March 4, 1945

Dearest Sylvia:

Today, I am just one step further along my route at a strange place with strange people. I had imagined that the things I found here would be as is, but reality is just a bit different from imagin-ation. All the land blossoms forth with fertility and green vegetation of [undecipherable] shades and are pleasant to behold. The climate is rather mild[,] and the damp[,] moist air from the

their bare feet. Old men, middle aged men, and boys tramp the sod with their thick flat calloused bare feet. Their clothes are made up of series of patches, that with their many colors and small pieces of cloth, they remind me of a patchwork quilt. They probably saw very little money before the yanks came and since they are a very thrifty people cannot understand our wasteful ways. Women are no-where to be seen and the only ones I have seen here were either red cross girls, nurses and flight nurses all who must feel like the Queen of Sheba among so many men. The native women stay indoors or are at other sections of the area where we cannot go.

We will probably remain here for a couple of days due to a clumsy accident caused by the ground crew. Our plane while going through one of many thorough inspections had one of its wing tips clipped as they were trying to get it in the hangar. The results were a severe gash in the wing tip which now must be replaced. The first night we slept in damp tents between two blankets that one of our men casually stated "I'd sure hate to spend another night sleeping here between these

sea causes it to be rather humid. We, as usual, are not allowed to visit the nearby villages but are restricted only to the limits of our base; that, naturally, spoils a good deal of the trip for me[,] since I can have only a one[-]sided[,] distorted view of the conditions and the people that exhist [sic] here.

All around the field, are farms that are managed by poor peasants with the aid of their oxen. Every square inch of land is not wasted but fenced in by neatly arrayed stone hedges. The people all are most of the time in [1R*] their bare feet. Old men, middle[-]aged men, and boys tramp the sod with their thick[,] flat[,] calloused bare feet. Their clothes are made up of [a] series of patches, that with their many colors and small pieces of cloth, they remind me of a patchwork quilt. They probably saw very little money before the Yanks came[,] and since they are a very thrifty people[,] cannot understand our wasteful ways. Women are no-where [sic] to be seen[,] and the only ones I have seen here were either [R]ed-[C]ross gals, nurses[,] and flight nurses[,] all who must feel like the Queen of Sheba among so many men. The native women stay indoors or are at other sections of the area where we cannot go.

We will probably remain here for a couple of days due to a clumsy accident caused by the ground crew. Our plane[,] while going through one of many thorough inspections[,] had one of its wing tips clipped as they were trying to get it in the hangar. The results were a severe gash in the wing tip[,] which now must be replaced. The first night[,] we slept in damp tents between two blankets that one of our men casually stated, "I'd sure hate

two wet wash rags (meaning blankets) Tonight we have been moved to barracks with many more comforts than the best of tents can offer.

As I happened by the P.X. yesterday, I noted among many things of interest a display of women's stockings. "Are they silk" I asked only as a wise remark. The P.X. clerk then had a time convincing me that they actually were. It didn't take too long to realize their value and on whom I would most like to see them. The shade may not be the best for I am no judge of that; I also know that I could be wrong on size but as for the shape that the stocking should fit, I believe I am a good judge of that.!?? Hmm Didn't think I noticed did you.?? (or did you?) I see the makings of a good hair pulling contest among the Jacob sisters to see who wears Sylvia's silk stocking."

Yesterday, we went down to the sea to fish, but the incoming tide and rough waters prevented us from getting close enough to the water's edge in order to cast a line. We did see many crabs and other such weird

to spend another night sleeping here between these [2*] two wet wash rags [sic] (meaning blankets)[.] Tonight[,] we have been moved to barracks with many more comforts than the best of tents can offer.

As I happened by the P.X. yesterday, I noted among many things of interest a display of women[']s stockings. "Are they silk?" I asked only as a wise remark. The P.X. clerk then had a time convincing me that they actually were.[263] It didn't take too long to realize their value and on whom I would most like to see them. The shade may not be the best[,] for I am no judge of that; I also know that I could be wrong on size[,] but as for the shape of the leg that stocking should fit[,] I believe I am a good judge of that??? Hmm[, d]idn't think I noticed did you?? ([O]r did you?) I see the makings of a good hair[-]pulling contest among the Jacobs sisters to see who wears Sylvia's silk stockings!![264]

Yesterday, we went down to the sea to fish, but the morning tide and rough waters prevented us from getting close enough to the water[']s edge in order to cast a line. We did see many crabs and other such weird [2R*] objects sunning themselves on the jagged rocks. The water was too cold for swimming.

We may try again tomorrow[,] but the wind seems to be blowing rather hard[,] and no doubt[,] the sea [would be] just as it was yesterday.

[263] See *supra* note 219.

[264] In 1945, as the war ended, the stocking shortage led to "nylon riots" in which women jostled with each other to obtain the rare commodity. One noteworthy riot was in Pittsburgh, Pennsylvania. Emily Spivack, "Stocking Series Part 1: Wartime Rationing and Nylon Riots," *Smithsonian Magazine*, September 4, 2012, https://www.smithsonianmag.com/arts-culture/stocking-series-part-1-wartime-rationing-and-nylon-riots-25391066/.

objects sunning themselves on the jagged rocks. The water was too cold for swimming.

We may try again today but the wind seems to be blowing rather hard and no doubt the road is just as it was yesterday.

The boys seem to be spending this rather quiet Sunday reading books. The movies are free of charge but consist of Monogram, Universal and Republic third rate thrillers that even as bad as they are can't entertain and cause us to relax after a strenuous flight.

Must bring this letter to a close and with you in my thoughts can't help but have a beautiful blissful sleep.

All my love
Tony

The boys seem to be spending this rather quiet Sunday reading books. The movies are free of charge but consist of Monogram, Universal[,] and Republic third[-]rate thrillers that even as bad as they are[,] can entertain and cause us to relax after a strenuous flight.

Must bring this letter to a close and with you in my thoughts[,] can't help but have a beautiful[,] blissful sleep.

All my love[,]
'Tony'

Free

MAR 18 1945
POSTAL SERVICE U.S. ARMY A.P.O.

Miss Sylvia Jacobs
2334 Avenue St.
Pittsburgh 12, Pa
U. S. A.

U. S. ARMY EXAMINER
PASSED BY U.S. ARMY EXAMINER 1198 S

March 6, 1945

Dearest Sylvia:

Gosh! at the rate I have
been going I'll probably spend a week
at every stop we make. I am still
here waiting for that plane of ours to
get the 'kinks' knocked out of it and to be
totally repaired before any other extensive
flight takes place.   We had
                    and no sooner did we reach
the end of the run way when
went out of order in   , so back
we went for further repairs. This
morning we were all set again and
were just about ready for take-off
when the
broke down
I am certainly thankful and grateful
that the good angel has been really
doing a splendid job of late and that
we have been able to discover these
difficulties on the ground rather

March 6, 1945

From: F./O. A.S. Mazza T-136514
                A.P.O. 19043 BT-15 c/o P.M.
                New York City, New York
                /s/ Anthony S. Mazza

To: Miss Sylvia Jacobs
                2334 Atmore St[.]
                Pittsburgh 12, Pa.
                U.S.A.

Postmark: [No Time]
                [No Month] 7, 1945
                U.S. Army Postal Service A.P.O.
                Passed by U.S. Army Examiner
                Base 1197
                Opened by U.S. Army Examiner

Letterhead: [No Letterhead]

[1*]   March 6, 1945

Dearest Sylvia:

Gosh! [A]t the rate I have been going[,] I'll spend a week at every stop we make. I am still here waiting for that plane of ours to get the 'kinks' knocked out of it and to be totally repaired before any other extensive flight takes place. We had [censored][265]

---

[265] The Army examiner cut out portions of the letter. "Censored" indicates the words that are missing. As the letter was written on both sides of the paper,

than in mid-air.

The past couple of afternoons were ~~spent~~ spent in the blissful atmosphere of this locality. Gee! but you and I would have been in a kind of heaven here on earth watching the blue sky, the white towering clouds, the rough choppy sea as it sprayed against solid rock, the totally green landscape neatly cultivated in beautifully and regularly divided terraces enclosed by stone fences that must have _____ the _____ area for ages; sea gulls g_____ grace and ease, a stray hawk searching for its prey, cattle grazing in such a manner that their owner could truthfully say his products soon and board

as local farmers dig in the rich soft earth with wooden plows that probably are handed down from one generation to another. All this I have noticed when alone but I guess I wouldn't

716

and no sooner did we reach the end of the run way [sic] when [censored] went out of order in [censored] so back we went for further repairs. This morning[,] we were all set again and were just about ready for take-off [sic] when the [censored] broke down [censored][.] I am certainly thankful and gratified that the good angel has been really doing a splendid job of late and that we have been able to discover the difficulties on the ground rather [1R*] than in mid-air [sic].

The past couple of afternoons were spent in the blissful atmosphere of this locality. Gee! [B]ut you and I would have been in a kind of heaven here on earth watching the blue sky, the white towering clouds, the rough[,] choppy sea as it sprayed against solid rock, the totally green landscape neatly cul-tivated in beatifully [sic] and regularly divided terraces enclosed by stone fences that must have [censored] area for ages; Sea gulls [sic] [censored] gl[ide] [censored] [with] grace and ease, a stray hawk searching for its prey, cattle grazing in such a manner that their owner truth [censored] his dairy products [censored]." Oxen hard [censored] [r]oom and board as local farmers digging the rich[,] soft earth as they guide their wooden plows that probably are handed down from one generation to another. All this I have noticed when alone[,] but I guess I wouldn't [2*] have seen a bit of it[,] if you had been at my side. No, I would have seen more than that in the color of your hair, the blue of your eyes[,] and the smile on your lips[,] but most of all[,] in the reassuring clasp of your hand in mine.

---

the offending word or words that were cut out on one side resulted in the inevitable omissions of benign words on the reverse side. For portions of the letter that were not the object of the censor's editing, partial letters from excised words may remain, making it possible at times to make reasonable guesses concerning the contents.

have
seen a bit of it if you had been at my
side. No, I would have seen more than
that in the color of your hair, the blue
in your eyes and the smile on your lips
but most of all in the reassuring clasp of
your hand in mine.

My evenings are spent at the movie
and last night saw a "Who dun it" mystery.
Believe it or not but I actually picked the
real murderer for a change. Tonight I
saw Bud Abbott & Lou Costello in "Lost
in a Harem." Who ever heard of a
Navigator getting lost? Come to think
of it I certainly have been for quite
some time almost 3 Easter Saturday's
ago. Good night Syl & dream of
me as I do of you
                    With love
                         Harry

My evenings are spent at the movie[,] and last night was a "Who[dunit]" mystery. Believe it or not[,] but I actually picked the real murderer for a change. Tonight[,] I saw Bud Abbott + Lou Costello in "Lost in a Haram [*sic*][.]"[266] Who ever heard of a [n]avigator getting lost? Come to think of it[,] I certainly have been for quite some time [since] almost 3 Easter Saturday[]s ago. Good night[,] Syl[,] + dream of me as I do of you[.]

With love[,]

'Tony'

---

[266] *Lost in a Harem*, directed by Charles Reisner, featuring Bud Abbott, Lou Costello, and Marilyn Maxwell (Metro-Goldwyn-Mayer, 1944).

Three

U.S. ARMY POSTAL SERVICE A.P.O.
7
1945

Miss Sylvia Jacobs
2304 Atmore St
Pittsburgh 19, Pa.
U.S.A.

T/5 A. J. Mazza T-136514
H.T.D. 17043 BT-15 Po.P.M.
New York City, New York

Anthony J. Mazza

PASSED BY
BASE
1197 S
ARMY EXAMINER

OPENED BY OPENED BY

720

March 9, 1945

Dearest Sylvia;

This evening I am writing to you
from North Africa, the scene of much
excitement and violent warfare but two
years back. The field here still shows
the effects of high explosive bombs and the
piles of 'cracked-up' planes seem to tell a
story of its own. The day before yesterday
was the first time we arrived on the Continent
and in but two days I have seen many
miles of this gigantic and somewhat majestic
region.

We had no trouble crossing the Atlantic
and when the distance across that ocean
is measured in Air Travel rate the Atlantic
doesn't seem to be so large after all. The
Ocean was clear and smooth all the way
and with but the stars to guide us, we
landed squarely over the middle of our
designated field. (I'll take a little credit
for that however) The contrast in climates
was terrific and a blazing hot African
sun soon had us working up quite

March 9, 1945

From: F./O. A.S. Mazza T-136514
               A.P.O. 19043 BT-15 c/o P.M.
               New York City, N.Y.
               /s/ Anthony S. Mazza

To: Miss Sylvia M. Jacobs
               2334 Atmore St.
               Pittsburgh 12, Pa.
               U.S.A.

Postmark: [No Time]
               763
               March 17, 1945[267]
               U.S. Army Postal Service

Letterhead: [No Letterhead]

[1*]   March 9, 1945

Dearest Sylvia:

This evening I am writing to you from North Africa, the scene of much excitement and violent warfare but two years back. The field here still shows the effects of high[ly] explosive bombs[,] and the piles of 'cracked-up' planes seem to tell a story of [their]

---

[267] The postmarked date of the envelope calls into serious question whether the envelope associated with this letter was the one that originally contained its contents. It may be noteworthy that neither the letter nor the envelope was the type of stationery ordinarily used for airmail.

a sweat the next afternoon. Suddenly, we saw a huge dark cloud approach our field, but hardly paid any attention to it for we have had quite a bit of weather phenomena the past several weeks. Then, I saw something new to me for the first time. A cloud of locust, millions of them, passed overhead, stopping now and then to eat every single blade of grass and the leaves on the trees that they could find. In a very short time, the poor farmers in this region were left very helpless and their crops completely gone.

   Across the northern area of Africa we noted many towns of entire Arabic inhabitance and origin. All cities have huge walls built (dry state) around them, something they could hardly have existed without not many years ago. Our base surely must have been a part of a French Colonial Army not so long ago. The Famous French Foreign Legion too had its quarters here once.

   For the first time in my life, I have seen filth and poverty at its lowest ebb.

own. The day before yesterday was the first time we arrived on the continent[,] and in but two days I have seen many miles of this gigantic and somewhat majestic region.

We had no trouble crossing the Atlantic[,] and when the distance across that ocean is measured in [a]ir [t]ravel rate[,] the Atlantic doesn't seem to be so large after all. The ocean was clear and smooth all the way[,] and with but the stars to guide us, we landed squarely over the middle of our designated field. (I'll take a little credit for that[,] however[.]) The contrast in climates was terrific[,] and a blazing hot African sun soon had us working up quite [1R*] a sweat the next afternoon. Suddenly, we saw a huge dark cloud approach our field, but hardly paid any attention to it[,] for we have had quite a bit of weather phenomena the past several weeks. Then, I saw something new to me for the first time. A cloud of locusts, millions of them, passed overhead, stopping now and then to eat every single blade of grass and the leaves on the trees that they could find. In a very short time, the poor farmers in this region were left very helpless[,] and their crops completely gone.

Across the northern area of Africa[,] we noted many towns of entire Arabic inhabitance and origin. All cities have huge walls built around them, something they (the cities) could hardly have existed without not many years ago. Our base surely must have been a part of a French Colonial Army not so long ago. The [f]amous French Foreign Legion[,] too[,] had its quarters here once.[268]

---

[268] "History," The French Foreign Legion, accessed June 20, 2020, https://french-foreign-legion.com/index.html.

The Arabs here have what were once white robes but perhaps have never taken them from their bodies since they first got them. Some wear garments that could hardly compare with burlap bag material and shuffle about in their filth on sandals made of wood. Many are employed by the U.S.A. to help improve this airfield, but there are still others who wander about aimlessly even searching the garbage cans for food.

Children here stop you for cigarettes, chewing gum, and candy. You just can't be kind to them but must ignore them or soon you will have a crowd of 30 or more followed by old men, practically digging from your pockets what little you have.

My quarters here are exceptionally good for according to some rumors this building was once the field headquarters of Gen. Rommel. Everything can be had here that is usually found in American quarters except one little American luxury;---- Indoor toilets!!

We were expected to leave this morning but when turning in our bedding

For the first time in my life, I have seen filth and poverty at its lowest ebb. [2*] The Arabs here have what were once white robes but[,] perhaps[,] have never taken them from their bodies since they first got them. Some wear garments that could hardly compare with burlap bag material and shuffle about in their filth on sandals made of wood. Many are employed by the U.S.A. to help improve this airfield, but there are still others who wander about aimlessly[,] even searching the garbage cans for food.

Children here stop you for cigarettes, chewing gum, and candy. You just can't be kind to them but must ignore them[,] or soon you will have a crowd of 30 or more followed by old men, practically digging from your jackets what little you have.

My quarters here are exceptionally good[,] for according to some rumors[,] this building was once the field headquarters of Gen. Rommel.[269] Everything can be had here that is usually found in American quarters except one little American luxury - - - - - [i]ndoor toilets!!

We were expected to leave this morning[,] but when turning in our bedding [2R*][,] one of the boys failed to get his slip and almost got charged for everything. The time we took in trying to clear that mess was long enough that it was impossible to leave at the time they indicated, so here we stay for another day.

All along the way here in North Africa, I have noted Italian [p]risoners of [w]ar at work in our Army bases. They drive trucks, serve us at [the] Officers [M]ess, make our beds[,] etc. I have been

---

[269] Field Marshall Erwin Johannes Eugen Rommel (b. November 15, 1891; d. October 14, 1944) was a successful German military commander in the North African campaign of 1941-1943. "Erwin Rommel," History, August 21, 2018, https://www.history.com/topics/world-war-ii/erwin-rommel-erwin.

one of the boys failed to get his slip and almost got charged for everything. The time we took in trying to clear that mess was long enough that it was impossible to leave at the time they indicated so here we stay for another day.

All along the way here in North Africa, I have noted Italian Prisoners of War at work in our Army bases. They drive trucks, serve us at Officers mess, make our beds etc. I have been trying out my Italian by conversing with them. What a sad picture I must make speaking quite broken Italian. I can make myself understood, however, but not without much effort. Gosh! but I'm sure sorry I didn't take my dad's advice and learned it thoroughly back home. How do you think you would make out Syl, if suddenly out of a whirl of commotion you found yourself in Slovakia?? My crew has gained better service though from my meager knowledge of that language and I'll learn with practice, I guess.

Here at the P.X's and Snack bars all waitresses are "Petit Femme France" (French Girls.) They look and act very much

trying out my Italian by conversing with them.[270] What a sad picture I must make speaking quite broken Italian. I can make myself understood, however, but not without much effort. Gosh! [B]ut I'm sure sorry I didn't take my dad's advice and learned it back home. How do you think you would make out[,] Syl[,] if suddenly out of a whirl of commotion[,] you found yourself in Slovakia??[271] My crew has gained better service[,] though[,] from my meager knowledge of that language[,] and I'll learn with practice, I guess.

Here at the P.X.'s [*sic*] and [s]nack bars[,] all waitresses are 'Petit Femmé Francé' [*sic*][272] (French [g]irls). They look and act very much [3*] like the ones we have back home except for slight difference in language. They are every bit as vivacious as I had heard. Too bad I happen to have a one[-]track mind that has a true + single bearing to Atmore St., nowhere else.

Last night, I attended another movie[,] and this time for a change I saw "Lost in a Harem" with Bud Abbott + Lou Costello

---

[270] Both of Anthony Mazza's parents immigrated to the U.S. as minors from the Calabrian town of Serrastretta in Southern Italy. In addition to fluent, non-accented English, both parents spoke Italian. For more information on the Mazza family, see Appendix B.

[271] Sylvia Jacobs' parents, George (György or Juraj) Jakubko, later anglicized to Jacobs, and Anna Kopcie Jacobs, immigrated to the United States in the late 19th century from villages in the Zemplín region (including the former Zemplén County) in what is today Eastern Slovakia. At the time, however, their homeland was a Slovak-speaking region in the upper portion of the Kingdom of Hungary, which was part of the Austro-Hungarian Empire. In addition to English, both of Sylvia Jacobs' parents spoke Slovak. For more information on the Jacobs family, see Appendix B.

[272] *Les petites femmes françaises.*

3.

like the ones we have back home except for a slight difference in language. They are every bit as vivacious as I had heard. Too bad I happen to have a one track mind that has a true bearing to Atmore St. nowhere else.

Last night, I attended another movie and this time for a change I saw "Lost in a Harem" with Bud Abbott & Lou Costello (for the second time.) We cannot get into town but I doubt very much if any harem exists in this area. If so, the women must be every bit as filthy as the men, in order to blend personalities and more of all roomis's. Have now added a couple more new bills to my "Short Snorter" and its beginning to be quite a little collection already. Suddenly, the French Franc is worth but 2¢ in our money.

Well, I must close quite a volume of material for a change and hope I haven't said too much.

Ti Amo (love)
"Tony"

730

(for the second time.)[273] We cannot get into town[,] but I doubt very much if any harem exists in this area. If so, the women must be every bit as filthy as the men, in order to blend personalities and most of all, aroma's [*sic*]. Have now added a couple more bills to my "Short Snorter[,]" and its [*sic*] beginning to be quite a little collection already. Incidently [*sic*], the French [f]ranc is worth but 2¢ in our money.

Well, I must close quite a volume of material for a change and hope I haven't said too much.

Ti Amo (love)[,]
"Tony"

---

[273] See *supra* note 266.

Miss Sylvia Jacobs
2334 Strand St.
Pittsburgh 12, Pa.
U.S.A.

Pvt. T.S. Mozza T-136514
APO. 19043 BT-15 BPM.
New York City, N.Y.

Anthony S. Mozza

732

March 14, 1945

Dearest Sylvia:

I tried my best, when I could, to write to you while en route here; but I'm afraid I hardly succeeded in getting out the number of letters I intended due to very strict censorship. The last letter was from North Africa but this one is from the place of my destination, Italy. Seems as though Uncle Sam had decided to send the Mazza's back to the old country, but from what I've already seen of this place I'll put up quite a struggle to get back to our good old U.S.A. and I can really understand too why my relatives left this region; it was a wise move for which I am utterly grateful.

My first stop in Italy was somewhere in the south where we stayed for a couple of days

734

March 14, 1945

From: F./O. A.S. Mazza T-136514
764 Bomb Sq Gp 461
A.P.O. 520 c/o P.M.
New York City; N.Y.
/s/ Anthony S. Mazza

To: Miss Sylvia M. Jacobs
2334 Atmore St[.]
Pittsburgh 12, Pa.
U.S.A.

Postmark: [The postmark is undecipherable other than the following partial words and numerals: "U.S. Army . . . A.," "16," "194," and "78." Based on later correspondence, one might read the postmark as follows:]
[No Time]
March 16, 1945
U.S. Army Postal Service A.P.O.
785
Air Mail

Letterhead: Air Mail

and it was from there that I
was placed here. For two nights
we slept in tents with nothing but
mother earth for a floor and no heat.
I had 9 blankets and heavy under-
whar and still was cold at night
because of the up draft which seemed
to go through our canvass cots.
Only from Yesterday, I arrived here at
App 461. As soon as we hit the
runway and came to a stop, I asked
the first person I saw where
App 451 was and he told me it
happened to be some 30 miles from
here. I felt pretty happy about
it all because now I thought I'd
get a chance to see Greg on some
week-end. I then went to Group
operations and asked them how to
contact my brother and pulled
out an old letter to show them
his address. My jaw dropped
several inches for a moment

March 14, 1945

Dearest Sylvia:

I tried my best, when I could, to write to you while en route here; but I'm afraid I hardly succeeded in getting out the number of letters I intended due to very strict censorship. The last letter was from North Africa[,] but this one is from the place of my destination, Italy. Seems as though Uncle Sam has decided to send the Mazza's [sic] back to the Old Country, but from what I've already seen of this place[,] I'll put up quite a struggle to get back to our good old U.S.A.[,] and I can really understand[,] too[,] why my relatives left this region; it was a wise move for which I am utterly grateful.

My first stop in Italy was somewhere in the south where we stayed for a couple of days[,] [2*] and it was from there that I was placed here. For two nights[,] we slept in tents with nothing but [M]other [E]arth for a floor and no heat. I had 9 blankets and heavy under-wear and still was cold at night because of the up draft [sic][,] which seemed to go through our canvas cots.

Only before yesterday, I arrived here at Grp[.] 461. As soon as we hit the runway and came to a stop, I asked the first person I saw where Grp[.] 451 was[,] and he told me it happened to be some 30 miles from here. I felt pretty happy about it all because now I thought I'd get a chance to see Greg on some week-end [sic]. I then went to [g]roup operations and asked them how to contact my brother and pulled out an old letter to show them his address. My jaw dropped several inches for a moment[,] [3*] but soon let up into a great big smile as I could hardly believe my eyes when I read Grp[.] 461 instead of 451; the same Grp[.] and field where I was located. Greg was in Squadron 766[,] and I [was] assigned to Squadron 764[;] that alone kept this coincidence or miracle from

but soon let up into a great big
smile as I could hardly believe
my eyes when I read Grp 461 instead
of 451; the same Grp and field where
I was located. Greg was in
Squadron 766 and I assigned to
Squadron 764, that alone kept this
coincidence or miracle from being
complete. I called him and
he happened to be out on a
mission. I left a message for
him to call my squadron and
spent a couple of hours in the
orderly room waiting for his
return call. I was beginning
to worry quite a bit since I hadn't
word from him for over one
month but suddenly who should
burst through the orderly room
but Greg himself. He and I

being complete.[274] I called him[,] and he happened to be out on a mission. I left a message for him to call my squadron and spent a couple of hours in the orderly room waiting for his return call. I was beginning to worry quite a bit[,] since I hadn't word from him for over one month[,] but suddenly who should burst through the orderly room but Greg himself. He and I [4*] could hardly

Gregory E. Mazza
(December 1942)

---

[274] Anthony Mazza was posted with the 15th Air Force at Torretta Field, which was about eight miles south of Cerignola, Italy. Gregory E. Mazza, "Chapter No. 8 Basic Flight," Memoir (n.d.) 25, 28 (on file with the editor); "Torretta Field," 461st Bombardment Group (H), accessed June 20, 2020, https://461st.org/Torretta/Torretta.htm; "Cerignola," 461st Bombardment Group (H), accessed June 20, 2020, https://461.org/Cerignola/Cerignola.htm.

4

Could hardly believe our eyes and
he kept repeating "I'll be danged".
Greg is just the same as he ever
was and although we haven't seen
each other for a couple of years, there
was little change I noticed in him.
For the past couple of days I've
been spending the nights at his
squadron while he has been over
to my squadron during the day.
We traveled all over the post in
a jeep that Greg was able to get
at his squadron. I read all
the last letters he got from home
since I probably can't get mail
here for a couple of weeks. One
of them happened to be from a girl
named Sylvia. Whats this I
hear about you deserting the Army
for the Navy in the Nurse draft?
Pure treason I call it; better have
a good reason!!

740

believe our eyes[,] and he kept repeating[,] "I'll be danged." Greg is just the same as he ever was[,] and although we haven't seen each other for a couple of years, there was little change I noticed in him. For the past couple of days[,] I've been spending the nights at his squadron while he has been over at my squadron during the day. We traveled all over the post in a jeep that Greg was able to get at his [s]quadron. I read all the last letters he got from home, since I probably can't get mail here for a couple of weeks. One of them happened to be from a girl named Sylvia. What[']s this I hear about you deserting the Army for the Navy in the nurse draft?[275] Pure treason I call it; better have a good reason!!

---

[275] In his State of the Union address in January of 1945, President Franklin D. Roosevelt proposed a nurse's draft to respond to the severe shortage of nurses in the U.S. military. The U.S. House of Representatives approved a bill for drafting nurses by a vote of 347 to 42 on March 28, 1945. The bill died in the U.S. Senate, however, based on changed circumstances, with the war coming to an end in Europe on May 8, 1945. Pamela D. Toler, "The First Time the U.S. Considered Drafting Women—75 Years Ago," *Washington Post*, March 21, 2019, https://www.washingtonpost.com/outlook/2019/03/21/first-time-us-considered-drafting-women-years-ago/.

Air Mail

So you are only now in Class 1A. I always thought you knew that you have always been in the 1A Class with me. Just you wait until I get my selective service system functioning properly!

In a little while I shall go to town to buy many items I need for Tent Comfort. This includes a couple of good mouse traps. In 3 hours yesterday with a single trap, I got 6 mice; quite a record, isn't it? So long for now and with oodles of love & kisses

"Tony"

[5*] So you are only now in Class 1A. I always thought you knew that you have always been in 1A Class with me. Just you wait until I get my selective service system functioning properly!

In a little while[,] I shall go to town to buy many items I need for [t]ent [c]omfort. This inclu[d]es a couple of good mouse traps. In 3 hours yesterday[,] with a single trap, I got 6 mice; quite a record, isn't it? So long for now and with oodles of love

+

Kisses[,]

"Tony"

UNITED STATES POSTAGE 3 CENTS 3

UNITED STATES POSTAGE 3 CENTS 3

U.S. ARM

Air Mail

F/o. A.S. Mazza F-136514
76th Bomb Sq. Sqd. #61
A.P.O. 520 c/o P.M.
New York City, N.Y.

Miss Sylvia Jacobs
2337 Atmore St
Pittsburgh 13, Pa.
U.S.A.

Anthony A. Mazza

744

March 16, 1945

Dearest Sylvia:

It is almost 8:00 PM and I have just returned from our outdoor movie, which is held every night in an old deserted building several hundred yards from my tent. Tonight we saw the movie "Show business" with Eddie Cantor and George Murphy. I sure enjoyed the show tonight for it certainly helped me to relax. As I sit on my cot, I can hear the steady patter pat of rain drops bouncing from our Canvas top. Inside we are rather Comfortable and cozy with the conveniences of a stove which I spoke of in my last letter and electric light since I brought bulbs and connections from the states at Gregs recommendation, two oil lamps that I made from tin cans, old jars, and an old woolen stocking for a wick. These

March 16, 1945

From: F./O. A.S. Mazza T-136514
764 Bomb Sq Gp 461
A[.]P[.]O. 520 c/o P.M.
N.Y.C., N.Y.
/s/ Anthony S. Mazza

To: Miss Sylvia Jacobs
2334 Atmore St.
Pittsburgh 12, Pa[.]
U.S.A.

Postmark: [No Time]
March 17, 1945
U.S. Army Postal Service A.P.O.
785
Air Mail

Letterhead: Air Mail

[1*]   March 16, 1945

Dearest Sylvia:

It is almost 8:00 PM[,] and I have just returned from our [s]quadron movie, which is held every other night in an old[,] deserted building several hundred yards from my tent. Tonight, we saw the movie "Show [B]usiness" with Eddie Cantor and

come in rather handy when the
electric power is cut off as it has
been tonight. On our candle
stove, I have my Canteen cup
filled with boiling water and will
make tea in a few minutes. I
have quite a number of small
tea tablets, the size of an aspirin,
which when dissolved makes a
rather tasty cup of that beverage.
I'll have you down here by
Telepathy to share some with me.
Otherwise — oh! Golly
it takes three whole minutes
for you to make the trip these
days. Not even out of breath
and just as wonderful as ever!
Too bad I can't have fancy
tea cups and saucers on a table
on which to pour the tea but
those will be forth coming after
we get settled a bit.

George Murphy.[276] I sure enjoyed the show tonight[,] for it certainly helped me to relax. As I sit on my cot, I can hear the steady pitter[-]pat of rain drops [sic] bouncing from our canvas top. Inside, we are rather comfortable and cozy with conveniences of a stove[,] which I spoke of in my last letter, an electric light[,] since I brought bulbs and connections from the [S]tates at Greg[']s recommendation, two oil lamps that I made from tin cans, old jars, and an old woolen stocking for a wick. These [2*] came in rather handy when the electric power is cut off[,] as it has been tonight. On our crude stove, I have my [c]anteen [c]up filled with boiling water and will make tea in a few minutes. I have quite a number of small tea tablets, the size of an aspirin, which when dissolved[,] makes a rather tasty cup of that beverage. I'll have you down here by [t]elepathy to share some with me. Swisssssssh! Golly[,] it takes three whole minutes to make the trip these days. Not even out of breath and just as wonderful as ever! Too bad I can't have fancy tea cups [sic] and saucers or a table on which to pour the tea[,] but those will be forthcoming after we get settled a bit. [3*] Instead[,] you'll have to drink your tea from the other

---

[276] *Show Business*, directed by Edwin L. Marin, featuring Eddie Cantor, George Murphy, and Joan Davis (RKO Radio Pictures, 1944).

Instead you'll have to drink your tea from the other end of this Cantara Cup. (No need for pouring.) How many lumps of sugar? Well, since we have a double portion and you are not impoverished, I'll use two lumps for you and I won't need any with all the sugar supplass right next to me. See these three chairs! Well, we made them today from old beat up scrap iron and a parachute pack for the seat. Over yonder in that corner is a wash stand under construction. The bowl consists of a helmet with a whole in the center that can be stopped. Tubing from an old oxygen mask will be used to drain the water from the bowl. Tomorrow we hope to build a drainage through the floor of our tent to the valley so that we won't have to carry the dirty

end of this [c]anteen [c]up. (No need for pouring.) How many lumps of sugar? Well, since we have a double portion[,] and you are here [undecipherable], I'll use two lumps for you[,] and I won't need any with all the sugar surplass [*sic*] right next to me. See these three chairs! Well, we made them today from old beat[-]up scrap iron and a parachute pack for the seat. Over yonder in that corner is a wash stand [*sic*] under construction. The bowl consists of a helmet with a hole in the center that can be stopped. Tubing from an old oxygen mask will be used to drain the water from the bowl. Tomorrow[,] we hope to build a drainage through the floor of our tent to the valley so that we won't have to carry the dirty [4*] water away. Weights with a con-structed pulley gives [*sic*]

water away. Wriglets with a con-
slanted pulley gives us a self
closing door while tin Ammunition
Cans serve as Cubboards for our
miscellaneous equipment. You
can readily see how busy we
have been and are using our spare
moments to some use. Enough
of all that kind of talk with you
near, Gee! After you wash
the cup and I dry it (mother
nature and the air as a dish
towel) We settle down to business?
This Cat is a poor substitute for
a candle but I'm still the same
old aggressor. Since now I think
we do pretty well in a 'Clinch',
don't you?? I'll sure have
my share of hugs and kisses
or know the reason Why not?
Navigator to Pilot hold a Heading
of 45° and pucker up. Smack!!
                            With love,

752

us a self[-]closing door[,] while tin ammunition cans serve as cubboards [*sic*] for our miscellaneous equipment. You can readily see how busy we have been[,] and we have been[,] and are[,] using our spare moments to some real use. Enough of all that kind of talk with you near. Gee! After you wash the cup and I dry it ([M]other [N]ature and the air as a dish tow[e]l)[, we can] settle down to business?? This cot is a poor substitute for a couch[,] but I'm still the same old aggressor. Some-how [*sic*] I think we do pretty well in a 'clinch;' don't you?? I'll sure have my share of hugs and kisses or know the reason why[] not?? Navigator to p]ilot[,] hold a [h]eading of 45° and pucker up. Smack!!

With love[,]

'Tony'

P.S. Have caught a total of 8 mice so far.

Air Mail

March 18, 1945

Dearest Sylvia:

Lying on the bed right beside
me are the treasures I have long
waited for. Letters from home
and from the girl I've left
behind. If letters such as these
could be evaluated, the heap right
be side me could not be measured
in terms of any price. I got 16 in
all with the latest one dated Feb 26
and the earliest Feb 17th. and have
already re-read the Jacobs deluxe
special ones twice. I'll be at them
for the next week re-reading and
finding something between the lines
I missed the first and second time.
Gosh! I'd sure like to answer
each one of them individually and
may later on but now I'll refer
to them in general terms.

Ah! Here's one dated the 17th
of Feb. and written on a Sat.

March 18, 1945

From: F./O. A.S. Mazza T-136514
764 Bomb Sq. Gp 461
A.P.O. 520 c/o P.M.
New York City; N.Y.
/s/ Anthony S. Mazza

To: Miss Sylvia Jacobs
2334 Atmore St.
Pittsburgh 12, Pa[.]
U.S.A.

Postmark: [No Time or Date]
U.S. Army Postal Service A.P.O.
Air Mail

Letterhead: Air Mail

[1*]   March 18, 1945

Dearest Sylvia:

Lying on the bed right beside me are the treasures I have long waited for. Letters from home and from the girl I left behind. If letters such as these could be evaluated, the heap right be-side [*sic*] me could not be measured in terms of any price. I got 16 in all[,] with the latest one dated Feb[.] 26 and the earliest Feb[.] 17th, and have already re-read [*sic*] the Jacobs deluxe special ones twice. I'll

2.

night. (That proves that one little girl I know isn't stepping out on me.) Gee! I have had those same lonely Sat. nights many times but just you wait until U.S.M. get truck'in on down Atmore St. again. He'll have something to say about the both of us. You sure did right by picking the P.O.E. instead of Topeka or I'd still be waiting for this particular letter. So the Army, Navy etc think you are "pretty popular girl" eh? Did you tell them you were Popular with me?? Your right about "I didn't think they cared." Well, they don't! They remind me of many people I know that never mean what they say and after hurting some-one very deeply pass it by with a couple of words "So Sorry!!"

Too bad you couldn't enjoy "The Cat" but with

be at them for the next week[,] rereading and finding something between the lines I missed the first and second time. Gosh! I'd sure like to answer each one of them individually and may later on[,] but now[,] I'll refer to them in general terms.

Ah! Here's one dated the 17th of Feb. and written on a Sat. [2*] night. (That proves that one little girl I know isn't stepping out on me.) Gee! I have had those same lonely Sat. nights many times[,] but just you wait until A.S.M. get[s] truck'n on down Atmore St. again[;] he'll have something to say about the both of us. You sure did right by picking the P.O.E. instead of Topeka[,] or I'd still be waiting for this particular letter. So the Army, Navy[,] etc[.] think you are a pretty popular girl[,] eh? Did you tell them you were popular with me?? Your [sic] right about "I didn't think they cared." Well, they don't! They remind me of many people I know that never mean what they say[,] and after hurting some-one [sic] very deeply[,] pass it by with a couple of words[,] "So [s]orry!!"

3"

The Bitman (me) at your
side I agree --- You wouldn't be
bored but you would be annoyed!!.
After looking at the program though
I see where you and I would have
bolted from the rest of the family
and gone to see "Faust." Yep, I
knew Carl Eoser who was Miss
Dusay's pride and joy at Oliver.
He was rather tall with big bulging
eyes and had a very deep voice.
If I remember correctly, he is bothered
with heart trouble of some sort and
one of his relatives owns a costume
store in town that provides props
for stage plays.

3 minutes with you?? Sucks!
that would hardly do. It would
take all of three minutes get over
the shock of seeing you but I'd
recover quick enough to have
at least one big hug + kiss and
would still be bargaining for

Too bad you couldn't enjoy "The Bat"[277] with [3*] "The Batman" (me) at your side[;] I agree - - - You [w]ouldn't be bored[,] but you would be annoyed!! After looking at the program[,] though[,] I see where you and I would have bolted from the rest of the family and gone to see "Faust." Yep, I know Carl Esser[,] who was Miss Disay's[278] pride and joy at Oliver. He was rather tall with big bulging eyes and had a very deep voice. If I remember correctly, he is bothered with heart trouble of some sort[,] and one of his relatives owns a costume store in town that provides props for stage plays.

[Three] minutes with you? Sucks![279] That would hardly do. It would take all of three minutes [to] get over the shock of seeing you[,] but I'd recover quick enough to have at least one big hug + kiss and would still be bargaining for [4*] more time in one and the same breath. See! I'm still normal and being over here hasn't changed me one bit.

---

[277] The reference appears to be to *Die Fledermaus* (*The Bat*), the 1874 operetta by Johan Strauss II. "Die Fledermaus," Guide to Light Opera and Operetta, accessed June 20, 2020, http://musicaltheatreguide.com/composers/straussjnr/fledermaus.htm.

[278] Ethel Disay taught music at Oliver High School. *The Omicron* (June 1939), 7.

[279] Perhaps the intended word is "Shucks!"

4

more time in one and the same
breath. See! I'm still normal and
being over here hasn't changed me
one bit.

Edna Susenda is still in
Florida. You see I get quite
a bit of detail on Eddie now that
I am in contact with Greg. Only
yesterday Greg showed me a wonderful snap shot that Edna sent him of
her. It sure was natural and
fitted very snugly in his wallet.

Yesterday, I received another
astonishing surprise. I had to
fly for a few hours in the afternoon
and just as soon as I got back
to my squadron who should I
see waiting for me none other
than Johnnie Yount. I don't
know if you happen to know
of Johnnie but George would
I'm sure.

Edna Surenda is still in Florida. You see I get quite a bit of detail on Eddie now that I am in contact with Greg. Only yesterday[,] Greg showed me a wonderful snap-shot [*sic*] that Edna sent him of her. It sure was natural and fitted very snugly in his wallet.[280]

Courtesy of Mazza Family Collection

Edna Surenda
(ca. 1945)

---

[280] Inexplicably, the photograph of Edna Surenda that Anthony Mazza mentions in his letter is enclosed. The gauzy, black-and-white photograph is of a young, attractive, self-possessed brunette with soft flowing hair and flawless skin. Her gaze is calm and steady; she is not smiling. She wears mabe pearl earrings and a white blouse with a ruffled lace collar. On the right side of her head, drawn in ink, is what appears to be a flower hair ornament. In the same ink as the drawing, an inscription appears at the lower right corner of the photograph: "Hi Greg, I hope I didn't scare you. Edna."

5

Yount graduated from High School
with us in June '39 and was one
of the celebrated members of the great
P.B.W. Fraternity. It was like old
times to see them and we had much
in common to talk about. Johnnie
is a Staff Sergeant on one the ground
crews here in the 765th Squadron
in our group and has been here
over one year. We shall see plenty
of each other at the moments when
I am free, but at present my
schedule is so irregular that I haven't
even seen Greg for the past couple
of days although we have had our
daily telephone conversations. Speaking
of telephone conversations, I wonder
how you and I would manage on
a hook up again after such a
long long time. I still chuckle
at the way I had those poor student
nurses on edge while I called

Yesterday, I received another astonishing surprise. I had to fly for a few hours in the afternoon[,] and just as soon as I got back to my squadron[,] who should I see waiting for me none other than Johnnie Yount. I don't know if you happen to know of Johnnie[,] but George would[,] I'm sure. [5*] Yount graduated from [h]igh [s]chool with us in June '39 and was one of the celebrated members of the great P.B.W. fraternity.[281] It was like old times to see him[,] and we had much in common to talk about. Johnnie is a [s]taff [s]ergeant on one of the ground crews here in the 765th Squadron in our group and has been here over one year. We shall see plenty of each other at the moments when I am free, but at present[,] my schedule is so irregular that I haven't even seen Greg for the past couple of days[,] although we have had our daily telephone conversations. Speaking of telephone conversations, I wonder how you and I would manage on a hook-up [sic] again after such a long[,] long time. I still chuckle at the way I had those poor student nurses on edge while I called [6*] Miss Sylvia Jacobs in the

---

[281] See *supra* note 213.

6

Miss Sylvia Jacobs in the middle of her peaceful shower bath at St. Johns Nurses Home 3334 Fleming Ave. Even comes natural now writing that old address.

I have also heard from home about my cousin getting up enough nerve for his second operation. I hope that it does come out O.K. I also received notice that his sister Margie is now a young married woman having married a sailor on but a short leave. His home is in Florida. All I can say to that is "That's my Cousin!!."

Well, I'd better close now for I could keep on and on but must save more comments for the next time. Everyone here in Italy, civilians and G.I.'s use the one word Multi extensively. It means colloquially "Lots of" or "Many" so I close this letter with

multi love
"Tony"

middle of her peaceful shower bath at St. John[']s Nurse Home [at] 3334 Fleming Ave. Even comes natural[ly] now[,] writing that old address.

I have also heard from home about my cousin getting up enough nerve for his second operation. I hope that it does come out O.K. I also received notice that his sister, Margie[,] is now a young married woman[,] having married a sailor on but a short leave. His home is in Florida. All I can say to that is[,] "That's my [c]ousin!!"

Well, I'd better close now[,] for I could keep on and on but must save more comments for the next time. Everyone here in Italy, civilians and GI's [*sic*] use the one word ["]Multi [*sic*]["] extensively. It means colloquially "Lots of" or "Many" so I close this letter with

Multi [*sic*] love[,]

'Tony'

March 20, 1945

Dearest Sylvia:

Received a call just a moment ago that Greg has arrived safe from another mission. I sure do sweat out every one that he is on. Later in the evening he will probably come over to my squadron and we'll have a toast on it. Airmen, after a bit become the most superstitious set of people that one can find anywhere, yet they will never admit it. Most of them wear a little charm of some sort, a scarf, a ring, cap, or go through a specific routine prior to each flight for 'luck'. Wonder what my reactions will be to that shortly.

This morning, out here in the wilderness, our entire crew had to dress in class A uniforms and meet the Commanding Officer. He welcomed us to the 15th Air Force

March 20, 1945

From: F./O. A.S. Mazza T-136514
               764th Bomb Sq 461 Gp
               A.P.O. 520 c/o P.M.
               N.Y.C., N.Y.
               /s/ Anthony S. Mazza

To: Miss Sylvia Jacobs
               2334 Atmore St[.]
               Pittsburgh 12, Pa[.]
               U.S.A.

Postmark: [No Time]
               March 22, 1945
               U.S. Army Postal Service
               785
               Air Mail

Letterhead: [No Letterhead]

[1*]   March 20, 1945

Dearest Sylvia:

   Received a call just a moment ago that Greg has arrived safe from another mission. I sure do sweat out every one that he is on. Later in the evening[,] he will probably come over to my squadron and we'll have a toast on it. Airm[e]n, after a bit,

and in a routine manner told us
of our great responsibilities and what
we must do to up hold the glorious
tradition of our group. Most of this
afternoon I spent chasing a soft-ball
over one of these fields near by, trying
to get in better physical condition and
tonight my bones are beginning to ache.

Yesterday, I finally got a chance
to go to town. Greg and I went to
Officers sales where I bought a new
O.D. shirt. Greg bought a mattress
cover and paid about $1.00 for it.
As we were walking further up the
village we were haunted by several
natives who were willing to pay
$15 for the same item. Clothing here
is terrifically scarce and these individuals were probably running a black
market of their own and would sell
the same cover for two or 3 times
what they paid for it. Under
strict orders we couldn't sell them
anything to them and wouldn't even

become the most superstitious set of people that one can find anywhere, yet they will never admit it. Most of them wear a little charm of some sort, a scarf, a ring, cap, or go through a specific routine prior to each flight for 'luck.' Wonder what my reactions will be to that shortly.

This morning[,] out here in the wilderness, our entire crew had to dress in [C]lass A uniforms and meet the [c]ommanding [o]fficer. He welcomed us to the 15th Air Force [2*] and in a routine manner[,] told us of our great responsibilities and what we must do to uphold the glorious tradition of our group. Most of this afternoon[,] I spent chasing a soft-ball [*sic*] over one of these fields nearby, trying to get in better physical condition[,] and tonight my bones are beginning to ache.

Yesterday, I finally got a chance to go to town. Greg and I went to [o]fficers['] sales where I bought a new O.D. shirt. Greg bought a mattress cover and paid $1.00 for it. As we were walking further up the village[,] we were haunted by several natives who were willing to pay $15 for the same item. Clothing here is terrifically scarce[,] and these individ–uals were probably running a black market of their own and would sell the same cover for two or 3 times what they paid for it. Under strict orders[,] we couldn't

3.

if we could for by so. doing some
one else would suffer. I wont go
into details on conditions in Italy
right now for that alone would
take volumes of material. Gradually
and little by little I'll have more
to write on that subject. The only
place we could go in town was to
the Officers club where we had
coffee and donuts and real honest
to goodness ice cream. We bought
the Stars & Stripes, a service mans newspaper and spent a quiet while reading
the latest news which looked very
favorable to us. We were back in
camp before supper.

I sure would like to see you
with your new hair cut and wished
I could have been with you to direct
operations. They would certainly leave
a job with me on hand for I'd
want your hair cut and waved
just so.

sell anything to them and wouldn't[,] even [3*] if we could[,] for by so-doing [sic] some one [sic] else would suffer. I won['']t go into details on conditions in Italy right now[,] for that alone would take volumes of material. Gradually[,] and little by little[,] I'll have more to write on that subject. The only place we could go in town was to the Officers Club[,] where we had coffee and donuts and real honest[-]to[-]goodness ice cream. We bought the *Stars [and] Stripes*,[282] a serviceman['']s news-paper, and spent a quiet while reading the latest news[,] which looked very favorable to us. We were back in camp before supper.

Sure would like to see you with your new hair cut [sic] and wished I could have been with you to direct operations. They would certainly have a job with me on hand[,] for I'd want your hair cut and waved just so.

---

[282] Italics added.

4

The stars at night are ever so bright
deep in the heart of Italy. Venus is
still the first heavenly body that can
be seen at night and when I usually
see it first I make just one little
wish! As I was going through some
of the letters, I couldn't help but
chuckle a little at the one item
that asks me to refrain from being
slighted since this one particular letter
makes up for two papers. Wow! I continuing
must be some Tyrant!! but if it
gets such marvelous results I'lleven
growl a little now and then.

Sylvia, if ever you do get into
the nurse Corps either army or Navy,
it will not alter and should not
alter that which exists between us.
As you have mentioned it could
change some people for the worse, but
since your personality and ideals
plus home training are similar
in many ways to mine, it should
not change you as it has had

[4*] The stars at night are ever so bright deep in the heart of Italy.[283] Venus is still the first heavenly body that can be seen at night[,] and when I usually see it first[,] I make just one little wish. As I was going through some of the letters from S[.]M[.]J[.], I couldn't help but chuckle a little at the one item that asks me to refrain from being slighted[,] since this one particular letter makes up for two papers. Wow! I must be some [t]yrant!! [B]ut if it continually gets such marvelous results[,] I'll even growl a little now and then.

Sylvia, if ever you do get into the nurse corps[,] either Army or Navy, it will not alter[,] and should not alter[,] that which exists between us. As you have mentioned[,] it could change some people for the worse[,] but since your personality and ideals plus home training are similar in many ways to mine, it should not change

---

[283] The description of Italy here is a parody of the lyrics from "Deep in the Heart of Texas," a song written by Don Wander and June Hershey in 1941. In 1942, four versions of the song were among the most popular recordings aired on the radio. "1942 Radio (Top 80 Playlist)," playback.fm, accessed June 20, 2020, https://playback.fm/year/1942.

5.

no effect on me. I'm not a perfect Angel by any means but I'm sure you know exactly what I mean. In a little while night will fall and another day will go into eternity. In the place of the sun's radiant rays, our meager oil lamps will burn, a cloud of smoke circles my head as I choke and sputter in my brave attempt to smoke a pipe. Will he make it?? Read the next thrilling episode of "The Tobaco Kid". (Incidently, don't go practicing how to fill pipes for I may not make the grade.) Good night Syl.

With Love

Tony

you[,] as it has had [5*] no effect on me. I'm not a perfect angel by any means[,] but I'm sure you know exactly what I do mean. In a little while[,] night will fall[,] and another day will go into eternity. In place of the sun's radiant rays, our meager oil lamps will burn; a cloud of smoke circles my head as I choke and sputter in my brave attempt to smoke a pipe. Will he make it?? Read the next thrilling episode of "The Tobacco Kid." (Incidently [*sic*][,] don't go practicing how to fill pipes[,] for I may not make the grade.) Good night[,] Syl.

With Love[,]
'Tony'

F/O. A. L. Mazza T-136514
7644 Bomb Sq. 461 Gp
A.P.O. 520 % P.M.
N. Y., N. Y.

Miss Sylvia Jacobs
2334 Atmore St
Pittsburgh 13, Pa
U. S. a.

Anthony L. Mazza

March 22, 1945

Dearest Sylvia:

Tonight, I am writing from our Squadron's Officers Club and at the same time have joined the boys in a treat. Good old U.S. beer that is rather hard to get in this neck of the woods. We are rationed to one bottle per man so I should get quite a hangover from this one bottle before me. My mail seems to again be falling off since neither I nor anyone from our crew has received a little since last Saturday. Incidently, it was then that I received 3 of them from a certain young lady who you should know rather thoroughly by now since you have been more than acquainted with her for almost 22 years.

Yesterday, Ming and I went to see John Yount and then the three of us spent the afternoon shooting

782

March 22, 1945

From: F./O. A.S. Mazza T-136514
             764th Bomb Sq 461 Gp
             A.P.O. 520 c/o P.M.
             N.Y.C., N.Y.
             /s/ Anthony S. Mazza

To: Miss Sylvia Jacobs
             2334 Atmore St[.]
             Pittsburgh 12, Pa[.]
             U.S.A.

Postmark: [No Time]
             March 23, 1945
             U.S. Army Postal Service
             785
             Air Mail

Letterhead: [No Letterhead]

[1*]   March 22, 1945

Dearest Sylvia:

Tonight, I am writing from our [s]quadron[']s Officers Club[,] and at the same time[,] have joined the boys in a treat. Good old U.S. beer that is rather hard to get in this neck of the woods. We are rationed to one bottle per man[,] so I should get quite a hangover from this one bottle before me. My mail seems to again be falling off[,] since neither I nor any-one from our crew

at a G.I. and German helmet with
a Tommy Gun. I was disappointed
that I hadn't my 45 cal Pistol with me
to give it a trial fire. The weapon
is still brand new but one of these
days soon when I get some extra ammunition
I find out whether or not it will stand
me in good stead.

I'm glad to hear that you got
to see "Winged Victory". It more than
any other picture I know of described
true Cadet days. The movie though
seemed to center upon Pilots and we
Navigators were slighted as usual.
How well I remember those old
guard duty days. Why it was then
that our old standby Mental Telepathy
was originated under a North
Carolina Moon and poor Sylvia
was dragged from her Comfortable
setting at home to trudge the lonely
nights at my side.

I sure got a kick out of the
Cartoon sheet you sent. "Good
Heavens! Don't you fighting men

has received a letter since last Saturday. Incidently [*sic*], it was then that I received 3 of them from a certain young lady who you should know rather thoroughly by now[,] since you have been more than acquainted with her for almost 22 years.

Yesterday, Greg and I went to see John Yount[,]and then the three of us spent the afternoon shooting [2*] at a G.I. and German helmet with a Tommy Gun. I was disappointed that I hadn't my 45 [c]al. [p]istol with me to give it a trial fire. The weapon is still brand new[,] but one of these days soon[,] when I get some extra ammunition[,] I'll find out whether or not it will stand me in good stead.

I'm glad to hear that you got to see 'Winged Victory[.']²⁸⁴ It[,] more than any other picture I know of[,] described the cadet days. The movie[,] though[,][seemed to center upon [p]ilots[,] and we [n]avigators were slighted as usual. How well I remember those old guard duty days. Why it was then that our old standby [m]ental [t]elepathy was originated under a North Carolina [m]oon[,] and poor Sylvia was dragged from her comfortable setting at home to trudge the lonely nights at my side.

I sure got a kick out of the [c]artoon sheet you sent. "Good Heavens! Don't you fighting men [3*] ever relax?" And there

---

²⁸⁴ *Winged Victory*, directed by George Cukor, featuring Lon McCallister, Jeanne Crain, and Red Buttons (20th Century Fox, 1944).

ever relax?" And there before me I see a couch with the usual scene that existed when Tony & Sylvia come together. The rest of the gags weren't so bad either.

I was very glad to hear that you met my dad at St. Johns. There is no question of doubt in my mind about me resembling him. I know too that I have also inherited many of his habits and moods and wished that I had acquired as much wit too. I was glad to hear that my dad was in the right frame of mind about my being obsessed.

Its too bad about Bob Strayne's sister's baby not being well. Perhaps, by this time it will be thriving normally and the family will be more at ease about its condition.

Say! I never expected my letters to get to you as soon as they actually did. Just taint fair is all I got to say, particularly since I had to

before me I see a couch with the usual scene that existed when Tony + Sylvia were together. The rest of the gags weren't so bad either.

I was very glad to hear that you met my dad at St. John[']s. There is no question of doubt in my mind about me resembling him. I know[,] too[,] that I have also inherited many of his habits and moods and wished that I had acquired as much wit[,] too. I was glad to hear that my dad was in the right frame of mind about my being overseas.

It[']s too bad about Bob Stroyne's sister's baby not being well.[285] Perhaps, by this time[,] it will be thriving normally[,] and the family will be more at ease about its condition.

Say! I never expected my letters to get to you as soon as they actually did. Just taint [*sic*] fair is all I got to say, particularly since I had to [4*] wait a while before yours could get to me.

---

[285] Robert S. Stroyne (b. October 6, 1921; d. December 10, 1999) was not only a high school classmate and friend of Anthony Mazza (see *supra* note 213), but he was also Sylvia Jacobs' maternal first cousin. He was the son of Mary Kopcie Stroyne. See Appendix B.

waits for a while before yours could get to me.

Already in the club a singing session is progressing. This usually indicates the coming end of another day, and same poor piece of furniture will be eventually blasted to bits. They began with "Mother Macree" and have settled down to "Rum Boogee". Get what I mean? So long for now with love a' plenty.

Love,
"Tony"

Already in the club[,] a singing session is progressing. This really indicates the coming end of another day[,] and some poor piece of furniture will be eventually blasted to bits. They began with "Mother Macree" [*sic*]²⁸⁶ and have settled down to "Rum Boogie [*sic*]." ²⁸⁷ [G]et what I mean? So long for now with love a'plenty [*sic*].

Love[,]
'Tony'

---

²⁸⁶ Rida Johnson Young, Chauncey Olcott, and Ernest Ball wrote the Irish-American ballad "Mother Machree" in 1910. "Collection of Irish Song Lyrics," Donal O'Shaughnessy, accessed June 20 2020, https://wwwirishsongs.com/index.php.

²⁸⁷ The Andrews Sisters, vocalists, "Rhumboogie," by Don Raye, Hughie Price, and Victor Schoen, recorded March 23, 1940, Decca, No. 67383; "The Andrews Sisters (Vocal Group)," DAHR, accessed June 20, 2020, https://adp.library.ucsb.edu/index.php/mastertalent/detail/301483/Andrews_Sisters_The.

F/O. A.S. MAZZA T-136514
764th Bomb Sq 461 Bgp.
A.P.O. 620 c/o P.M.
N.Y.C., N.Y.

Miss Sophia Jacuba
2334 Athone St.
Pittsburgh 14, Pa.
U.S.A.

Anthony S. Mazza

790

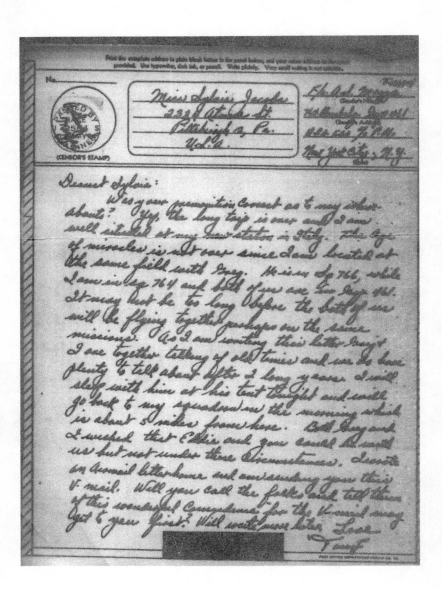

No._____

PASSED BY
NAVAL
CENSOR
(CENSOR'S STAMP)

Miss Sylvia Jacobs
233 Atwood St.
Pittsburgh 13, Pa.
Vol. 4.

Dearest Sylvia:

Was your premonition correct as to my whereabouts? Yep, the long trip is over and I am well situated at my new station in Italy. The age of miracles is not over since I am located at the same field with Irving. He is in Sq. 766, while I am in Sq. 764 and both of us are in Group 461. It may not be too long before the both of us will be flying together perhaps on the same missions. As I am writing this letter Irving & I are together talking of old times and we do have plenty to tell about after 4 long years. I will sleep with him at his tent tonight and will go back to my squadron in the morning which is about 5 miles from here. Both Irving and I wished that Eddie and you could be with us but not under these circumstances. I wrote an airmail letter home and am sending you this V-mail. Will you call the folks and tell them of this wonderful coincidence for the V-mail may get to you first? Will write more later. Love
Tony

March 23, 1945 (V-Mail)

From: F./O. A.S. Mazza
                     764th Bomb Sq 461 Gp
                     A.P.O. 520 c/o P.M.
                     New York City, N.Y.

To: Miss Sylvia Jacobs
                     2334 Atmore St.
                     Pittsburgh 12, Pa.
                     U.S.A.

Postmark: War & Navy Departments
                     V-Mail Service[288]
                     Official Business
                     10:00 AM
                     March 23, 1945
                     U.S. Postal Service

Letterhead: V-Mail Form

---

[288] The U.S. Post Office Department initiated V-Mail (Victory Mail) service on June 15, 1942. Members of the armed services posted overseas could send microfilmed letters to the U.S. that were transported by air and then printed out for the recipient. "V-Mail," U.S. Postal Service, July 2008, https://about.usps.com/who-we-are/postal-history/v-mail.pdf.

PENALTY FOR PRIVATE USE TO AVOID
PAYMENT OF POSTAGE, $300

WAR & NAVY
DEPARTMENTS
V-MAIL SERVICE

OFFICIAL BUSINESS

[1*]

Dearest Sylvia:

Was your premonition correct as to my where-abouts [*sic*]? Yep, the long trip is over[,] and I am still situated at my new station in Italy. The age of miracles is not over[,] since I am located at the same field with Greg. He is in Sq[.] 766, while I am in [S]q[.] 764[,] and both of us are in Grp. 461. It may not be too long before the both of us will be flying together[,] perhaps on the same missions.[289] As I am writing this letter[,] Greg + I are together talking of old times[,] and we do have plenty to talk about after 2 long years. I will sleep with him at his tent tonight and will go back to my squadron in the morning[,] which is about 5 miles from here. Both Greg and I wished that Eddie and you could be with us[,] but not under these circumstances. I wrote an airmail letter home and am sending you this V-mail. Will you call the folks and tell them of this wonderful [undecipherable][,][290] for the V-mail may get to you first? Will write more later, Love[,]

'Tony'

---

[289] See Appendix A: Record of Missions, No. 4.
[290] Perhaps the word is "correspondence."

March 27, 1945

Dearest Sylvia:

I finally have driven myself
to the desk at the Officers Club and will
write letters tonight or surely bust in
the attempt. For the past couple of
days, since I've been flying, I haven't
had that normal urge to write to
anyone. A rather paradoxical occurence
has been to put things off until the next
time.

Now that I have started, I just
don't know where to begin with all
the many things I have to tell you. Ah!
I know I'll start by telling my
Cheri that I love her. How's that for
a rather fast start? Why don't I
tell you something new? Repitition
has its advantages in certain fields
only??

The night before the night before
last night F/O. Mazza was assigned
as the "Officer of the day" for

March 27, 1945

From: F./O. A.S. Mazza T-136514
764th Bomb Sq[.] 461 Gp.
c/o P.M. A.P.O. 520
New York City, N.Y.
/s/ Anthony S. Mazza

To: Miss Sylvia Jacobs
2334 Atmore St[.]
Pittsburgh 12, Pa[.]
U.S.A.

Postmark: [No Time]
March 29, 1945
U.S. Army Postal Service
785
Air Mail

Letterhead: [No Letterhead]

[1*]   March 27, 1945

Dearest Sylvia:

I finally have driv[e]n myself to the desk at the Officers Club and will write letters tonight or surely bust in the attempt. For the past couple of days, since I've been flying, I haven't had the normal urge to write to anyone. Another laxadasical[291] [sic] occurrence has been to put things off until the next time.

---

[291] The intended word is most likely lackadaisical.

2.

squadron 764. With a command car at my disposal I had quite a time bumming all over our area. I was charged with all activities until the wee hours of morning. One of my many jobs was to censor all the ground crews mail. That indeed was some job for I had to lick all the envelopes closed (seal'em). My tongue and lips got pretty sore after the first 50 or so. I just sort of glanced through the letters in order to hunt out any important information that should not be there but could not help notice many other things. I am glad to say our letters struck a very happy medium compared to some I have seen where dearie, darling, honey, etc are used after every other word and the "mush" becomes rather slushy at times to be actually used by grown men and women. These

Now I have started, I just don't know where to begin with all the many things I have to tell you. A[h]! I know[,] I'll start by telling my [chérie] that I love her. How[']s that for a rather fast start? Why don't I tell you something new? Repetition has its advantages in certain fields only.

The night before the night before last night[,] F./O. Mazza was assigned as the "Officer of the [D]ay" for [2*] [S]quadron 764. With a command car at my disposal[,] I had quite a time bouncing all over our area. I was charged with all activities until the wee hours of morning. One of my many jobs was to cens[o]r all the ground crew[']s mail. That indeed was some job[,] for I had to lick all the envelopes closed (seal 'em). My tongue and lips got pretty sore after the first 50 or so. I just sort of glanced through the letters in order to hunt out any important information that should not be there but could not help notice many other things. I am glad to say our letters strike a very happy medium compared to some I have seen[,] where dearie, darling, honey, etc[.] are used after every other word[,] and the 'mush' becomes rather 'slushy' at times to be actually used by grown men and women.

3.

were others that I thought too stiff and still others I thought were down-right silly. Some after each sentence write Ha!Ha! until it becomes a chronic habit. One particular letter had Tsk! Tsk! after each wise remark and on some pages the tsk printed and pasted at the end of a sentence in bold type. The author had one sentence that said "I guess this is rather silly. I wonder what the censor thinks about this." I tried very hard to refrain from doing what I did but the temptation was too great. At the end of his sentence in different colored ink and in parenthesis I wrote "in one word what I thought in exactly his terms" (TSK!).

Say! That must be some slick card player I have for a girl. I'll have to watch she don't slip an ace on me. Winner at the Ladys' Aide

There [3*] were others I thought too stiff[,] and still others I thought were down right [*sic*] silly. Some after each sentence write Ha! Ha! until it becomes a chronic habit. One particular letter had Tsk! Tsk! after each wise remark[,] and on some pages the Tsk printed and pasted at the end of a sentence in bold type. The author had one sentence that said[,] "I guess this is rather silly; I wonder what the censor thinks about this." I tried very hard to refrain from doing what I did[,] but temptation was too great. At the end of his sentence in different colored ink and in parenthes[e]s[,] I wrote in one word what I thought in exactly his terms (TSK!).

Say! That must be some slick card player [*sic*] I have for a girl. I'll have to watch she don't [*sic*] slip an ace on me. Winner at the

Card party? It was good to hear that you did beat the Old Maid Winner anyway?? I'll let you build up the 'hope chest' while I do all the Hopeing.

I can see where the male shortage is still rather serious back home when people go about Calling a picture of me "Some Movie Star". I don't think I'm smart about something like that; some one must be blind is all I can say.

"When Irish Eyes are Smiling" still can be heard from the miniature juke box I sent?? Just as long as the tune reminds you of us, it will ~~have this~~ served magnificent purpose. (I hope.)

Have read a clipping that Lucille sent me about another Pittsburgh Flood. That wouldn't stop me though for I can already picture Sylvia and I going on our 'date' across town via "skiff" or "Piper Cub". I'll

Lady's Aide [4*] card party? It was good to hear that you did beat the [o]ld [m]aid [w]inner anyway?? I'll let you build up the 'hope chest' while I do all the Hopeing [sic].

I can see where the male shortage is still rather serious back home when people go about calling a picture of me "Some Movie Star." I don't think I'm smart about something like that; some one [sic] must be blind is all I can say.

"When Irish Eyes are Smiling" still can be heard from the miniature juke box [sic] I sent?? Just as long as the tune reminds you of us, it will have served a magnificent purpose. (I hope.)

Have read a clipping that Lucille sent me about another Pittsburgh [f]lood.[292] That wouldn't stop me[,] though[,] for I can already picture Sylvia and I [sic] going on our date across town via "sciff" [sic] or "Piper Cub."[293] I'll [5*] let you have your choice.

---

[292] "Flood Crest Near 35 Feet Seen," *Pittsburgh Post-Gazette*, March 7, 1945.
[293] A skiff is a flat-bottomed boat; a Piper Cub is a light American aircraft of the era.

5.

let you have your choice.

I haven't seen Issy the past
Couple of days although I did receive
a telephone Call from him today.
It is now getting a bit late and
our electricity has been cut off. This
letter is being finished by Candle light.
As steady as that flame burns before
me so steady too does the flame
exist in my heart for you

With Love

"Issy"

I haven't seen Greg the past couple of days[,] although I did receive a telephone call from him today. It is now getting a bit late[,] and our electricity has been cut off. This letter is being finished by candle light [*sic*]. As steady as that flame burns before me[,] so steady[,] too[,] does the flame exist in my heart for you.

With Love[,]
"Tony"

Air Mail

F/O. A. J. Mygge T-136514
764 Bomb Sq.
To P.M. H.P.O. 520
New York City 3, N.Y.

Miss Sylvia Jacobs
2334 Atmore St
Pittsburgh 13, Pa.
U. S. A.

USMygge

Anthony L. Mazza.

Record of Missions

#1.
Flew to Brescia, Italy where we hit a small arms plant. No flak whatsoever. We went a route different than briefed and I locked as Toews sectional. Mission time approx 6 hrs.

Appendix A: Record of Missions

Anthony S. Mazza

#1.

Flew to Brescia, Italy[,] where we hit a small arms plant. No flack whatsoever. We went a route different than briefed[,] and I lacked a Torino sectional.[294] Mission time approx[.] 6 hrs.

---

[294] A Sectional Aeronautical Chart is the primary reference for visual navigation for aircraft traveling at slow or medium speed. "Sectional Aeronautical Chart," Federal Aviation Administration, accessed June 20, 2020, https://www.faa.gov/air_traffic/flight_info/aeronav/productcatalog/vfrcharts/sectional/. Torino is the Italian name for the City of Turin. In his notes, Anthony Mazza is recording that because his aircraft had to take a different route than planned on its mission to Brescia, he did not have a Sectional Aeronautical Chart or "sectional" for the City of Turin, which he would have liked to have had during the flight. See "Mission No. 208, 6 April 1945, Bescia–Breda Small Arms Works, Italy," 461st Bombardment Group (H), accessed June 20, 2020, https://461st.org/Missions/April1945.htm.

#2.

This was a big day
for us as 15th heavies
participated in bombard-
ment of Enemy ground
forces and our armies
began push to Po valley.
Dropped 20 frag clusters
12 in one cluster. Our
ground forces had neat
system of markings for
us to drop in baited
area. We had plenty of
trouble over target when
one bomb stuck in

bomb rack. The propellor
was off and it kept revving
against sides of bomb bays.
Removed it by dropping
it by hand over our own
lines. It was a question
of it blowing up on us
and maybe someone else.
We dropped the bomb and
proceeded homeward
with a deep sigh of relief.
Saw 2 parachutes from
a plane that went
down in the group
ahead. Light flack
and low. Mission
Time 5 hrs.

#2.

This was a big day for us[,] as 15th heavies[295] participated in bombard-ment of [e]nemy ground forces and our armies began a push to [the] Po [V]alley. Dropped 20 frog clusters[,] 12 in one cluster. Our ground forces had [a] neat system of markings for us to drop in [the] briefed area. We had plenty of trouble over target when one frog bomb stuck in [the] bomb rack. The propeller was off and it kept swinging against [the] sides of [the] bomb bays. Removed it by dropping it by hand over our own lines. It was a question of it blowing up on us and maybe someone else. We dropped the bomb and proceeded homeward with a deep sigh of relief. Saw 2 parachuted from a plane that went down in group ahead. Light flack and low. Mission Time 5 hrs.

---

[295] See *supra* note 178. The reference may be to aircraft from the 15th Air Force. Anthony Mazza flew with the 461st Bombardment Group (H), which was part of the 15th Air Force during World War II. See *supra* note 274.

#3.

Flew again to same area near Rimini as we dropped another load of frags on the Jerries. Flak increased in intensity and we saw one plane in the 2F ahead go down in flames. One parachute only was seen by our tail gunner. No bomb trouble this time.

#3.

Flew [a]gain to same [a]rea near Rimini as we dropped another load of frogs on the Jerries.[296] Flak increased in intensity and we saw one plane in the Gp[.] ahead go down in flames. One parachute only was seen by our tail gunner. No bomb trouble this time.

---

[296] Germans.

#4

Went to notorious Brenner
Pass today about 5 miles
south of Bolzano. Our
flight was to hit a
R.R. marshaling yd. Flak
was light but extremely
accurate. Meg flew
in the flight along side
of ours. One plane
in the group ahead
disintegrated from
a direct hit on the
bomb run. Went
through more flak
probably mobile

stuff north of Venzio.

#4[.]

Went to notorious Brenner Pass today about 5 miles south of Bolzano.[297] Our flight was to hit a R[.]R. mar[shal]ling] yd.[298] Flak was light but extremely accurate. Greg flew in the flight alongside of ours. One plane in the group ahead disintegrated from a direct hit on the bomb run. Went through nose flak probably [undecipherable] stuff north of Venezia.[299]

---

[297] "Mission No. 212, 11 April 1945, Bronsolo Marshalling Yard, Italy," 461st Bombardment Group (H), accessed June 20, 2020, https://461st.org/Missions/April1945.htm.

[298] A marshalling yard is "a place or depot where railway wagons are shunted and made up into trains and where engines, carriages, etc[.], are kept when not in use." "Marshalling Yard," *Collins*, accessed June 20, 2020, https://www.collinsdictionary.com/us/dictionary/english/marshalling-yard.

[299] The reference is most likely to Venezia (Venice), but the writing is not clear.

5

Today I flew with another Crew-Arnholt. Ship #11 oldest plane in Squadron. Everything went smooth up to target when we started around 2nd time our engines started to sputter. We left formation as Pilot gave us the "buzz" Stand by for bail -out" I hurriedly picked out emergency landing strip and gave him the new heading.

The engines then acted up again and we proceeded on to the base. Oil poured from one engine and it was miraculous that the #2 engine did not catch fire. I sure sweat this trip out all the way back. Got the Air medal award to-day for the effort. Target was a marshalling yd near Lake Garda & Verona.

#5[.]

Today I f[l]ew with another [c]rew[,] Arnholt[.]³⁰⁰ Ship #11 [is the] oldest plane in [s]quadron. Everything went smooth[ly] up to target[;] when we started around [the] 2nd time[,] our engine started to sputter. We left formation as [the p]ilot gave us the buzz[,] "Stand by for bail-out [*sic*][.]" I hurriedly picked out [an] emergency landing strip and gave him the new heading. The engine then acted up again[,] and we proceeded on to the base. Oil poured from one engine[,] and it was miraculous that the #2 engine did not catch fire. I sure sweat[ed] this trip out all the way back. Got the Air [M]edal award to-day [*sic*] for the effort.³⁰¹ Target was a mar[sha]lling yd[.] near Lake Ga[r]da + Verona.

---

³⁰⁰ The crews were named after the pilot. At the time, in the 764th Squadron of the 461st Bombardment Group (H), one of the pilots was Robert (Bob) C. Arnholt. "Arnholt - #155," 461st Bombardment Group (H), accessed June 20, 2020, https://461st.org/Crews/764th%20Crews/Arnholt.htm.

³⁰¹ The citation for the Air Medal was as follows: "for meritorious achievement in aerial flight while participating in sustained operational activities against the enemy . . . ." General Order No. 3058, Headquarters Fifteenth Air Force (May 6, 1945) (on file with the editor).

#6.
This was the toughest mission to date and our Target was Linz Austria, the north marshalling yds. Everything worked according to plan up to our I. P. when one Me-109 attacked our formation and was promptly chased by 4 P-51's. Over the Target we were hit with many bursts of accurate flak! One piece came through the window on my right and the Plexi glass shattered causing

small glass splinters to strike my helmet and eye's or the lids and below the right eye causing a gash which bled freely. 4 Planes went down in our Gp and one in our Sqn. Ross flying right along side of us. Bursts and yellow flame could be Plainly seen. Plane #4 Ross's crew was in trouble & started to drop flak helmets to one starting fling #7 causing them to lose #3 engines; our plane had many holes and our engineer was almost hit by a piece of flak that whizzed by him. Was treated when I got down + grounded for 3 days.

#6.

This was the roughest mission to date and our [t]arget was Linz[,] Austria, the north mar[sha]lling yds.[302] Everything worked accord-ing to plan up to our I.P.[303] when one Me-109[304] attacked our formation and was promptly chased by 4 P-51's [*sic*].[305] Over the [t]arget[,] we were hit with many bursts of accurate flak. One piece came through the window on my right and the [p]lexiglass shattered[,] causing small glass splinters to strike my helmet and eye[s] on the lids and below the right eye[,] causing a gash[,] which bled freely. [Four p]lanes went down in our [Gp.] and one in our squadron flying right alongside of us. Bursts and yellow flame could be plainly seen. Plane #4[,] Ross's crew[,][306] was in trouble

---

[302] "Mission No. 222, 25 April 1945, Linz Main Marshalling Yard, Austria," 461st Bombardment Group (H), accessed June 20, 2020, https://461st.org/Missions/April1945.htm.

[303] I.P. here most likely stands for Initial Point. DOD *Dictionary of Military and Associated Terms*, June 2020, https://www.jcs.mil/Portals/36/Documents/Doctrine/pubs/dictionary.pdf, 286. An initial point is "[a] well defined point, easily distinguishable visually and/or electronically, used as a starting point for the bomb run to target." "Initial Point Definition (US DoD)," Military Factory, accessed June 20, 2020, https://www.militaryfactory.com/dictionary/military-terms-defined.asp?term_id=2663.

[304] The Messerschmitt Bf 109 shot down more Allied airplanes in World War II than any other aircraft. "Messerschmitt Bf 109," Howstuffworks, accessed June 20, 2020, https://science.howstuffworks.com/messerschitt-bf-109.htm.

[305] The Boeing P-51 Mustang was a U.S. fighter aircraft that was successful in destroying Axis defenses in Italy during World War II. "P-51 Mustang Fighter: Historical Snapshot," Boeing, accessed June 20, 2020, http://www.boeing.com/history/products/p-51-mustang.page.

[306] The reference is likely to the crew of Roger S. Ross, a pilot in the 764th Squadron at the time. "Ross - #115R," 461st Bombardment Group (H), accessed June 20, 2020, https://461st.org/Crews/764th%20Crews/ross.htm.

+ started to drop flak [undecipherable][,] one striking ship #17[,]
causing [it] to lose #3 engines [*sic*]; our plane had many holes[,]
and our engineer was almost hit by a piece of flak that whizzed
by him. Was treated when I got down + grounded for 3 days.[307]

---

[307] According to the medical report of Captain Emil J. Koenig, the flight
surgeon, dated April 30, 1945, Anthony Mazza sustained wounds on
April 25, 1945, that were the basis for awarding the Purple Heart. The
medal, earned by those who "are wounded in action against an enemy of
the United States," was conferred on May 9, 1945. General Orders No.
18, Headquarters 461st Bombardment Group (H) Army Air Forces (May
9, 1945) (on file with the editor); "The Purple Heart," U.S. Department
of Veterans Affairs, accessed June 20, 2020, https://www.va.gov/opa/
publications/celebrate/purple-heart.pdf.

Sylvia Jacobs and Anthony Mazza during their courtship (ca. 1945)

Anthony Mazza and Sylvia Jacobs Mazza being celebrated with rice as they leave St. Gabriel Church on the North Side of Pittsburgh, Pennsylvania, on their wedding day, June 26, 1948.

Anthony Mazza and Sylvia Jacobs Mazza pose for a formal portrait on their wedding day at the Allegheny Observatory in Riverview Park, 159 Riverview Avenue, Pittsburgh, Pennsylvania (June 26, 1948).

The bridal party for Anthony Mazza and Sylvia Jacobs Mazza consisted of their brothers and sisters: Julius Mazza, Elizabeth Jacobs, George Jacobs, Gertrude Jacobs, Anthony Mazza, Sylvia Jacobs Mazza, Gregory Mazza, Irene Jacobs, Joseph Mazza, and Lois Jacobs (June 26, 1948).

Anthony Mazza and Sylvia Jacobs Mazza cut their wedding cake at the wedding breakfast held in their honor at Sylvia Jacobs' home, 2334 Atmore Street, Pittsburgh, Pennsylvania (June 26, 1948).

Appendix B: Brief History of the Mazza and Jacobs Families

"Please tell me about yourself" is often one of the first requests that people who want to get to know each other make. In telling one's own story, where does one begin? Does one start with oneself, with one's parents, with one's grandparents, or with even more distant ancestors? Although each of us is autonomous, families play a key role in our coming to an understanding of ourselves. In the wartime correspondence between Anthony Mazza and Sylvia Jacobs, they are revealing to each other who they are, which is an essential part of courtship. The process entails sharing not only individual stories but family stories as well.

To place their correspondence in context, this section offers a brief sketch of the more recent history of the Mazza and Jacobs families. This outline has multiple limitations. It only hints at a unifying narrative, where two people meet, fall in love, marry, and build their own family. The larger dynamics, not only concerning the broader historical context but also internal family relationships, are stories left for another time. What is presented here is a rough genealogy, consisting of the names of relatives and ancestors, and where possible, relevant dates and places. The compilation is a work in process, as some of the names and related information are not easily verifiable through supporting documentation. Moreover, there are admittedly many omissions, as both families are large and supplying information about spouses and cousins through multiple generations became unworkable. Nonetheless, an effort has been made to identify key family members and provide the dates on which they were born and died. Others may be able to expand this skeletal outline, correct the inevitable errors, and supply missing information.

Anthony S. Mazza

Anthony Samuel Mazza was born in Pittsburgh, Pennsylvania, on February 6, 1921, and died in Munster, Indiana, on February 2, 2004. He was the eldest son of Louis (Luigi) Mazza (b. August 29, 1896; d. January 13, 1973) and Pauline (Pasqualina) Guzzi (b. September 30, 1904; d. September 4, 1993).

Anthony had five siblings, Gregory E. Mazza (b. March 10, 1922; d. June 18, 2007), Joseph L. Mazza (b. November 7, 1924; d. December 22, 2015), Lucille Mazza Lopez (b. June 2, 1928; d. December 22, 1989), Julius A. Mazza (b. August 26, 1929; d. August 1, 2010), and Marie Antoinette Mazza Sudarich (b. June 13, 1931; d. February 14, 2001).

Louis (Luigi) Mazza, born in Serrastretta, Italy, emigrated to the United States from Naples, Italy, at the age of 17, arriving in New York City aboard the *Luisiana* on June 28, 1913.[308] At the age of 22, Louis (Luigi) Mazza enlisted in the U.S. Army and served overseas during World War I, becoming a naturalized citizen during his military service on August 29, 1918.[309]

---

[308] "Passenger Search," Statue of Liberty – Ellis Island Foundation, accessed June 20, 2020, https://www.libertyellisfoundation.org/passenger.

[309] Louis Mazza, Certificate of Naturalization, No. 1116113 (August 29, 1918) (duplicate on file with the editor). Louis (Luigi) Mazza enlisted in the Army on July 31, 1918. He served overseas from September 9, 1918, to August 13, 1919. He was discharged on August 19, 1919. Louis Mazza, Commonwealth of Pennsylvania Veteran's Compensation Application, No. 19094 (March 9, 1934) (on file with the editor). Based on Louis (Luigi) Mazza's service

Pauline (Pasqualina) Mazza, born in Serrastretta, Italy, emigrated with her parents to the United States from Naples, Italy, at the reported age of five months, arriving in New York City aboard the *Weimar* on May 8, 1905.[310]

Louis (Luigi) Mazza had five siblings: Gregorio Mazza (b. March 7, 1894; d. August 7, 1976), Antoinette (Antonia) Mazza Talarico (b. March 3, 1898 (1897); d. October 1979),[311] Angeline Rose (Angelarosa) Mazza Ventura Branca (b. April 14, 1899; d. March 2, 1983),[312] Joseph (Giuseppe) Mazza (b. ca. 1900; d. unknown),[313] and Gaetano (Guy) Mazza (b. September 6, 1902; d. January 1, 1981).

---

overseas during World War I, his direct descendants may be eligible for the LaVerne Noyes Scholarship, a stipend for undergraduate studies.

[310] The age listed on the manifest of the *Weimar* states that Pauline Guzzi Mazza was five months old in May of 1905, which does not correspond to her birthday in 1904. See *supra* note 308.

[311] Records for Antoinette (Antonia) Mazza Talarico present her first name with a variety of spellings, including Antonietta (i.e., on a 1973 Social Security application, which is the source of the birthdate, if this is the same person), Antonitta (i.e., on the death certificate of her son, Angelo Talarico; see Angelo Talorico [*sic*], State of Ohio Department of Health Division of Vital Statistics Certificate of Death, File No. 30729, Registered No. 1782 or 1762 (October 5, 1936)), Antonetic/Antonetia/Antonete (i.e., 1940 U.S. Census in Cleveland, Ohio), and Annettea (i.e., in a newspaper article, "Ready for the Elements," *Tucson Daily Citizen*, February 28, 1977). The 1940 U.S. Census records her living in Cleveland, Ohio, with her husband, Louis Talarico. The only other record readily available is for a gravesite in Arizona, listing Louis Talarico (b. 1898; d. 1980) and Antoinette Talarico (b. 1897; d. 1979).

[312] Lou Anne Kirby, "Everybody Cooks: Red Wine Cookies," *Arizona Daily Star*, July 15, 1963 (featuring Angeline Rose Branca).

[313] With immigration policies in the U.S. becoming tighter following World War I, Joseph Mazza was unable to immigrate to the U.S. along with the rest of his immediate family. He chose instead to relocate to Argentina.

Louis (Luigi) Mazza's parents were Antonio Mazza and Lucia (Lucy) Gigliotti (b. June 29, 1868; d. June 29, 1938). Lucia (Lucy) Gigliotti, along with three of her children, Gaetano (Guy) Mazza, Antonia (Antoinette) Mazza, and Angelerosa (Angeline Rose) Mazza, immigrated to the United States from Serrastretta, Italy, on board the *Patria*, departing from Naples and arriving in New York City on February 15, 1920.[314]

As of the writing of this summary, information about Joseph Mazza and his life in Argentina is limited. A newspaper clipping in the Mazza family's collection, however, provides a photograph with a brief caption, reporting the reunion of the Mazza brothers in Pittsburgh after fifty years. Unfortunately, the clipping is missing the date and title of the newspaper, and a database search of the *Pittsburgh Post-Gazette* and the *Pittsburgh Press* did not locate the source. The date of the reunion was ca. 1970. The clipping shows four elderly men with wineglasses raised to toast each other. The caption reads as follows:

> Toasting [t]ogetherness and fulfilling a 50-year dream of Guy Mazzi [*sic*], seated left, the Brothers Mazzi [*sic*]—Guy, 68, and Joseph, 70, seated right, and standing left, Gregory 76, and Louis, 73—are all together again for the first time since 1919. All but Joseph left Italy to live and raise families in the U.S. A victim of the U.S. quota system, he emigrated to Argentina, but, through the efforts of his brothers here, finally got to Pittsburgh for a three-month stay. Guy and Gregory live in Sheraden and Louis in Woods Run.

[314] "Passenger Search," Statue of Liberty – Ellis Island Foundation, accessed June 20, 2020, https://www.libertyellisfoundation.org/passenger. A reference in the ship's manifest to the marital status of Lucia Gigliotti is unclear, with a printed *w*, indicating that she was a widow, but with a handwritten *d* next to it, indicating that she was divorced. The Ellis Island Foundation's passenger database lists her as a divorcée. It is unclear whether the use of her maiden name on the passenger list might also indicate her marital status. Her son Louis (Luigi) Mazza, however, often recounted

Antonio Mazza's parents were Giuseppe Mazza and Maria Stella. Lucia Gigliotti's parents were Gaetano Gigliotti and Angelarosa Talarico. Gaetano Gigliotti's mother was Rosario [Rosaria] Gigliotti.

Pauline (Pasqualina) Guzzi Mazza's parents were Pasquale Guzzi (b. March 7, 1877; d. April 14, 1971) (designated here as the elder) and Antonia (Antoinette) Mascaro (b. October 22, 1879; d. January 21, 1919).[315]

Pauline Mazza had four full siblings: Angeline/a Guzzi Mazza (b. January 3, 1906; d. May 27, 1981), Florence Guzzi Facio Perrone Barbetta/i (b. April 22, 1907; d. December 20, 1974), Rose Guzzi Patello Ali (Alie) (August 26, 1911; d. January 11, 1994), and William Louis Guzzi (b. February 1, 1916; d. December 13, 1978).

After the death of Pauline Mazza's mother, her father married Elvira (Elvera) Massimi (also Missimi or Mousini) (b. April 25,

---

that his family's fortunes in Italy declined with the death of his father, prompting his own immigration to the U.S. as a teenager.

[315] There is a death record for Antionette [sic] Guzzi née Mascaro for a married woman who died in the midst of the influenza pandemic on January 21, 1919, in Stowe Township, which is located within Allegheny County, Pennsylvania, and who resided at 1317 Roschelle [sic] Street. Antionette [sic] Guzzi, Certificate of Death, Commonwealth of Pennsylvania Department of Health, File No. 5620, Registered No. 25 (January 22, 1919). The document is misfiled in databases of death certificates for Pennsylvania under the surname Luzzi. The 1930 U.S. Census lists her remarried husband, Pasquale Guzzi, residing at 1317 Rochelle Street in Pittsburgh, Pennsylvania, with his second wife and children. The 1930 U.S. Census appears to confirm that the death certificate is generally correct. The death certificate also lists Antonia Mascaro Guzzi's father as Anton (Antonio) Mascaro, which is, for the most part, consistent with other family sources, but the name of her mother differs. Instead of having the surname of Costanza, the death certificate lists her mother's name as Rosaro [Rosaria/o] Muraco.

1895; d. March 23, 1952). Pasquale Guzzi, the elder, had four additional children with his second wife: Alma Guzzi Secka (b. March 21, 1917; d. May 5, 1993), Adeline Guzzi Hall Brown (b. January 11, 1924; d. November 24, 1989), Pasquale (Patsy) J. Guzzi (b. August 16, 1927; d. September 12, 2008), and Anthony (Tony) E. Guzzi (b. November 10, 1928; d. December 31, 1990).[316]

The parents of Pasquale Guzzi, the elder, were Felice Antonio Guzzi and Angela Gallo. Antonia Mascaro's parents were Antonio Mascaro and [Name Unknown] Costanzo.

When Anthony Mazza departed home for the Army Air Forces in August of 1943, his family was living at 817 Woods Run Avenue in Pittsburgh, Pennsylvania.

Sylvia M. Jacobs

Sylvia Mary Grace Jacobs Mazza was born in Pittsburgh, Pennsylvania, on June 2, 1923. When she died on December 14, 1994, she was living in Munster, Indiana. She was the next to the youngest child of George (György) Jakubko (anglicized to Jacobs) (b. December 27, 1881; d. March 24, 1955) and Anna Kopcie (Kopczej or Kopciej) Jacobs (b. April 7, 1887; d. October 24, 1980).[317] Sylvia Jacobs had nine siblings. Her two oldest sisters, Mathilda Anna (b. November 4, 1904; d. March 18, 1912) and Agnes (b. February 19, 1907; d. January 7, 1912), died as children

---

[316] "Four Sheraden Homes Burn in 2-Alarm Fire," *Pittsburgh Press*, January 24, 1935.

[317] The baptismal records for the Roman Catholic Church in Nižný Hrušov, which in the 19th century was within the Michalovce District of the Kingdom of Hungary, state that Anna Kopczej was born on April 6, 1886, and baptized on April 7, 1886. Her parents are listed as János Kopczej and Anna Sztulyak. Nižný Hrušov is today within the Vranov nad Topľou District in the Prešov Region of Eastern Slovakia.

within months of each other during a typhoid epidemic. Sylvia Jacobs grew up with six sisters and one brother: Gertrude E. Jacobs (b. March 3, 1909; d. March 25, 1975), Alice Jacobs Soltis (b. February 9, 1911; d. April 21, 1999), Mathilda Jacobs Ilcisin (b. March 24, 1913; d. November 24, 1983), Irene M. Jacobs (b. April 24, 1915; d. February 5, 2003), Elizabeth C. Jacobs (b. December 27, 1918; d. January 28, 1988), George J. Jacobs (January 18, 1921; d. March 12, 2015), and Lois Jacobs Talotta Droney (b. June 4, 1931).

According to the passenger records from the Ellis Island Foundation, György Jakubko (George Jacobs) emigrated to the United States at the age of 17 from the town of Vehecz in Hungary (present-day Vechec, Slovakia), departing from Bremen, Germany, on board the *Lahn* and arriving in New York City on December 6, 1900.[318]

The Ellis Island Foundation has no passenger records that correspond with the names of Anna Kopcie or her parents, John J. Kopcie (b. December 27, 1860;[319] d. March 8, 1938) and Anna (Annie) Stulyak[320] Kopcie (b. June 9, 1860; d. January 2,

---

[318] "Passenger Search," Statue of Liberty – Ellis Island Foundation, accessed June 20, 2020, https://www.libertyellisfoundation.org/passenger.

[319] The birthdate for John Kopcie is from his Declaration of Intention in the naturalization process. Declaration of Intention, U.S. Department of Labor Naturalization Office, No. 61245 (November 10, 1919). The same document states that he immigrated from Bremen, Germany, aboard the *Vera* and arrived in New York City on January 15, 1887. The Ellis Island Foundation database has no entry for either the Kopcie (Kopczej) surname or the *Vera*. John Kopcie also states on the Declaration of Intention that he was born in Hrusov, Zamplinzka, which at the time of the filing of the document was identified as being within the new nation of Czechoslovakia. Ibid.

[320] The maiden name has alternative spellings in various records, including Sztulyak, Stulak, Stulyok, and Iztulyak. The name here is from the

1944).[321] The 1900 U.S. Census states that both John and Annie Kopcie were 38 years old at the time of the survey and had been married for 14 years (i.e., married ca. 1886). According to the 1900 U.S. Census, Anna, the daughter, and Annie, the mother, immigrated to the United States in 1892, whereas the 1910 U.S. Census states they immigrated in 1893 and the 1930 U.S. Census states they immigrated in 1894.

According to the records from the Roman Catholic Church in Vechec, György Jakubko was born on December 27, 1881; other documents list his birthyear as 1882, 1884, or 1885, but church records in the United States (e.g., the entry for his marriage) support the 1881 date.[322] The church records in Vechec state that he was baptized on December 30, 1881. His parents were György (Georgius) Jakubko, here designated as the elder, and Ilona (Helena) Mihalcsin.[323]

Ilona Mihalcsin was born in 1848; her parents were Andras Mihalcsin and Anna Kirik. She married György Jakubko, the elder, on June 4, 1865, and she died on June 2, 1892, at the age of 44. At the time of her marriage, she was 17, and György Jakubko, the elder, was a 32-year-old widower. György Jakubko, the elder,

---

Certificate of Death, Commonwealth of Pennsylvania, Department of Vital Statistics, File No. 9238, Registered No. 115 (January 5, 1944).

[321] Various records, including U.S. Census data, give a later birthyear. The birthdate here is from the Certificate of Death. Ibid. The Certificate of Death also states that the name of Anna Stulyak's father was John. Ibid.

[322] See *infra* note 324.

[323] The church in Vechec, Slovakia, initially recorded baptisms, marriages, and deaths with Latinized names, but toward the end of the 19th century, influenced by the Kingdom of Hungary's Magyarization policy, the church recorded the names of its Slovak-speaking parishioners in Hungarian rather than Latin.

had previously married Anna Bacso on October 29, 1854; she died at the age of 30 on November 8, 1864.

After the death of Ilona Mihalcsin, György Jakubko, the elder, married a third time, wedding Maria Harcsar on August 4, 1892. György Jakubko, the elder, died on December 6, 1893, at the age of 60.

According to the archives of St. Gabriel Church, maintained by the Roman Catholic Diocese of Pittsburgh, the marriage record of Sylvia Jacobs' parents is as follows:

23 Jan 1904 Georgius Jakubko; Vechelz, com. Zemplin, Hung.; son of Georgius Jakubko and Helena Mihalesik; age 22 married to Anna Kopciej, Hrusovo, com. Zemplin, Hung.; daughter of Joannes Kopciej and Anna Iztulyak; age 18. Witnesses: Joannes Chavanesak, Michael Csekos.[324]

Information about the Kopcie family is difficult to trace in the absence of reliable immigration records. The petition of George Jacobs, Sylvia Jacobs' father, for naturalization in the U.S. District Court for Western Pennsylvania, filed on June 15, 1925, states that his wife's hometown in Slovakia was Zrusen, whereas previously noted, other records in the United States identified her family's town as Hrusov or Hrusovo. The baptismal record for Sylvia Jacobs' mother, Anna Jacobs, may be the most reliable source, which ties the Kopcie (Kopczej) family to Nižný Hrušov in present-day Slovakia. The distance between Nižný Hrušov and

---

[324] Letter to George Mazza from Burris E. Esplen, IV, associate archivist, Diocese of Pittsburgh Archives and Record Center (March 18, 2010) (on file with the editor).

Vechec, the ancestral village of Sylvia Jacobs' father, is about 17 kilometers or 11 miles.

Anna Kopcie Jacobs had four younger siblings: Mary Kopcie Stroyne (b. June 2, 1894; d. February 14, 1978), John Kopcie (b. December 27, 1896; d. November 4, 1952), Lillian Kopcie Slobodnik (b. January 18, 1899; d. November 18, 1991), and Michael Kopcie (b. October 9, 1902; d. May 24, 1980).

By the time of the 1910 U.S. Census, Sylvia Jacobs' parents, George and Anna Jacobs, with their names anglicized, were living with two children at 2334 Atmore Street in Pittsburgh, Pennsylvania, the place where Sylvia Jacobs grew up, and the address that appears on many of the letters that Anthony Mazza wrote to her between August 1943 and March 1945. The distance between the houses of the Jacobs family and the Mazza family on the North Side of Pittsburgh was less than two miles.

Descendants of Anthony S. Mazza and Sylvia M. Jacobs

Anthony Mazza and Sylvia Jacobs married on June 26, 1948, at St. Gabriel Church in Pittsburgh, Pennsylvania. They had five children: Mary Ann Mazza Mast Crawford (b. May 21, 1950), Louis Anthony Mazza (b. September 20, 1951), Mark George Mazza (b. March 7, 1954), George Jacobs Mazza (b. July 3, 1955), and Michelle Marie Mazza Robertson (b. December 6, 1963).

Mary Ann Mazza married Eric Lamont Mast (b. August 12, 1949; d. July 11, 2011) on October 7, 1977, in Munster, Indiana. The marriage ended in divorce in November of 1993. Mary Ann Mazza married Stephen Crawford (b. December 29, 1955) on January 29, 2000, in Bremen, Indiana.

Mary Ann Mazza and her first husband, Eric Mast, had three children: Jennifer Mast Sellers (b. May 31, 1978), Elizabeth (Liz) Mast (b. May 11, 1980), and Mathew Mast (b. August 16, 1987).

Jennifer Mast married Douglas Sellers (b. December 1, 1984) on May 26, 2001. The marriage ended in divorce in September 2007. They had one son, Luke Sellers (b. October 17, 2004). Elizabeth Mast married Levi Gamble on March 13, 1999; the marriage ended in divorce.

Louis Anthony Mazza married Rita Lorraine Norton (b. March 9, 1959) on August 14, 1982, in Pineville, Louisiana. The marriage ended in divorce on September 13, 1993. Louis Anthony Mazza's life partner is Elizabeth Karen Vogel (b. August 14, 1946).

Louis Anthony Mazza and Rita Lorraine Norton had three children: Louis Edward Mazza (b. October 3, 1983), Alessandra Rose Mazza Medrano (b. February 27, 1986), and Angelica (Jelly) Terese Mazza Nigam (b. May 14, 1988).

Louis Edward Mazza is affianced to Mallory Westfall; they plan to marry on August 15, 2021, in Temecula, California.

Alessandra Rose Mazza married Justin Medrano (b. July 8, 1984) on November 5, 2010, in Munster, Indiana. They had three children: Nolan David Medrano (b. March 30, 2012), Penelope Rose Medrano (b. September 29, 2013), and Xander John Medrano (b. December 15, 2017).

Angelica (Jelly) Terese Mazza married Avneesh Nigam (b. February 23, 1978) on June 15, 2013, in San Francisco, California. They had two children: Nina Sol Nigam (b. January 10, 2017) and Sonali Rita Nigam (January 15, 2019).

Mark George Mazza was ordained a Roman Catholic priest on October 2, 1980, for the Diocese of Gary, Indiana, at St. Thomas More Church in Munster, Indiana. He moved to San Francisco, California, in January 2003 and became a priest of the Archdiocese of San Francisco. He is currently the pastor of the Church of the Immaculate Heart of Mary in Belmont, California.

George Jacobs Mazza was ordained a Roman Catholic priest on May 23, 1981, for the Archdiocese of Louisville, in Louisville, Kentucky. He received regularization with permission to marry from the Catholic Church in May of 1997. He married Cherie Roseanne Brown (b. December 4, 1949) on June 1, 1997, in Washington, District of Columbia.

Michelle Marie Mazza married Rick Alan Robertson (b. March 7, 1952) on July 4, 1992, in Indianapolis, Indiana. They had two children: Sylvia Rae Robertson (b. May 5, 1996) and Carl Mazza Robertson (b. October 10, 1997).

Editor's Notes

The Mazza Family

During a December cruise to the Bahamas in 2009, I decided to reread Bocaccio's *Decameron*. While reading his amusing stories set in Italy, I found myself wanting to learn more about my Italian ancestors. The little I knew at the time was that both of my fraternal grandparents immigrated to the United States from the small hillside village of Serrastretta in Calabria, which is located in the instep of the Italian "boot." With a bit of online research, I discovered the work of Rabbi Barbara Aiello.[325] Rabbi Barbara, as she prefers to be called, and her husband, Dr. Enrico Mascaro, are leading figures in recovering the Jewish history of Southern Italy. Her Jewish family emigrated from Serrastretta to the United States and settled in Pittsburgh, Pennsylvania, where she grew up. She, too, wanted to reconnect to her Italian roots, but they were Italian Jewish roots. As a second career, she became a rabbi and returned to Serrastretta. She has written extensively about

---

[325] Rabbi Barbara, accessed June 20, 2020, https://www.rabbibarbara.com/.

what that return meant, uncovering the history of the town and founding the first synagogue in Southern Italy in over 500 years, Synagogue Ner Tamid del Sud.[326]

I was intrigued by her story and her work in Serrastretta. I contacted her by email and set up a telephone call in January of 2010. At the time, I asked her, "Does the Jewish history of Serrastretta have anything to do with my family?" I later realized that this was the wrong question. The more appropriate question would have been, "How could the Jewish history of Serrastretta not have anything to do with my family?"

Rabbi Barbara patiently told me the documented history of the town. When the Catholic Monarchs, Isabella I of Castile and Ferdinand II of Aragon, issued the Alhambra Decree on March 31, 1492, which expelled Jews from Spain, many Jews fled to Sicily, which was a territory still within the Spanish orbit. When the Inquisition followed them, they retreated to the Italian mainland. Some Sephardic (Iberian) Jewish families decided to relocate to the mountains of Calabria, a protected place that would allow them to see any advancing forces from either the Ionian or Tyrrhenian Seas. The founders of Serrastretta were Sephardic Jewish families. By the 1530s, the Inquisition had come to Serrastretta, forcing the residents to choose among three options: execution, conversion, or exile. Some chose to leave, many reportedly going to Greece. My ancestors, of course, chose neither execution nor exile but conversion. Some *conversos* or *anusim*[327] in Serrastretta practiced Catholicism openly but maintained Jewish identity and customs

---

[326] Barbara Aiello, "The Jews of Sicily and Calabria: the Anusim that Nobody Knows," Italian Jewish Cultural Center of Calabria, accessed June 20, 2020, https://www.rabbibarbara.com/wp-content/uploads/2020/02/The_Jews_of_Sicily_and_Calabria.pdf.

[327] Hebrew for coerced ones.

privately. As Rabbi Barbara writes, some *anusim* families held on to their Jewish identity over centuries, even to the present day.[328] Others, like my family, lost touch with their Jewish heritage.

In the summer of 2015, my wife, Cherie Brown, who is Jewish, and I visited Rabbi Barbara in Serrastretta. When we met her in the town's piazza, she greeted us with open arms, saying to me, "Giorgio, welcome home!" We attended a *bat mitzvah* service at the synagogue, which involved an American family, who had chosen to travel to Serrastretta to celebrate with their daughter, as she identified with a community that was reclaiming its Jewish identity. The family welcomed us to join their celebration, bestowing on us the roles of honorary grandparents. Afterward, with my father's family tree in hand, I asked members of the congregation if they might have any connection to the listed ancestors. Although none could identify any particular person, everyone in the synagogue bore one of the surnames on the chart.

It has taken time to absorb this relatively new information about the Mazza family. For most of my life, I thought of my father's family as being proud Italian Catholics who immigrated to the United States and built successful lives despite harsh conditions. What is missing from this remarkable story is an earlier, centuries-long oppression, one that had forced the family to relinquish its Sephardic Jewish identity for the sake of survival. I wish at times that I could have had a conversation with my father and grandparents about the Jewish heritage of the family, but those conversations were not possible.

The story of the reclamation of the Mazza family's Jewish identity took an unexpected turn in 2015 when the Spanish government passed a law offering citizenship to those who could

---

[328] See *supra* note 326.

show that they were descendants of Sephardic families exiled from Spain in 1492.[329] One of the requirements of the original law was that the opportunity to apply for citizenship was limited. The deadline for submitting an application was October of 2018, which the Spanish government extended one year. I was struck by the irony that I would not have known about my Sephardic Jewish background earlier in my life and that the Spanish government was providing a way to reclaim this heritage within only a relatively short window of time. I decided to apply for Spanish citizenship, enlisting Rabbi Barbara's support in providing the necessary documentation and taking classes in Spain to pass the required language and cultural examinations. In June of 2018, I appeared before the notary in Málaga, Spain, to petition for citizenship based on the Mazza family's Sephardic heritage, and the notary accepted the petition.

My Spanish attorneys have advised me that the slow bureaucratic process, confounded by the coronavirus pandemic, has delayed the issuance of the citizenship papers, but there is every reason to expect that the granting of Spanish citizenship is forthcoming.

The Jacobs Family

My research of the Jacobs family began with studying the manifest of the *Lahn*, the ship that brought my grandfather, George Jacobs (György Jakubko), to the United States in 1900. The manifest indicated that his hometown was Vehecz, Hungary. I discovered that the Hungarian name of the town corresponded to the

---

[329] Kiku Adatto, "Spain's Attempt to Atone for a 500-Year-Old Sin," *The Atlantic*, September 21, 2019, https://theatlantic.com/international/archive/2019/09/spain-offers-citizenship-sephardic-jews/598258/.

present-day town of Vechec, which is in the Vranov nad Topl'ou District in the Prešov Region of Eastern Slovakia. With the assistance of genealogical materials available through FamilySearch, a resource provided by the Church of the Latter-day Saints,[330] I was able to access the church records of the Catholic Church in Vechec and piece together information about my grandfather and his family.

During a trip to Europe in June 2016, I arranged to travel to Slovakia—the first time, to my knowledge, any member of the family had been to the country since my mother's parents immigrated to the United States. I chose to stay at a hotel in Košice, the principal city of Eastern Slovakia, which is about 44 kilometers or 27 miles from Vechec. As I knew no one in Vechec, and as any family ties to relatives in Slovakia were long severed, my idea was to find a driver who could take me to the village, where I imagined I could have a leisurely stroll through the town and then return to Košice within a few hours.

In arranging the excursion to Vechec, I called the manager of the hotel in Košice and explained the family connection to Vechec and the short outing I had planned. I asked for help in soliciting a driver who would accompany me. The manager of the hotel kindly listened and asked me for more information about the Jakubko family, which I provided. She promised to help me retain a driver for the trip to Vechec.

I traveled by train from Budapest to Košice and arrived at the hotel in the afternoon. I met briefly with the hotel manager, and she assured me all was in order for the following morning.

---

[330] "About," FamilySearch, accessed June 20, 2020, https://www.familsearch.org/en/home/about.

After breakfast, I waited in the hotel lobby for my driver. When he appeared, he said, "I have some good news for you. Your cousins are waiting for you. They can't wait to meet you."

"Cousins?"

On his own initiative, the driver, based on the information I provided to the hotel manager, called ahead to the town hall in Vechec and discovered a family who had lived in the village for generations with the surname of Jakubko. He provided members of the family with the information he had, and one of the family members, Veronika Jakobková, a young woman in her early twenties at the time, who not only spoke English but who was also aware of her family's history, immediately recognized the connection. Based on her own independent research, she knew that there was a relative who had left Vechec for the United States in the early 20th century, but the family had lost contact with him.

When I arrived in Vechec, Pavol (Paul) Jakubko (b. ca. 1962) and his daughter, Veronika Jakobková, welcomed me into their home, where we were joined by Pavol's two living siblings: his sister, Agnesa (Agnes) (b. ca. 1948) and his brother, Michal (Michael). Pavol's wife was away, and I met his son only briefly, as he stopped me as I was already on the road driving back to Košice.

Veronika explained that she and her family members in Vechec were related to me and the Jacobs family in the United States through György Jakubko, the elder. She and her family are descendants of György Jakubko, the elder, and his first wife, Anna Bacso, whereas the Jacobs family are descendants of György Jakubko, the elder, and his second wife, Ilona Mihalcsin.

Over Agnesa's homemade cake and Pavol's home-distilled pear spirits, we toasted our reunion. Afterward, the Jakubko family gave me a tour of the rural town, stopping directly in front of the doors of the village church to point out the prominent stone

843

monument memorializing members of the Jakubko family. The family also showed me the farmlands, reaching into the town center, that the Jakubko family traditionally held.

I have been in contact with Veronika Jakobková and her family via email since my visit to Vechec, often exchanging greetings and presents at Christmas and Easter. She married Pavol (Paul) Samsely from Dlhé Klčovo on October 10, 2020, in Vechec. She and her husband currently reside in Vrano nad Topľou, Slovakia.

G.J.M.

Addendum

The Anthony S. Mazza family donated the original letters, record of missions, and related materials that appear in this volume to the archives of the National World War II Museum, 945 Magazine Street, New Orleans, Louisiana.